CONTEMPORARY
MARRIAGE

Comparative Perspectives on a Changing Institution

edited by
Kingsley Davis

in association with
Amyra Grossbard-Shechtman

RUSSELL SAGE FOUNDATION   NEW YORK

The Russell Sage Foundation

The Russell Sage Foundation, one of the oldest of America's general purpose foundations, was established in 1907 by Mrs. Margaret Olivia Sage for "the improvement of social and living conditions in the United States." The Foundation seeks to fulfill this mandate by fostering the development and dissemination of knowledge about the political, social, and economic problems of America. It conducts research in the social sciences and public policy, and publishes books and pamphlets that derive from this research.

The Board of Trustees is responsible for oversight and the general policies of the Foundation, while administrative direction of the program and staff is vested in the President, assisted by the officers and staff. The President bears final responsibility for the decision to publish a manuscript as a Russell Sage Foundation book. In reaching a judgment on the competence, accuracy, and objectivity of each study, the President is advised by the staff and selected expert readers. The conclusions and interpretations in Russell Sage Foundation publications are those of the authors and not of the Foundation, its Trustees, or its staff. Publication by the Foundation, therefore, does not imply endorsement of the contents of the study.

Library of Congress Cataloging-in-Publication Data

Contemporary marriage.

Bibliography
Includes index.
1. Marriage—Cross-cultural studies—Congresses.
2. Marriage—United States—Congresses. I. Davis,
Kingsley, 1908-   . II. Grossbard-Shechtman, Amyra.
HQ734.C75   1985   306.8'1   85-62452
ISBN 0-87154-221-8

Cover and text design: Huguette Franco

CONTRIBUTING AUTHORS

Grace Ganz Blumberg

Dr. Blumberg is a professor of law at the University of California at Los Angeles. Her recent publications include "Intangible Assets: Recognition and Valuation," "Legal Issues in Nonsurgical Human Ovum Transfer," and "Cohabitation Without Marriage: A Different Perspective." In 1983 Dr. Blumberg argued *Sullivan v. Sullivan* before the California Supreme Court, which addressed the question of whether a professional education acquired during marriage is community property subject to division at divorce.

Elwood Carlson

Dr. Carlson is an assistant professor in the Sociology Department at the University of South Carolina. In addition to his work on cohabitation in France, he has written about cohabitation in the United States and is involved in original analysis of German *Mikrozensus* results concerning marriage and family patterns in Germany. Other research has focused on divorce, childbearing outside marriage, and infant mortality.

Kingsley Davis

Kingsley Davis is Distinguished Professor of Sociology at the University of Southern California and a senior research fellow at the Hoover Institution on War, Revolution and Peace, Stanford University. A native Texan, he received his undergraduate education at the University of Texas and his Ph.D. at Harvard University.

Thomas J. Espenshade

Dr. Espenshade was a senior research associate in the Human Resources Policy Center at The Urban Institute, but has recently been appointed to a professorship at Brown University. He received his Ph.D. in economics from Princeton University and served on the faculties of the University of California at Berkeley, Bowdoin College, and Florida State University before joining the Institute in 1980. His research interests include family demography, the cost of children, population mathematics, and immigration to the United States.

Amyra Grossbard-Shechtman

Amyra Grossbard-Shechtman studied economics and sociology at the Hebrew University in Jerusalem and obtained her Ph.D. in economics at the University of Chicago. She is associate professor of economics at San Diego State University, has taught at Bar-Ilan and Tel Aviv universities and at the Claremont Colleges, and has been a fellow at the Center for Advanced Study in the Behavioral Sciences, Stanford. Her article, "A Theory of Allocation of Time in Markets for Labor and Marriage," was published in *Economic Journal* in 1984. She has published additional articles on marriage-related issues in economics, sociology, and anthropology journals.

Joy Hendry

Dr. Hendry is lecturer in social anthropology at Oxford Polytechnic in Oxford, England. She received a B.Sc. in General Science from Kings College, London University, and a Diploma, B.Litt., and D.Phil. in social anthropology from Lady Margaret Hall, Oxford University. She did research in Japan in three separate periods in the years 1975 to 1980 and published *Marriage in Changing Japan* in 1981. She has just completed work on a new book, *Becoming Japanese*.

Adam Kuper

Dr. Kuper studied at the University of the Witwatersrand and at Cambridge, where he was awarded a Ph.D. in 1966. He has taught at universities in Uganda, England, the Netherlands, Sweden, and the United States, and is currently professor of social anthropology and head of the Department of Human Sciences at Brunel University, England. Dr. Kuper is the author of *Kalahari Village Politics: An African Democracy*, *Changing Jamaica*, and *Wives for Cattle: Bridewealth and Marriage in Southern Africa*.

John Modell

Dr. Modell is a professor of history at Carnegie-Mellon University. He received his Ph.D in history from Columbia University. He spent a postdoctoral year in Population Studies at the University of Pennsylvania and became interested in "the new social history." His major work is in the historical study of immigration, urbanization, and the family.

Rachel Pasternack

Dr. Pasternack was a graduate student at Tel Aviv University when the study of Israeli socialization was carried out. During 1983–1984 she was a visiting scholar at the State University of New York at Stony Brook. At present Dr. Pasternack is on the faculty of the Levinsky Teacher's College in Tel Aviv.

Yochanan Peres

Dr. Peres completed his studies at the Hebrew University of Jerusalem. His main areas of interest are ethnic relations and the family in Israeli society. He has taught at Columbia, Harvard, the University of Michigan, and the University of Southern California. At present he is an associate professor in the Department of Sociology at Tel Aviv University.

James E. Smith

Dr. Smith received a Ph.D. in sociology from the University of Southern California in 1979. From 1976 to 1983 he was a member of the sociology faculty, and an associate of the Family and Demographic Research Institute, at Brigham Young University; more recently he was a fellow at the Cambridge Group for the History of Population and Social Structure. He is currently engaged in research concerning contemporary Chinese population and family structure.

Graham B. Spanier

Dr. Spanier is professor of sociology and psychiatry and vice provost for undergraduate studies at the State University of New York at Stony Brook. He was previously on the faculty at the Pennsylvania State University. His most recent books are *Parting: The Aftermath of Separation and Divorce* (with Linda Thompson) and *Recycling the Family: Remarriage after Divorce* (with Frank Furstenberg). His research interests focus on the quality and stability of marriage across the life course and family demography.

Alan A. Stone

Dr. Stone is a psychiatrist who became director of residency training at McLean Hospital and began teaching law and psychiatry at Harvard Law School in 1970. He is now the Touroff-Glueck Professor of Law and Psychiatry there. Dr. Stone's most recent book is *Law, Psychiatry and Morality.*

Donald Symons

Dr. Symons has taught in the Department of Anthropology at the University of California at Santa Barbara since 1970, where he is currently associate professor. He received a B.A. in psychology (1964) and a Ph.D. in physical anthropology (1973) from the University of California at Berkeley. He conducted a study of play among free-ranging rhesus monkeys (*Play and Aggression*). Dr. Symons has since been interested in developing a Darwinian approach to the study of the human mind and has published *The Evolution of Human Sexuality.*

Lenore J. Weitzman

Dr. Weitzman was recently a member of the Institute for Advanced Study in Princeton, New Jersey, on leave from Stanford University where she is an associate professor of sociology (for research). Her research focuses on sociological aspects of family law. She has analyzed legal marriage and alternatives to marriage in her book, *The Marriage Contract: Spouses, Lovers and the Law,* and has written on divorce law reforms in "The Alimony Myth" and "The Economics of Divorce." She has just completed a book, *No-Fault Divorce and the Transformation of Marriage.*

Margery Wolf

Margery Wolf is a professor of anthropology at the University of Iowa and chair of the Women's Studies Program at that university. She has done extensive anthropological field work in Taiwan and the People's Republic of China, resulting in the publication of several books, including *The House of Lim* and most recently *Revolution Postponed: Women in Contemporary China.*

PREFACE

It is a curious irony that marriage, which holds great importance and interest in human lives, receives almost no attention in social science. Although it provides the very stuff of which novels, movies, and television serials are made, although it plays a prominent role in assaults, homicides, and suicides, and although it continuously affects people's daily lives and deepest emotions, it is given short shrift as an object of scientific investigation. Far more money goes into research on a particular disease—say, AIDS—than on marriage. The average university has a few courses on marriage and the family scattered around the campus, but engineering and business have whole schools of their own.

The causes of this hiatus between public interest and scientific attention lie deep in the sociology of science, but whatever they are, the situation calls for some rectification. It calls for giving a greater share of scholarly attention to marriage, especially at a time when that institution, at least in the industrial societies, is changing more rapidly and experiencing more difficulty than ever before.

The present volume is a modest attempt to help correct the imbalance. Its history goes back to a seminar and a conference. The seminar was conducted at the Center for Advanced Study in the Behavioral Sciences at Stanford, California, during the 1980–1981 academic year. The fellowships of participants in the seminar, and the seminar itself, were supported in part by funds from the National Science Foundation and the Foundation's Fund for

ix

Research in Psychiatry. Late in the seminar, an ad hoc group was convened for two days at the Center, to plan a conference on contemporary marriage. Funded by the Research and Planning Committee of the American Academy of Arts and Sciences, this meeting was attended by Bert N. Adams, University of Wisconsin; John H. Bishop, University of Wisconsin; Elizabeth Colson, University of California, Berkeley; Amyra Grossbard-Shechtman, San Diego State University; Barbara Laslett, then at the University of Southern California; and John Modell, then at the University of Minnesota. The conference itself, generously funded by the Russell Sage Foundation, took place at the Center for Advanced Study in the Behavioral Sciences on August 23–25, 1982. Most of the chapters in the present volume were first presented at the conference and a few have been added, but in every case the contribution has been edited and revised, in some cases several times.

One can readily see that the book owes its existence to numerous individuals and organizations. In addition to Professor Grossbard-Shechtman, whose enthusiasm for the study never flagged, special thanks must go to the following: Alida Brill, Program Officer of the Russell Sage Foundation, who attended the conference and all along has given helpful encouragement and good ideas; Muriel Bell, Staff Associate of the American Academy of Arts and Sciences, Western Center, who handled with rare competence the organization and logistics of the conference; members of the staff of the Center for Advanced Study, who helped cheerfully when called upon (which was often); and Nancy Williams, who was the first-round editor for most of the chapters. By way of organizations, the book's debt to the Russell Sage Foundation, the Center for Advanced Study in the Behavioral Sciences, and the American Academy of Arts and Sciences is plain and is cheerfully acknowledged. A special debt is also owed to the Hoover Institution and the University of Tel Aviv for facilitating editorial work on the symposium.

Kingsley Davis
The Hoover Institution, Stanford University
The University of Southern California

CONTENTS

The Meaning and Significance of Marriage in Contemporary Society

KINGSLEY DAVIS

THE ASSUMPTION UNDERLYING the present volume is that in industrial countries today the institution of marriage is experiencing unprecedented but poorly understood changes. Whether or not these changes ultimately threaten the institution of marriage itself, as often stated, they are surely disturbing the lives of hundreds of millions of people. For humane as well as scholarly reasons, then, they deserve careful study.

Given this focus, the logic of the arrangement in the book is clear. The first task is to document the major changes themselves. What has happened to marriage since World War II? What are the trends with respect to such matters as age at marriage, permanent celibacy, cohabitation, single parenthood, divorce, wives' employment, and fertility? This task is addressed in the first part of the symposium, where trends in the United States and in industrial societies generally are presented, and in the third part, where case studies are made of particular societies or countries.

The second task is to analyze possible causes and consequences of the trends and to use the results to assess potential future developments in marriage. This is done mainly in the second, fourth, and fifth parts of the book, where legal, economic, and sociological theories are used to probe into the nature of marriage and its presumed alternatives.

The overall aim of the symposium is thus a wide-ranging analysis of a basic but troubled institution in the advanced nations. Needless to say, the purpose is not to reach an overall conclusion or consensus. Although there is general agreement on the statistical and descriptive facts, the focus of attention, the interpretation, the whole way of looking at marriage varies from one author to another. John Modell sees contemporary marriage in America as extending a long tradition, while Amyra Grossbard-Shechtman sees it as a market system affected by current conditions. James Smith finds marriage to be very strong in a religious community that is highly successful economically—thus challenging the thesis that problems of the marital institution come from prosperity. Joy Hendry holds that the patterns of change in Japanese marriage are determined to some extent by Japanese culture rather than by modern economic development, while Lenore Weitzman sees family legislation as a source of change that is partly independent of both culture and development.

Disciplines, Relevance, and Words

These differences in approach are not disagreements (most of the authors have had little chance to confront one another) but contrasting ways of looking at marriage. To a certain extent they reflect the diversity of disciplines from which the authors come. There are seven sociologists, five anthropologists, two economists, one historian, one psychiatrist, and one law professor. But the influence of the formal disciplines should not be exaggerated. There are other, more personal, bases of difference among the authors, including contrasts in style and experience.

In fact, given the diversity of fields and backgrounds represented, what is surprising is not the differences but the overall cohesion and complementarity. The symposium maintains a common focus for two main reasons—first, a willingness of the authors to keep their attention on contemporary marriage without being drawn off onto tangential subjects; second, an effort to avoid disputes over disciplinary boundaries and vocabularies.

The common focus means that, although the authors see contemporary marriage with different eyes, they nevertheless see the same reality. Any particular topic is dealt with only insofar as it somehow enlightens the reader about marriage today in a changing world. When people from different fields thus pursue a common empirical topic, they tend to forget disciplinary affiliations unless reminded of them and put on the defensive. In the present case an effort was made to avoid disciplinary claim-staking. It was made clear that the project had no interest in disciplines as such, but only in contemporary marriage. To the extent that a discipline threw light on this topic, it was welcome, but not if it merely *claimed* that it *could* do so. In other words, the interdisciplinary character of this work is a result not of preference but of necessity. If only one discipline were required to understand the basics of contemporary marriage, the others could be omitted, but that is not the case.

Terminological disputes seem more difficult to avoid than disciplinary territoriality. As everybody knows, scholars in the natural and social sciences have to communicate mainly with words, but words can obstruct as well as facilitate communication because they often have fuzzy or vague meanings and mean different things to different people or even to the same people at different times. To avoid confusion, scientists try in each field to establish a technical vocabulary; but in social science the task is complicated by the fact that ordinary language already has terms for social phenomena and by the further fact that social scientists, like laymen, react emotionally to particular words and phrases. As a result, many disputes that are ostensibly scholarly are really disputes over the meaning of words.

The Meaning of Marriage

One can well imagine that unless precautions are taken, a conference or symposium on contemporary marriage can be stalled by debate over the proper definition of "marriage." Does it mean a duly registered and celebrated union between a man and a woman, with sexual intercourse and reproduction in mind, or simply a protracted arrangement whereby a couple live and sleep together? Can homosexuals "marry" each other? Do subhuman primates (apes) get married? Are people who are legally separated still legally married? Is a marriage a marriage if it is never consummated? Is it a real marriage if the couple intend to remain childless? These questions can be hotly and fiercely debated for hours on end.

Obviously, scholars must constantly try to get behind the words to the reality that words so confusingly represent. In the present case, an effort was made to avoid arguments over the meaning of "marriage." In certain chapters changing legal and social definitions are dealt with, but these are part of the phenomena being studied, not the imposition of the observer's own definition. The reader will also find certain operational definitions made for statistical purposes, to achieve clarity and consistency.

Types of Union

Avoidance of disputes over definitions should not, however, preclude useful distinctions. With respect to our subject, one can readily concede that what is commonly called marriage has as one of its features that it is a sexual union. It is not, however, the only kind of sexual union. It differs from other kinds in terms of other criteria. At bottom the existence of other kinds of sexual unions depends on the fact that in human societies male–female relations have two components, the biological and the normative. The fact that a couple *can* reproduce without public approval—in fact, with distinct disapproval—is far from pure biology (mankind has evolved so long in a cultural setting that even the act of intercourse must be learned), but it is nevertheless heavily biological, and it underlies the classification of unions in Figure I.1. In that chart, five types of union are distinguished according to six traits, or criteria. Marriage is the only kind of union that meets all six criteria. In five of the criteria, it shares the trait with one or more other kinds of union, but it is the sole kind of union that satisfies the sixth criterion—public approval and recognition. It is this trait, then, that constitutes the unique character of what we call marriage.

Figure I.1

Schematic Representation of Elements in Five Types of Unions

	Sex Relations Expected	Common Residence	Division of Labor	Children Expected	Permanence Assumed	Public Recognition
Marriage	X	X	X	X	X	X
Common-Law	X	X	X	X	X	
Consensual Union	X	X	X	X	?	
Cohabitation	X	X	?			
Liaison	X					

Although the details of getting married—who chooses the mates, what are the ceremonies and exchanges, how old are the parties—vary from group to group, the principle of marriage is everywhere embodied in practice. Just as every elephant is different from all other elephants, so each marriage system is different from all others; nevertheless, in spite of the variations, we can identify elephants in general and marriage systems in general. No matter how bizarre or peculiar the marriage customs of a given society, they are still recognizable as *marriage* customs. In any particular society there may be individuals, couples, or even groups who reject marriage as a norm, but these, being in the minority, do not determine the norms of the whole society. Other people may fail to marry because of conditions beyond their control, but the institution of marriage is present in the society.

Granted that the unique trait of what is commonly called marriage is social recognition and approval, one still must ask, approval of what? The answer is that it is approval of a couple's engaging in sexual intercourse and bearing and rearing offspring. Of course, approval is given only when the couple meet certain conditions. These vary from one society to another, but generally the couple must be committed to a durable relationship that begins with public ceremonies and involves a common residence, a division of labor based on gender, and a set of rights and obligations with respect to each other and to their children.

Public approval, however, should not be construed too narrowly. In industrial societies there are two kinds of approval—official and unofficial—which sometimes clash. Officially, a marriage requires a license certifying that the couple meet certain requisites for marriage and a record that a suitable ceremony was performed. These bare-bones requirements can be satisfied bureaucratically and impersonally, without the knowledge of friends and relatives, without the exchange of gifts, without the wedding feast, honeymoon, or other manifestations of community recognition and involvement. In this case, public approval is quite different from that signalized by a church wedding celebrated by friends, relatives, and neighbors. But the legal status of the union is the same: the couple are married. To get unmarried requires a divorce. Soon, too, friends and relatives learn about the marriage and react accordingly.

Few would deny the term "marriage" or "wedlock" to a union with all the six attributes shown in Figure I.1—that is, a socially approved, durable, heterosexual relationship in which reproduction and child care are assumed and there is a common residence and a division of labor. But the question arises as to what unions are called that lack some of these attributes. For instance, as noted already, one of the oldest dilemmas in human morality is how to handle couples who openly live together and bear children without having satisfied the legal and public formalities of marriage. What their relationship is called depends in part on social policy. One might think that since an unauthorized union flouts the norms and, in more advanced societies at least, makes enforcement of connubial rights and obligations more difficult, it would be outlawed and called by an opprobrious name. Some societies do try to ban such unions, but seldom are the sanctions severe enough to dissolve a relationship already established. If the undocumented union possesses the other four ingredients of a regular marriage—that is, if it is open and durable and involves offspring, a common residence, and a customary division of labor—there is little to be gained and much to be lost (especially for children) by breaking it up. A simpler remedy is to have the couple go through a *belated* marriage ceremony, thus "legitimizing" the children. The union is then a marriage. Still more simple is a law declaring de facto unions to be marriages, with all the rights and obligations thereto pertaining. This is the famous common-law marriage of countries with an English legal tradition. The name signifies a marriage entered into by a designated path, but a path different from that usually taken.

Slightly further away from normal marriage is the "consensual union," which is widely tolerated but not ordinarily given official or religious recognition. In some parts of Latin America it constitutes a majority of all unions. Unlike common-law marriage, the consensual union, unless recognized by statute, has no legal standing. To dissolve it, one does not need a divorce. The man is not required to support the woman or her offspring. The only enforcement of family obligations therefore comes from public opinion, which may be sufficient in small communities but not in cities. Unlike parties to a common-law marriage, a partner in a consensual union can be married to someone else, in which case the relationship can be called concubinage or de facto polygamy.

Unions other than full marriage generally lack more than formal recognition and approval. For instance, if a couple openly live together and establish a division of labor but do not (at least for the time being) intend to stay permanently together and have children, they are missing three and possibly four of the attributes of true marriage in Figure I.1. On the other hand, they do share a common residence, which gives their relation the name "cohabitation." If this trait is also missing, the relationship is harder to name, but the term *liaison* perhaps comes the nearest.

Why Sexual Unions?

If this conceptual analysis of marriage and its alternatives is useful, it leads us to the question of why the various kinds of union exist and why they differ in normative standing. For example, why is it that all five of the unions named in the stub of Figure I.1 have one trait in common, namely, a sexual relationship of some duration? The answer: this is what we mean by "unions," and it is unions that we are discussing. But why is it that, of all five types of union, marriage is the only one entered with full public approval and ceremonial recognition? The answer is again simple: that is what is called "marriage." The family is the part of the institutional system through which the creation, nurture, and socialization of the next generation is mainly accomplished. If these vital and extremely demanding tasks are to be performed efficiently, some individuals must be held responsible for them and rewarded for the effort. The genius of the family system is that, through it, the society normally holds the biological parents responsible for each other and for their offspring. By identifying children with their parents, and by penalizing people who do not have a stable reproductive relationship, the social system powerfully motivates individuals to settle into a sexual union and take care of the ensuing offspring.

To make the family system work, however, a weak link in the system needs to be strengthened. The weak link is, of course, the father. While the mother is tied to her offspring by physiological and psychological bonds, the same cannot be said of the father. To be sure, he has a sexual bond of sorts with the mother, but as time goes by he tends to feel more attraction to new or younger females. As a consequence, human societies have evolved strong controls, or incentives, that attach the male to the family. These are particularly evident when a new family is formed, that is, at marriage. At that moment advantage is taken of the youthfulness of the bride and groom to emphasize their togetherness, to impress upon them the importance and social approval of their sexual contact, and to stress the durability of the relationship and its connection with children. At this moment, too, the match—the tradeoff of traits, interests, and assets that binds the two sides together—is finalized. The long-run commitment of the male, regardless of his tendency to roam, is reinforced in ritual and in the involvement of his relatives and allies. In sum, not only does the public and ceremonial recognition of the new union instill a sense of permanence, but it also provides a basis for enforcement later on. To the extent that new bonds are created by marriage, it is difficult to cancel the marriage when sexual ardor has waned.

Nonmarital Unions

What are ordinarily called marriages are therefore sexual unions established with public approval and control and normally involving the other four traits in Figure I.1. Competing kinds of unions exhibit some of these traits but lack matrimony's unique public and ceremonial recognition. They coexist with marriage not only because of biology but also because of social conditions affecting the advantages and disadvantages of nonconformity. If marriage is so highly regulated that it is difficult to enter or to leave, couples will be tempted to forget the controls and form unrestrained sexual unions. On the other hand, if marriage is made so trivial that it can be entered or left at a moment's notice, young people will become indifferent as to whether they are married or not. Actual social systems represent a compromise between these extremes. As we have seen, unions established without the prescribed formalities are not necessarily outlawed. To remedy them, a society has two options. It can legitimate the maverick union by a belated ceremony (often when the bride is pregnant), or it can declare the union to be legal by virtue of having existed for a specified period. Only if neither option is taken are the consequences of unwed cohabitation serious. In that case, the unmarried couple may soon separate, may "live in sin" indefinitely, or may have children or not; but since the male will have little incentive to remain in the menage, the chances of permanence are slight, and the children, if any, will probably be reared by the mother alone.

To avoid such consequences, most societies provide disincentives to forming such unions in the first place. One stratagem is to seclude women, preventing contact with males other than close relatives. Another is to marry off girls at puberty, leaving no time for premarital pregnancy. A third is to penalize masculine sexual advances toward respectable women so heavily that few men will venture them.

The Urban-Industrial Erosion

Thus we can see how traditional societies buttress marriage in spite of the male's promiscuous character and the competition of other kinds of sexual union. In times of crisis, the family may revert to a mother-offspring unit, but in general the advantages of full marriage are great enough to pull the male into the domestic unit. The same can be said of urban-industrial societies in their early history. Marriage not only remained prevalent but involved an unusually sharp and reciprocal division of labor between husband and wife (Davis 1984). Now, however, in the late stages of modernization, controls over sexual and reproductive behavior have become ineffective. The loss of local surveillance, the employment of women outside the home, the rise of bureaucratic authority over children, and the increase in divorce all have undermined the norms and lessened the advantages of marriage. Projection of

Table I.1

Percent Unmarried Among Swedes Aged 30–39

	Men	Women
1972	24.2	17.3
1981	40.2	31.3

such trends leads many observers to predict either a disappearance of marriage as it has been known or a failure of industrial societies to survive.

Certainly, if a nation, say, were to abandon its preference for marriage in favor of a completely laissez-faire policy—that is, if it made no effort to discourage or transform de facto unions—the system of marriage as traditionally known would be jeopardized. This may already be happening in Sweden. There, in 1981, among people aged 30–39, four-tenths of the men and nearly a third of the women were unmarried. The swift rise of Swedish nonmarriage can be seen by comparing 1981 with 1972 (see Table I.1).[1]

At the rate of change shown by these figures, Swedish men aged 30–39 would be 100 percent unmarried by 1997, and Swedish women by 1999. No wonder Sweden has a high proportion of births out of wedlock (39.7 percent in 1980). In other countries the ratio is lower, but it has been rising.

Why do governments in most advanced countries take a laissez-faire attitude toward marriage? One factor, it seems, is the sheer size of modern states. With millions of citizens, a country finds it difficult to regulate personal intimacy. Further, each nation generally includes a diversity of ethnic and religious groups that have strong but often conflicting mores. Facing intense lobbying by these warring groups, the regime in power finds it difficult to take a strong stand of its own. Instead, it takes the easier path of letting people behave according to their consciences. This presumably means letting each ethnic or religious group practice its own marital mores, but since such groups lack enforcement powers (unless delegated to them), they cannot guarantee control. Gradually, then, there is a drift toward permissiveness. Official policies move in the direction of sexual freedom, no-fault divorce, open homosexuality, subsidized illegitimacy, teenage contraceptive services, tolerated pornography, and free abortion. The general public does not welcome these developments, which more or less tend to undermine marriage, but it finds itself paralyzed by its own internal conflicts.

Even when a government enacts into law the views of a conservative constituency, evasion tends to nullify the effort. For instance, in various ways people evade the absolute ban on divorce that some Roman Catholic countries still impose. They either avoid legal marriage in the first place and simply live together, thus making de facto divorce easy, or if they are legally married, they obtain an annulment, secure a divorce in a foreign country, or simply separate and cohabit with someone else. Whatever the marriage laws, it is seldom to anybody's direct interest (other than spouse and children) to have the laws enforced, whereas there is often strong interest in evasion. Further, vigorous enforcement may hurt the child. To penalize a woman for bearing a child out of wedlock hardly benefits the child, but encouraging the parents to get married may do so. The current tendency in advanced societies to give the unwed mother special attention and special financial support benefits the child but strikes a long-run blow at marriage, especially when the solicitude exceeds that shown for married mothers. In the United States in 1981, Aid to Families with Dependent Children (AFDC) amounted to $7.8 billion (*Statistical Abstract of the United States 1984*, pp. 371, 396). The proportion of the recipients who were unmarried was 42 percent, and rising rapidly.[2] Although some states in the United States have tried to track down illegitimate fathers and force them to pay child support, the predominant tendency has been for the government itself to play father and to treat the unwed mother as a special person needing help precisely because she has no husband. Thus irresponsible rather than responsible parenthood is encouraged.

A Substitute for Marriage?

If contemporary societies are failing to support the institution of marriage, does this mean that a substitute is on the way? If so, what is it?

The answer is not to be found in our list of unions in Figure I.1, simply because these are unions. If reproduction and socialization are to be accomplished by means of a sexual union, then that union is marriage, for marriage alone, among the various man–woman relations, has the traits that facilitate that accomplishment. So, if there is to be a substitute for marriage, it cannot be any kind of sexual union, but must be instead some kind of asexual arrangement. The most likely candidate is a reversion to the basic primate unit of mother and offspring. If this unit were publicly recognized and supported, and if effective incentives were provided for mothers, it could certainly perform the function of population replacement. Women could be selected, trained, and paid for childbearing and child care. Motherhood would thus become a profession like other professions. Other women would be free to enter any other occupation, just as men would be, without the handicap of family ties. Sexual relations, freed from their connection with reproduction, could be pursued without restraint.

Although the rise of single-parent households seems to portend such a development, especially in Scandinavian countries, there are good reasons for skepticism. For one thing, the professionalization of parenthood would be too expensive. In the past, by protecting parenthood from market forces, societies have obtained, without pay, the most dedicated, difficult, and yet important work that individuals can do. They have induced people to be parents out of love, pride, and duty, not out of greed. If governments now try to reverse themselves and pay women for motherhood, they will find the bill staggering. Thomas J. Espenshade (1984, p. 3) has estimated the expenditure of families per child in the United States in 1981 prices. For children under 18, and excluding college, the average expenditure comes out to about $82,400, which is $4,578 per year. Multiplying this by the number of children in 1981, we get over $289 billion per year, which is 10 percent of the GNP. This, however, includes neither college costs nor the expenditures the government already makes for the education, health, and welfare of children. In 1981, public education alone accounted for $102.5 billion (*Statistical Abstract of the United States 1984*, p. 153). Also, the expenditures per child by parents, even if wholly covered by the government, would not be a reward, but would merely cover the costs. To make parenthood profitable, the government would have to pay much more than the current parental expenditures per child. It would have to pay, say, three times that amount, because expenditures on children constitute over a third of family income. If we add the average college costs to the expenditures on children under 18, we arrive at a total of $356 billion per year. Three times this would be $1,068 billion, which is 36 percent of the GNP. This, of course, would not be all that the government would have to pay, for there would still be school, welfare, and health costs that are not included in parental expenditures. Including these would bring the total hypothetical expenditure on children to roughly $1,205 billion, or 41 percent of 1981 GNP. I conclude that no government is likely to pay a "reproductive wage" high enough to induce single women to have enough children to replace the population.

A further ground for not expecting a wholesale shift to single parenthood is the virtual universality of durable sexual unions. Although sexual attraction is generally ephemeral or at least wanes with familiarity, it often initiates a bond that later turns into durable companionship. Indeed, one has only to observe new groups of singles to see how quickly the pairing off begins. Given an enduring man/woman relationship, there is hardly any way of preventing the man from taking an interest in the woman's offspring, especially if they are his as well. A regime of female-headed households would therefore tend to revert to a system of nuclear families.

If the nuclear family is to disappear, a more drastic change will have to occur. One such change could be the breaking of the parent/child bond rather than the man/woman bond. If children were reared together in special quarters by professional child-tenders, and if their paternal and maternal parentage were unknown, a recrudescence of the nuclear family would be prevented. As far as I know, however, such a system has never emerged. It was imagined by Plato in the *Republic*, and it was partially instituted by the radical kibbutzim in Israel, but it has not become a working principle in any society. The Israeli kibbutzim successfully collectivized child-rearing but did not eliminate the parent/child identity, with the result that the nuclear family resurrected itself, as shown by Melford Spiro in his famous book, *Venture in Utopia* (1956).[3]

Marital Instability and Its Consequences

Plainly, the features of marriage in Figure I.1 are interdependent. It is easier to cooperate in rearing children if there is, for example, a common residence and a division of labor between husband and wife. It is also easier if the marriage lasts. In a traditional society, close relatives help to give permanence to the milieu surrounding the children, regardless of what happens to the marriage; but with the growth of cities and industrialism, child care has become much more concentrated in the nuclear family. As a result, the high divorce rate characterizing the industrial nations is particularly significant. It is defeating the newly developed importance of marriage as a stable agency for the nurture and socialization of children. It is contributing not only to confused child-rearing but also to low fertility as couples limit births as a hedge against divorce.

Torn between condemning divorce as a disaster and excusing it as a liberation from old-fashioned restraints, modern governments resort to a wide variety of divorce laws. On the one hand, as noted above, some countries still ban absolute divorce altogether, while others permit divorce unilaterally, at the request of either party. Attempts to ban divorce entirely cannot succeed because, in the modern world, couples find ways of evasion. So contemporary governments are more commonly bowing to liberal demands by making divorce easier, reducing the role of marriage as a stable agency for children.

One might think that liberal divorce laws would diminish the need for extralegal unions. If divorce is available on request, marriage carries little risk, so why not get married? Actually, however, the opposite is true. The rise in divorce has been accompanied by a rise, not a fall, in cohabitation, as documented in the chapters by Carlson, Davis, and Spanier. Evidently, when divorce becomes very easy, as in the American no-fault system, the law is contrary to public sentiment. If marriage is trivialized by such legislation, individuals of course take advantage of the newly found permissiveness for their own purposes, but the public does not in principle approve of such moral abdication. If the young like to cohabit in temporary childless unions, they nevertheless refuse to dignify these relationships by calling them marriage.

Marriage and Public Opinion

This conclusion is buttressed by the strength of public sentiment favoring marriage. Curiously, at a time when cohabitation, divorce, illegitimacy, sexual deviancy, and low fertility are prevalent—when, in fact, marriage as an institution seems on the skids—surveys reveal that the public views marriage with strong approval, faith, and satisfaction. It resists policies and trends that erode marriage and insists on treating marriage as a goal in itself rather than as a means to something else. Further, the satisfaction with marriage is greater when people are reporting on their own personal situation than when they are reporting on society at large. The polls therefore suggest that the public clearly distinguishes between the ideal of marriage, which it strongly supports and enjoys, and social and demographic facts about contemporary trends, which it deplores.

On the ideal side, the polls uniformly attest to a very high value being placed on marriage and the family. In a Roper survey in 1981, no less than 92 percent of all respondents, and 89 percent of those under age 30, said they would welcome "more emphasis on traditional family ties" (Gallup Report No. 197, p. 6). In another survey of the same year, Gallup found that in a list of nineteen "social values," the one called "good family life" was rated as more important by more respondents (78 percent of men and 84 percent of women) than any other social value (Gallup Report No. 198, p. 4).

The approval of marriage is matched by a corresponding disapproval of cohabitation. In a Virginia Slims poll in 1979, only 19.2 percent of respondents would find it acceptable if their daughter were to live with someone outside of marriage, and only 10.5 percent would find it acceptable if their daughter were to have a baby outside of marriage (The 1980 Virginia Slims American Women's Opinion Poll). In the same poll, only 11.1 percent agreed that society could survive without marriage.

This very high regard for marriage does not rest solely on unrealistic idealism but on personal experience as well. To a surprising degree (given the actual problems of marriage) respondents regard their own marriages as satisfactory. According to an NORC (National Opinion Research Corporation) poll in 1982, 96 percent of respondents described their marriage as happy. In the same year 79 percent of 5,000 readers of Better Homes and Gardens said that their expectations of happiness in marriage were being fulfilled, and 81 percent said that if they had to do it over again, they would choose the same marital partner (Hastings and Hastings 1984, pp. 285, 288, 289).

Given this high regard for the institution of marriage and the personal satisfaction derived from it, people are alarmed by trends felt to be weakening marriage. Some 80 percent of the *Better Homes and Gardens* readers agreed that "family life in America is in trouble" (Hastings and Hastings 1984, p. 285). The Virginia Slims respondents overwhelmingly (69.2 percent) believed that marriage was weaker than it had been ten years before. They evidently thought that the forces weakening marriage can be stopped or reversed (the Virginia Slims study found only 22.9 percent predicting that the idea of marriage to the same person for life would disappear), but their diagnosis of the problem and its remedy was somewhat vague. When asked to specify "the greatest threat to family life today," the readers of *Better Homes and Gardens* gave "absence of religious foundation" as the main reason, followed by "inattentive parents," "divorce," and "moral decay," in that order (Hastings and Hasting 1984, p. 285).

In general in the polls, the public favors liberal causes, but when a liberal cause conflicts with marriage in some way, the cause loses support. For instance, public sentiment favors raising the status of women. An NORC poll in 1982 found that 68 percent favored the Equal Rights Amendment (Hastings and Hastings 1984, pp. 471–472). In the Virginia Slims poll, 64.5 percent of the respondents favored efforts to strengthen women's status in society. But when marriage or the family is brought into the picture, the support for female emancipation falls off. In the Virginia Slims poll, only 15 percent favored Ms. rather than Miss or Mrs. as a form of address for women, and 50.8 percent of women preferred to stay at home and take care of house and family rather than take a job outside the home. In regard to abortion, support of unrestricted abortion immediately falls if the husband and family are brought into the picture. In the Virginia Slims poll, 75.2 percent agreed that the abortion decision should be left to *the woman and her doctor*, but when asked if the father should have the right of veto, 43.2 percent said yes.

Similarly, the attitude toward government intervention in the family depends on what people think it will do to marriage. If they think it will strengthen marriage, they are for it. Thus a 1984 Gallup Poll found that only 10 percent of respondents favored "making up for past discrimination" by affirmative action for women (*Gallup Report* No. 224, p. 29). Apparently the public feels that affirmative action pulls women into the labor force who would otherwise stay at home and take care of their families. As late as 1982 in Canada, 55 percent of respondents thought a mother's working had "a harmful effect on family life." In answer to the same question in the same year, 69 percent of 5,000 readers of *Better Homes and Gardens* said the effect would be harmful (Hastings and Hastings 1984, pp. 290–291). But when the question of a wife's working is posed without reference to the family or affirmative action, the response is overwhelmingly one of approval. According to the 1982 NORC study, 84 percent of respondents would vote for a woman if she were nominated for president by the respondent's party, and in South Africa 90 percent of a sample of whites thought that a woman can perform in a job as well as a man (Hastings and Hastings 1984, p. 472). If the job involves close friendships with men, however, the response is less positive: in the *Better Homes and Gardens* survey, 53 percent of male householders said this would make them uncomfortable (Hastings and Hastings 1984, p. 287). That the public resents government interference unless it favors marriage and the family is shown in France, where in 1982 some 74 percent of a sample favored creation of a government fund to guarantee divorced women their alimony (Hastings and Hastings 1984, p. 278), and West Germany where a majority in 1983 were against military service for women (*World Opinion Update*, p. 36).

Idealism versus Reality

The profound faith and personal satisfaction in marriage shown by the polls raise a significant question. How can people cherish marriage, believe in its continuance, and think of themselves as being or becoming happily married when in fact the odds are against them? How can their idealism be reconciled with the grim world of reality, or do the polls misrepresent the public mind?

The answer, I think, is not that the polls lie. There is always, in human society, a contrast between ideal and actual behavior. If norms are to be effective in organizing social behavior, they must be supported, and the life-course they project for the individual must be felt as desirable. But the very existence of the norms indicates that there is something to be regulated, something to be overcome. In the case of marriage, the norms have to contend with atavistic sexual instincts, interpersonal conflicts, and competing social bonds. Enforcement of the norms therefore requires constant surveillance and strong incentives. At best, it will never be perfect.

People know there are potential hazards, but they also realize that without the norms the hazards would be worse. They therefore cling to moral ideals in the face of enormous adversity. In modern societies, urban living, culture clash, and intellectual sophistication have destroyed most of the consensus and much of the enforcement that formerly existed, but despite all the difficulties, adults keep trying to instill the norms in the young and to shield youth from realism and cynicism.

One of the first decisions the young make for themselves, with little input from parents, is how to handle the opposite sex. This usually precedes marriage by some years, so that by the time the decision to marry is made the idealism of mating is already tarnished but not completely gone. It is not necessarily banished by a knowledge of the odds against a successful marriage, because young couples tend to view themselves as exceptions to the rule. They thus realize or anticipate negative trends in the society and still retain their faith in their own marriage. In the Virginia Slims poll, 77 percent predicted that cohabitation will increase and 72 percent said that it will weaken marriage, but they themselves overwhelmingly favored sexual fidelity in marriage and love as a basis for marriage. Although they are aware of changing conditions, people obviously make a distinction between statistical reality on the one hand and moral preference on the other.

Social Change and the Future of Marriage

Faith in norms does not, however, stop social change. As industrialism continuously alters the way people live, it weakens the foundations of the old norms without creating a consensus on new ones. Instead of living in villages where one's behavior is constantly under surveillance by friends, relatives, and neighbors, people now live mostly in cities where few care about their behavior except policemen, creditors, and landlords. Instead of remaining in one milieu where their character and reputation are known, individuals can now move swiftly from one milieu to another and thus take advantage of pluralistic ignorance.

The role of special interest groups in eroding marital mores deserves particular attention. In industrial democracies, the theory is that each person votes as an independent individual, but in reality he usually votes as a member of a bloc whose leaders wield power behind the scenes and represent the bloc's interest rather than that of the society at large. Such interest groups often justify their advocacy of violating a particular norm by appealing to a supposedly higher norm. For example, as shown by numerous polls, the public rejects homosexuality. In the Virginia Slims poll, 71 percent of respondents said they would not accept a homosexual daughter. From this one could conclude that homosexuals would be excluded from employment giving them access to youths; but no, the opposite is true: in a number of states, under the banner of nondiscrimination but evidently in quest for homosexual votes, legislators have outlawed such exclusion.

That new conditions engender new attitudes is indisputable, but the important question is not change per se but its direction. Nothing in history is comparable to the changes wrought by the continuing Industrial Revolution, and the general direction of the changes is clear: it is toward the use of inanimate energy and scientific technology to produce ever more goods and services per person. The transformation has taken a species that evolved in small face-to-face groups and put it in cities and societies with millions of inhabitants. It has given an animal once satisfied with food and rudimentary shelter and clothing a magical ability to fill new wants.

How has this fantastic transformation of human existence affected marriage? Has it altered marriage in fundamental ways? Has it increased the productivity, or efficiency, of marriage? The answer, I think, is that compared to most other aspects of human society, marriage has changed surprisingly little. As an institution, contemporary wedlock bears an indubitable likeness to marriage three centuries or three millennia ago. It still has the same essential character that it had then. The main reason for this remarkable continuity is that marriage is not simply a means to other goals but is a goal in itself. The industrial transformation has multiplied the means, not the goals, of human existence.

The general direction of the changes in marriage that the present book documents during the last forty years is toward a weakening of marriage as an institution. If this goes far enough, and if no satisfactory substitute for marriage emerges, industrial societies will not survive. In fact, they are not replacing themselves now, in either number or quality of the next generation. The nonindustrial two-thirds of the world, ill equipped to provide adequate education, is producing 92 percent of the world's next generation. There is thus no assurance that industrial societies, as we have known them, will survive.

In this regard, the country to watch may not be Sweden, the United States, or any advanced country, but China. More than any other nation, China has altered and regulated the institution of marriage for state purposes. It is the one Third World country that has succeeded in reducing the birth rate *ahead* of economic development, and as Margery Wolf brings out in her chapter, this has been accomplished through its control of marriage. The government has successfully discouraged sexual relations outside of marriage and thus maintained marriage as a sexual union, but it has reduced the significance of marriage for kinsmen, has raised the average age at marriage, has put wives to work outside the home, and has drastically reduced marital fertility. China has thus tried to achieve the demography of a highly developed society while still being primarily an agrarian society. Its policy has had more success in towns and cities than in the countryside, but even so, the program has been more effective than anyone predicted. The Chinese example thus indicates that in the future there may be more regulation of marriage for purposes of reaching some desired level of fertility. The rate of reproduction may become too important to be left to folk mores and religious doctrines. James Smith, in his chapter on the Mormons, shows how religious control can produce a high birth rate even when the sect is surrounded by a society with a low rate. Mormonism has incorporated marriage into its theological system as no other religion has, and this, in addition to its unique missionary system, has given the Mormon church an extremely rapid growth in membership. Yet the data show that, after a lag, Mormons follow trends evident in the surrounding society.

In the past, marriage has been a resilient institution. Several chapters, especially those by Kuper, Stone, and Modell, show its remarkable survival power under adverse or changing conditions. Although marriage reflects both the policies and the conditions of the time, it does not do so as a mirror. Like any other social institution, it has a life of its own and makes its own contribution to society. It therefore influences as well as reflects the rest of society.

At no time in history, with the possible exception of Imperial Rome, has the institution of marriage been more problematic than it is today, but nevertheless, none of our authors predicts its abandonment or even radical changes in its form in the future.

NOTES

1. Calculated from United Nations, *Demographic Yearbook 1982*, pp. 946–947, 950–951.

2. Estimated on the basis of the trend from 1975 to 1979.

3. See also Tiger and Fox (1971).

REFERENCES

Davis, Kingsley. "Wives and Work: Consequences of the Sex Role Revolution." *Population and Development Review*, 10 (September 1984):401–405.

Espenshade, Thomas J. *Investing in Children: New Estimates of Parental Expenditures*. Washington, D.C.: The Urban Institute Press, 1984.

Gallup Report No. 197 (February 1982).

Gallup Report No. 198 (March 1982).

Gallup Report No. 224 (March 1984).

Hastings, Elizabeth Ham, and Hastings, Philip K. (eds.). *Index to International Public Opinion, 1982–1983* (Westport, Conn.: Greenwood Press, 1984).

New York Times, November 23, 1984, p. 13.

Plato. *Republic*. Oxford: Oxford University Press, 1945.

Spiro, Melford E. *Kibbutz: Venture in Utopia*. Cambridge, Mass.: Harvard University Press, 1956.

Statistical Abstract of the United States 1984.

Tiger, Lionel, and Fox, Robin. *The Imperial Animal*. New York: Holt, Rinehart & Winston, 1971.

United Nations, *Demographic Yearbook 1982*.

The 1980 Virginia Slims American Women's Opinion Poll: A Survey of Contemporary Attitudes. New York: Roper Organization, 1980.

World Opinion Update, Vol. VII, Issue 3 (March 1984), p. 36.

PART I

The Revolution in Marital Behavior: The Factual Study

1 *The Future of Marriage*

KINGSLEY DAVIS

THE LAST WORLD WAR, like the one that preceded it, was so cataclysmic that it established a common starting point for the industrial nations. From that point on, social trends were surprisingly similar from one country to another. For instance, all the industrial nations had a marriage boom right after the war, followed soon afterward by a baby boom; and they nearly all had a second baby boom in the late 1950s and early 1960s, followed in turn by the most drastic drop in fertility ever known. Similarly, they had a postwar divorce peak and later, after a lull, a steady rise in divorce. There were, of course, minor differences between countries, and these tended to widen as distance from World War II increased, but still there was remarkable similarity. One can therefore learn a great deal about contemporary marriage by analyzing the similarities and differences between advanced nations.

The analysis that follows will, where data permit, deal with informal (nonlegal) unions as well as legal ones. It will also deal with important aspects of life relevant to marriage—such as work, reproduction, parenthood, divorce, and widowhood. And, to give focus to the treatment, it will ask apparently simple questions: Is marriage somehow weakening as an institution? Is it occupying a less important place in people's lives? If so, when we turn to the quantitative evidence, we would expect to find postponement of marriage, fewer people ever getting married, a smaller proportion of life being spent in wedlock, and a rising preference for competing types of relationship. Admittedly, these signs are not all conclusive. Postponement of marriage, for example, could mean that people are taking marriage *more* seriously, not less. A lesser proportion of life spent in wedlock might reflect nothing motivational but rather a change in sex differences in mortality. In reviewing the evidence, then, one must test the interpretation of one kind of data by assessing its consistency with other kinds.

Postponement of Marriage

A strategic topic to start with is entry into marriage, and in this regard some instructive comparisons can be made. The first is geographical and cultural: Western Europeans have long entered marriage later than other peoples and have married later in Europe than in the New World. In most industrial countries the age at marriage declined noticeably through most of the twentieth century, especially after World War II, but recently there has been a reversal, with the average age at first marriage rising almost everywhere.

Figures 1.1–1.4 show the postwar trend for several industrial countries, with either the mean or the median age at first marriage as the index. Regardless of the starting level, the slope is always downward until about the 1970s, when the trend reverses itself. Although the reversal has not gone far, it marks a turning point, coming as it does after a long decline that evidently started in most industrial countries around the turn of the century or even earlier. Further, the recent upsurge is quite rapid. How long the reversal will last cannot be judged by these curves alone. Other data suggest that it will last for a considerable time.

Figure 1.1

Mean Age at First Marriage: Male

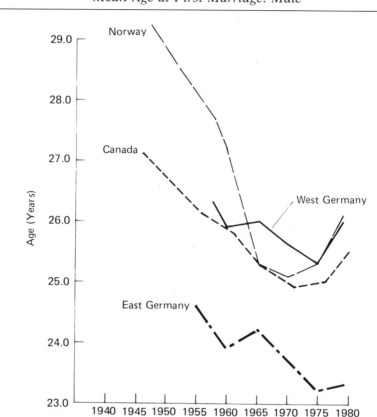

SOURCES: Statistical abstracts and yearbooks for the four countries, various years.

The Propensity to Marry

The average age at marriage tells us how old the people who marry are when they marry, but nothing about people who never marry. If marriage is weakening, we would expect weddings not only to be postponed but, in a substantial number of cases, to be forgone entirely.

Since, however, the proportion who never marry cannot be known until the people in question are old, the evidence arrives too

Figure 1.2

Mean Age at First Marriage: Female

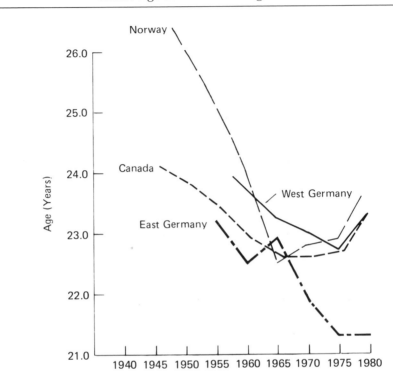

SOURCES: Statistical abstracts and yearbooks for the four countries, various years.

late to throw light on the present and future propensity to marry. For example, among people aged 45–49, the proportion never married has been falling, not rising, but these people were in the prime marrying ages twenty to twenty-five years ago; they therefore reflect behavior at that time, not at present.

If instead of age 45–49, we take a younger age—say, age 25–29—we obtain more up-to-date information, but at the cost of mixing postponement with permanent nonmarriage. The trend of the proportion never married at this age is shown in Table 1.1 for several countries. Every country except Japan manifested a declining trend in nonmarriage at this age until about 1965 or 1970. After that, except in Ireland, the trend reversed itself. The reversal has been particularly sharp in Sweden and the United States. Japan

Figure 1.3

Median Age at First Marriage: Male

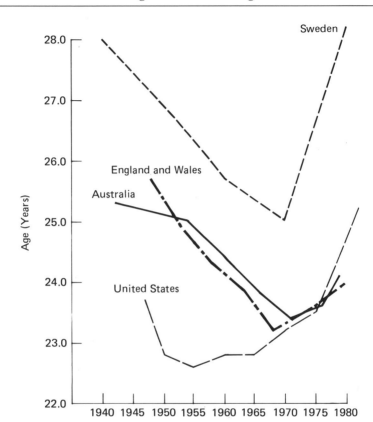

SOURCES: For first three countries, statistical abstracts and yearbooks, various years; for the United States, Bureau of the Census, "Marital Status and Living Arrangements: March 1982," *Current Population Reports*, Series P-20, No. 380 (May 1983), p. 2.

had a rise in nonmarriage right after World War I corresponding to a period when the birth rate was drastically reduced, but after that the proportion married at age 25–29 remained rather stable, rising slightly for both males and females between 1970 and 1975 but sharply after that. Ireland, which had the highest nonmarriage rate of any country in the world, deflated this rate speedily after the war. The direction of its trend thus conformed to that of industrial countries in general, but with a speed indicating that it was catch-

Figure 1.4

Median Age at First Marriage: Female

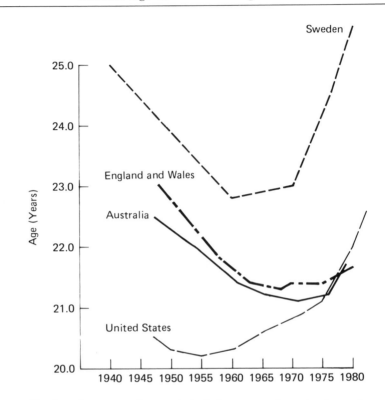

SOURCES: For first three countries, statistical abstracts and yearbooks, various years; for the United States, Bureau of the Census, "Marital Status and Living Arrangements: March 1982," *Current Population Reports*, Series P-20, No. 380 (May 1983), p. 2.

ing up. Far from reversing itself, the downward trend in Irish non-marriage has continued up to the present, which one would expect if the country is still catching up with mainstream industrial nations.

Other things equal, the proportion of people never married tends to be reduced by a high divorce rate: the rapid formation and breakup of marriages throws more people onto the marriage market (that is, people who have been married but are unmarried again). This broadened market increases the marital opportunities of single people. Accordingly, the recent rise in the proportion

Table 1.1

Proportion of Population Aged 25–29 Who Have Never Married,
Selected Countries, 1950–1980

Year and Sex	Percent Never Married						
	Sweden	U.S.A.	Japan	Canada	France	Ireland	New Zealand
Males							
1950	48.6	23.8	41.1[a]	35.1[b]	37.4[c]	76.6[b]	36.8[b]
1960	41.2	20.8	46.1	29.6[b]	38.1	67.2	29.6
1965	37.9	NA	45.7	27.4[b]	NA	58.5	26.7
1970	40.8	19.6	46.4	25.6[b]	32.6	49.2	NA
1975	56.3	22.3	48.3	27.0[b]	30.89	NA	23.0
1980	68.5	32.4	55.1	33.2	31.4	39.1[d]	29.4[b]
1982	70.7[d]	36.1	NA	NA	NA	NA	NA
Females							
1950	26.4	13.3	20.6[a]	20.7[b]	22.7	54.4	18.9
1960	20.7	10.5	21.6	15.4[b]	19.8	45.1	12.5
1965	20.2	NA	18.9	14.9[b]	NA	37.8	11.8
1970	23.0	12.2	18.1	15.4[b]	18.1	31.2	NA
1975	35.0	13.8	20.9	16.3[b]	19.6	NA	11.8
1980	48.8	20.8	24.0	20.2	20.7	26.3[d]	15.7[b]
1982	51.3[d]	23.4	NA	NA	NA	NA	NA

[a] 1955 instead of 1950.
[b] Dates are one year later.
[c] French dates are 1954 instead of 1950, 1962 instead of 1960, 1968 instead of 1970.
[d] Dates are for previous year.
SOURCES: United Nations, 1982, p. 810, Table 40; ibid., 1979, Table 12.

never married is all the more impressive since it has occurred at a time of climbing divorce rates.

The Rising Proportion of the Unmarried

The "unmarried" category includes not only those who have never married but also those who have been widowed or divorced and have not remarried. As the divorce rate rises, this category tends to expand, but not proportionately, because the number of the unmarried depends on rates of widowhood and remarriage as well. For this reason, the number of the unmarried tends to rise with age, because at older ages people are widowed more and remarry less.

Table 1.2

Proportion of Population Unmarried, By Age and Sex, United States and Sweden, 1940–1980

Year	Males				Females			
	20–24	25–29	30–34	35–39	20–24	25–29	30–34	35–39
Sweden								
1940	91.6	59.5	36.4	27.0	71.8	40.4	29.3	28.0
1950	84.6	49.6	28.6	22.2	60.2	28.3	18.8	18.4
1960	81.2	41.3	25.9	21.3	56.3	22.3	15.2	14.9
1965	80.9	39.2	23.3	20.0	58.0	22.5	14.6	13.9
1970	83.9	43.3	24.7	20.2	61.8	26.8	16.8	15.0
1975	91.7	58.9	34.3	25.2	77.0	40.2	24.4	18.9
1979	94.2	68.3	42.8	30.7	83.0	50.8	31.3	25.0
1980	94.8	70.9	44.9	32.2	84.5	53.4	33.3	26.1
1981	95.3	73.0	46.9	33.8	85.8	55.8	35.2	27.4
United States								
1950	61.3	27.4	17.3	15.0	36.6	19.3	16.3	17.2
1960	55.4	24.3	16.0	13.4	32.8	16.6	14.1	14.6
1970	58.3	24.8	16.2	14.0	42.1	20.8	17.3	16.8
1977	69.9	34.4	21.5	15.8	53.2	29.6	22.5	21.5
1982	74.4	44.3	29.5	22.4	60.0	37.0	29.0	26.1

SOURCES: Central Bureau of Statistics of Sweden, Tables 1–4: "The Whole Country and the Counties, etc."; United Nations, 1979, Table 12; ibid., 1982, pp. 846–877, 950–951; U.S. Bureau of the Census, October 1981, p. 7; ibid., April 1978, p. 7.

Table 1.2 and Figures 1.5 and 1.6 show more strikingly than the previous figures the revolution that is taking place. Until 1960, in the industrial nations, being married was becoming more universal. But during the 1960s and particularly the 1970s, a rapid reversal occurred. In one decade, for example, Sweden's proportion unmarried rose so fast that it wiped out a decline that had taken thirty years to accomplish. In the United States in 1982, 29.0 percent of women aged 30–34 were unmarried compared to only 14.1 percent in 1960. At ages over 30 most of the change has been due to the rise in divorce, but a substantial part of it has arisen from a growing unwillingness to marry in the first place, as noted earlier. At present, then, a weakening of marriage is certainly occurring, at least in the sense that matrimony is rapidly becoming less prevalent. At the rate of change occurring among women 30–34 in the United States in the period 1970–1982, it will take only thirteen years for half the women in that age group to be unmarried.

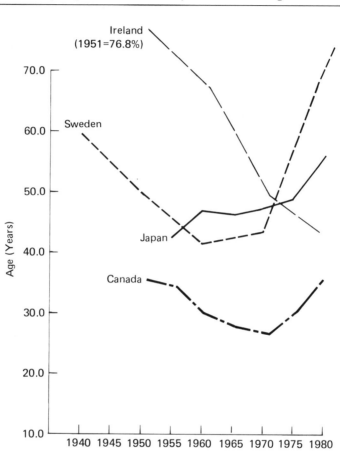

Figure 1.5

*Proportion of Population **Currently** Unmarried: Age 25–29 Male*

The Cohabitation Trend

Some observers will argue that this explosive decline of marriage
is a change more in form than in substance, a change offset by a
corresponding and equally explosive rise in informal unions, vari-
ously called consensual unions, de facto marriages, or cohabiting
couples. To this argument, however, there are two answers: first,
statistically the two kinds of unions do not behave similarly; second, even if they are comparable, there are not enough de facto
unions to compensate for the loss of legal ones.

Figure 1.6

Proportion of Population Currently Unmarried: Age 25–29 Female

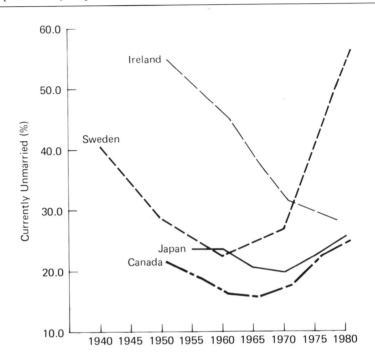

How Many Consensual Unions?

Precisely because informal unions are nonlegal and hence not re-corded in registration systems, it is difficult to obtain quantitative information on them.[1] However, data on households and living ar-rangements throw some light on such relationships, and occasion-ally a question is asked bearing directly on such unions. In the United States, for instance, the annual survey of "Marital Status and Living Arrangements" now obtains information on unmarried couples living together. The surveys show that between 1970 and 1980 the number of such couples rose by 12 percent per year, and between 1980 and 1983 by 6 percent per year.

Much has been made of this rapid increase, but as yet the pro-portion of consensual unions among all unions is small: it was only 1.1 percent in 1970, 3.1 percent in 1980, and 3.6 percent in 1983. If the 1970–1983 change in the percent were to continue, in thirty years cohabitation would represent half of all unions. There is of course no good ground for extrapolating the trend far into the future, but already the tendency to live together without marriage is retarding or reversing the growth of the married population. Between 1970 and 1983 the number of married couples in the United States increased by 12 percent, while the number of unmarried heterosexual couples living together increased by 262 percent. Further, persons living alone proliferated by 77 percent, and households of two unrelated adults of the same sex, by 239 percent. Same-sex couples now rival opposite-sex informal couples; the two together make up 6.2 percent of all couples. Doubtless many of the same-sex couples are merely sharing living quarters (the American data do not say how many), but altogether, by 1983, households with a legally married couple had fallen to 59 percent of all households, from 71 percent in 1960.

Other countries show a similar retreat from legal marriage. In Sweden, in the twelve years from 1968 to 1980, the number of first marriages for women dropped by 37 percent, while the number of cohabiting couples rose rapidly. As Jan Trost has pointed out, in 1960 unmarried cohabiting couples were 1 percent of all couples and thus 99 percent were married; but by 1970 the proportion of unmarried cohabiting couples had reached 7 percent, and the estimate for 1979 was 15 percent. A survey in Norway in 1970 showed that at age 18–19, among all women living with a man, 43 percent were not married; at age 20–24, 26 percent were not married; and at age 25–29, 6 percent were not married. At age 23, of all women who had ever lived with a man, only 58 percent had done so only within legal marriage. At young ages, then, consensual unions in Norway are competing with marriage. Most women eventually enter a legal marriage, usually with the man they are living with at the time, but legalization is increasingly postponed.

If young people were merely substituting de facto marriage for legal marriage, the total union rate—that is, the combined rate of unions, whether legal or not—should be holding up. People in consensual unions should also be behaving in the same way people do in legal unions, and they should have the same attitudes and expectations, but the data do not fulfill these expectations. In the United States the percentage of women age 15 or above in any kind of union has been declining. It was 61.6 percent in 1970, 58.2 percent in 1977, and 55.6 percent in 1982, despite the rise in the number of unmarried couples. This drop in the proportion in any kind of union could occur only because of an increase in the number of people living alone. Between 1970 and 1983 in the United States, persons living alone increased by 4.5 percent per year. Since the absolute number of such persons greatly exceeds those living in unmarried unions, this rapid increase has more than canceled the expansion of cohabitation. In 1983, for example, the number living alone was five times the number living with a nonrelative of the opposite sex (U.S. Bureau of the Census, May 1983, pp. 6, 36).

How Similar Are Marriage and Cohabitation?

Logically, if cohabitation were simply marriage without trivial formalities, the displacement of marriage by cohabitation would lack significance. If, on the other hand, the two differ in essentials, the substitution tendency, if carried much further, may have socially important implications. Such evidence as we have suggests that the two kinds of union are different.

For instance, participants in consensual unions are younger than married couples. In 1982 the ratio of informal heterosexual unions to legal marriages in the United States was much higher for the young than for those over 35, as the following figures show (U.S. Bureau of the Census, May 1983, pp. 46–48).

Age	Informal Unions as Percent of Marriages
Under 25	18.4
25–34	6.8
35–44	2.4
45–64	1.3
65 +	1.4

Between 1976 and 1982, the fastest increase in the proportion of informal unions in the United States was for people under 45. Similarly, in Norway cohabiting women tend to be younger than married women. In 1977, 59 percent of women in consensual unions were below age 25, whereas only 14 percent of wives were in those ages (Central Bureau of Statistics of Norway, p. 52).

From these data on age, it can be argued that consensual

unions are a form of trial marriage. Young people live together for a while. If things work out in the "relationship," they ultimately decide to have children and to marry legally; thus at older ages they are overwhelmingly married. This seems plausible, but the data can be interpreted in another way—namely, that the cohorts now in the young adult ages are setting a new lifetime pattern, a pattern different from that of their parents.

A second difference between cohabitation and regular marriage—and one that lends some support to the trial marriage interpretation—is that consensual unions are much less fertile than legal marriages. In the United States in 1982, for instance, the proportion of couples with own children under 18 was lowest for consensual unions (*Statistical Abstract of U.S.*, 1984, p. 52; U.S. Bureau of the Census, May 1983, p. 6):

Households Headed by	Percentage with Children Under 18
A lone person	57.5
A married couple	49.3
An unmarried couple	25.5*

*Refers to households with children under 15.

The facts are compatible with the hypothesis that men and women in nonmarital unions tend either to remain childless, to break up the union, or, if they decide to have children, to marry.

In Norway, where some 13 percent of women under age 30 who live with a man do so without being married, only 4 percent of mothers at first birth are in such a situation. Further, childbirth seldom leads women in consensual unions to become legally married. What appears to be true in Norway is that consensual unions, whether fruitful or not, are overwhelmingly abandoned for legal marriage within a few years. If they are abandoned, it is not because a child has been born but because one is on the way. According to the 1977 survey in Norway, only 8 percent of first births are to women in a consensual union or no union at all, while 40 percent are conceived before wedlock but born legitimately.

If consensual unions are tending to replace marriage, especially at younger ages, and if they are less fertile than legal marriage, then one of the causes of low fertility in industrial nations is the rise of consensual unions.

Still another difference between consensual and legal unions is that the consensual ones are less stable. To the extent that consensual unions are trial marriages, this is automatically true, for on the average it would be the more stable unions that turn into marriages. But again, if there is a trend toward displacement of marriage by consensual unions, a result may be an overall marginal rise in instability of unions. In Norway, according to the 1977 fertility survey, "cohabitation without marriage which does not change into marriage is notably less stable than a formal marriage . . . . On the average, a terminated cohabitation without marriage has had a duration of 1.2 years compared with 7 years for terminated marriages."

The Function of Consensual Unions

All told, the differences between consensual unions and formal marriages seem great enough to defeat the equivalence argument. Although marriage in recent decades has evolved in the direction of consensual unions, it has not become identical to them, and it is possible that the two kinds of union will never coalesce. If so, one has to ask if they serve different functions. I have already made reference to one functional difference, namely, that consensual unions serve as trial balloons, turning into marriages if they prove congenial. Logically, this function was more necessary when marriage itself was quite formal, because trial unions would have helped save people from lifelong mistakes. When marriage itself is made easy to enter and leave, as it has been, then it can serve as its own trial arrangement. Since cohabitation became popular *after* the historical period when the marriage bond began to weaken, it must serve some function other than that of trial balloon. One possibility is that cohabitation is an ephemeral pairing based on sexual attraction, one that allows young people considerable postponement of marriage without loss of a convenient sexual partnership. In other words, we may be moving toward a widened separation of sex from reproduction, not so much in the form of adultery and mistresses (as in earlier times) as in the form of youthful and elderly (postreproductive) sexual freedom. If so, consensual unions compete not only with marriage but also with institutionalized "singles" groups. The advantage of consensual unions is that they imply some stability and security without childbearing or a long-term personal commitment; their disadvantage is that they limit the variety provided by the singles world. In recent years cohabitation has certainly been gaining on legal marriage but doing little more than holding its own in competition with singles groups.

Declining Marital Output

As the main institutional relationship through which societies license and encourage childbearing and child care, formal marriage is usually more productive of children than cohabitation or any other kind of sexual relationship. But in industrial societies two circumstances are undermining that preeminence: first, unlike marriages in the past, those of today are not producing enough children, by and large, to replace the population; second, the restriction of reproduction to wedlock is declining. Something thus seems to be amiss with the main societal function of marriage.

The Sinking Birth Rate

In the industrial world, as Table 1.3 shows, fertility has been falling for almost twenty-five years. It fell quite rapidly in the late 1960s and in the 1970s, after which it dropped at a slower pace. On a steady-state basis, the nineteen industrial countries as of 1980 would be reducing their population by 17 percent per generation.

The less developed the country, the higher the birth rate. Some European countries such as Spain, Portugal, Ireland, Poland, and Iceland still have replacement rates near or above unity, but not the more advanced nations. Were it not for immigration from the Third World, industrial countries such as the United States, Britain, Sweden, and Australia would have fertility rates still lower than those they actually have. Even the East European Communist states, which have pursued pronatalist policies (Andorka 1982, pp. 139–156), are below replacement. In the past, pronatalist policies in countries like Belgium, France, and the Netherlands have not noticeably increased the birth rate. The European parts of the Soviet Union are now below replacement.

The decline of fertility below replacement is all the more impressive in view of the fact that, compared to the past, "replace-

Table 1.3

Change in Average Fertility Rates for Nineteen Industrial Countries,
from 1945–1949 to 1980

	Gross Reproduction Rate		Net Reproduction Rate	
Period	Mean	Percent Change	Mean	Percent Change
1945–1949	1.41		1.27	
1950–1954	1.27	− 10.0	1.23	− 3.0
1955–1959	1.35	6.9	1.29	4.5
1960–1964	1.38	1.8	1.32	2.4
1965–1969	1.24	− 9.7	1.20	− 8.9
1970–1974	1.05	− 15.1	1.03	− 14.9
1975–1979	.85	− 15.9	.88	− 16.4
1980	.85	− 4.5	.83	− 4.5

NOTE: The countries are as follows: Australia, Austria, Belgium, Canada, Czechoslovakia, Denmark, England and Wales, Finland, France, Germany (West), Italy, Japan, Netherlands, New Zealand, Norway, Scotland, Sweden, Switzerland, United States. The means are arithmetic, unweighted by population. All percentages are calculated on the basis of figures less rounded than those shown. Some estimates were made by the author for 1979 and 1980. The last percent change is on a five-year basis.

SOURCES: United Nations, various years; *Population Index*, Vol. 47, pp. 402–411.

ment" today requires very little childbearing. In the United States in the mid-nineteenth century, a woman would have had to bear approximately 3.3 children on average to assure replacement (Davis 1976, p. 3). By 1980 the requirement was 2.1 children. Yet, while the nineteenth-century women produced more children than the high requirement of their time, those of today produce fewer than the low number now required.

Births per U.S. White Woman

	Actual	Required for Replacement
1855	5.31	3.32
1980	1.75	2.11

When people in industrial societies are asked how many children they want, or consider ideal, they respond on average with a figure higher than the number they actually have. For instance, in eight countries of northwestern Europe in 1979 the mean number of children regarded as ideal was 2.21, which if achieved would be enough to replace the population; but the actual rate of reproduction at the time was 1.65 per woman, only about three-fourths of replacement rate (Girard and Roussel 1982, p. 330).

A careless interpretation of this discrepancy might suggest an increase in the birth rate, since people will naturally strive to achieve their ideal. However, when the distribution of ideal numbers of children is analyzed, it shows that people overwhelmingly want two or three children. For instance, a French survey in 1975 found that 91 percent of families surveyed found either two or three children ideal (ibid., p. 334). Almost no couple wants to be childless or to have only one child, and very few want families of four or more children. In fact, however, according to fertility tables published by The National Center for Health Statistics (1976, pp. 246–248), a substantial number of women—23.9 percent of U.S. women born in 1925—will be childless or have only one child in spite of their desire for more. In the past, the deficiency of these women was overcome by other women who had large families, but today there are virtually no such large families. Thus a low fertility ideal inevitably means still lower fertility in practice, and the fact that the ideal is now itself barely at replacement suggests a depressed birth rate in the future. In 1980, American wives age 18–24 "expected" to have an average of only 2.09 births during their lifetime (*Statistical Abstract of the United States*, 1984, p. 67). It seems unlikely that they will replace the population.

The fact that in the United States birth rates have recently risen among women in their late 20s and early 30s has been hailed as the beginning of a new pattern whereby women assure their careers at an early age and, once established, start having children. This is certainly true of a substantial number of women, because women aged 30-plus had 21.7 percent of the U.S. births in 1982 as compared to 16.5 percent in 1975. However, mothers under age 25 still had 47 percent of all births in 1982. Some women doubtless prefer to have their children early and then return at a young age to their career. In any case, a shift in the age of childbearing represents a change in timing rather than a recrudescence of overall fertility.

The Rise of Nonmarital Reproduction

If nonreplacement fertility suggests weakness in the marital institution, so does the tendency of marriage to lose its monopoly of
births. In 1950, in the United States white population, only 1.7 percent of the births were to unmarried women, but by 1982 the percentage had risen to 12.1. A similar evolution has occurred elsewhere. In eighteen industrial countries the average ratio rose from
8.1 percent in 1966 to 14.8 percent in 1980. In some of these countries the percent of illegitimate births has reached staggering proportions—22.8 percent in East Germany, 33.2 percent in Denmark,
39.7 percent in Sweden. The trend is all the more surprising since
one could have expected an opposite change. Recalling that for two
decades after World War II the age at marriage dropped, the propensity to marry increased, and contraception was improved and
more widely diffused, one could have expected illegitimacy to diminish. The reason it did not diminish is that the illegitimate birth
rate—the number of illegitimate births per 1,000 unmarried
women—kept on rising or, if it fell, fell at a slower rate than legitimate fertility. In the United States white population, for example,
the illegitimate birth rate rose consistently from 6.1 per 1,000 unmarried women in 1950 to 18.8 in 1982. Since the legitimate birth
rate *fell* consistently after the 1950s, it can be seen that unmarried
women are coming closer and closer to equaling married women in
reproduction. In 1950, in the white population of the United States,
a thousand married women had 16.8 times more offspring than a
thousand unmarried women; by 1982 the ratio had dropped to
only 3.0 times. In the black population, age for age, an unmarried
woman is now about as likely to give birth as a married woman.

Perhaps many nonmarital births occur to couples who have a
stable relationship, but as noted already, in industrial societies the
fertility of cohabitational unions is low. It seems more likely that
most of the births called nonmarital really are nonmarital, and
that if their rise continues, they will rival marital births to a degree not exactly known in past history except in disorganized
societies such as the Caribbean.

The increasing proportion of births out of wedlock means that
a larger number of children will be cared for by only one parent.
In this sense, marriage in industrial societies is losing not only its
monopoly of births but also its monopoly of child care. I shall re-

turn to this point in a moment, but first it is necessary to consider another index of marital distress—divorce—which also gives rise to single-parent families.

The Exploding Divorce Rate

As industrialism advances, so does divorce. In the United States the divorce rate has exhibited a rising trend ever since the first data were gathered in 1867. In that year there was one divorce for every 3,333 inhabitants, while in 1981 there was one for every 189 inhabitants. A peak rate was reached in the immediate postwar years. The rate then declined to a low point in 1958, after which it resumed its climb and in 1973 surpassed the postwar peak. According to the age-specific divorce rates of 1976–1977 in the United States, 49.6 percent of marriages would end in divorce in the absence of mortality (Weed 1980).

Most other advanced countries have exhibited the same trends, but with a lag. Table 1.4 shows the postwar crude divorce rates for seventeen developed nations, and Table 1.5 shows the rate of change in the mean rate. The period immediately after World War II was one of high divorce rates, as always happens after a war, but after a lull in the 1950s the rate shot up to unprecedented levels. The mean rate for all eighteen countries was around 40 percent of the United States rate throughout the whole period—a very stable ratio. With respect to divorce, one can say that as the United States goes, so about twenty years later, goes the rest of the industrial world.

The remarriage rate after divorce is high; indeed, in the United States it is higher than the first-marriage rate for males of all ages and for females under age 30 (National Center for Health Statistics, 1981, pp. 17, 23). This penchant for remarriage has often been cited as evidence of people's enthusiastic confidence in marriage and hence evidence for the strength of the marital institution. Be that as it may, there is one qualification. As the divorce rate rises, the proportion of all marriages that are remarriages also rises. In the United States in 1930–1932, for instance, only 13.1 percent of the marriages involved a previously married woman. By 1981, 32.7 percent involved such a woman (National Center for Health Statistics, 1984, p. 8; *Statistical Abstract of U.S.*, 1981, p.

Table 1.4

Average Crude Divorce Rates per Half Decade in Seventeen Industrialized Countries, from 1945–1949 to 1975–1979

Country	1945–1949	1950–1954	1955–1959	1960–1964	1965–1969	1970–1974	1975–1979	1980–1982
Australia	.97	.84	.70	.67	.84	1.15	2.97	2.72[a]
Austria	1.68	1.42	1.21	1.14	1.25	1.36	1.57	1.78[a]
Belgium	.67	.50	.49	.53	.62	.82	1.29	1.51[a]
Canada	.53	.39	.38	.39	.66	1.58	2.38	2.69[a]
Czechoslovakia	.89	.97	1.11	1.19	1.46	1.92	2.14	2.24
Denmark	1.66	1.54	1.46	1.40	1.52	2.48	2.59	2.78
England and Wales	.83	.68	.54	.61	.88	1.84	2.66	2.96[a]
France	1.09	.73	.70	.66	.74	.90	1.37	1.62[b]
FRG	1.61	1.13	.83	.85	1.06	1.40	1.31	1.67[a]
GDR	2.05	1.81	1.29	1.40	1.65	2.04	2.59	2.79[a]
Japan	1.01	.93	.81	.74	.84	1.00	1.13	1.26[a]
Netherlands	.80	.57	.49	.49	.60	1.11	1.57	1.99
New Zealand	1.13	.79	.69	.72	.82	1.23	1.76	2.92
Norway	.68	.65	.60	.67	.76	1.07	1.50	1.68[a]
Sweden	1.03	1.17	1.19	1.17	1.37	2.10	2.63	2.46
Switzerland	.91	.90	.87	.84	.89	1.18	1.57	1.72[a]
USA	3.35	2.47	2.23	2.26	2.74	4.04	4.99	5.19
Mean	1.23	1.03	.92	.93	1.10	1.60	2.12	2.35

[a] No data for 1982.
[b] Estimate 1980 only.
SOURCE: United Nations, 1968, 1969, 1979, 1982.

Table 1.5

Percent Change in Mean Divorce Rates for Seventeen Industrial Countries, from 1945–1959 to 1980–1982

Period	Mean Rate	Annual Percent Change from Prior Period
1945–1949	1.23	
1950–1954	1.03	− 3.64
1955–1959	.92	− 2.11
1960–1964	.91	.17
1965–1969	1.10	3.53
1970–1974	1.60	7.80
1975–1979	2.12	5.77
1980–1982	2.35	2.64[a]

[a] Calculated on a five-year basis.

SOURCE: See Table 1.4.

80). It is well known among demographers that higher-order marriages are more unstable than first marriages. According to the age-specific divorce rates for 1975 in the United States, 30.4 percent of first marriages would be broken by divorce within ten years, while for remarriages the proportion would be 38.5 percent (Weed 1980). Divorce thus feeds on itself. The more there is, the more there will be, other things being equal. This means that some people—those who marry and divorce several times—contribute disproportionately to the divorce rate. If everybody who got divorced stayed divorced and did not remarry, the divorce table would be similar in method to a life table; instead, it is like a life table in which people die and get resurrected, some several times. For this reason, in figuring probabilities, one should keep first marriages and remarriages separate.

The statistics just discussed concern formal marriages. There is far less information on the breakup of informal unions, but such information as we have indicates that such unions are less stable than formal unions. In many cases the trauma of parting is surely just as great. This being true, the official divorce rate understates the force of divorce in a society. If cohabitational unions serve as trial marriages, we could expect that as such unions increase in relative importance, the official divorce rate would decline. The fact that this has not happened, at least as yet, suggests either that the trial-marriage theory of consensual unions is not accurate or that counterforces are at work undermining the stability of legal marriage.

One-Parent Households

It used to be that death was the main terminator of marriages; now it is divorce, and the divorce rate has climbed so high that it has pushed death into a relatively small role, especially at younger ages. According to U.S. age-specific rates for 1976–1977, of 100,000 marriages begun, 44,380 would be terminated either by death or by divorce in the first nineteen years. Of these, 82.5 percent would be terminated by divorce, 17.5 percent by death (Weed 1980).

Divorce has thus become the main cause of single-parent households. The other great cause is the relative rise of nonmarital parenthood (illegitimacy). The two together have caused the proportion of families with only one parent or with a stepparent to skyrocket. In 1970 in the United States 14.8 percent of children under 18 years of age were not living with both parents; by 1982 the proportion had risen to 25.0 percent. The greatest increase is in the illegitimate factor. In 1970, 6.8 percent of the parents in single-parent housholds had never been married; by 1982 this proportion had climbed to 21.0 percent. But though it had a less rapid increase, the divorced or separated factor accounted for most one-parent households—60.5 percent in 1970 and 66.5 percent in 1982 (U.S. Bureau of the Census, May 1983, p. 5). Increasingly, marriage is becoming less synonymous with having children. In 1970 in the United States 42.9 percent of married couples had no own children under 18 living with them; by 1983 the figure was 51.2 percent. Meanwhile, the proportion of family households without a married couple that had own children under 18 went up from 47.5 percent in 1970 to 56.2 percent in 1983 (U.S. Bureau of the Census, May 1982, p. 2; ibid., 1984, p. 2).

Work

One-parent families generally mean that the lone parent (usually the mother) must work. Divorce and illegitimacy thus contribute to female employment, and the reverse may also be true. An analysis of marriage would therefore be incomplete without a study of women's work.

Marriage has generally been characterized by cooperation between husband and wife. Sometimes this cooperation has involved doing the same work together, as when both husband and wife participated in planting or harvesting the crop. More commonly, it has involved doing different tasks which, to some degree, dovetail with one another. Such complementarity has taken two forms. First, it has involved a differential commitment to childbearing and child care, meaning that these activities fell almost exclusively to the wife and related women. Second, it has involved a division of economic labor, with husband and wife pursuing different activities in the production of goods. These different activities could require husband and wife to work together, as when the male plowed and the female planted, but more usually it involved their working separately, as when the husband hunted and the wife gathered nuts and fruit. In general, the assignment of economic tasks was such as to give the woman those that were most compatible with repeated pregnancies and continual child care, which usually meant tasks that could be done in or near the home.

The evolution of human societies from a hunting-and-gathering economy to industrialism required the development of an elaborate division of labor based on learned skills, differential access to resources, and exchange of products facilitated by an exchange medium. As a market for labor emerged that went far beyond what the age and sex differences of the nuclear family could provide, there arose in most societies a two-tiered system—a market for female labor, generally inferior in reward though not necessarily in productivity, and a market for male labor. The market for female labor created a conflict between the commitment of women to pregnancy and child care, on the one hand, and their value as labor in the extrafamilial labor market, on the other. In a purely agrarian economy, this conflict was reasonably well resolved, because the work of women outside the family tended to be an extension of the work they did in their own family—most definitely when they were employed as domestics. Furthermore, agricultural work was seasonal, lent itself to being interrupted, and was fairly close to home.

With industrialism, however, the conflict between participation in the outside labor market and duties at home has never been

Table 1.6

Recent Labor Force Participation Rates for Women Aged 20–59, by Marital Status, Selected Industrial Countries

Country and Date	Labor Force as Percent of Female Population Aged 20–59			
	All Women	Single	Married	Divorced or Widowed
Bulgaria, 1975	82.1	69.0	83.8	74.2
England and Wales, 1971	54.6	87.2	47.1	NA
Finland, 1975	66.8	68.1	65.6	73.4
France, 1975	54.2	75.3	47.8	71.8
Hong Kong, 1976	49.3	90.3	37.7	49.6
New Zealand, 1976	43.0	81.1	37.2	45.1
Sweden, 1975	81.7	72.6	62.9	86.0
United States, 1982	62.2	76.7	57.0	69.6

SOURCES: United Nations, 1979, Tables 12 and 43; ibid., 1976, Table 41; ibid., 1972, Table 15; *Statistical Abstract of the United States*, 1984, p. 412; U.S. Bureau of the Census, May 1983, p. 8.

satisfactorily resolved. Adaptive mechanisms such as withdrawal from the labor market during the childbearing years, part-time work for married women, and extrafamilial day-care facilities for children have certainly lessened the conflict, but they have not eliminated it. Nevertheless, the participation of married women in the labor force has had a remarkable increase. Table 1.6 shows the level reached recently in a number of advanced countries. By now in most industrial countries, participation in the labor force has become the norm for married women. Simultaneously, there is a strong movement to eliminate the two-tiered labor market, putting men and women in direct competition with each other. The incompatibility of this development with childbearing is indicated not only by the low birth rates in industrial societies but also by special studies of the influence of labor force participation on fertility.[2] Also, the growing employment of women outside the home has contributed to the high divorce rate in three ways: first, by throwing wives into prolonged contact with men other than their husbands; second, by making wives financially independent of marriage; and third, by encouraging low fertility and hence less commitment to marriage.

Conclusion: Marriage in Future Years

Some of the trends we have described represent recent reversals and others represent continuations of long-term changes. Regardless of which they are, they seem to indicate a weakening of formal marriage as it has been known in the past, but how long into the future the trends will continue is not certain. Among the trends that appear to be continuations of long-term changes are the rising share of births out of wedlock, the rising divorce rate, the greater employment of married women outside the home, and the fall in fertility. These are perhaps more fundamental than the recent changes in direction, such as the rather sudden upturn in the age at marriage after a long decline, the recent tendency to avoid marriage altogether, the fast rise of consensual unions, and the multiplication of one-parent households.

One can gain perspective on future developments by trying to imagine what will stop or reverse each current trend. For instance, the age at marriage obviously cannot rise indefinitely. It will either get too late in the reproductive span for marriage to perform its reproductive function, or some other kind of union, with a lower age of entry, will take its place. In this regard, the case of Ireland is instructive. The age at marriage there became about the highest ever known, and the propensity to marry the smallest. In 1945–1946 the average age at marriage was 33.1 years for men and 28.0 years for women, and 30 percent of women age 35–44 had never married at all. At that time, extrapolating the trend toward late marriage and celibacy, one might have concluded that marriage would disappear in Ireland. Far from disappearing, however, it staged a comeback. By 1979 the average age at marriage had fallen to 26.1 years for men and 24.0 years for women, and by 1971 the proportion of never-married women age 35–44 had dropped to 17.5 percent. Thus marriage has recovered in Ireland. Interestingly, however, the birth rate has shown almost no change. In other words, there are more marriages now in Ireland, but they produce fewer children per marriage, which means that contraception rather than marital postponement is being used to limit offspring.

Looked at in comparative perspective, Ireland's demographic behavior is what one might expect. As a country where Roman Catholicism and nationalism reinforced each other, a country that in effect was a rural part of a larger industrial economy, Ireland relied more than other countries on marital postponement and emigration as methods of population limitation. Eventually, however, as in other northwestern European countries, the age at marriage began to fall. Doubtless a reversal will occur, but since Ireland is behind other European countries, the reversal has not yet started. In the meantime, the secular decline in marital fertility characterizing advanced countries was slow to come to Ireland, but it was strong enough to muffle the postwar baby boom, giving the country almost no change in birth rate in the entire postwar period.

Another trend that cannot continue for long is the rise in labor force participation by married women, because if the current rise continues, it will soon reach its upper limit. For instance, at the pace of increase exhibited between 1960 and 1980 in the United States, the participation rate for married women age 25–44 would reach the married male rate (97.1 percent) in only fifteen years![3]

For different reasons, the divorce rate also seems to have a limit, but the limit is indeterminate and very high. The reason for the limit is that to marry and to divorce takes time. If we assume that under maximum divorce conditions the average duration of a marriage is two years, and that the average time in the unmarried state between marriages is one year, then each divorce uses up three years of life. If a woman's active marital and reproductive span is from age 20 to 49, she can have a total of ten divorces. This would represent about 330 divorces per year per 1,000 women in the prime ages, which is nearly ten times the actual rate in the United States. In other words, the theoretical potential for divorce is much greater than the maximum so far reached. Of course, one must keep in mind that if the break-up of consensual unions is counted as divorce, the actual divorce rate is much higher than the official one, but still not ten times as high. In any case, there is no automatic shut-off that would prevent the divorce rate from climbing still higher. It will certainly climb higher in the industrial countries as a whole if the rest catch up with the present United States figure, but in the meantime the United States figure could stabilize or start to fall.

A more fundamental question concerns the future of the birth rate. If the labor force participation of married women continues its upward course, if the divorce rate continues its rise or even stabilizes at the present level, if women in increasing numbers gain admission to higher occupations and reach higher levels of formal education, it seems doubtful that the birth rate will remain even at its present level, which in most industrial countries is the lowest in history. In short, although people value children very highly, it seems likely that they will not exceed replacement-level fertility unless incentives for childbearing and child care are systematically improved and disincentives are alleviated, which in large part means reforming the institution of marriage. Failing such a development, it seems likely that the population of the industrial nations will increasingly be sustained by immigrants from the Third World.

NOTES

1. In Latin American countries, where consensual unions are common, they are usually treated as a separate marital category in census enumerations.

2. For a summary of these studies, see Kupinsky 1977, especially Chapters 6–12.

3. The percent of married women aged 25–44 in the labor force in 1960 was 33.1; in 1980 it was 60.2 (*Statistical Abstract of the United States*, 1981, p. 386).

REFERENCES

Andorka, Rudolf. "Comparative Demographic Analysis of Socio-Cultural Determinants of Fertility in European Socialist Countries Where Fertility Is Around Replacement Level." *International Population Conference: Solicited Papers, Manila 1981*. Liège, Belgium: International Union for the Scientific Study of Population, 1982.

Central Bureau of Statistics of Norway. *Fertility Survey, 1977*. Oslo (1981).

Central Bureau of Statistics of Sweden. *Population Changes, 1980*. Stockholm (1981).

Davis, Kingsley. "The Changing Family in Industrial Societies." In R. C. Jackson and J. Morton (eds.), *Family Health Care: Health Promotion and Illness Care*. Berkeley: University of California, School of Public Health, 1976.

Girard, Alain, and Louis, Roussel. "Ideal Family Size, Fertility, and Population Policy in Western Europe." *Population and Development Review*, 8 (June 1982).

Kupinsky, Stanley. *The Fertility of Working Women: A Synthesis of International Research*. New York: Praeger, 1977.

National Center for Health Statistics, *Fertility Tables for Birth Cohorts by Color, United States, 1917–1973* (Washington, D.C., April 1976).

National Center for Health Statistics. "Marriage and Divorce." *Vital Statistics of the United States, 1977*, Vol. 3 (1981).

National Center for Health Statistics. "Advanced Report of Final Divorce Statistics, 1981." *Monthly Vital Statistics Report*, Vol. 32, No. 9, Supplement 2 (January 1984).

Population Index, Vol. 47, No. 2 (Summer, 1981).

Statistical Abstract of the United States, 1984.

Statistical Abstract of the United States, 1981.

Trost, Jan. "Changing Family and Changing Society." In Jan Trost (ed.), *The Family in Change*. Västerås, Sweden: International Library, 1980.

United Nations. *Demographic Yearbook*. New York: United Nations, 1968, 1969, 1972, 1976, 1982.

United Nations. *Demographic Yearbook, Historical Supplement*. New York: United Nations, 1979.

U.S. Bureau of the Census. "Household and Family Characteristics: March, 1981." *Current Population Reports*, Series P-20, No. 371 (May 1982).

U.S. Bureau of the Census. "Household and Family Characteristics: March, 1983." *Current Population Reports*, Series P-20, No. 388 (May 1984).

U.S. Bureau of the Census. "Marital Status and Living Arrangements: March 1977," *Current Population Reports*, Series P-20, No. 323 (April 1978).

U.S. Bureau of the Census. "Marital Status and Living Arrangements: March, 1980," *Current Population Reports*, Series P-20, No. 365 (October 1981).

U.S. Bureau of the Census. "Marital Status and Living Arrangements: 1982." *Current Population Reports*, Series P-20, No. 380 (May 1983).

Weed, James A. "National Estimates of Marriage Dissolution and Survivorship: United States." In National Center for Health Statistics, *Vital and Health Statistics*, Series 3, No. 19 (November 1980).

2 The Recent Decline of American Marriage

Blacks and Whites in Comparative Perspective

THOMAS J. ESPENSHADE

THE PURPOSE OF THIS CHAPTER is to investigate whether marriage is declining as a social institution in the United States and, if so, whether it is declining at a faster pace among blacks than among whites. Evidence suggests that in the United States the institution has been declining since at least 1960. To be sure, how-

NOTE: This paper draws on research supported by NICHD Contract No. NO1-HD-02849 from the Center for Population Research, U.S. Department of Health and Human Services. Conversations with Urban Institute colleagues Kristin Moore, June O'Neill, and Douglas Wolf have contributed to this paper. Helpful comments were also received from James Cramer and William Nye. The careful programming of Thy Dao and the technical assistance of Tracy Ann Goodis, Bobbie Mathis and Terri Murray are also gratefully acknowledged. The views expressed here are the sole responsibility of the author and do not necessarily reflect the opinions of The Urban Institute or any of its sponsors.

ever, we first need criteria by which to judge the strength of marriage. For this purpose, I adopt the criteria developed by Kingsley Davis in Chapter 1. According to him, if marriage is weakening as an institution, "we would expect to see postponement of marriage, fewer people ever getting married, a lesser proportion of life spent in wedlock, and a shorter duration of marriage."

Cross-Sectional Evidence

Data from the U.S. decennial censuses of population and from the monthly *Current Population Surveys* conducted by the Bureau of the Census since the late 1940s furnish the necessary information on these trends (see Table 2.1). Since 1900 the median age at first marriage for both men and women in the United States has moved in a slow, pendulumlike fashion, first falling to a low during the 1950s and then rising up to the present. The figure of 22.5 years registered by women in 1982 is the highest median age at first marriage for females since 1890. For men, the 1982 figure is the highest since 1910, when it was 25.1 years. Commenting on these changes, the U.S. Bureau of the Census (1983b) observed, "It now appears that men and women are returning to the pattern of timing of first marriage that characterized the United States in the early decades of this century [p. 1]."[1] Accordingly, the proportion never married is rising.

For women 20 to 24 years old, the percent never married was 53.4 in 1982, up from 35.8 percent in 1970. For women aged 25 to 29, the percent never married in 1982 was 23.4, more than double the percentage for 1970 (10.5). Men exhibit similar patterns. Sharp race differences exist in these proportions. In March 1982 half (50.5 percent) of the white women in the age group 20 to 24 had never married, compared to 71.5 percent of black women. Seven out of ten (70.1 percent) of white men in the same age group were never married, compared to more than eight out of ten black men (82.3 percent).

Evidence from Longitudinal Data

The cross-sectional evidence reviewed gives only a snapshot of the population at different points in time. Individual-level longitudinal

Table 2.1

Marital Status Distributions of Persons 15 Years Old and Over, by Race and Sex: 1982, 1970, 1960

Marital Status	All Races			White			Black		
	1982[a]	1970[a]	1960[a]	1982[a]	1970[a]	1960[a]	1982[a]	1970[a]	1960[a]
Women									
Number, 15 years and over[b]	92,228	77,202	64,607	79,591	68,512	57,860	10,511	7,921	6,747
Single (never married)	22.5%	22.1%	19.0%	20.8%	21.3%	18.7%	35.1%	28.0%	21.6%
Married, husband present	54.5	58.4	62.2	57.2	60.2	63.9	33.4	42.0	48.2
Married, husband absent	3.8	3.6	3.7	2.9	2.6	2.8	10.2	12.1	11.6
Separated	3.0	2.2	2.0	2.2	1.3	1.3	9.2	10.0	8.3
Widowed	11.7	12.5	12.5	11.7	12.4	12.3	12.4	13.5	14.3
Divorced	7.5	3.5	2.6	7.3	3.4	2.5	8.9	4.3	4.3
Men									
Number, 15 years and over[b]	83,958	70,270	60,273	73,285	62,613	54,130	8,614	6,907	6,143
Single (never married)	29.7%	28.2%	25.3%	28.1%	27.1%	24.5%	41.2%	36.6%	32.4%
Married, wife present	59.9	64.1	66.7	62.2	66.0	68.3	41.7	48.6	53.0
Married, wife absent	2.7	2.5	2.6	2.3	1.9	2.0	6.3	7.5	7.9
Separated	1.9	1.3	1.5	1.5	0.9	1.0	5.3	5.0	5.5
Widowed	2.2	3.0	3.5	2.1	2.9	3.4	3.5	4.3	4.8
Divorced	5.5	2.2	1.8	5.3	2.2	1.8	7.3	2.9	2.0

[a] Numbers in thousands.
[b] For 1970 and 1960, data are for persons 14 years old and over.

SOURCE: U.S. Bureau of the Census, *Current Population Reports*, Series P-20, No. 380, "Marital Status and Living Arrangements: March 1982," 1983; *Current Population Reports*, Series P-20, No. 212, "Marital Status and Family Status: March 1970," 1971; and *Current Population Reports*, Series P-20, No. 105, "Marital Status and Family Status: March 1960," 1960.

data not only show the lifetime incidence of marriage, marital dissolution, and remarriage but also allow removal of the influence of the age composition. Such data were collected by the Census Bureau in a special Marital and Fertility History supplement to the June 1980 Current Population Survey. Roughly 125,000 respondents (nearly 60,000 men and over 65,000 women) between the ages of 15 and 75 were asked to report to an interviewer their complete marital histories. Altogether seven different marital status categories were recognized: never married, married for the first time, separated from a first marriage, remarried, separated from a remarriage, divorced, and widowed. Using these data I have made multiple increment-decrement life tables by race and sex for each five-year period between 1940 and 1980.[2] Such tables decompose a cohort's life expectancy at birth into the average number of years expected to be lived in each marital status. Results for white and black women are shown in Tables 2.2 and 2.3.

For the white female population, 1960 represents a watershed in terms of marital activity. For twenty years before that date, the proportional distribution of life expectancy at birth in alternative marital statuses changed little, except for a decline in the percent of time never married, attributable to a fall in the age at first marriage. After 1960, the percent of life expectancy spent as never married began to rise as the age at marriage increased. A rising age at first marriage also meant proportionately less time spent in a first marriage. This decline in first marriage duration has been so sharp that, despite the growing experience of white women with remarriage, the total time white women spend married (including first and subsequent marriages) has been declining both in absolute and in relative terms. Since 1960 there has been an acceleration in the amount of time white women spend separated and divorced, although by 1975–1980 relative to the total, the separated state consumed just 1.5 percent of total life expectancy, or an average of just 1.2 years.

Black women have generally exhibited the same trends as whites, but earlier and more conspicuously. For them, the significant threshold occurred not in 1960 but in the early 1950s when the percent of total lifetime spent never married increased and the proportionate amount of time in first marriages started to fall.

Despite the growth in the total time in the divorced status,

Table 2.2

Distribution of Life Expectancy at Birth by Marital Status: White Women, 1940–1980

Time Spent in Each Marital Status (in years)

Period	Total Life Expectancy at Birth ($\overset{\circ}{e}_0$)	Never Married (N)	First Marriage (M1)	Separated, Formerly First Married (S1)	Divorced (V)	Widowed (W)	Remarriage (M2)	Separated, Formerly Remarried (S2)
1975–1980	76.8	26.0	23.6	0.8	7.5	8.9	9.7	0.4
1970–1975	76.5	24.4	27.1	0.7	5.7	9.5	8.9	0.3
1965–1970	75.7	23.1	30.3	0.6	4.1	9.7	7.6	0.2
1960–1965	74.9	23.0	33.3	0.6	3.2	9.3	5.5	0.2
1955–1960	74.2	22.1	34.8	0.5	1.9	9.8	5.0	0.2
1950–1955	73.1	22.4	34.2	0.4	1.8	9.3	5.1	0.1
1945–1950	71.1	21.8	33.2	0.3	1.3	9.3	5.0	0.2
1940–1945	68.2	23.9	29.6	0.3	1.1	9.2	4.1	0.1

Percentage Distribution

Period	($\overset{\circ}{e}_0$)	(N)	(M1)	(S1)	(V)	(W)	(M2)	(S2)
1975–1980	100.0	33.8	30.8	1.0	9.8	11.6	12.6	0.5
1970–1975	100.0	31.9	35.4	0.9	7.5	12.4	11.6	0.4
1965–1970	100.0	30.6	40.1	0.8	5.4	12.9	10.0	0.2
1960–1965	100.0	30.7	44.4	0.8	4.2	12.4	7.3	0.3
1955–1960	100.0	29.7	46.9	0.6	2.6	13.2	6.7	0.2
1950–1955	100.0	30.6	46.8	0.5	2.4	12.7	6.9	0.1
1945–1950	100.0	30.7	46.7	0.5	1.9	13.0	7.0	0.2
1940–1945	100.0	35.0	43.4	0.4	1.6	13.5	6.0	0.1

SOURCE: The Urban Institute, Washington, D.C.

Table 2.3

Distribution of Life Expectancy at Birth by Marital Status: Black Women, 1940–1980

Time Spent in Each Marital Status (in years)

Period	Total Life Expectancy at Birth ($\overset{\circ}{e}_0$)	Never Married (N)	First Marriage (M1)	Separated, Formerly First Married (S1)	Divorced (V)	Widowed (W)	Remarriage (M2)	Separated, Formerly Remarried (S2)
1975–1980	73.4	34.5	12.5	4.7	9.5	7.2	3.8	1.1
1970–1975	71.3	30.2	15.3	5.2	6.0	8.2	5.5	0.8
1965–1970	69.2	27.1	16.5	5.2	6.7	7.6	5.6	0.6
1960–1965	68.5	24.9	21.1	4.3	3.7	7.7	6.4	0.5
1955–1960	67.7	24.2	22.4	2.7	3.7	8.0	6.1	0.6
1950–1955	65.5	22.5	24.2	1.9	3.1	8.1	5.4	0.5
1945–1950	61.6	22.9	20.8	2.5	2.7	8.6	3.9	0.2
1940–1945	57.7	23.2	18.9	1.8	1.0	7.0	5.3	0.5

Percentage Distribution

Period	($\overset{\circ}{e}_0$)	(N)	(M1)	(S1)	(V)	(W)	(M2)	(S2)
1975–1980	100.0	47.1	17.1	6.5	12.9	9.8	5.1	1.5
1970–1975	100.0	42.4	21.5	7.4	8.4	11.5	7.6	1.2
1965–1970	100.0	39.2	23.8	7.5	9.7	10.9	8.1	0.8
1960–1965	100.0	36.3	30.7	6.3	5.4	11.3	9.3	0.7
1955–1960	100.0	35.7	33.1	4.0	5.4	11.9	9.0	0.9
1950–1955	100.0	34.4	36.9	2.9	4.7	12.3	8.2	0.6
1945–1950	100.0	37.2	33.8	4.1	4.3	13.9	6.4	0.3
1940–1945	100.0	40.1	32.8	3.2	1.8	12.1	9.1	0.9

SOURCE: The Urban Institute, Washington, D.C.

black women (unlike whites) are spending less time remarried. They are also spending significantly larger proportions of time in the separated status. In 1975–1980 this status occupied a total of 8.0 percent of their life expectancy, versus just 1.5 percent of that of white women. Perhaps the most remarkable difference between black and white women is in the total amount of lifetime spent married. In 1975–1980, less than one-quarter (22.2 percent) of black female life expectancy was spent married, 17.1 percent in first marriages and 6.1 percent in remarriages. In contrast, white women spent a total of 43.4 percent of their lifetimes in the married state, 30.8 percent in first marriages and 12.6 percent in remarriages. In terms of total years married, white women are outliving blacks by a ratio of two to one.

Information identical to that in Tables 2.2 and 2.3 is shown in Tables 2.4 and 2.5 for men. With few exceptions, the patterns are the same as those for women. One difference is the steadily rising percentage of time for black men in the remarried state. This percentage reached 11.1 by 1975–1980, whereas for black women the figure crested at 9.3 in 1960–1965 and then fell off sharply.

Data for the 1975–1980 period indicate that white men are the only population subgroup for whom marriage comprises more than half (52.9 percent) of total life expectancy at birth. At the other extreme, black women are spending a total of just 16.3 years on average in the married state, or 22.2 percent of a total life expectancy of 73.4 years.

Demographic Determinants

Demographic changes contributing to the declining centrality of marriage are the tendency to postpone marriage and, perhaps, to avoid it altogether, the rise in the probability of divorce, and the decline of remarriage among black women. It is worthwhile examining each of these demographic factors in detail because subsequent interpretation presumes a familiarity with them.

Patterns of First Marriage.   One way of assessing the prevalence of marriage is to consider the percent of life table cohort members surviving to age 50 who have married at least once. For white women this figure rose slightly after World War II to a high

Table 2.4

Distribution of Life Expectancy at Birth by Marital Status: White Men, 1940–1980

Period	Total Life Expectancy at Birth ($\overset{\circ}{e}_0$)	Never Married (N)	First Marriage (M1)	Separated, Formerly First Married (S1)	Divorced (V)	Widowed (W)	Remarriage (M2)	Separated, Formerly Remarried (S2)
				Time Spent in Each Marital Status (in years)				
1975–1980	69.1	27.1	25.4	0.5	3.3	1.4	11.1	0.3
1970–1975	68.2	25.7	28.2	0.5	2.6	1.4	9.5	0.3
1965–1970	68.0	25.0	31.1	0.4	1.9	1.4	8.1	0.1
1960–1965	67.9	24.6	33.7	0.4	1.6	1.5	5.9	0.2
1955–1960	67.7	24.4	34.9	0.4	1.2	1.7	5.0	0.1
1950–1955	67.2	24.7	33.8	0.3	1.0	1.8	5.6	0.0
1945–1950	65.7	24.2	33.3	0.2	1.1	2.4	4.3	0.2
1940–1945	63.6	25.6	29.7	0.3	0.9	3.0	4.0	0.1
	($\overset{\circ}{e}_0$)	(N)	(M1)	(S1)	(V)	(W)	(M2)	(S2)
				Percentage Distribution				
1975–1980	100.0	39.3	36.8	0.7	4.7	2.0	16.1	0.4
1970–1975	100.0	37.7	41.4	0.7	3.8	2.1	13.9	0.4
1965–1970	100.0	36.7	45.8	0.6	2.8	2.0	11.9	0.2
1960–1965	100.0	36.2	49.7	0.5	2.4	2.2	8.7	0.2
1955–1960	100.0	36.0	51.5	0.6	1.8	2.6	7.4	0.1
1950–1955	100.0	36.8	50.3	0.4	1.5	2.6	8.3	0.1
1945–1950	100.0	36.8	50.6	0.3	1.7	3.6	6.6	0.3
1940–1945	100.0	40.3	46.8	0.4	1.4	4.8	6.3	0.1

SOURCE: The Urban Institute, Washington, D.C.

Table 2.5

Distribution of Life Expectancy at Birth by Marital Status: Black Men, 1940–1980

Period	Total Life Expectancy at Birth ($\overset{\circ}{e}_0$)	Never Married (N)	First Marriage (M1)	Separated, Formerly First Married (S1)	Divorced (V)	Widowed (W)	Remarriage (M2)	Separated, Formerly Remarried (S2)
				Time Spent in Each Marital Status (in years)				
1975–1980	62.8	29.6	17.9	2.2	3.6	1.8	7.0	0.8
1970–1975	61.1	27.9	19.8	2.2	3.0	1.6	5.9	0.6
1965–1970	59.6	26.8	18.9	2.4	3.1	2.1	5.8	0.6
1960–1965	61.5	26.2	24.2	1.8	1.9	1.6	5.4	0.3
1955–1960	60.6	28.2	21.1	1.7	2.5	2.4	4.6	0.1
1950–1955	59.6	25.1	22.4	1.5	2.1	3.1	5.3	0.2
1945–1950	57.1	24.6	21.3	0.9	2.5	3.9	3.6	0.2
1940–1945	53.2	26.7	16.8	1.1	1.1	3.5	4.0	0.0
	($\overset{\circ}{e}_0$)	(N)	(M1)	(S1)	(V)	(W)	(M2)	(S2)
				Percentage Distribution				
1975–1980	100.0	47.1	28.5	3.4	5.8	2.9	11.1	1.3
1970–1975	100.0	45.7	32.4	3.6	5.0	2.6	9.7	1.0
1965–1970	100.0	45.0	31.6	4.0	5.2	3.4	9.7	1.0
1960–1965	100.0	42.7	39.4	2.9	3.1	2.6	8.8	0.5
1955–1960	100.0	46.6	34.9	2.7	4.1	4.0	7.5	0.1
1950–1955	100.0	42.0	37.5	2.5	3.5	5.3	8.9	0.3
1945–1950	100.0	43.1	37.3	1.6	4.4	6.8	6.4	0.3
1940–1945	100.0	50.1	31.6	2.1	2.1	6.5	7.5	0.0

SOURCE: The Urban Institute, Washington, D.C.

of 97.5 percent in 1955–1960, and then remained well above 90 percent in 1975–1980. Marriage among black women also increased in the 1940s and early 1950s, but since 1960 a sharp decline has occurred. The proportion ever marrying was 78.5 percent by 1975–1980, well below the corresponding proportion for white women (93.1 percent).

The mean age at first marriage for white women fell to a minimum of 21.4 in the 1950s, then rose to a post-World War II peak of 23.0 years in 1975–1980. The mean age for black women underwent a strikingly different pattern. It rose steadily from the end of World War II, reaching 26.1 years by 1975–1980. During the 1940s, blacks married at about the same or even at an earlier age than whites but, by the end of the 1970s, they were marrying for the first time three years later than their white counterparts.[3]

Marital Dissolution.   For white women the probability of a marriage ending in divorce increased from 14.0 percent in 1940–1945 to 45.2 percent by 1975–1980. Most of the rise over the past forty years occurred in the last two decades. Black women have exhibited even higher probabilities of divorce. Their proportion of marriages terminating in divorce grew from 17.6 percent in 1940–1945 to 47.1 percent in 1975–1980.[4]

For both black and white women, the accelerating rise in divorce from 1960 to 1980 is the driving force behind the reduction in the average length of a marriage. In Table 2.6 the average duration of a marriage or a separation has been computed by dividing the total number of person-years lived in each status by the number of times that status is entered over the lifetime of the cohort. By 1975–1980 the average black female marriage lasted less than fifteen years, compared to an average of 22.5 years for white women.

Remarkable black/white differences also exist in the average length of a marital separation. Black women spend considerably more time in the separated state before divorce than do whites, as noted also by McCarthy (1978). For the period 1975–1980, for example, separated white women, at any given age, are about five times as likely to divorce as separated black women.

Remarriage.   As a social phenomenon, remarriage is becoming increasingly common. Our life table data indicate that in the late

Table 2.6

Average Duration of Marriages and Separations, by Race: 1940–1980[a]

	Marriages			Separations		
Population	Total	First Marriages	Remar-riages	Total	Following First Marriage	Following Remar-riage
White women						
1975–1980	22.5	25.7	17.1	1.9	1.8	1.9
1970–1975	25.7	29.1	18.9	2.1	2.0	2.4
1965–1970	28.5	32.2	19.6	2.4	2.5	2.1
1960–1965	32.6	35.5	21.7	3.3	3.0	4.9
1955–1960	33.8	36.8	21.6	3.6	3.3	4.9
1950–1955	34.0	36.6	22.7	3.0	2.9	3.9
1945–1950	33.3	35.6	23.2	3.5	2.8	7.6
1940–1945	32.2	33.3	25.8	3.4	3.0	7.1
Black women						
1975–1980	14.6	16.2	10.9	9.8	10.6	7.6
1970–1975	17.8	18.5	16.2	12.7	13.1	10.9
1965–1970	19.2	19.7	17.8	12.7	13.2	9.5
1960–1965	23.0	24.1	20.1	12.4	12.2	14.9
1955–1960	23.7	25.7	18.5	9.0	8.7	10.5
1950–1955	25.6	27.3	20.0	8.4	8.0	11.9
1945–1950	24.4	24.6	23.3	11.7	12.2	7.7
1940–1945	22.6	23.7	19.5	11.3	10.3	16.8

[a] Durations in years.

SOURCE: The Urban Institute, Washington, D.C.

1970s nearly two out of every five white female marriages and almost one-third of all black female marriages were remarriages. Since 1940 the proportion of all marriages that are remarriages has risen for both blacks and whites, but especially for white women.

A detailed analysis reported in Espenshade (1983), shows that the surge in remarriages is due to the rise in divorce itself rather than to an increasing prevalence of remarriage after divorce. Despite a recent leveling in the remarriage rate following divorce among whites and a continued decline in this rate among black women, remarriages constitute a growing fraction of all marriages for both races because the divorced population likely to remarry has expanded so rapidly.

After this review of the demographic evidence we can conclude that, at least since 1960 in the United States, a weakening of marriage has been underway. The fading centrality of marriage in the lives of American men and women is more noticeable for blacks than for whites and, within the black population, black women exhibit the weakest attachment to marriage.

Further Indications

Further indications of a weakening of marriage are rises in out-of-wedlock childbearing and in incomplete families.

Trends in Illegitimacy

Since a postponement of marriage or an increase in divorce expands the number of unmarried women at risk of having an out-of-wedlock birth, the *ratio* of illegitimate births to all births could be expected to increase, regardless of whether the illegitimacy *rate* (births per 1,000 unmarried women) increases or not. Table 2.7 shows that both the rate and the ratio have risen, but the ratio has risen faster. For all races combined, the illegitimacy rate rose from a modest 7.1 per thousand unmarried women in 1940 to 29.4 by 1980. The rate for whites followed the trend for all races, but at a lower level. By sharp contrast, the illegitimacy rate for nonwhites has been dropping since 1960 and for blacks as far back as the data go. It seems that out-of-wedlock birth rates are now moving in opposite directions for whites and blacks.

As for the ratio, the proportion of all births that occurred out of wedlock increased from less than 4 percent in 1940 to over 18 percent in 1980. The proportion of black births to unmarried mothers reached 55 percent, five times the white ratio. By 1982 the overall illegitimacy ratio had climbed higher—to 19.4 percent. This increase was accompanied by gains in the ratios for both whites and blacks (National Center for Health Statistics, 1984a).

The relative absence of change in the white illegitimacy ratio before 1960 reinforces our previous observation that 1960 marked a threshold in white marital behavior. Before 1960, the distribution of life expectancy at birth across different marital statuses changed little for white families, but much thereafter. The large jump between 1965 and the early 1970s in the nonwhite illegitimacy ratio

Table 2.7

Estimated Numbers, Rates, and Ratios of Births to Unmarried Women by Race: United States, 1940–1980

| Year | Number | | | | Rates per 1,000 Unmarried Women[a] | | | | Ratio per 1,000 Live Births | | | |
| | All Races | White | All Other | | All Races | White | All Other | | All Races | White | All Other | |
			Total	Black			Total	Black			Total	Black
1980	665,747	320,063	345,684	325,737	29.4	17.6	77.2	82.9	184.3	110.4	484.5	552.5
1975	447,900	186,400	261,600	249,600	24.8	12.6	80.4	85.6	142.5	73.0	441.7	487.9
1970	398,700	175,100	223,600	215,100	26.4	13.9	89.9	95.5	106.9	56.6	349.3	375.8
1965	291,200	123,700	167,500	—	23.4	11.6	97.4	—	77.4	39.6	263.2	—
1960	224,300	82,500	141,800	—	21.6	9.2	98.3	—	52.7	22.9	215.8	—
1955	183,300	64,200	119,200	—	19.3	7.9	87.2	—	45.3	18.6	202.4	—
1950	141,600	53,500	88,100	—	14.1	6.1	71.2	—	39.8	17.5	179.6	—
1940	89,500	40,300	49,200	—	7.1	3.6	35.6	—	37.9	19.5	168.3	—

[a] Rates computed by relating total births to unmarried women, regardless of age of mother, to unmarried women aged 15–44 years.

SOURCE: 1940–1978, National Center for Health Statistics, *Vital Statistics of the United States, 1978*, Vol. I—Natality, 1982; 1979, National Center for Health Statistics, *Monthly Vital Statistics Report*, "Advance Report of Final Natality Statistics, 1979," Vol. 30, No. 6, Supplement (2), September 29, 1981; 1980, National Center for Health Statistics, *Monthly Vital Statistics Report*, "Advance Report of Final Natality Statistics, 1980," Vol. 31, No. 8, Supplement, November 30, 1982.

accords well with our finding of a substantial increase (2.8 years) in the mean age at first marriage for black women between 1965–1970 and 1970–1975.

An explanation of the rise in illegitimacy ratios must take trends in marital as well as nonmarital fertility into account, because the illegitimacy ratio is influenced by both. Actually, the two have been moving in opposing directions: marital fertility falling, nonmarital fertility rising. Between 1960 and 1978 the fertility rate of married women fell from 156.3 to 96.8 per thousand (Fuchs 1983), while the rate for unmarried women rose from 21.6 to 26.2 per thousand. This fact alone would have caused the illegitimacy ratio to rise in the absence of other changes. The trend away from marriage naturally accentuated this rise.

This general picture needs qualification when considered by race. Nonmarital fertility rates for black women have been dropping, not increasing, and this undoubtedly explains part of the slowdown in the growth of the black illegitimacy ratio. Nevertheless, the black ratio is still higher than that for whites, and an important part of the explanation is that in the black population, age for age, an unmarried woman is now about as likely to give birth as a married woman (Davis 1982). In 1978, for women 15–44 years of age, the marital fertility rate was 95.8 per thousand married women compared to the nonmarital rate of 83.1 per thousand unmarried women (National Center for Health Statistics 1982). Among the white population in 1950, married women were 16.8 times as fertile as unmarried women (Davis 1982), but by 1979 the ratio had dropped to 4.3 (Davis 1982).

How much has the decline in marriage contributed to the rise in out-of-wedlock births? Chapman (1983) provides a partial answer: "The increase in out-of-wedlock births, from 400,000 in 1970 to 600,000 in 1979, is not the result of an increased rate of childbearing among unmarried women, but rather, an increase in the number of unmarried women who could potentially have an out-of-wedlock birth" (pp. 202–203). The number of nonmarital births increased by roughly 50 percent during this period, but the nonmarital fertility rate went up by only 5.3 percent. However, the National Center for Health Statistics (1981), analyzing the change between 1978 and 1979, finds that the increase of 9.9 percent is due both to a higher rate of childbearing by unmarried women and to more unmarried women of childbearing age. For all ages combined, the rate increased more sharply than did the number. Turning to racial differences, we find that for blacks, since illegitimate birth rates have generally fallen, the rise in the number of nonmarital births comes exclusively from delayed marriage, higher rates of divorce and separation, and a lesser tendency to remarry— all of which combine to provide more years of exposure to the risk of an out-of-wedlock birth. For whites, however, rates are generally up, along with the age at marriage.

Family Characteristics and Economic Welfare

The trends in marriage and divorce have promoted an unusually large increase in female-headed families with dependent children. Such families typically rank near the bottom in measures of family income. It would not be a mistake to blame the weakening of marriage for a large share of the poverty currently experienced by families in the United States.

Table 2.8 shows the growth in the number of households by type between 1970 and 1982. Four points are worth noting. First, the proportion of all households that are family households has declined. Between 1970 and 1982, the number of family households grew by 19.1 percent in comparison to a 91.3 percent growth in nonfamily households. Second, the proportion of all family households that are married-couple households has gone down—from 86.7 percent in 1970 to 81.3 percent in 1982. Third, the number of non-married-couple family households with a female head increased faster than all households combined. And fourth, the number of female-headed households with dependent children under age 18 doubled, causing this family type to increase its share of all households from 4.7 percent in 1970 to 7.0 percent in 1982. So conspicuous was the latter trend that it prompted the U.S. Bureau of the Census (1983a) to remark: "The increase in one-parent households has been one of the major changes in household composition over the past decade" (p. 2).

The 1970–1982 increase in female-headed families with dependent children was about the same for white as for black women (95.6 percent for whites and 102.8 percent for blacks), but such families comprised one in five black households in 1982 compared to 5.4 percent for whites. Nevertheless, it is still the case that the

Table 2.8

Household Composition, by Presence of Own Children Under 18, Race, and Marital Status: 1982 and 1970 (Numbers in Thousands)

| | 1982 | | | | | | 1970[a] | | | | | | Change, 1970–82 | |
| | All Races | | White | | Black | | All Races | | White | | Black | | All Races | |
Subject	Number	Percent	Number	Percent	Number	Percent	Number	Percent	Number	Percent	Number	Percent	Number	Percent
All households	83,527	100.0	72,845	100.0	8,961	100.0	62,874	100.0	56,248	100.0	6,053	100.0	20,653	32.8
Family households	61,019	73.1	53,269	73.1	6,413	71.6	51,237	81.5	46,022	81.8	4,774	78.9	9,782	19.1
Married-couple family	49,630	59.4	45,007	61.8	3,535	39.4	44,436	70.7	40,802	72.5	3,249	53.7	5,194	11.7
Other family, male householder	1,986	2.4	1,642	2.3	273	3.0	1,221	1.9	1,036	1.8	176	2.9	765	62.7
Other family, female householder	9,403	11.3	6,620	9.1	2,605	29.1	5,580	8.9	4,185	7.4	1,349	22.3	3,823	68.5
No own children under 18	3,535	4.2	2,694	3.7	784	8.7	2,655	4.2	2,178	3.9	452	7.5	880	33.1
With own children under 18	5,868	7.0	3,926	5.4	1,821	20.3	2,925	4.7	2,007	3.6	898	14.8	2,943	100.6
Married, spouse absent	1,503	1.8	953	1.3	523	5.8	1,093	1.7	639	1.1	445	7.4	410	37.5
Separated	1,332	1.6	818	1.1	492	5.5	768	1.2	390	0.7	373	6.2	564	73.4
Widowed	582	0.7	407	0.6	144	1.6	647	1.0	503	0.9	140	2.3	−65	−10.0
Divorced	2,692	3.2	2,219	3.0	418	4.7	952	1.5	798	1.4	148	2.4	1,740	182.8
Never married	1,092	1.3	347	0.5	735	8.2	232	0.4	68	0.1	163	2.7	860	370.7
Non-family households	22,508	26.9	19,576	26.9	2,548	28.4	11,765	18.7	10,319	18.3	1,309	21.6	10,743	91.3

[a]Individual items may sum to slightly more than the total in 1970 because the count of all families includes both primary and secondary families. Thus, a household may contain more than one family. Beginning with the 1980 CPS, unrelated subfamilies (i.e., secondary families) are no longer included in the count of families.

SOURCE: U.S. Bureau of the Census, *Current Population Reports*, Series P-20, No. 218, "Household and Family Characteristics: March 1970," 1971; and *Current Population Reports*, Series P-20, No. 381, "Household and Family Characteristics: March 1982," 1983.

majority of black families are married-couple families (Matney and Johnson 1983). At the same time, however, less than half (42.4 percent) of all black children under 18 lived with two parents in 1982 (U.S. Bureau of the Census 1983b).

Two demographic phenomena cause the number of female-headed families with children to grow: the separation or divorce of married couples with children and out-of-wedlock childbearing. Most of the growth in single-parent families headed by women arises through divorce or separation, and a smaller fraction through unwed motherhood (Guttentag and Secord 1983). For example, of the 2,943,000 net additions to the number of female single-parent families in 1970–1982, 1,740,000 occurred to divorced women and 564,000 to separated women. A total of 860,000 (or about 30 percent) were due to illegitimacy. The picture for whites is similar, but for blacks the relative contribution of these two factors is reversed. The number of black female-headed families with children increased by 923,000 between 1970 and 1982, and 62 percent of the growth (572,000) came from never-married mothers.

Table 2.9 includes information on the incomes of the families in Table 2.8. Married-couple families in which the wife is in the labor force have the highest incomes, whereas the incomes of female householders with dependent children come at the bottom. The poverty rates in Table 2.10 show that poverty depends on the presence of young children. Poverty is not much more commonplace in female-headed families without children than it is in families in general; it is concentrated in single-parent families headed by women. Close to one-half (44.3 percent) of all such families were poor in 1981, and the proportion who were poor rose dramatically with the number of children. Similar conclusions emerge when either white or black families are considered alone, although poverty is overall greater among black families.[5]

Single-parent mothers face a double financial burden. Not only do they not have access to a male's income within the family, but having dependent children makes it more difficult for them to work outside the home. The financial advantages to women of being married have been summarized by Fuchs (1983): "Measured purely in income terms, most women are best off when they are married and share in the higher earnings of their husbands.". Women who become divorced in mid-life or beyond complain that some of the most important losses or adjustments they experience

Table 2.9

Number of Families and Median Family Income in 1981, by Family Type and Race (Families as of March 1982)

Family Type	All Races Number (thousands)	Median Income (dollars)	White Number (thousands)	Median Income (dollars)	Black Number (thousands)	Median Income (dollars)
All families	61,019	22,388	53,269	23,517	6,413	13,267
Married-couple families	49,630	25,065	45,007	25,474	3,535	19,624
Wife in labor force	25,002	29,247	22,252	29,713	2,114	25,040
Wife not in labor force	24,628	20,325	22,755	20,880	1,421	12,341
Male householder, no wife present	1,986	19,889	1,642	20,421	273	14,489
Female householder, no husband present	9,403	10,960	6,620	12,508	2,605	7,506
Without related children under 18 years[a]	2,916	15,741	2,383	16,986	487	10,622
With related children under 18 years	6,487	9,330	4,237	10,688	2,118	7,015

[a] "Related" children in a family includes own children.

SOURCE: U.S. Bureau of the Census, Current Population Reports, Series P-60, No. 137, "Money Income of Households, Families, and Persons in the United States: 1981" (March 1983), and unpublished Census Bureau tabulations.

Table 2.10

Poverty Status in 1981 of Families, by Race, Type of Family, and Presence of Related Children Under 18 Years Old (Numbers in Thousands; Families as of March 1982)

Family Type	All Races Total	Below Poverty Number	Percent of Total	White Total	Below Poverty Number	Percent of Total	Black Total	Below Poverty Number	Percent of Total
All families	61,019	6,851	11.2	53,269	4,670	8.8	6,413	1,972	30.8
Married-couple families	49,630	3,394	6.8	45,007	2,712	6.0	3,535	543	15.4
Without related children under 18 years[a]	24,353	1,195	4.9	22,672	989	4.4	1,333	186	13.9
With related children under 18 years	25,278	2,199	8.7	22,334	1,723	7.7	2,202	357	16.2
Other families, male householder	1,986	205	10.3	1,642	145	8.8	273	52	19.1
Without related children under 18 years[a]	1,164	90	7.7	990	69	7.0	138	19	13.4
With related children under 18 years	822	115	14.0	652	75	11.6	135	34	25.0
Other families, female householder	9,403	3,252	34.6	6,620	1,814	27.4	2,605	1,377	52.9
Without related children under 18 years[a]	2,916	375	12.9	2,383	250	10.5	487	117	23.9
With related children under 18 years	6,488	2,877	44.3	4,237	1,564	36.9	2,118	1,261	59.5
1 child	2,932	950	32.4	2,108	599	28.4	769	336	43.7
2 children	2,082	919	44.1	1,399	522	37.3	639	381	59.6
3 children	903	574	63.6	478	272	56.9	401	290	72.3
4 children	361	260	72.1	180	122	67.9	175	133	76.2
5 or more children	209	173	82.9	71	49	69.0	134	121	90.1

[a]"Related" children in a family include own children.

SOURCE: U.S. Bureau of the Census, *Current Population Reports*, Series P-60, No. 134, "Money Income and Poverty Status of Families and Persons in the United States: 1981" (July 1982); and *Current Population Reports*, Series P-60, No. 138, "Characteristics of the Population Below the Poverty Level: 1981" (March 1983).

involve economic factors, including financial losses through dividing property and other resources, the need to develop new labor market skills, and the need for greater financial resources to offset the loss of husband's income (Berardo 1982).[6]

The Panel Study of Income Dynamics (PSID) conducted at the University of Michigan constitutes one of the most informative data sets for studying the relationship between changes in family composition and economic welfare. The PSID began in 1968 with a group of families that oversampled poor and minority households. Since then it has followed all family members, even when they were separated by divorce or by children leaving home, or when they entered new unions through marriage or cohabitation. Analyses of the longitudinal data indicate that changes in marital status are the most important factor governing changes in economic status for women and children. According to Duncan (1983): "Family composition changes, such as divorce, marriage, and remarriage are more important than any other single factor in accounting for fluctuations in economic fortunes" (p. 233).[7]

Factors Contributing to the Decline in Marriage

If marriage has been declining as a social institution since at least 1960 for the white population and perhaps since somewhat earlier for blacks, what is its future course? Will the trends observed over the past two decades continue, or can a reversal be expected? To achieve more than armchair speculation, we need a theoretical explanation for the decline in marriage. The purpose of this section is to review three competing explanations proposed by economists and sociologists to account for events of the last two decades. In the order that we will consider them, these theories emphasize the gains to marriage, the changes in the relative income of young adults, and the influence of modernization on family functioning.

The Gains to Marriage

The theory of the gains to marriage is most closely associated with Gary Becker, an economist (Becker 1981; see also Becker, Landes, and Michael 1977). The basic idea is an application of the principle of comparative advantage derived from international trade theory.

The application of this theory to marriage is straightforward. Single men and women represent potential trading partners. They marry only if the gains to marriage are positive, that is, if each partner perceives that he or she will be better off (or at least no worse off) by being married than by remaining unmarried. Typically, in the past the wife traded part of her domestic services (including childbearing and child-rearing) to the husband in exchange for part of the husband's income. The key question is whether fundamental economic and social changes are undermining this sexual division of labor and the comparative advantage that men and women historically had.

Male/Female Differences in Labor Market Advantage. Over time, with the rise in female education and the growth of a service economy, women have become more like men in terms of their labor market skills and activity. In addition, technological improvements in the home and the overall lowering of fertility not only leave women with fewer domestic chores but also reduce women's alleged greater efficiency over men in performing these chores. If this argument is correct, it implies a narrowing of the competitive advantage of men over women in market work and also a smaller competitive advantage of women over men in home production. These developments would signify a reduction in the gain to marriage and would help to account for the fading centrality of marriage in America today.

As a reason for the greater family disorganization among blacks than among whites, some writers cite the legacy of slavery. Slaveowners discouraged marriage while encouraging high fertility. Slaves had no legal recognition of marriage, and a matriarchal family structure was a natural consequence (Reid 1982). Other historical factors that have had adverse consequences for black families include legal segregation, discrimination, urbanization, ghettoization, and the inability of large numbers of blacks, especially men, to find work (Joint Center for Political Studies 1983).

Becker (1981) argues that black families should be less stable than white families "if only because blacks are much poorer and black women earn much more relative to black men than white women do relative to white men" (p. 231; see also Smith 1977, 1979). Ross and Sawhill (1975) furnish evidence that black/white differences in income, earnings, and unemployment explain much of the difference in marital stability in recent years.[8]

This reasoning suggests that in the labor market women have been gaining on men faster among blacks than among whites. Thus women, especially black women, have less to gain from marriage than before. Never-married women come closer to duplicating the incomes of never-married men among blacks than among whites. Data on job tenure also show greater similarities between black men and women than between white men and women.

From 1960 to 1970, black occupational status distributions improved for both men and women, but more for women. In 1970, one in every three black women had a white-collar job, compared to only one in six black men.

Welfare Programs, Marital Dissolution, and Illegitimacy.
Some scholars believe that another factor discouraging marriage is the availability of public assistance, the most well-known being Aid to Families with Dependent Children (AFDC). This program guarantees an income to single-parent mothers and thereby reduces the gain to marriage. Unmarried women may have less incentive to marry if they become pregnant, and married mothers may have less incentive to stay married.

Table 2.11 shows selected data on the AFDC program, including the number of AFDC families, the number of recipients, and the level of cash payments since 1950. Over time, at least until 1980, the number of families in the AFDC program has increased, especially between 1965 and 1971 when the number of AFDC families nearly tripled. This period also coincides with the extraordinary jump of 2.8 years in the mean age at first marriage for black women. Several reasons have been given to explain this growth in the recipients of AFDC (Economic Report of the President, 1976). First, information about the program became more widespread, due in part to the efforts of poverty-concerned organizations. Second, eligibility criteria were relaxed, making it possible for more people to qualify for the program. Third, the rising level of payments made participation more attractive. Between 1965 and 1971, real AFDC payments per recipient increased by 22 percent, versus a 10 percent rise in real hourly earnings. In addition, the introduction of Medicaid in 1966 and the growing availability of food

Table 2.11

AFDC Families, Recipients, and Cash Payments,
Selected Years, 1950–1982

Year	AFDC Recipients (thousands)	AFDC Families		AFDC Cash Payments Monthly Average per Recipient[a]	
		Number[a] (thousands)	Percent of All Female-Headed Families with Children[b]	Current Dollars	December 1974 Dollars[c]
1982	10,370	3,546	50.3	104.53	55
1981	10,607	3,629	57.0	103.15	57
1980	11,101	3,843	72.0	100.53	60
1979	9,868	3,444	65.1	93	63
1975	11,300	3,395	77.1	71	68
1974	11,006	3,219	78.9	66	66
1973	10,815	3,068	80.8	57	64
1972	11,065	3,005	83.5	54	66
1971	10,653	2,783	83.5	52	66
1970	9,659	2,394	81.8	50	65
1965	4,396	996	40.2	33	54
1960	3,073	803	38.3	28	49
1955	2,192	602	32.2	24	46
1950	2,233	651	51.3	21	44

[a] The number of AFDC families as well as the monthly average per recipient is for December of each year except 1975, which is for September, and 1982, which is for October.

[b] The percentages are based on the number of female-headed families in March of each year except for 1975, which refers to April.

[c] Deflated by the consumer price index.

SOURCE: 1950–1975: *Economic Report of the President, 1976*, Table 29, p. 97; 1979: estimates furnished by June O'Neill, The Urban Institute; 1980–1982: Committee on Ways and Means, U.S. House of Representatives, *Background Material and Data on Major Programs Within the Jurisdiction of the Committee on Ways and Means*, February 8, 1983, Table 8, p. 267.

stamps after 1965 also added to the benefits that could be obtained. By 1975 the level of income available to AFDC families, while low compared to that of the average family, had risen sufficiently to be high relative to the potential earnings of the AFDC participants. A hypothetical AFDC family of four (consisting of a woman and three children), with no earnings or other income, had the equivalent of $5,348 in taxable income in 1974 and $5815 in 1975 from AFDC benefits, food stamps, and Medicaid (for which

AFDC families were automatically eligible). The median income of all families was $12,836 in 1974, but AFDC-related benefits compared favorably with what many women earned. In 1974 women with the same level of education as those on AFDC but who worked full-time earned $6,175 (Economic Report of the President, 1976).

Since the early 1960s the number of female-headed families has increased rapidly, and to some extent this rise may be related to AFDC changes. According to the Economic Report of the President (1976): "It is possible that the rising benefit levels and more liberal standards of eligibility in the AFDC program make it easier for women to form their own households" (p. 98). The report goes on to argue that studies have shown that women are more likely to form their own households when their earnings improve, while some respond in a similar way to increases in the AFDC stipend. AFDC also provides an additional incentive for women to remain family heads, since eligibility for AFDC is conditioned upon the absence of a husband.

Microeconomic theory lends support to these contentions. Relaxed AFDC eligibility criteria act like an income effect, permitting more people to come into the program with no necessary change in behavior regarding marital circumstances. On the other hand, rising benefit levels act like a price or substitution effect (the incentive to marry would now be reduced if a women has a child). In other words, a rise in average monthly benefit levels increases the price of being married, so at the margin one would expect to see a shift away from marriage.

Becker (1981) feels that the growth of the welfare state has been "a powerful force that has changed the family in recent decades" (p. 251). He cites the AFDC program as contributing to an increase in the fertility of eligible women, and to a rise in divorce and a decline in marriage because the financial well-being of recipients is increased by children and decreased by marriage. "In effect, welfare is the poor woman's alimony, which substitutes for husband's earnings. The expansion of welfare, along with the general decline in the gain from marriage, explains the sizeable growth in the ratio of illegitimate to legitimate birth rates despite the introduction of the pill and other effective contraceptives" (p. 252).[9] Fuchs (1983) also maintains that the large increase in the size of the AFDC payment, the relaxation of eligibility requirements, and the growing availability of other subsidies probably contributed to the chances that a mother of small children would opt for divorce. In addition, he suggests that the decline since the late 1960s in the remarriage rate following divorce, particularly noticeable for black women, may be the result either of improved employment opportunities for women or of the growth of government transfer programs such as AFDC. Fuchs notes the study by Hutchens (1979) who, he says, in a carefully controlled study of families in twenty states, found that the higher the level of AFDC payments, the lower the rate of remarriage. The Economic Report of the President (1976) adds that women on welfare are only half as likely to remarry within a four-year period as all women heading families with children (p. 98).

Despite what may seem to be the overwhelming logic of this argument, some analysts find little evidence that AFDC payments are a factor in either promoting divorce or preventing remarriage (Duncan 1983). Similar conclusions are reached by Bishop (1980). In a notable exception, however, it was found in the Seattle/Denver Income Maintenance Experiment that the five-year negative income tax treatment significantly increased the dissolution rates for black and white couples, by 57 percent for blacks and by 53 percent for whites (SRI International 1983, p. 291).

The economic perspective on marriage also suggests that illegitimacy should rise as AFDC payments increase, either by making marriage a less attractive option or by increasing the incentive to have an out-of-wedlock birth. The illegitimacy ratio rose particularly rapidly during the 1960s—the same decade in which the average monthly payment per AFDC recipient grew fastest. Fuchs (1983) cites other factors as well. First, there has been an expansion of employment opportunities for women, especially in the growing service industries. Second, the ability of women to raise children without a husband has been aided not only by the growth of the AFDC program but also by poverty health programs, subsidized housing, food stamps, day-care centers, and other transfers. Finally, women have access to better fertility control through more effective contraceptive methods and legalization of abortion (pp. 58–59). All of these, but especially the first two, make women less dependent on the economic security of marriage.

Leibowitz, Eisen, and Chow (1980) furnish evidence to substantiate the connection between welfare and illegitimacy. They analyze the behavior of 297 pregnant teenagers who, from 1972 to

1974, visited health care providers in Ventura County, California, for either prenatal care or abortions. In this self-selected sample, 15 percent married before delivery, 62 percent chose abortion, and 23 percent were unwed at delivery. With age, school enrollment, grades, religion, and ethnicity held constant, being eligible for public assistance significantly increased the likelihood of delivering out of wedlock.[10]

On the other hand, Vining (1983) points out that in southern states, despite welfare payments that are substantially lower than in the rest of the country, the black illegitimacy ratio is only slightly lower than in the rest of the country.

Relative Income Hypothesis

Easterlin's concept of relative income is a ratio between the earnings potential of a couple and the level of their material aspirations. The numerator is determined largely by the husband's job opportunities, wage rates, and speed of advancement and promotion on the job. The denominator depends on one's experiences as a child in the parental home. A high and comfortable living standard there leads to similar expectations for onself as a young adult, and vice versa. As the relative income of young adults rises, they will feel less economic pressure and therefore will feel freer to marry and to have children. As their relative income falls, they will feel increasing economic stress, causing marriage and fertility to decline. In more general terms, relative income can be thought of as the couple's economic outlook. High potential earning power relative to aspirations makes for an optimistic outlook, and vice versa.

Relative cohort size is important in determining relative income. Easterlin (1980) contrasts persons born during low birth rate periods (the 1930s) with those from high birth rate periods (the 1950s). Those born during low birth rate periods find that when they reach working age, they are in scarce supply relative to the number of older workers. Since the young adults are in relatively scarce supply, they find plenty of job openings, comparatively good wage rates, and rapid advancement. This situation favorably affects the relative income of young adults by creating good earnings prospects.

To measure relative income for the period 1957 to 1978, Easterlin uses the ratio of young men's income to their parents' income. In 1957 relative income stood at 73 percent but it had fallen to 54 percent by 1978, a situation that Easterlin says is putting young adults today under considerably greater economic stress than those in the late 1950s (p. 46). For the period before 1957 Easterlin uses the relative unemployment experience of fathers and sons as a proxy for relative income.

As evidence for this theory, Easterlin graphs the total fertility rate from 1940 to 1978 against his measure of relative income. The two curves coincide nicely. In the late 1950s, both the relative economic position of young adults and childbearing peaked. When a couple's economic outlook was exceptionally good, as in the late 1950s, the rate of marriage and the rate of childbearing increased. Conversely, when the outlook was more pessimistic, as before World War II and in the late 1970s, couples tended to defer marriage and to postpone childbearing within marriage, thereby depressing the total fertility rate.

When Easterlin applies his theory to divorce, he relies on the preservation of traditional sex roles. The man is valued for his work outside the home, whereas the woman's job as parent is paramount. Whereas couples from a small generation will find it relatively easy to fulfill their expected social roles, those from a larger generation will experience greater economic pressure. Wives may feel they have to work to support the family; the couple may not have as many children as they would like; husbands may feel guilty because they are unable to support their families as they had hoped; and wives may experience resentment. These marital strains resulting from economic pressure may result in marital dissolution. Two related factors compound the probability of divorce. Since children often help to hold a marriage together, a couple's reduced childbearing increases the chances of divorce. With the wife working outside the home, her feelings of financial independence may grow. Thus, high relative income makes for a lower probability of divorce, and low relative income adds to the likelihood of divorce.

Easterlin argues that recent divorce trends in the United States have two components to them: (1) an underlying secular trend that has tended upward; and (2) cyclical fluctuations or deviations from the trend. The upward secular trend Easterlin attributes to such longer-term forces as the so-called sexual revolution and the decreasing role that religion plays in shaping family attitudes. Other elements (for example, recent liberalizing of divorce laws) also have had a sporadic influence. However, generation size modifies this rising trend so that when a small generation is in the family-forming ages, divorce rates rise less steeply than the secular trend by itself would suggest, and when a large generation is at this state, large cohort size aggravates the rise in divorce. Thus small birth cohorts of the 1930s slowed down the divorce rates of the 1950s, but the large generations born during the 1950s served to accelerate the trend in divorce during the 1970s. Easterlin concludes that "the experience of the last two decades may give a distorted idea of the long-term trend—the traditional family may not be going down the drain quite so fast as some think" (p. 80).

What empirical evidence supports this theory on divorce? Easterlin cites a study by Coombs and Zumeta (1970) who surveyed intact families in the Detroit metropolitan area and then examined those factors that subsequently precipitated divorce. The authors demonstrated the importance of the wife's expectations about her husband's economic performance as a cause of divorce. A significantly larger proportion of the wives whose marriages ended in divorce considered their income to be inadequate and felt that their husbands were doing less well than others with similar work and education. A second bit of supporting evidence comes from a study by Preston and McDonald (1979), who examined the probability of divorce among successive five-year first-marriage cohorts between 1910 and 1914 and 1955 to 1959. These authors found that divorce was unusually high in periods when many couples had earnings that were low compared with the incomes of the families in which they grew up, and vice versa.

Modernization

Another explanation of the decline in marriage focuses on the loss of functions that society expects families to perform as industrialization and economic growth advance. Westoff (1983) views fundamental changes in the economic system as propelling a later age at marriage and an accompanying decreasing fertility. These have caused a loss in family functions, including economic, religious, and educational functions. Nevertheless, the family continues to survive, albeit in altered and somewhat attenuated form, because its essential functions of reproduction and socialization have remained (Westoff 1983, p. 102).

Economists also have drawn attention to the fading role of the conjugal family as the major institution in U.S. society (Fuchs 1983). Individuals appear to be relying less on their families today than in the past for the production of essential goods and services and for financial and emotional support. As economic growth has increased the advantages of both large-scale and specialized production units, the market and the government have assumed many of the family's former functions. Fuchs (1983) cites as examples the processing of food, making of clothes, and education of children. The market provides day-care centers for children and hospital and nursing homes for the elderly. The government has also taken over social insurance for widows and orphans, the sick, and the elderly (Fuchs 1983).

Many observers agree that the growth in the earning power of women and the emerging economic equality between men and women have important implications for marriage as a social institution. The near universality of marriage has traditionally been explained by the fact that marriage is a "complementary economic exchange system" (Westoff 1983, p. 102), but Westoff questions whether full economic equality between the sexes would undermine one of the most basic ingredients of marriage. He speculates that "such economic independence for women would certainly have the effects of postponing marriage even further and of increasing considerably the opportunity costs of childbearing and child rearing" (p. 102). Fuchs (1983) also raises as an issue what would happen to families if women became as continuously attached to the labor force and as varied in their occupatitonal choices as men.

The Future of Marriage

If trends in marriage and divorce from 1960 to 1980 indicate that marriage has been declining along a number of different dimensions, can these trends be expected to continue or not? The available evidence is rather mixed. Etzioni (1983) projects that if we continue to dismantle the American family at the accelerating pace observed since 1965, "[t]here will not be a single American family left by the year 2008" (p. 26). The U.S. Bureau of the Census (1983b) estimates that the number of unmarried-couple households has more than tripled during the 1970–1982 period, growing from 523,000 in 1970 to 1,863,000 in 1982—an increase of 256.2 percent. To the extent that young people think of living together or cohabiting as a natural prelude to marriage or as "trial marriage," the rising number of unmarried couples is retarding the growth of the married population (Davis 1982).

The delay in marriage may, however, presage a decline in divorce rates, or at least slow their rise, since the probability of divorce is inversely related to the age at marriage (Carlson and Stinson 1982). Moreover, remarriage rates remain high, at least for the white population. This suggests that high divorce should not be interpreted as a rejection of the institution of marriage but rather of particular marriage partners (Davis 1972). Many young people still believe that self-fulfillment and happiness can be found more easily by sharing one's life with another (U.S. News and World Report 1983).

Linear Theories of Change.   Becker (1981) believes that the rise in the earning power of women and (for poorer women) the growth in the welfare state lie behind the gradual diminution in the gain to marriage. He predicts less rapid increases in divorce if economic development continues to slow and if the expansion of the welfare state continues to moderate (p. 255). Westoff (1978), citing low fertility, trends in premarital cohabitation, and the rising status of women, argues that "[t]he future seems less and less compatible with long-term traditional marriage" (p. 82); he speculates that a massive postponement of marriage may portend "a radical change in the family as we know it" (p. 79). Westoff (1983) says that none of the primary forces of social change conducive to later marriage and low fertility is likely to be reversed and that the growing independence of women has not run its full course. Fuchs (1983) also feels that the future of the conjugal family is uncertain.

Cyclical Theories of Change.   Easterlin's (1980) theory of marriage anticipates a continuous series of ups and downs in marriage rates. With rising relative income of young adults between now and the 1990s due to low fertility in the 1960s and 1970s, Easterlin predicts a gradual shift to earlier marriage, increased childbearing within marriage, an upturn in the birth rate, and a below-average growth in divorce rates. Some of these changes may already be occurring. Easterlin cites as possible evidence the fact that the rate of childbearing has remained nearly constant since 1974 and that there has been a slowdown in the growth of the divorce rate in the period 1973 to 1977 in comparison to the period 1967 to 1973.[11] Implicit in his relative-income theory is a self-generating swing in fertility and marriage lasting about forty years. Persons from low birth rate cohorts marry early and have above-average numbers of children; persons born during times when birth rates are high have few children and marry late. Thus, the low birth rate cohort of the 1930s produced the high birth rate cohort of the 1950s, which in turn produced the low birth rate cohort of the 1970s.

Summary

Marriage, separation, divorce, and remarriage are significant choice variables for individuals. In recent years there have been considerable shifts in the decisions made by American adults regarding family formation and dissolution, and these shifts are consistent with the view that marriage is weakening as a social institution. Beginning in 1960 or earlier and continuing through 1980 there has been an increasing tendency to postpone marriage and perhaps to avoid it altogether; the probability that a marriage will end in divorce has risen steadily and has even accelerated during the 1970s; and rates of remarriage following divorce have either leveled off or continued to decline. In the early 1950s white women were spending more than half (54 percent) of their life expectancy at birth in the married state, but this proportion dropped to 43 percent by the late 1970s. For black women the shift away from marriage has been more dramatic. Black women in the early 1950s were spending 45 percent of total lifetime in the married state in comparison to just 22 percent by the late 1970s.

Numerous theories exist to explain this recent behavior. Some economists argue that women have less to gain from marriage since their earning power in the marketplace has increased and since government has taken over part of the responsibility for insuring minimal economic welfare for poorer families. Other economists trace the cause of declining marriage to a downward trend in the relative income of young adults. Since the income earning prospects of today's young adults are low in relation to their material aspirations, marriage is deferred and fertility is reduced. Some sociologists believe that the weakening of marriage is due to longer-term forces of social change that are gradually eliminating many of the functions marriage and families were once expected to perform.

Whatever its cause, the decline in marriage is having substantial repercussions. The proportion of all children born out of wedlock is rising; more than one out of every five American children is currently living with only one parent, and the number of single-parent families headed by women is increasing rapidly. Families headed by women typically have the lowest levels of household income, and this is especially so if young children are present. Much of contemporary poverty in the United States can be accounted for by female-headed families with dependent children.

What one projects for the future is likely to depend on whether one subscribes to linear or to cyclical theories of social change. Linear theories anticipate that the future will be a continuation of the recent past, whereas cyclical theories expect marriage to rebound over the next decade either because smaller birth cohorts of young adults will be entering the labor force or because the current imbalance in the sex ratio of eligible marriage partners can be expected to rectify itself.

NOTES

1. Cherlin (1981) makes this same point, but so rapid has the postponement of marriage been since the late 1970s, when Cherlin observed the American scene, that it is now necessary to go back to the turn of the twentieth century to find patterns of first marriage similar to today's.

2. The interested reader may consult Rogers (1975), Willekens and Rogers (1978), or Willekens et al. (1982) for a discussion of the methodology.

3. Black women expect to marry later than white women. In a 1975

survey of low-income high school students from six southern states, 311 juniors and seniors were asked, "How old do you think you will be when you get married?" Findings indicated that 42 percent of the white young women, but only 13 percent of the black young women, expected to marry at age 19 or younger. On the other hand, 18 percent of the white students and 43 percent of the black female students expected to be 24 or older (Kenkel 1981).

4.   As Davis shows in Chapter 1, the United States has the highest divorce rate of any industrial nation. Haskey (1982) demonstrates that if current divorce rates were to continue at their present levels, one in three marriages in England and Wales would eventually end in divorce.

5.   In recent years about one-half of all families below the poverty level were maintained by women with no husband present. In the early 1960s the proportion was about one in four (Chapman 1983). The "feminization of poverty" has been particularly evident among black families. The number of black female-headed families that were poor increased from 834,000 in 1970 to 1.4 million in 1981. These families accounted for 70 percent of all poor black families in 1981, compared with 56 percent in 1970 (Matney and Johnson 1983).

6.   A more detailed examination of the economic consequences of divorce including a discussion of the distribution of the economic hardship associated with divorce can be found in Espenshade (1979).

7.   Findings from the Panel Study of Income Dynamics on changes in family well-being are summarized in Duncan and Morgan (1981), in Duncan (1984), and in Bane (1976).

8.   Both Reid (1982) and Bane (1976) come to a similar conclusion. Without denying that the black–white income differential is a factor, Fuchs (1983) says that regional differences in the United States cast doubt on this explanation. The black–white difference in income is much greater in the South than in the Northeast, but the race differential in the percentage of children not living with both parents is greater in the Northeast than in the South (p. 58).

9.   Becker (1981) believes that a negative income tax system would also raise separation and divorce rates among eligible families in that the incomes of divorced and separated persons are raised relative to the incomes of married persons. Divorce rates of participants in negative income tax experiments are analyzed in Hannan et al. (1977) and in Keeley (1980). The effect of aid to mothers with dependent children on the number of female-headed households is considered in Honig (1974).

10.   This study's findings are reported in Fuchs (1983).

11.   The crude divorce rate was 5.0 divorces per thousand population in 1976 and 1977. It spurted to a new high of 5.3 in 1979 and 1981, but has receded since then. For 1983 it had fallen back to 5.0, and the rate was 4.9 divorces per thousand population for the first eight months of 1984 (National Center for Health Statistics 1984b, 1984c). One must be careful

not to rely too heavily on the fact that the crude divorce rate is declining as evidence that marriages have a better chance of holding together. Trends in the crude divorce rate tend to follow (with a lag of two or three years) trends in the crude marriage rate. The fact that the marriage rate has shown signs of leveling off may explain much of the recent behavior in the crude divorce rate.

REFERENCES

Akers, Donald S. "On Measuring the Marriage Squeeze." *Demography* 4(1967):907–924.

Albrecht, S. L. "Reactions and Adjustments to Divorce: Differences in the Experiences of Males and Females." *Family Relations* 29(1980):59–68.

Aries, Philippe. "Two Successive Motivations for the Declining Birth Rate in the West." *Population and Development Review* 6(1980):645–650.

Bane, Mary Jo. *Here to Stay: American Families in the Twentieth Century.* New York: Basic Books, 1976.

Becker, Gary S. *A Treatise on the Family.* Cambridge, Mass.: Harvard University Press, 1981.

Becker, Gary S.; Landes, Elizabeth; and Michael, Robert. "An Economic Analysis of Marital Instability." *Journal of Political Economy* 85(1977):1141–1187.

Berardo, Donna H. "Divorce and Remarriage at Middle Age and Beyond." In *Middle and Late Life Transitions.* Philadelphia: American Academy of Political and Social Science Annals, Vol. 464 (November 1982), pp. 132–139.

Bishop, John L. "Jobs, Cash Transfers, and Marital Instability: A Review and Synthesis of the Evidence." *Journal of Human Resources* 15(1980):301–334.

Carlson, Elwood, and Stinson, K. "Motherhood, Marriage Timing, and Marital Stability: A Research Note." *Social Forces* 61(1982):258–267.

Chapman, Bruce. "Prepared Statement on Broken Families." In *Hearings Before the Subcommittee on Family and Human Services of the Committee on Labor and Human Resources, U.S. Senate, March 22 and 24, 1983*, pp. 199–227. Washington, D.C.: U.S. Government Printing Office, 1983.

Cherlin, Andrew J. *Marriage, Divorce, and Remarriage.* Cambridge, Mass.: Harvard University Press, 1981.

Coombs, Lolagene C., and Zumeta, Zena. "Correlates of Marital Dissolution in a Prospective Fertility Study: A Research Note." *Social Problems* 18(1970):92–101.

Davis, Kingsley. "The American Family in Relation to Demographic Change." In Charels F. Westoff and Robert Parke, Jr. (eds.), *Demographic and Social Aspects of Population Growth*, pp. 235–265. Washington, D.C.: U.S. Government Printing Office, 1972.

Davis, Kingsley. "Changes in Marriage Since World War II." Paper presented at the conference on "Contemporary Marriage: Comparative Perspectives on a Changing Institution." Center for Advanced Study in the Behavioral Sciences, Stanford, California, 1982.

Duncan, Greg J. "Prepared Statement on Broken Families." In *Hearings Before the Subcommittee on Family and Human Services of the Committee on Labor and Human Resources, U.S. Senate, March 22 and 24, 1983*, pp. 233–238. Washington, D.C.: U.S. Government Printing Office, 1983.

Duncan, Greg J., and Morgan, James N. "Persistence and Change in Economic Status and the Role of Changing Family Composition." In Martha S. Hill, Daniel H. Hill, and James N. Morgan (eds.), *Five Thousand American Families—Patterns in Economic Progress*, Vol. 9. Ann Arbor, Mich.: Institute for Social Research, 1981.

Duncan, Greg J. *Years of Poverty, Years of Plenty: The Changing Economic Fortunes of American Workers and Families*. Ann Arbor, Mich.: Institute for Social Research, University of Michigan, 1984.

Easterlin, Richard A. *Birth and Fortune: The Impact of Numbers on Personal Welfare*. New York: Basic Books, 1980.

Economic Report of the President. Washington, D.C.: U.S. Government Printing Office, 1976.

Espenshade, Thomas J. "The Economic Consequences of Divorce." *Journal of Marriage and the Family* 41(1979):615–625.

Espenshade, Thomas J. "Black–White Differences in Marriage, Separation, Divorce, and Remarriage." Paper presented at the annual meeting of the Population Association of America, Pittsburgh, Pennsylvania, 1983.

Etzioni, Amitai. "Prepared Statement on Broken Families." *Hearings Before the Subcommittee on Family and Human Services of the Committee on Labor and Human Resources, U.S. Senate, March 22 and 24, 1983*, pp. 25–29. Washington, D.C.: U.S. Government Printing Office, 1983.

Fuchs, Victor R. *How We Live*. Cambridge, Mass.: Harvard University Press, 1983.

Glick, Paul C., and Norton, Arthur J. "Perspectives on the Recent Upturn in Divorce and Remarriage." *Demography* 10(1973):301–314.

Goldin, Claudia. "Female Labor Force Participation: The Origin of Black and White Differences, 1870 and 1880." *Journal of Economic History* 37(1977):87–108.

Grady, W. R. "Remarriages of Women 15–44 Years of Age Whose First Marriage Ended in Divorce: United States, 1976." *Advanced Data from Vital and Health Statistics*, No. 58. DHEW Publication No. (PHS) 80–1250. Washington, D.C.: U.S. Government Printing Office, 1980.

Green, Gordon, and Welniak, Edward. "Changing Family Composition and Income Differentials." U.S. Bureau of the Census, Special Demographic Analyses, CDS-80-7. Washington, D.C.: U.S. Government Printing Office, 1982.

Greene, W. H., and Quester, A. O. "Divorce Risk and Wives' Labor Supply Behavior." *Social Science Quarterly* 63(1982):16–27.

Gutman, Herbert G. *The Black Family in Slavery and Freedom, 1750–1925.* New York: Pantheon Books, 1976.

Guttentag, Marcia, and Secord, Paul F. *Too Many Women? The Sex Ratio Question.* Beverly Hills, Calif.: Sage Publications, 1983.

Hannan, Michael T.; Tuma, Nancy B.; and Groeneveld, Lyle P. "Income and Marital Events: Evidence from an Income-Maintenance Experiment." *American Journal of Sociology* 82(1977):1186–1211.

Haskey, J. "The Proportion of Marriages Ending in Divorce." *Population Trends* 27(1982):4–8.

Hauser, Philip M. "Demographic Factors in the Integration of the Negro." *Daedalus* 94(1974):847–877.

Honig, Marjorie. "AFDC Income, Recipient Rates, and Family Dissolution." *Journal of Human Resources* 9(1974):303–322.

Hutchens, Robert M. "Welfare, Remarriage, and Marital Search." *American Economic Review* 69(1979):369–379.

Joint Center for Political Studies. *A Policy Framework for Racial Justice.* Washington, D.C.: Joint Center for Political Studies, 1983.

Keeley, Michael C. "The Effects of Alternative Negative Income Tax Programs on Marital Dissolution." Paper presented at the Workshop in Applications of Economics, University of Chicago, 1980.

Kenkel, William F. "Black–White Differences in Age at Marriage Expectations of Low Income High School Girls." *The Journal of Negro Education* 50(1981):425–438.

Keyfitz, Nathan. "The Mathematics of Sex and Marriage." *Proceedings of the Sixth Berkeley Symposium on Mathematical Statistics and Probability*, Vol. 4. Berkeley: University of California Press, 1972.

Lane, Jonathan P. "The Findings of the Panel Study of Income Dynamics About the AFDC Program." Unpublished manuscript, Assistant Secretary for Planning and Evaluation, Department of Health and Human Services, 1981.

Leibowitz, Arleen; Eisen, Marvin; and Chow, Winston. "Decision-Making in Teenage Pregnancy: An Analysis of Choice." Working draft WD-421-3-HEW. Santa Monica, Calif.: Rand Corporation, 1980.

MacDonald, Maurice M., and Rindfuss, Ronald R. "Earnings, Relative Income, and Family Formation." *Demography* 18(1981):123–136.

McCarthy, James. "A Comparison of the Probability of the Dissolution of First and Second Marriages." *Demography* 15(1978):345–359.

Matney, William C., and Johnson, Dwight L. "America's Black Population: 1970 to 1982. A Statistical View." U.S. Bureau of the Census, Special Publication, PIO/POP-83-1, 1983.

Michael, Robert T. "Two Papers on the Recent Rise in U.S. Divorce Rates." National Bureau of Economic Research. Working Paper No. 202, 1977.

Michael, Robert T. "Causation Among Socio-Economic Time Series." National Bureau of Economic Research. Working Paper No. 246, 1978.

National Center for Health Statistics. "Advance Report of Final Natality Statistics, 1979." *Monthly Vital Statistics Report* 30(1981), Supplement 2.

National Center for Health Statistics. "Natality." *Vital Statistics of the United States, 1978*, Vol. 1. DHHS Pub. No. (PHS) 82-100. Washington, D.C.: U.S. Government Printing Office, 1982.

National Center for Health Statistics. "Advance Report of Final Natality Statistics, 1982." *Monthly Vital Statistics Report* 33 (1984a), Supplement.

National Center for Health Statistics. "Annual Summary of Births, Deaths, Marriages and Divorces: United States, 1983." *Monthly Vital Statistics Report* 32 (1984b).

National Center for Health Statistics. "Births, Marriage, Divorces and Deaths for August 1984." *Monthly Vital Statistics Report* 33 (1984c).

Norton, Arthur J. "Sociodemographic Trends and the 1980 Census." Paper presented at the annual meeting of the Population Association of America, Pittsburgh, Pennsylvania, April 14–16, 1983.

O'Hare, William. "Income and Wealth: The Real Status of American Blacks." Unpublished manuscript. Washington, D.C.: Joint Center for Political Studies, 1983.

O'Neill, June. "The Trends in Sex Differential in Wages." Paper presented at the Conference on Trends in Women's Work, Education and Family Building. White House Conference Center, Chewood Gate, Sussex, England, May–June 1983.

Parke, Robert Jr., and Glick, Paul C. "Prospective Changes in Marriage and the Family." *Journal of Marriage and the Family* 20(1967):249–256.

Philliber, William W., and Hiller, Dana V. "Relative Occupational Attainments of Spouses and Later Changes in Marriage and Wife's Work Experience." *Journal of Marriage and the Family* 45(1983):161–170.

Population Reference Bureau. "U.S. Population: Where We Are; Where We're Going." *Population Bulletin* 37(1982).

Preston, Samuel H., and McDonald, John. "The Incidence of Divorce Within Cohorts of American Marriages Contracted Since the Civil War." *Demography* 16(1979):1–25.

Reid, John. "Black America in the 1980s." *Population Bulletin* 37(1982).

Rogers, Andrei. *Introduction to Multiregional Mathematical Demography.* New York: John Wiley, 1975.

Ross, Heather L., and Sawhill, Isabel V. *Time of Transition.* Washington, D.C.: The Urban Institute, 1975.

Ryder, Norman B. "The Family in Developed Countries." *Scientific American* 231(1974):123–132.

Ryder, Norman B. "Cohort and Period Orientations to Measurement of Marital Formation and Dissolution." In *International Population Conference: Solicited Papers, Manila 1981*, Vol. 1. Liège, Belgium: International Union for the Scientific Study of Population, 1982.

Smith, James P. "Family Labor Supply over the Life Cycle." *Explorations in Economic Research* 4(1977):205–276.

Smith, James P. "The Distribution of Family Earnings." *Journal of Political Economy* 87(1979):S163–192.

SRI International. *Final Report of the Seattle/Denver Income Maintenance Experiment*, Vol. 1. Washington, D.C.: U.S. Government Printing Office, 1983.

U.S. Bureau of the Census. *Statistical Abstract of the United States: 1981.* Washington, D.C., 1981.

U.S. Bureau of the Census. "Households, Families, Marital Status, and Living Arrangements: March 1982 (Advance Report)." *Current Population Reports*, Series P-20, No. 380. Washington, D.C.: U.S. Government Printing Office, 1983a.

U.S. Bureau of the Census. "Marital Status and Living Arrangements: March 1982." *Current Population Reports*, Series P-20, No. 380. Washington, D.C.: U.S. Government Printing Office, 1983b.

U.S. News and World Report. "Marriage: It's Back in Style!" June 20, 1983.

Vining, Daniel R., Jr. "Illegitimacy and Public Policy." *Population and Development Review* 9(1983):105–110.

Westoff, Charles F. "Some Speculations on the Future of Marriage and Fertility." *Family Planning Perspectives* 10(1978):79–83.

Westoff, Charles F. "Fertility Decline in the West: Causes and Prospects." *Population and Development Review* 9(1983):99–104.

Willekens, Frans, and Rogers, Andrei. *Spatial Population Analysis: Methods and Computer Programs*. RR-78-18. Laxenburg, Austria: International Institute for Applied Systems Analysis, 1978.

Willekens, Frans; Shah, I.; Shah, J.M.; and Ramachandran, P. "Multi-State Analysis of Marital Status Life Tables: Theory and Application." *Population Studies* 36(1982):129–144.

Zelnik, Melvin, and Kantner, John F. "First Pregnancies to Women Aged 15–19: 1976 and 1971." *Family Planning Perspectives* 10(1978):11–20.

3 *Cohabitation in the 1980s*

Recent Changes in the United States

GRAHAM B. SPANIER

SOCIAL SCIENTISTS CAN POINT to few trends in contemporary American society that have manifested such a dramatic pace of change and that have exhibited such consistent upward growth as the trend in unmarried cohabitation. The objective of this chapter is to document and explain this development and to test the explanations against some characteristics of cohabiting couples.

About four million American adults are living with a partner of the opposite sex whom they have not married (U.S. Bureau of the Census 1983a, 1984). Some observers may regard the number as small in a population of 238 million. Yet cohabitation usually involves persons who are eligible for an important life transition—marriage—or who have recently experienced another critical tran-

---

NOTE: *Some of the material in this chapter is also presented in* "Married and Unmarried Cohabitation in the United States: 1980," *Journal of Marriage and the Family, May 1983, pp. 277–288.*

sition—divorce. Thus the study of the features of marriage entails at least some study of cohabitation.

By definition, an unmarried cohabiting individual is an adult sharing living quarters with one unrelated adult of the opposite sex. No other adult may be present in the household although children may or may not be present. The data are drawn primarily from the March 1980 *Current Population Survey* conducted by the U.S. Bureau of the Census and secondarily from more recent *Current Population Surveys*. It is reasonable to assume that most heterosexual unmarried couples with no other adults in the household live together because they are romantically involved. This assumption is important to note because the data featured here are demographic and do not provide the respondents' reports of their attitudes, motivations, and plans. The demographic data, however, do allow us to address many of the questions raised in this chapter. For example, although our definition of unmarried cohabitation encompasses such arrangements as an elderly woman who rents a room to a male college student or an elderly man who employs a live-in nurse or housekeeper, fewer than 1 percent of unmarried cohabiting couples fit this profile. Most unmarried couples differ in age by no more than a few years.

Trends in Unmarried Cohabitation

A profound increase in unmarried cohabitation occurred during the 1960s and 1970s and has continued into the 1980s; only recently are there signs that the rate of increase may be leveling off.

Table 3.1 compares figures for 1970, 1980, and 1984. In 1980 three times as many unmarried couples lived together as in 1970, the number nearly doubling between 1975 and 1980. In 1980 the trend continued to grow, showing a 14 percent increase by 1981. In 1984, there were two million unmarried-couple households (U.S. Bureau of the Census 1984), a 25 percent increase since 1980. About 4 percent of all couples living together in the United States are unmarried.

Table 3.1 also reveals that about 27 percent of all unmarried-couple households have at least one child in the household. When

Table 3.1

*Households with Two Unrelated Adults of Opposite Sex
Sharing Living Quarters, by Presence of Children:
1970, 1980, 1984*

	1984		1980		1970	
	Number (in thousands)	Percent	Number (in thousands)	Percent	Number (in thousands)	Percent
Total	1,988	100.0	1,589	100.0	523	100.0
No children present	1,373	69.1	1,159	72.9	327	62.5
Children present[a]	614	30.9	431	27.1	196	37.5

[a] For the year 1970, children in unmarried-couple households are under 14. For the years 1980 and 1984, children are under 15.

SOURCE: U.S. Bureau of the Census, *Current Population Reports*, Series P-20, No. 391, 1984.

children as well as adults are included, more than 4.6 million persons live in the households of unmarried couples.

Table 3.2 verifies a finding noted in earlier data, namely that primarily young adults find unmarried cohabitation attractive as a living arrangement. One-fourth of the men and nearly two-fifths of the women are under 25 years old; two-thirds of the men and three-fourths of the women are under 35. Although unmarried couples consist of persons of all ages, the phenomenon continues to involve younger persons disproportionately.

Between 1970 and 1981 one particularly noteworthy trend was a significant decline in the proportion of unmarried couples involving persons 65 and over. The absolute number of elderly persons remained relatively constant. For example, in 1970 approximately 115,000 persons 65 or older were unmarried and cohabiting, constituting 22 percent of all households with no children present. In 1981 there were approximately 120,000 such couples, only 7 percent of those with no children present. Given a possibly greater reluctance to report such a living arrangement in 1970 than in 1981, the negligible change in the number of unmarried cohabiting older persons during a period when the elderly population increased significantly is noteworthy. Changes in Social Secu-

Table 3.2

Partners in Unmarried-Couple Households, By Sex, Age, and Marital History: 1981 (Numbers in Thousands)

	Men		Women	
	Number	Percent	Number	Percent
Total	1,808	100.0	1,808	100.0
Age				
Under 25	435	24.1	687	38.0
25–34	780	43.1	686	37.9
35–44	252	13.9	151	8.4
45–64	232	12.8	181	10.0
65 years or more	111	6.1	99	5.5
Marital history				
Never married	958	53.0	991	54.8
Ever married	850	47.0	817	45.2

SOURCE: U.S. Bureau of the Census, *Current Population Reports*, Series P-20, No. 372, 1982.

rity regulations, which make remarriage more practical for the elderly, may account for some of the inertia in cohabitation.

Another interesting subgroup are persons legally married to someone other than the person they live with. In 1981 there were an estimated 282,000 such individuals—about 8 percent of the total number of persons cohabiting. The partners of individuals in this category most frequently either have never married or have been divorced. To a lesser extent, the partners share the same status, namely, still married to someone else.

Contrary to previous speculation suggesting that unmarried couples typically involve never-married persons, Glick and Spanier (1980) found that about half of the individuals living together had been married previously. More recent data confirm this finding. Although never-married cohabiting individuals tend to be young (81 percent of the men and 88 percent of the women are under 35), those who have been married are more evenly distributed across the adult years—40 percent of the men and 31 percent of the women are 35–54 years old, and 24 percent and 22 percent, respectively, are 65 or older. One of the more notable changes between 1975 and 1980 is the increase in the proportion of cohabitants under 35 who have been married. In other words, among the ever-married, a larger share of the increase can be attributed to those under 35. This change undoubtedly stems somewhat from the continuing high divorce rate, which rose from 4.9 to 5.2 per 1,000 population during the period (National Center for Health Statistics 1981, 1982). The change may also reflect a possibly longer period between divorce and remarriage, although such a trend has not yet been established. Since divorce disproportionately affects younger adults, a growing pool of previously married individuals now has the option of remarrying or of living with someone as an unmarried couple.

Glick and Spanier (1980) reported that between 1960 and 1975 the number of unmarried couples in households with children present had not varied much. The increase in nonmarital cohabitation was accounted for primarily by young couples without children. This pattern changed between 1975 and 1980 when both the number and the proportion of households with children increased. Thus, the recent growth in nonmarital cohabitation comes both from couples with children and from couples without children.

As with married couples, most young unmarried cohabiting adults live with someone of the same race. In 1980 nearly 98 percent of married couples and 95 percent of unmarried couples were of the same race. In 1980 about 2.2 percent of all marriages with the woman under 35 involved persons of different races, compared to 1.2 percent in 1975. The largest share of this increase occurred among couples with a white man or woman married to a person who designated a race other than black or white. Black men are far more likely to be living with white women than are black women to be living with white men. Individuals neither black nor white are as likely to have a partner of a different race as of the same race.

Unmarried partners generally are in the same or an adjacent age group. The ages of the partners tend to be widest apart when the man was previously married and least widely apart when he was never married. Whereas 45 percent of the previously married cohabiting men are in an older five-year age cohort than their wives, 71 percent of the previously married cohabiting men are in an older category than their unmarried partners. These findings reflect a tendency for men either to live with and then marry younger women or simply to live with a younger woman following a disrupted marriage.

It is interesting to point out that whereas only 4 percent of married women are in an older five-year cohort than their husbands, about 12 percent of the couples with a never-married man, and about 6 percent with one previously married, have such a profile. In general, therefore, young unmarried women, regardless of their marital history, are more likely than married women to be older than their partners.

The increase in cohabitation in recent years has encompassed persons of all educational backgrounds, but particularly has involved those with less than a college degree. In 1975, for example, 25 percent of the men and 21 percent of the women of cohabiting couples involving a never-married man were college graduates; in 1980 the percentages had dropped to 18 and 16.

Unemployment in 1980 was about twice as high for unmarried cohabiting women as it was for married men. An unmarried working man or woman exhibits a much higher tendency to live with an unemployed partner than does his or her married counterpart. However, unemployment does not seem to afflict both members of a cohabiting relationship simultaneously. Only 2 percent of unmarried-couple households possessed both an unemployed man and an unemployed woman.

The statistics are similar for both partners' participation in the labor force. In 1980, in only 3 percent of unmarried-couple households both the man and the woman were not in the labor force. However, unmarried women are much more likely than married women to be supporting a man who is not in the labor force. On the other side of the coin, married men are more likely than their cohabiting counterparts to support a woman not in the labor force.

Of all unmarried couples in which the woman is under 35 years old, nearly half are ones in which neither partner has ever been married. This represents an increase (48 percent compared to 43 percent) between 1975 and 1980. In another 15 percent of the cases, both the man and the woman have been divorced and in another 23 percent one partner has never been married while the other has been divorced.

Among these relatively young couples, widowhood is rare, as are relationships involving individuals still married to another partner. Cohabiting men and women who are still married to another person are much more frequent among couples in which the woman is over 35.

In 1980 in unmarried households, the proportion of separated persons was only half of what it had been in 1975, while the proportion of divorced persons was larger. This shift suggests that individuals are now more likely than before to terminate a failing marriage by divorce rather than to allow it to continue legally. Divorce may be sought sooner by persons who wish to live with someone else; moreover, divorce laws now more readily permit a speedy dissolution of a marriage.

Explaining the Trend

Increased unmarried cohabitation suggests that attitudes have changed. Cohabitation is viewed as a more acceptable form of living, and individuals are now more willing to live together. If so, if both attitude and behavior have changed, what are the causes of the change?

One factor has been the increase in the average age at first marriage, which has accompanied the rising incidence of cohabitation. After the 1950s, when the median age at first marriage reached a low for both men and women in the United States, the marital age rose steadily. In the most recent twenty-five-year period the median age climbed by more than two full years for both men and women (U.S. Bureau of the Census 1983a). It can be argued that among never-married persons cohabitation provides a contemporary extension of the courtship process, perhaps contributing to the postponement of marriage. Of course, if individuals first decide to postpone marriage, then cohabitation has more time to flower. Thus additional explanations are in order as to why these trends have covaried.

Several trends pertaining to sexual behavior and fertility have been well-documented during the last twenty-five years. In particular, the incidence of premarital coitus has increased, effective contraception is more readily available, fertility rates among young women have declined, and young married women are waiting longer after the wedding to commence childbearing (U.S. Bureau of the Census 1983b; Zelnik and Kantner 1980).

The prospect of sexual intimacy probably offered young adults of a generation ago a powerful incentive to consider marriage and to schedule it with some dispatch. Since the significant upward trend in cohabitation appears to have begun in the early 1960s, let us consider the 1950s as a period of comparison with today. In the 1950s, as Andrew Cherlin points out (Cherlin 1981), home and family life were highly regarded. It was a period of prosperity, high birth rates, and geographical dispersion to family-centered suburbs. In these and other ways, society provided a climate conducive to early marriage, early childbearing, and relatively high birth rates. Cohabitation had no prominent place given the norms of the time. Since the public consciousness largely disapproved of sexual intercourse outside of marriage—although it was fairly common—marriage provided young people with the only pragmatic route to sexual intimacy on a continuing basis. Since the 1950s, however, premarital sexual activity has become more prevalent, has involved less risk, and has tended to begin earlier. Society accepts such behavior more readily. Contraception more readily available to young people reduces or even eliminates the fear of pregnancy. The availability of abortion and the increased awareness of abortion as a method of controlling fertility undoubtedly also play some role.

Society's changing views of sex and marriage have made it possible to deemphasize or even to eliminate access to a sexual partner as a primary motivation for marriage. With this motivation removed, it is logical on the average that marriage would tend to occur later. Simultaneously, the period during which cohabitation can occur has extended and there now exists a diminished need for a cohabitational relationship to be formalized. Since a woman can almost completely eliminate the risk of pregnancy, the couple also can avoid what in the 1950s would have been a very compelling reason for early marriage—a birth out of wedlock or premarital pregnancy.

Society has changed in another way that may contribute to increased unmarried cohabitation. In the 1950s people assumed that women would marry relatively early, in part to begin childbearing, and that most mothers would remain at home to raise the children. The impressive movement of women into the labor force during the intervening years has changed this picture. Women now possess a much greater propensity to have attended college in order to pursue a career or to have an interest in working during their early adult years. Consequently, they have a diminished desire to marry during their early twenties or to have children at a time when their careers are being launched. With the internal and external pressures to marry and have children lessened, it is likely that young women would want to consider other options, such as cohabitation without marriage, during the years when their counterparts a generation ago were already married and beginning families.

Higher education, in its own right, may also influence cohabitation in two ways. First, since more young women leave home for college today than did so in the 1950s, they are more likely to become socially independent of their parents. The contemporary woman has increased opportunities to interact with eligible men, usually in an environment that tends to be less restrictive than that at home. Second, women attending college today expect to integrate both family and career, whereas women a generation ago viewed college as a transition to marriage. The college climate today directs women toward careers, not toward mate selection and marriage.

Urbanization, similarly, may be conducive to nonmarital cohabitation. The urban environment and its characteristic anonymity allow for cohabitation with fewer sanctions than a small town or rural environment might provide. Men and women may live together out of wedlock with little concern about what others will think. With urbanization, the level of surveillance of personal behavior has declined, thus making cohabitation easier to consider.

Finally, we may cite the increased prospect of divorce as a contributor to the upward trend in cohabitation. Although few brides and grooms expect to get divorced, there is now a very real awareness of the increased propensity to divorce. Many young men and women have experienced a divorce in their own families of orientation. The delay in marriage and the increased likelihood of cohabitation as a temporary alternative to marriage reflect to some degree a reluctance to rush into a relationship that runs some risk of divorce. In other words, young couples today may be weighing the prospects for marriage more carefully, deciding to marry only after reaching a degree of commitment higher than that required two or three decades earlier.

Although the discussion above focuses on young adults never

yet married, parallel arguments can be presented for the phenomenon of divorced persons cohabiting after their marriages have been dissolved. One common trend in all of these explanations is that couples do not necessarily equate living together with a permanent and lasting alternative to marriage, but rather associate it with a postponement of marriage or regard it as a temporary matter of convenience without an explicit understanding of what lies ahead. Indeed for many couples, the link between cohabitation and marriage is unclear from the outset because of other overriding concerns such as educational or job mobility. Couples may wish to delay marriage because one individual is preparing to go to graduate school and views marriage as a distant possibility. They may delay marriage because of job offers in differing locations. Economic concerns also suggest why a couple may prefer temporary cohabitation. They may be reluctant to marry before they are financially secure or when one or both partners are unemployed. Cohabitation can thus be viewed as an extension of the traditional courtship process, having many of the same conceptual features as engagement.

This discussion suggests that nonmarital cohabitation increased over the course of a generation when other fundamental changes also took place in society. Cohabitation, I believe, is best viewed not as a cause or effect of such changes, but rather as a phenomenon that occurred simultaneously and logically with other changes. We may generalize that cohabitation allows for intimacy without the commitment of marriage, providing for some couples the opportunity to satisfy the needs traditionally met in a family context. Cohabitation also affords the opportunity to terminate a relationship without the messy legal tangles (although they are not always avoided) and without the stigma that can accompany divorce. Cohabitation may serve an important economic function, since two individuals living together can usually live more cheaply than two individuals living apart. It may also be more economical than living together as a married couple due to the structure of our income tax system. Unmarried cohabitation may be like engagement in that it signifies to others that a formal, committed relationship short of marriage exists. It can be a period where the advisability of marriage is determined. Unlike engagement, however, which implies an imminent wedding, cohabitation may function in a contrary manner, allowing the indefinite postponement of a wedding date.

Some aspects of the demography of cohabitation must be viewed in a broader historical context. For example, the racial differences in social and economic characteristics of unmarried cohabitants are so substantial that they cannot be explained solely in terms of contemporary history. It is likely that nonmarital unions have different meanings for blacks and whites. The history of black family life in Africa and during the period of slavery in the United States suggests that black women and men possessed a greater degree of independence than did men and women in traditional European society. Of course, other fundamental differences exist between blacks and whites that may be responsible for the cohabitational variation. Differing employment patterns for black men and women, a higher rate of economic instability for blacks than for whites, the higher rate of illegitimate births among blacks, and the sex ratio resulting in fewer black men available for marriage to black women as compared to whites may all play some role in explaining the differences presented.

The following sections highlight the social and economic characteristics of unmarried cohabiting men and women compared with married men and women of similar age categories. We can look to these data to verify some of the tentative ideas presented above.

Profile of Social Characteristics

Table 3.3 presents a broad view of individual social characteristics in three types of living arrangements. Individuals are classified by sex and age, and are cross-classified by education, metropolitan-nonmetropolitan residence (sizes of the Standard Metropolitan Statistical Area), and race. The estimates for unmarried cohabiting individuals include persons married to someone other than their current partner. The Current Population Survey assigns weights, determined by sampling variability, to individual and household records to allow for population estimates. Estimates for unmarried men and women are based on weights associated with their own individual records, whereas estimates for unmarried couples are

Table 3.3

Selected Social Characteristics of Adults According to Living Arrangements, by Sex and Age: 1980

| | Living with Unrelated Person of Opposite Sex | | | | | | Married, Living with Spouse | | |
| | Never Married | | | Ever Married | | | | | |
Characteristic[a]	Under 35 Years	35–54 Years	55+ Years	Under 35 Years	35–54 Years	55+ Years	Under 35 Years	35–54 Years	55+ Years
Men									
Education									
0–11 years	18.3	39.9	77.3	21.6	33.0	59.6	14.9	25.0	47.2
12 years	36.6	21.2	9.9	37.7	38.4	27.6	40.5	36.2	28.8
13–15 years	27.2	12.4	b	22.9	14.5	4.4	21.3	14.9	10.6
16 years or more	18.0	26.6	12.8	18.0	14.2	8.4	23.2	24.0	13.4
SMSA size									
3 million or more	18.1	31.2	17.4	20.1	21.6	27.7	14.0	16.0	15.5
1–3 million	29.3	31.6	37.9	24.1	25.4	23.1	20.6	21.8	19.7
Less than 1 million	25.7	21.4	15.0	30.3	30.5	19.7	28.4	26.0	26.1
Not in SMSA	26.9	15.8	29.7	25.5	22.5	29.5	37.1	36.1	38.9
Race									
White	83.7	53.6	67.8	87.8	69.5	70.8	90.7	91.2	92.6
Black	14.8	44.1	32.2	10.9	28.9	28.5	7.2	7.0	6.4
Other	1.5	2.3	b	1.3	1.6	0.7	2.1	1.8	1.0
N (in thousands)	808	121	71	376	420	250	13,898	18,550	15,139
Total (in thousands)	999			1,046			47,587		

Women

Education									
0–11 years	17.6	44.8	21.9	25.3	39.3	61.9	16.2	23.1	42.2
12 years	41.3	29.6	15.0	45.2	34.1	29.3	48.6	48.6	39.0
13–15 years	21.9	6.9	1.3	19.9	17.3	5.0	19.0	14.3	10.5
16 years or more	19.2	18.8	61.9	9.4	9.4	3.9	16.2	14.1	8.4
SMSA size									
3 million or more	19.6	44.6	58.3	20.0	16.7	21.5	14.3	16.1	15.4
1–3 million	30.3	24.5	12.8	21.4	26.5	22.9	10.8	21.6	19.6
Less than 1 million	26.0	14.6	15.5	30.1	31.5	19.0	27.6	26.3	26.2
Not in SMSA	24.2	16.3	13.3	28.5	25.3	36.0	37.3	36.1	38.9
Race									
White	82.2	74.9	90.7	88.5	78.3	72.9	90.6	91.1	93.3
Black	15.6	21.6	9.3	9.3	18.8	26.6	7.1	7.1	5.7
Other	2.3	3.5	b	2.2	2.9	0.5	2.3	1.9	1.0
N (in thousands)	805	64	47	424	285	204	16,899	18,262	12,425
Total (in thousands)	916			914			47,587		

a Total for each characteristic is 100 percent.
b Zero or rounds to zero.
SOURCE: March 1980 *Current Population Survey.*

based on weights for the male cohabitor. This procedure results in totals for unmarried men and women that are not precisely comparable.

One of the several generalizations that can be offered is that the numbers of never-married and ever-married cohabiting women are approximately equal, whereas the number of men show a somewhat more heavy representation in the ever-married category. Thus, a previously married man has a greater tendency to cohabit with a never-married woman than vice versa. This trend may imply an increase in the proportion of never-married women in this living arrangement. This change may stem from the recent rise in the median age at first marriage (U.S. Bureau of the Census 1981a) and the greater acceptance of unmarried cohabitation for young women.

In '975 Glick and Spanier (1980) found significant educational differences between married and unmarried persons. By 1980 many of the differences still existed, although they had tended to diminish. For example, in 1975 only three in ten of the married women in the youngest age group had attended college, compared to one-half of the never-married cohabiting women. By 1980 the gap had narrowed from both directions to the corresponding figures of 35 and 41 percent. In all age categories married men are more likely than unmarried cohabitating men to have graduated from college and less likely to have dropped out of high school. These differences also characterize married women in relation to previously married cohabiting women. However, never-married cohabiting women fail to fit into any of these generalizations. Such women are more likely than women in any other living arrangement to have a college degree. The differences are particularly large among the never-married women over age 55, of whom 62 percent are college graduates.

Where do unmarried couples live? The figures for 1980 maintain the 1975 finding that unmarried couples have a greater tendency than their married counterparts to reside in metropolitan areas. For example, for people under 35 years old, about half of all never-married cohabitants lived in communities with at least one million residents, compared to only 35 percent of married persons.

In 1975 blacks, relative to whites, showed a disproportionate representation among unmarried couples. The cohabitation rate among blacks was three times that of whites. Although such differences continue to persist, they have moderated somewhat to a cohabitation rate about twice as high for blacks as for whites. In 1980 only 15 percent of never-married cohabitants and 10 percent of ever-married cohabitants under 35 were black. These figures represent significant declines over the five-year period. Among persons in the 35–54 and 55-and-above age groups, however, blacks continue to be quite heavily represented relative to whites and contrast sharply with the relative proportion of whites and blacks among married couples.

Profile of Economic Characteristics

Table 3.4 presents information on three economic correlates of living arrangements. Comparisons with 1975 data reveal that, although the proportion of married men in the labor force under age 35 remained virtually unchanged in 1980, the proportion employed increased in all other categories. Employment of married women in this age group increased from 44 to 55 percent; unmarried couples with a never-married man showed increases from 71 to 78 percent for men and from 68 to 72 percent for women; and unmarried couples with the man ever-married jumped from 77 to 85 percent for men and from 59 to 73 percent for women.

These developments reflect two changes. The first change is the rather familiar pattern of young women continuing to move into the labor force. The second change stems from an incipient convergence of the social and economic characteristics of married and unmarried couples. As suggested earlier, unmarried couples apparently are being drawn more fully into the mainstream of society, and people are more willing to ignore marital status, or at least are more willing to consider unmarried cohabitation as a regular living arrangement, if only on a temporary basis.

Despite the changes, unmarried cohabiting men are still less likely to be employed than married men, and unmarried cohabiting women are still more likely to be employed than married women. In the more recent data, differences also persist in the occupational categories of employed persons. Married men continue to be more likely than unmarried cohabiting men to have white-collar jobs. The reverse is true of service-worker jobs.

For women, differences in occupational group by living ar-

Table 3.4

Selected Economic Characteristics of Adults According to Living Arrangements, by Sex and Age: 1980

| | Living with Unrelated Person of Opposite Sex | | | | | | Married, Living with Spouse | | |
| | Never Married | | | Ever Married | | | | | |
Characteristic[a]	Under 35 Years	35–54 Years	55+ Years	Under 35 Years	35–54 Years	55+ Years	Under 35 Years	35–54 Years	55+ Years
Men									
Employment status									
Employed	78.0	80.4	31.6	84.7	84.0	45.2	92.1	92.4	48.1
Unemployed or not in labor force	22.0	19.6	68.4	15.3	16.0	54.8	7.6	7.6	32.0
Occupational group									
White collar	30.7	30.3	10.0	33.4	32.3	17.4	39.0	46.3	25.6
Blue collar	54.0	45.0	15.9	56.8	49.5	23.1	50.8	41.8	21.9
Service workers	10.4	7.9	9.5	7.1	10.4	9.5	6.0	5.4	4.9
Farm workers	1.4	1.5	0.4	0.6	1.1	1.5	2.5	3.0	3.6
Never worked or not in labor force	3.5	15.4	64.3	2.0	6.8	48.5	1.8	3.6	44.0
Family income									
Less than 10,000	53.3	46.4	97.8	34.4	34.7	68.6	12.5	7.8	27.6
10,000–14,999	25.8	30.3	1.6	30.3	25.6	10.4	16.8	8.9	19.2
15,000–19,999	12.4	12.0	0.7	16.7	18.4	4.2	20.7	13.7	12.8
20,000 and over	8.5	11.3	b	18.5	21.3	16.8	50.0	69.7	40.4
N (in thousands)	808	121	71	376	420	250	13,398	18,550	15.139
	999			1,046			47,587		
Total (in thousands)				47,587					

Women

Employment status									
Employed	72.1	57.3	37.9	73.3	72.3	28.2	55.2	57.2	23.7
Unemployed or not in labor force	27.9	42.7	62.1	26.7	27.7	71.8	44.8	42.8	76.3
Occupational group									
White collar	53.4	28.5	12.0	52.6	43.4	11.3	47.4	43.0	18.0
Blue collar	14.1	17.8	3.7	12.5	11.3	5.3	9.9	9.8	4.2
Service workers	20.0	17.6	22.2	19.1	20.9	17.4	12.4	11.0	6.1
Farm workers	0.8	b	b	1.1	1.2	0.2	0.9	1.2	0.7
Never worked or not in labor force	11.8	36.1	62.1	14.8	22.8	65.8	29.5	35.0	70.7
Family income									
Less than 10,000	77.5	71.9	96.0	68.3	57.7	84.9	12.3	8.2	30.7
10,000–14,999	14.7	8.9	4.0	22.8	26.5	9.9	15.9	9.0	20.6
15,000–19,999	5.2	12.2	b	6.8	9.9	3.5	20.0	13.0	12.8
20,000 and over	2.6	7.0	b	1.5	6.0	1.7	51.8	69.9	36.0
N (in thousands)	805	64	47	424	285	204	16,899	18,262	12,425
Total (in thousands)		916			914			47,587	

[a] Total for each characteristic is 100 percent.
[b] Zero or rounds to zero.

SOURCE: March 1980 *Current Population Survey*.

rangement are harder to find. Fewer unmarried women have never worked or are not in the labor force. This difference may reflect the more tenuous nature of unmarried cohabitation, which requires more independence and more financial self-reliance. Of course, it is also likely that some women who are a priori more independent and financially self-reliant experience less pressure or less motivation to marry. They are therefore more willing to consider unmarried cohabitation. Apart from this difference, however, the distribution of job types is roughly similar for all women. In all three living arrangements most women have white-collar jobs; service work is the next most prevalent form of employment, followed by blue-collar work.

Table 3.4 includes information on income, a variable that reveals perhaps the most profound difference between married couples and unmarried couples. Table 3.4 combines the incomes of the man and the woman into "family income" for married couples but not for unmarried couples. Yet this procedure does not negate the differences between the two groups, partially because the differences are so profound. In 1975 and again in 1980 low income was found to be especially characteristic of unmarried couples. The recent data reveal, for example, that approximately half of cohabiting men receive less than $10,000 per year, compared to fewer than one in eight families of married men.

In addition, whereas more than half of married men have family incomes surpassing $20,000, about one in twelve never-married cohabiting men and about one in five ever-married cohabiting men fall in this income category.

Conclusion

Our data on the social and economic characteristics of couples provide some confirmation of our explanation for the upward trend in cohabitation. The data presented here, when compared with similar data prepared five years earlier, suggest an overall picture of consistency in the demographic characteristics of unmarried couples. However, differences between unmarried couples and married couples are diminishing. Unmarried couples are evidently being drawn more fully into the mainstream of society. Society is more willing to ignore marital status in its evaluation and treatment of individuals, and those already in the mainstream of society are more willing to consider unmarried cohabitation as an acceptable living arrangement.

Much of our earlier discussion about the trend in nonmarital cohabitation probably makes the most sense from the perspective of middle and upper-middle class Americans—people who have benefited from clear norms governing mate selection and from a college education and job mobility. But our profile of social and economic characteristics, while not contradicting any of these explanations, suggests that most unmarried cohabitants are not in the middle or upper-middle class at all. A disproportionate share of such persons have a high school diploma at best, are blue-collar or service workers—or are unemployed—and earn less than $10,000 per year. Blacks are overrepresented. Thus, we must examine the possibility that two simultaneous phenomena have provided the force for changes in nonmarital cohabitation. The first relies on the dynamics cited already in this chapter and applies mostly to middle class young adult men and women who have never been married or who were previously married. The other explanation of the trend must focus on the large working class and lower class population, particularly blacks, for whom cohabitation may be principally a response to economic hardship, family disruption, and elusive mate selection and marriage norms.

When applied to the second group, the upward trend in unmarried cohabitation correlates with the high level of illegitimacy, single parenthood, and divorce among individuals in the lowest socioeconomic statuses. Among blacks, for example, only 42 percent of children live with two parents. Among black children with one parent, the largest share live with a never-married mother. The incidence of such arrangements has increased substantially over the past decade, paralleling the increase in nonmarital cohabitation (U.S. Bureau of the Census 1983b).

What lies in the future? An overall increase in cohabitation is likely to occur, although more slowly than in recent years, since the conditions that have been conducive to nonmarital cohabitation or that perhaps have contributed to its increase will continue to be present. Since the age at first marriage probably will continue its increase, cohabitation will remain prominent in our society. If the divorce rate continues at its current level, or even declines slightly, a large population of previously married individuals will be free to cohabit, many in a transition to remarriage. The beginnings of a trend toward postponement of remarriage, undoubtedly corresponding with the trend in postponement of first marriage, is likely to continue, thus increasing unmarried cohabitation arrangements.

Although the pace of the increase shows signs of deceleration, the large numbers of individuals who now cohabit and who have caused significant changes in our society have bequeathed to us a demographic history that will not go unnoticed by the next generation. Future cohorts will find the freedoms and flexibility of cohabitation attractive, and, almost certainly, behavior across social class lines will converge. To the extent that social and economic conditions improve, cohabitation for lower-status individuals should level off or decline. Yet a continuing increase in cohabitation due to other factors mentioned certainly will compensate for this leveling effect. The collective outcome is likely to be one of convergence among social classes within the larger framework of a continuing increase nationally in cohabitation. A comparison of 1975, 1980, and later data indicates that this prediction may have some merit.

REFERENCES

Cherlin, A. J. *Marriage, Divorce, Remarriage*. Cambridge, Mass.: Harvard University Press, 1981.

Glick, P. C., and Spanier, G. B. "Married and Unmarried Cohabitation in the United States." *Journal of Marriage and the Family* 42(1980):19–30.

National Center for Health Statistics. "Annual Summary of Births, Deaths, Marriages, and Divorces: United States, 1980." *Monthly Vital Statistics Report*, Vol. 29, No. 13, September 17. Washington, D.C.: Department of Health and Human Services, 1981.

National Center for Health Statistics. "Births, Marriages, Divorces, and Deaths for 1981." *Monthly Vital Statistics Report*, Vol. 30, No. 12, March 18. Washington, D.C.: Department of Health and Human Services, 1982.

U.S. Bureau of the Census. "Marital Status and Living Arrangements: March 1980." *Current Population Reports*, Series P-20, No. 365. Washington, D.C.: U.S. Government Printing Office, 1981a.

U.S. Bureau of the Census. "Household and Family Characteristics: March

1980." *Current Population Reports*, Series P-20, No. 366. Washington, D.C.: U.S. Government Printing Office, 1981b.

U.S. Bureau of the Census. "Marital Status and Living Arrangements: March 1981." *Current Population Reports*, Series P-20, No. 372. Washington, D.C.: U.S. Government Printing Office, 1982.

U.S. Bureau of the Census. "Marital Status and Living Arrangements: March 1982." *Current Population Reports*, Series P-20, No. 380. Washington, D.C.: U.S. Government Printing Office, 1983a.

U.S. Bureau of the Census. "Fertility of American Women: June 1981." *Current Population Reports*, Series P-20, No 378. Washington, D.C.: U.S. Government Printing Office, 1983b.

U.S. Bureau of the Census. "Households, Families, Marital Status, and Living Arrangements: March 1984 (Advance Report)." *Current Population Reports*, Series P-20, No. 391. Washington, D.C.: U.S. Government Printing Office, 1984.

Zelnik, M., and Kantner, J. F. "Sexual Activity, Contraceptive Use and Pregnancy Among Metropolitan-Area Teenagers: 1971–1979." *Family Planning Perspectives* 12(1980):230–237.

4 *Couples Without Children*

Premarital Cohabitation in France

ELWOOD CARLSON

THE TIDE OF EARLY MARRIAGES that swept in upon many Western nations in the mid-twentieth century (Hajnal 1953; Davis 1958; Festy 1973) has receded. In recent years, a delayed marriage trend (Wunsch 1973; Glick and Norton 1977; Munoz-Perez 1979) has followed in these same nations. As a consequence, there is an expanding life-space in early adulthood where informal premarital unions may flourish. "Indeed there have been few developments relating to marriage and family life which have been as dramatic as the rapid rise in unmarried cohabitation" (Glick and Spanier 1980, p. 19).

In French society, where the spread of premarital unions has advanced to a level intermediate among Western nations, such informal cohabitation generally amounts to a form of "partial marriage" with reproduction actively delayed or avoided. These are couples without children. This way of looking at premarital cohabitation also leads to a useful framework for comparing changes in marriage and family life in the broader international community.

Delayed Marriage and Cohabitation

A delayed marriage trend is in fact the first prerequisite for the spread of informal unions. When marriages are early and universal, premarital cohabitation has little chance to occur. On the other hand, while such a shift in marriage timing is necessary for the spread of premarital cohabitation, it is not sufficient. It would be a serious error to maintain that the European tradition of late marriage (Hajnal, 1965) also was a tradition of extensive premarital cohabitation such as can be witnessed today. The "European marriage pattern" delayed *all* unions, formal and informal.

Today the delayed marriage trend also has expanded the ranks of young people "at risk" of cohabiting in many nations that have no previous history of delayed marriage. By the late 1970s the average age at marriage for women was nearly the same (about 24) in Sweden, Switzerland, Italy, and Greece, for example. As of 1975, the shares of women still unmarried at ages 25 to 29 were 23 percent, 22 percent, 23 percent, and 26 percent in each of these countries, respectively (United Nations 1976).

Despite such similarity in marriage timing, patterns of informal cohabitation in these countries were quite different. According to Trost (1975) nearly all Swedish couples reported that they had cohabited before marrying. About 60 percent of surveyed Swiss citizens married in Geneva in 1974 and 1975 had lived together before their marriages (Perrin, Kellerhals, Voneche, and Steiner, unpublished data cited in Roussel and Festy 1979). By contrast, premarital cohabitation in Italy and Greece remains infrequent and unusual (Roussel and Festy 1979). Thus cohabitation should not be viewed as a cause of marital delay. Why do informal unions precede marriage to such a different extent, in societies which all have experienced delayed marriage trends?

Even within French society as studied here, late marriage is not a sufficient explanation for high rates of premarital cohabitation. As a result of unfavorable economic conditions and prospects (Jegouzo 1979) the French farm population marries quite late. Yet they also exhibit the lowest level of cohabitation before marriage of any French occupational or size-of-place-of-residence group (Roussel 1978).

This analysis seeks to explain why, within a social climate of widespread postponement of marriages, informal premarital cohabitation becomes increasingly common for *some* segments of a population.

Social Correlates of Cohabitation

Previous research about cohabitation (Trost 1975; Clayton and Voss 1977; Roussel 1978; Glick and Spanier 1980; Spanier 1983) has explored the positions young adults occupy in society as correlates of informal unions. For example, cohabitation is predominantly an urban phenomenon. It is more common among those with higher levels of education. It occurs much more among persons with only weak or nonexistent ties to formal religious groups.

All these comprehensive studies, however, examine such social correlates of premarital cohabitation on a simple bivariate basis, which does not allow us to untangle possible interactions between the various dimensions of social structure.

As a first step toward understanding premarital unions, then, consider Table 4.1. The results of a Multiple Classification Analysis demonstrate the independent contributions of five aspects of French social structure to the tendency to cohabit before marriag

The respondents shown in this table were selected in 1977 by the Institut National d'Etudes Démographiques in Paris and were representative of all young adults in France between the ages of 18 and 29. Included are reports of past premarital unions for married respondents as well as past and present unions among those still unmarried at the time of the survey.

Table 4.1 reveals four separate, direct links between incidence of cohabitation and social structure. Urban residence (particularly in Paris), advanced education, geographic separation from parents, and weak or nonexistent religious involvement each display an *independent* association with a higher incidence of informal unions. On the other hand, the influence of family socioeconomic status is not directly evident. When viewed in a simple bivariate context, the father's socio-professional activity shows a strong relation to

Table 4.1

*Proportion of Respondents Ever Cohabiting Before Marriage
by Selected Social Characteristics, 1977
(Multiple Classification Analysis Results)*

	Females	(N)	Males	(N)
Proportion for total	.39	(1234)	.37	(1243)
Father's socio-professional activity				
Cadres supérieurs	.45	(245)	.40	(197)
Artisans/commerçants	.38	(185)	.44	(205)
Techniciens	.35	(159)	.32	(134)
Employés	.40	(168)	.34	(188)
Ouvriers	.35	(288)	.37	(335)
Cultivateurs	.39	(189)	.33	(184)
Proximity of parental family				
Same commune	.28	(526)	.24	(593)
Elsewhere	.48	(708)	.48	(650)
Education				
Primary	.27	(214)	.33	(274)
Trade school	.32	(295)	.33	(352)
Secondary	.37	(366)	.36	(226)
Postsecondary	.54	(360)	.44	(391)
Religious practice				
Nonpracticing	.45	(874)	.34	(1012)
Practicing	.24	(360)	.25	(231)
Residence				
Paris	.59	(346)	.56	(358)
Other in France	.31	(888)	.31	(885)
Explained variance (R^2)	28.2%		22.2%	

the incidence of informal unions (Roussel 1978) but in Table 4.1 little or none of this relation remains when the other four variables are taken into account. Because family status comes before these other variables temporally and logically, one should say that the social and economic position of the parental family *is* linked to cohabitation, but only indirectly through association with the other four intervening variables.

Such multivariate analysis helps to sort out patterns of cohabitation in French society but does not help to explain the rapid increase of such informal unions in recent years. There have been no upheavals such as dramatic increases in young adults enrolled in school, sudden mass defections from religion, new waves of migration to cities, or sudden upward shifts in the socioeconomic distribution of families. Although cross-sectional variations often receive the most attention in studies of cohabitation, variations such as those observed in Table 4.1 cannot be translated into diachronic explanations of change (a point that applies to patterns of cohabitation in many other nations as well as in France). In fact, increases in cohabitation generally have occurred *within* categories such as urban residence and higher education, as we shall see later.

In his study of these same respondents, Roussel concluded that premarital cohabitation in France was "mostly a preliminary stage to marriage, which was put back by at least six months" (Roussel 1978, p. 42). One further detail in the lives of these young French men and women furnishes the key to the timing of the transition from cohabitation to marriage—the birth of a child.

Cohabitation and the Avoidance of Parenthood

Nearly forty years ago, Murdock (1949) suggested that marriages provide socially guaranteed sexual contact, produce and care for children, and foster division of labor among family members. He implied that the formation of marriages "activated" all of these functions at once. Indeed, it was precisely this binding together of functions into one social unit that provided Murdock's rationale for his much-debated claim that the nuclear family is universal.

Murdock's analysis never has offered a very accurate picture of how intimate unions work. For most people who have ever lived in most human societies, the premier function of marriage has been reproduction. In traditional societies, "[i]ndividuals not only use children for labor and depend on them for care and assistance later in life, they also gain the only rewarded statuses in the kinship system through having children and, thereby, becoming parents" (Blake 1972, p. 283).

This primacy of the reproductive function of marriage has been clearly documented with examples from Africa (Caldwell 1968; Sween and Clignet 1978), from Latin America (Camisa 1975), and from Asia (Morgan and Rindfuss 1984). In some instances conception precedes the nuptial rites; after the arrival of infants, couples may perhaps find love and companionship in marriage, but a union without babies is often dissolved. Marriage exists to produce children.

In a number of nations today, at least among certain young adults, this worldwide historical rule has been turned on its head. Marriages no longer exist principally to produce children. Today it is the arrival of children that produces marriages, among couples who came together initially for personal intimacy rather than reproduction. This pattern has been observed in Germany, where the incidence of informal unions has increased in recent years.

> The small number of unmarried mothers living with their children seems surprising, given the strong increase in cohabiting couples. . . . Apparently it is very rare for these couples to have children. The opinion that an infant should have parents who are legally married is still very widespread (translated from Schwarz 1983, p. 571).

Similarly in France, in connection with the same respondents who figured in Table 4.1, Roussel observed:

> The young who are living together seem thus to have a lifestyle very near to that of married persons. One important point distinguishes them from each other, however: for the most part cohabitants have no children and do not envisage having any without getting married (translated from Roussel 1978, p. 35).

Based on 1980 census data, Davis (1983, p. 27) makes much the same judgment concerning American cohabitation and parenthood: "The facts are compatible with the hypothesis that men and women in nonmarital unions tend either to remain childless, to break up the union, or if they decide to have children, to marry."

Table 4.2 documents this aspect of the French respondents' lives in more detail than was presented in earlier analyses by Roussel and his colleagues in Paris. Only one out of seven cohabiting couples had any children after four years of living together. The situation is exactly reversed for married couples; only one out of seven had still not had a child after four years of marriage.

Thus the real difference between cohabitation and marriage is made clear. It is the prospective arrival of an infant that transforms one state into the other. It seems that the word "marriage" is more and more reserved for those who are parents, at least for

Table 4.2

Proportion of Respondents with Any Children, by Types and Duration of Unions (with base N's)

Duration (in completed years)	Cohabitation Without Marriage	
	Men	Women
0	.01 (76)	.04 (76)
1	.05 (64)	.05 (58)
2	.05 (56)	.06 (65)
4	.16 (48)	.14 (55)

	Marriages			
	Men		Women	
Duration (in completed years)	Never Cohabited	Ever Cohabited	Never Cohabited	Ever Cohabited
0	.06 (17)	.22 (16)	.00 (18)	.06 (18)
1	.40 (62)	.42 (36)	.27 (47)	.35 (49)
2	.70 (50)	.64 (51)	.71 (51)	.29 (31)
3	.80 (45)	.52 (49)	.73 (36)	.75 (20)
4	.87 (39)	.94 (49)	.89 (56)	.86 (21)

certain young people in France. The birth of a child marks the conclusion of their informal "partial marriages"—marriages in which only the companionate function has been activated and in which parenthood has been at least temporarily avoided.

In Sweden and Denmark, however, this rule apparently does not hold (Hofsten 1978). In these two countries, where informal cohabitation has become all but normative, many cohabiting couples seem willing to have children without marrying in the short term, although most still marry eventually (Lewin 1982). It is important to recognize, then, that the social meaning of cohabitation as advanced here applies chiefly in societies where informal unions occur with considerable frequency but do not receive overt societal recognition as "normative"—that is, there is no preferential access to child care for unmarried mothers, no joint tax returns for cohabiting parents, no social security for cohabiting women based on the man's earnings.

Symptoms of the Decline of Consanguine Family Systems

Delayed marriage, premarital unions, and avoidance of parenthood all are symptoms of a deeper current of social change, the general character of which is the decline of consanguine family systems. The consanguine family is the wider kinship group, defined mainly by emphasizing filial relationships. Strictly speaking, marriage is not included among consanguine relationships; it is a different sort of social bond. The filial character of consanguine relations gives rise to hierarchies of age, generation, and sex. These tend to control the marriage rites of culture after culture. Marriage traditionally has existed as obedience to one's parents. The choice of marriage partners and the timing of marriage have reflected the interests of those at the top of kin-based hierarchies. Caldwell (1976) captured this hierarchical principle of obedience when he described the traditional "flow" of wealth, obligations, and services from children to parents in such systems. Lesthaege and Wilson (1982) used this same idea when they explained the long-term decline of European fertility as the result of a decline or perhaps even a reversal of the flow of wealth and services from children to their parents.

Within such a family system there is usually little direct coercion. Rather, conformity is accomplished through transmission of a body of pronatalist and pronuptial norms. These not only generate the consanguine family but place it at the heart of the social order and allocate to it the material wealth of society.

In many contemporary societies, however, the consanguine family seems to have loosened its grip upon the lives of people. Roles and obligations derived from consanguine families no longer constitute the foundation of social organization. Sometimes the explanation of this change has been economic. For Hall (1974) consanguine family connections proved insufficient to conduct rapidly expanding commercial enterprises, spelling the end of cross-cousin marriages in New England merchant families. Tilly, Scott, and Cohen (1976) showed how migration of young women to expanding urban labor markets attenuated protection by kin and led to rising illegitimacy.

On the other hand, Boli-Bennett and Meyer (1978) maintain

that neither consanguine families themselves nor the new economic system actually "turned off" the flow of wealth and services
from children to consanguine families. Families caught up in the
industrial transformation at first simply translated children from
obedient unpaid servants and farm laborers into obedient wage
laborers (Baker 1964; Modell, Furstenberg and Hershberg 1976). It
was called the "family system." The same tendency for consanguine families to adapt to the urban industrial context (rather than
simply falling apart) is apparent in contemporary non-Western
societies as well.

> Under the demographic and economic circumstances, working
> daughters [in Hong Kong] are expected to contribute to their fami-
> lies' income. This virtually forced family survival mechanism actu-
> ally enables the family to improve its living standard. Since family
> needs are socially defined, they can be shifted upwards. From food,
> shelter and clothing, higher educational standards are the next step
> The period during which women must contribute to their families'
> budgets is thereby rather flexibly extended [Salaff 1976, pp. 410–
> 411].

Boli-Bennett and Mayer (1978) point to the increasing political power of the state as the root of declining family systems. By
intervening in testamentary procedures, by legislating against
child labor, by making formal schooling mandatory, and by a host
of related acts, the early Western nation-states began four or five
centuries ago to transform children from economic assets to economic liabilities. When the state attains a certain level of power
with its citizens, it dispenses with intermediaries such as kin
groups and hence abandons its age-old alliance with the family as
an agent of social control.

Other scholars (Dumont 1981; Goody 1983) push the origins of
eroding consanguine family influence even further into the past,
wholly rejecting the politico-economic "modernity" approach to
this process. "Some historical accounts of the rise of the modern
family read as if the authors thought that conjugality, marital affection, and attachment to children were inventions of bourgeois
capitalism" (Goody 1983, p. 26).

Instead, Goody and others trace the origins of these changes
all the way back to the emergence of the Church in the late Roman
Empire, as a social institution seeking to assert itself through regu-

lation of the morality of individuals (and incidentally, acquisition of considerable amounts of their property in the process).

Whatever the explanation, it is clear that the determination of individual life-chances has shifted out of the hands of consanguine families. Consanguine family members no longer dictate marriage choices. Marriage and babies no longer "matter" to relatives in the sense that their own life-chances are significantly improved or damaged by an individual's marital choice and reproductive behavior. The conjugal bond itself becomes the basis for marriage.

Because such social change does not proceed evenly at all levels of a complex society, patterns of behavior and attitudes are not uniform. Thus the tendency to limit births, to delay marriages, and to live together without marriage—as illustrated by Table 4.1 for France—differs in diverse social strata.

In the same way, images of formal marriage vary between those who cohabit and those who do not. Respondents in the French survey were asked to decide whether marriage would remain the most widespread form of living together, would become only one lifestyle among others, or would eventually disappear. Their answers are shown in Table 4.3.

The table, which classifies respondents by marital status and experience with cohabitation, shows that currently cohabiting couples are least convinced of the continued dominance of marriage and most likely to guess that it may eventually disappear. Their attitudes reflect the temporary ascendancy of what may be called the conjugal family system in their lives. The conjugal family involves a social bond between two adults without social responsibilities to kin. In place of hierarchy, such a man and woman seek equality. They consider each other "partners" in their union. Considered as an ideal type, the conjugal family would be a system of affinity without consanguinity.

Married couples in Table 4.3 who never cohabited are twice as likely to foresee the continued dominance of formal marriage. These couples—less urban, less educated, more religious—are more closely tied to consanguine family tradition, including marriage and childbearing.

What is less predictable and more interesting, however, is that the considerably younger unmarried respondents who had never cohabited perceived marriage in a more traditional light. This finding plainly suggests it is *not* an ideology of individualism

Table 4.3

French Respondents' Attitudes about the Future of Marriage

Past and Present Living Arrangements	(N)	Proportion Saying Marriage Will		
		Continue Dominant	Be One Form of Many	Gradually Disappear
Single, never cohabited				
Men	(501)	50%	37%	13%
Women	(394)	46%	39%	15%
Cohabiting at survey				
Men	(252)	23%	49%	28%
Women	(279)	26%	50%	24%
Single, formerly cohabited				
Men	(66)	42%	42%	16%
Women	(41)	24%	52%	24%
Married, formerly cohabited				
Men	(153)	42%	46%	12%
Women	(181)	40%	46%	14%
Married, never cohabited				
Men	(336)	66%	26%	8%
Women	(411)	59%	31%	10%

and conjugal independence that propels young adults into informal unions. Shorter's (1975) image of a "surge of sentiment" as the motor for family transformation does not fit these facts. Rather, young adults continue to grow up with the values of the consanguine family system. Though political, economic, religious, and even demographic circumstances have considerably reduced the power that kin exercise over one another in adult life, the nuclear family's responsibility for (and thus control over) children has been less affected. Until the end of childhood, parents still exert powerful controls over life-chances. Then, particularly for more highly educated, urban, and less religious youth, the material circumstances of their lives *release* them from the family environment. They move away from parents, attend schools, practice birth control, drift away from religion, and become economically independent. In this social space, at arm's length from consanguine ties, they form informal unions and the ideology of the conjugal family emerges, at least temporarily.

Thus, in French society today one can observe the rapid but

not uniform spread of the conjugal family as a new collective ideal of family life, excluding or abandoning consanguine family ties. At the leading edge of change, each of the activities formerly bound together in families as facets of formal marriage separate into independent, more limited, specialized relationships. This process of temporal "unbinding" of the functions of marriage, including the decline in fertility, touches principally the prosperous, educated urban classes (Blake 1972; Lesthaege and Wilson 1982; see also Table 4.1). For others in the same society the functions of marriage are not thus separated or arranged in temporal steps.

But Table 4.3 also suggests that "traditional" attitudes about marriage begin to reappear among couples when an informal union comes to an end through marriage or through dissolution and a return to single status. It appears that the emergence of conjugal family ideals and informal unions in France is as yet confined to a temporary period in young adulthood, and a key to this timing is the birth of infants. The conjugal bond does not now draw its purpose or stability from obedience to consanguine relatives, but from the affections of the conjugal pair for each other. *Such a bond does not require infants.* In fact, infants bring a sort of tension into a purely "conjugal" union. With infants come the old questions about relations between generations.

We could even say that babies are the "agents-provocateurs" of the consanguine family. Newborn infants and little children, by their very presence, force at least a partial return to the rules of the consanguine family. A newborn does not make a good "partner." Equality between generations will not suffice for rearing a child. It is an inescapable fact that the relationship of a child to a parent is a *consanguine* tie, complete with hierarchical role requirements which contradict the whole conjugal ideology.

Clearly, infants and children cannot play by the rules of the conjugal family. To such internal role incompatibility we also must add growing state interest in and regulation of children, including any household in which they happen to appear. Whatever else happens to the social ties in these households, informality is sharply curtailed.

Once the prospective arrival of infants is recognized as the central factor in transforming informal unions into formal marriages (or sometimes into single-parent households as an alternative), we also obtain the key to the riddle of why cohabitation has increased so rapidly in recent years among some segments of the population. Until the last two decades, social and economic changes (higher education, female labor force participation, rising standards of living, separation from parental households) released some young adults from the consanguine family, but they promptly plunged themselves back into it again by creating new consanguine relationships. Greater independence from parents and other kin simply led to earlier marriage and childbearing, which re-introduced consanguine relationships into households. Only the ability to avoid parenthood by contraceptive practices made "conjugal" relationships a viable alternative (Hofsten, 1978) since young adults seem determined to form intimate unions whether consanguine kin are guiding them or not.

> ". . . towards the extinction of the passion between the sexes, no progress whatever has hitherto been made. It appears to exist in as much force at present as it did two thousand or four thousand years ago" (Malthus 1970(1798), p. 71).

For a section of French youth, then, formal marriage is becoming a ceremony of retreat from the new conjugal family image. It is at least a partial surrender to social norms drawn from the battered but persistent consanguine family system.

Different perceptions of marriage by cohabiting and non-cohabiting couples highlight this surrender. In Table 4.4, response patterns are shown for a question about getting married: "Among the following reasons why people continue to get legally married today, which do you feel is the most decisive?" The choices involved "external" social constraints (relatives, more general social pressure), the interests of a child, and the desire of the couple themselves to add something to their union.

It is evident that individuals who have cohabited or are doing so feel differently about marriage than those who have never cohabited before marriage. The cohabiting couples are less than half as likely to see marriage as something chosen for its own sake. They are nearly twice as likely to perceive marriage as a response to external social pressure. As in Table 4.3, attitudes of the young who have never married or cohabited suggest that alienation from marriage is a by-product of cohabitation. Their views of marriage as something to be chosen for its own sake were closer to "traditional" attitudes, particularly among women in the sample.

Table 4.4

French Respondents' Attitudes about Why People Marry

Past and Present Living Arrangements	(N)	Percent Choosing Reasons for Marriage		
		Satisfy Society	Interest of Child	Couple's Own Desire
Single, never cohabited				
Men	(503)	45%	37%	18%
Women	(393)	39%	39%	22%
Cohabiting at survey				
Men	(250)	59%	30%	11%
Women	(271)	55%	35%	10%
Single, formerly cohabited				
Men	(65)	40%	40%	20%
Women	(43)	40%	53%	7%
Married, formerly cohabited				
Men	(153)	55%	31%	14%
Women	(184)	49%	42%	9%
Married, never cohabited				
Men	(345)	37%	38%	25%
Women	(411)	26%	45%	29%

Women are more likely than men to advocate marriage for a child's sake, perhaps because legal and normative arrangements drawn from consanguine family principles bind their fates more closely to children. Overall, cohabiting couples who eventually marry feel more alienated from marriage and more coerced into it than couples who marry without first living in an informal union. For the cohabiting couples, formal marriage means parenthood, a status they avoid because life with children produces fundamental, unavoidable conflicts with the ideology of the conjugal family. Though through some eyes their unions may seem to undermine "family life," in fact only the consanguine family system is being avoided. In a sense, informal cohabitation without children is the ultimate expression of the conjugal family system. This system's great flaw is that it does not reproduce itself, since reproduction intrudes as an alien element.

Cohabitation and Anomie

Unless an alternative to the institutional linkage of parents and children is adopted, the supplanting of the consanguine family by the conjugal family will remain a temporary feature of young adulthood. One man and one woman may for a time abandon the hierarchies of age and sex, but only if they maintain themselves as an isolated couple, free of children and of any other "treaties" with the consanguine family system. In industrial nations prosperity allows us to leave our parents' homes at earlier ages than in times past. We participate in the economic system as individuals, freed from economic duties to kin. What is more, contraceptive technology allows us to regulate the arrival of infants. These conditions allow people to live as isolated couples and give the conjugal family ideology at least a limited realm of existence.

In semidirected interviews, however, the young French respondents say that they regard solitude and isolation as the greatest tragedy in life (Roussel 1979). Since they also resist the entangling commitments of consanguine family ties, they are in a serious dilemma. For most people, sooner or later, the little "agents provocateurs" and the inertia of social pressures provide at least an existential resolution. In the future, will their social environment change in such a way as to eliminate the disquiet that young people experience in the transition to adult life?

We cannot return to a life controlled by the hierarchy of consanguine families, despite the recommendations of Le Play (1878), Zimmerman (1947), and others. Such a retreat is incompatible with a complex, urban, mobile, bureaucratic society.

Durkheim, also convinced we could not turn back, insisted we must go forward. But what is "forward"? To preserve conjugal family ideals in the face of the arrival of babies, some alternative means of support must be found to replace consanguine family structures. Perhaps the Swedish model of increasing state recognition and support offers one substitute for consanguine kin. It even appears that with such social recognition and support, informal unions themselves can become important *nomos*-generating relationships (Lewin 1982). Will France move in this fiscally demanding direction, replacing unpaid obligations of kin with contractual exchanges involving more government bureaucracy, taxation, and the money economy? The answer may depend in part upon whether the power of the state to dictate the conditions of individuals' lives continues to increase, replacing the authority of consanguine kin.

Given the structure of contemporary French society, French youth will continue to live in a problematic social position. Premarital cohabitation will be possible for them, even frequent, but not socially supported. They will continue to flee from a life of loneliness and isolation, but also will continue to avoid consanguine family commitments which demand more than the sentiment of the moment.

Particularly if they are well-educated and prosperous and reside in urban centers, they will continue to form "partial marriages," to live at least for a time as couples without children. These circumstances will continue to produce a temporary efflorescence of attitudes that we may label as the conjugal family ideology. Responses from this French sample suggest that this ideology is a by-product of the actual lifestyle it reflects.

These informal unions also will continue to be transformed into traditional marriages. The watershed event for this transformation is the birth of a child. In the context of French society today, conjugal ideals emphasizing equality and independence can be sustained by most couples only so long as they remain couples without children.

REFERENCES

Baker, Elizabeth. *Technology and Woman's Work.* New York: Columbia University Press, 1964.

Blake, Judith. *Fertility Control and the Problem of Voluntarism.* Berkeley, Calif.: Institute of International Studies, Population Reprint No. 442, 1972.

Boli-Bennett, John, and Meyer, John. "The Ideology of Childhood and the State: Rules Distinguishing Children in National Constitutions, 1870–1970." *American Sociological Review* 43(1978):797–812.

Caldwell, John. *Population Growth and Family Change in Africa: The New Urban Elite in Ghana.* Canberra: Australian National University Press, 1968.

Caldwell, John. "Toward a Restatement of Demographic Transition Theory." *Population and Development Review* 3–4(1976):321–336.

Camisa, F. *Fecundidad y Nupcialidad.* Encuesta Demografica Nacional de Honduras. Vol. 3. Santiago: CELADE, 1975.

Clayton, R., and Voss, H. "Shacking Up: Cohabitation in the 1970's." *Journal of Marriage and the Family* 39(1977):273–282.

Davis, Kinglsey. "The Early Marriage Trend." *What's New* 207(1958): 36–39.

Davis, Kinglsey. "The Future of Marriage." *Bulletin of the American Academy of Arts and Sciences* 36(1983):15–43.

Dumont, L. "La Genèse chrétienne de l'individualisme: Une vue modifiée de nos origins." *Le Débat* 15(1981):124–146.

Farbar, Bernard. *Family and Kinship in Modern Society*. Glenview, Ill: Scott, Foresman, 1973.

Festy, Patrick. "Canada, United States, Australia and New Zealand: Nuptiality Trends." *Population Studies* 27(1973):479–492.

Glick, Paul, and Norton, Arthur. "Marrying, Divorcing, and Living Together in the U.S. Today." *Population Bulletin* 32(1977).

Glick, Paul, and Spanier, Graham. "Married and Unmarried Cohabitation in the United States." *Journal of Marriage and the Family* 41(1980): 19–30.

Goode, William. *World Revolution and Family Patterns*. New York: Free Press, 1963.

Goody, Jack. *The Development of Marriage and the Family in Europe*. Cambridge: At the University Press, 1983.

Hajnal, John. "The Marriage Boom." *Population Index* 19(1953):80–101.

Hajnal, John. "European Marriage Patterns in Perspective." In D. V. Glass and D. E. C. Eversley (eds.), *Population in History*. London: Edward Arnold, 1965.

Hall, Peter. "Marital Selection and Business in Massachusetts Merchant Families, 1800–1900." In R. Coser (ed.), *The Family and Its Structure and Functions*. New York: St. Martin's Press, 1974.

Hofsten, Erland. "Non-Marital Cohabitation—How to Explain Its Rapid Increase, Particularly in Scandinavia." In *International Union for the Scientific Study of Population*. Proceedings of the Helsinki Conference, Vol. 3. Liège, Belgium: IUSSP, 1978.

Jegouzo, Guenhael. "Le Célibat paysan en 1975." *Population* 34(1979): 27–41.

Le Play, Frederic. *Les Ouvriers Européens*, 2nd edition. Paris: Mame et Fils, 1878.

Lesthaege, Ron, and Wilson, Chris. "Les Modes de production, la laicisation et le rythme de baisse de la fécondité en Europe de l'Ouest." *Population* 37(1982):623–645.

Lewin, Bo. "Unmarried Cohabitation: A Marriage Form in a Changing Society." *Journal of Marriage and the Family* 44(1982):763–774.

Malthus, Thomas. *An Essay on the Principle of Population*. Harmondsworth, England: Penguin, (1798) 1970.

Modell, John; Furstenberg, Frank; and Herschberg, Theodore. "Social Change and Transitions to Adulthood in Historical Perspective." *Journal of Family History* 1(1976):7–32.

Morgan, S. Philip, and Rindfuss, Ronald. "Household Structure and the Tempo of Family Formation in Comparative Perspective." *Population Studies* 38(1984):129–140.

Munoz-Perez, Francisco. "L'Evolution récente des premiers mariages dans quelques pays européens." *Population* 34(1979):649–694.

Murdock, George. *The Social Structure*. New York: Macmillan, 1949.

Roussel, Louis. "La Cohabitation juvenile en France." *Population* 32(1978): 15–42.

Roussel, Louis. "Générations nouvelles et mariage traditionnel." *Population* 34(1979):141–162.

Roussel, Louis, and Festy, Patrick. *Recent Trends in Attitudes and Behavior Affecting the Family in Council of Europe Member States*. Strasbourg, France: Council of Europe, 1979.

Salaff, Janet. "The Status of Unmarried Hong Kong Women and the Social Factors Contributing to Their Delayed Marriage." *Population Studies* 30(1976):391–412.

Schwarz, Karl. "Les menages en République Fédérale d'Allemagne 1961–1972–1981." *Population* 38(1983):565–583.

Shorter, Edward. *The Making of the Modern Family*. New York: Basic Books, 1975.

Spanier, Graham. "Married and Unmarried Cohabitation in the U.S.: 1980." *Journal of Marriage and the Family* 45(1983):277–288.

Sween, J., and Clignet, R. "Female Matrimonial Roles and Fertility in Africa." In C. Oppong et al. (eds.), *Marriage, Fertility, and Parenthood in West Africa*. Canberra: Australian National University Press, 1978.

Tilly, Louise; Scott, Joan; and Cohen, Miriam. "Women's Work and European Fertility Patterns." *Journal of Interdisciplinary History* 6(1976): 447–476.

Trost, Jan. "Married and Unmarried Cohabitation: The Case of Sweden with Some Comparisons." *Journal of Marriage and the Family* 37(1975): 677–682.

United Nations. *Demographic Yearbook*. New York: United Nations, 1976.

Watkins, Susan. "Regional Patterns of Nuptiality in Europe 1870–1960." *Population Studies* 35(1981):199–216.

Wunsch, Guillaume. "Recent Trends of Nuptiality in Some European Countries." In B. Frijling (ed.), *Social Change in Europe. Some Demographic Consequences*. Leiden, Netherlands: E. J. Brill, 1973.

Zimmerman, Carl. *Family and Civilization*. New York: Harper & Brothers, 1947.

PART II

The Limits of Variation
in Marital Patterns

5 *Darwinism and Contemporary Marriage*

DONALD SYMONS

> *I see no marriages that sooner are troubled and fail*
> *than those that progress by means of beauty*
> *and amorous desires.*
>
> ✦
>
> *A good marriage, if such there be,*
> *rejects the company and conditions of love.*
> *It tries to reproduce those of friendship.*
>
> ✦
>
> *Love hates people to be attached to each other except by*
> *himself, and takes a laggard part in relations that are set*
> *up and maintained under another title, as marriage is.*
> *Connections and means have, with reason, as much*
> *weight in it as graces and beauty, or more. We do not*
> *marry for ourselves, whatever we say; we marry just as*
> *much or more for our posterity, for our family.*
>
> Montaigne, *Essays* III:5

CHARLES DARWIN DISCOVERED neither evolution nor natural selection. The idea of organic evolution was clearly in the air at the end of the eighteenth century, and long before Darwin, Lamarck hypothesized that human beings had evolved from apelike creatures. The role of natural selection, or differential reproduction, in culling deviant organisms also was well known. Bishop Samuel Wilberforce, Darwin's antagonist, argued that natural selection is God's way of maintaining species' perfection. (Wilberforce was largely correct: natural selection does, for the most part, preserve

NOTE: *I am grateful to D. E. Brown, Kingsley Davis, and Gordon Orians for helpful comments on an earlier draft of this essay and to John Townsend for supplying important references.*

133

the status quo.) It was Darwin's genius to see that natural selection also is the creative evolutionary process responsible for adaptive design. Other processes—mutation, migration, genetic drift (chance)—change the composition of gene pools, but they are random with respect to adaptation.

A complete understanding of a species-typical trait, biologists agree, entails an understanding of the trait's adaptive significance (function) and evolutionary history (phylogeny) as well as its development (ontogeny), physiology, and stimulus control. This presumably applies to human beings as much as to other species and to psychological traits as much as to morphological and behavioral traits. Stated thus, it is easy to imagine one group of scientists—comprising those interested in questions of adaptation and evolution—tilling one field while a second group—comprising those interested in questions of development, physiology, and stimulus control—tills another. Since each group is addressing a different set of questions, they need not impinge on each other's territory.

This is the traditional view of the matter, and there is much truth in it, but it is not the whole truth. In this chapter I shall argue that Darwin's view of life—that is, the view that organisms evolved by natural selection—can be useful even to scientists with no special interest in questions of adaptation and evolution, and, more particularly, that a Darwinian perspective can shed at least a faint glow on some of the questions of concern to students of contemporary marriage. The main question I want to address is: Can marriage be based primarily on erotic gratification?

On the Uses of Darwinism

Of what use is the knowledge that organisms evolved by natural selection? Lloyd (1979) puts the matter succinctly:

> Simple genetic logic is followed, or rather is pushed through to its seeming endpoint. The conclusion, as to what should or should not be, is not final or binding on nature: it merely provides a guide and prevents certain kinds of errors, raises suspicions of certain explanations or observations, suggests lines of research to be followed, and provides a sound criterion for recognizing significant observations on natural phenomena [p. 18].

A Darwinian perspective provides a general set of expectations about human beings. The view that organisms have been designed to promote the survival of their genes implies that individuals who are not genetically identical, including mates (Trivers 1972) and parents and their offspring (Trivers 1974), are to some extent reproductive competitors and, hence, do not have identical interests. This view of life thus raises suspicions of explanations which imply that individuals have been designed to perpetuate either groups or abstractions such as culture and society (Ghiselin 1974). Darwinists are more likely to focus on human psychology as the cause of social forms than the reverse and to ask, with regard to a given tradition or practice: who benefits (Alexander 1979)? Darwinists also anticipate the existence of species-typical sex differences in psychology: since men and women have always encountered very different reproductive opportunities and constraints, someone who viewed *Homo sapiens* as the product of evolution by natural selection would surely be astonished if male and female brains turned out to be identical (Symons 1979, forthcoming). Similarly, unlike many feminists, Darwinists would not expect womankind to form a cooperative unit vis-à-vis mankind, since womankind does not have common interests, any more than the females of other species do: females, like males, achieve their goals in part at one another's expense (Symons 1982).

Darwinists, of course, are not unique in viewing individuals as, in some sense, self-interested competitors and social forms as the outcomes of individual strivings, and they are not alone in anticipating the existence of species-typical sex differences in psychology. Many psychologists and economists, for example, share these views. The special contribution of Darwinism is to emphasize that the psychological mechanisms underpinning human action were designed to promote the survival of genes. This view of the mind can suggest new questions and inspire research. For example, Hames (1979) showed that among Ye'kwana Indians of southern Venezuela degree of genetic relatedness is a good predictor of the frequency of interaction between individuals, a much better predictor, in fact, than Ye'kwana kin terms. Although evolutionary theory in no sense "predicted" this finding, it would never have been discovered had Hames not been inspired to analyze his data in a non-traditional way by W. D. Hamilton's (1964) theoretical work in evolutionary genetics.

Perhaps Darwinism's most important contribution to the study of human affairs will be in helping to answer the most vexing question of all: what species-typical mental mechanisms—that is, what basic psychological traits—underpin human action? Alexander (1979) writes:

> In general, evolutionary biologists proceed as follows: First they identify phenotypic traits in organisms, then they study the adaptive (reproductive) significance of those traits, almost as if the traits had no ontogenies—as if there were no proximate physiological or developmental mechanisms on which they depend. Evolutionists postpone the analysis of ontogenies because their initial interest is only how the trait is expressed in the usual environment of the species, which is what determines its evolutionary adaptiveness [p. 96].

In this passage Alexander emphasizes the separate-fields point of view mentioned above. But note that the scientific enterprises in both fields depend crucially on identifying, demarcating, or characterizing traits. If what constitutes a "useful" trait is the same in both fields, then in this critical respect everyone is working on the same problem.

Consider two species-typical human traits: (1) human blood is red; and (2) each time a person swallows his larynx rises, shutting off the passage to his lungs. Both the physiologist and the evolutionist are likely to consider the latter trait to be more "useful" than the former. The redness of blood is simply an incidental effect or by-product of the chemical natures of hemoglobin and oxygen: redness per se has no functional significance and was never specifically selected for. The rise of the larynx during swallowing, on the other hand, has obvious functional significance; it certainly was produced and is maintained by natural selection.

Although this example may be a bit trivial, it nonetheless illustrates some key points. First, the physiologist and the evolutionist agree in the matter of the usefulness of traits. I suspect that agreement about what constitutes a useful trait will prove to be the rule. Second, the notion of function—the assumption that (useful) traits were designed to achieve some specific goal or goals, pervades physiology just as it does evolutionary biology, though function often is implicit in the former and explicit in the latter. In fact, implicit assumptions of function also pervade the social and behavioral sciences. The study of living things is *inherently* teleological. And, third, the evolutionist's contribution to the study of swallowing is likely to be minimal. Even were the physiologist operating under the erroneous assumption that human beings have been designed to promote their own survival as individuals or the survival of their species, such an assumption would probably not hinder his research on the physiology of swallowing, nor would knowledge of modern evolutionary theory be of much help to him. Other disciplines, however, have more to gain from Darwinism. Already the study of nonhuman animal social behavior, for example, has been revolutionized by the evolutionary perspective, and for good reason: while the "ideal" design for a swallowing mechanism is probably much the same whether the mechanism's goal is to promote gene, individual, or species survival, this is not at all true of the "ideal" design for, say, the neural and hormonal mechanisms that underpin intraspecific fighting. The burgeoning interest in infanticide among free-ranging animals is the result not only of more sophisticated field work but also of the growing realization that, from the standpoint of gene survival, the existence of a physiological mechanism designed to kill infants in certain circumstances is not more surprising than a mechanism designed to prevent choking during swallowing. For similar reasons, I suspect that Darwinian psychology—the study of the adaptive significance of human mental mechanisms (Ghiselin 1973)—will come to play an important role in the study of human affairs.

Darwinian Psychology

To exemplify Darwinian psychology and its uses, I would like to consider Gordon Orians's (1980) argument that human beings have a species-typical emotional response to a particular kind of landscape:

> we enjoy being in savannah vegetation, prefer to avoid both closed forests and open plains, will pay more for land giving us the impression of being a savannah, mold recreational environments to be more like savannahs, and develop varieties of ornamental plants that converge on the shapes typical of tropical savannahs [p. 64].

Orians supports his "savannah hypothesis" with data on real estate prices, journals recording the emotional responses of early explorers to new regions, and worldwide similarities in the way vegetation is manipulated for purely aesthetic reasons in parks and yards.

Hypotheses like the savannah hypothesis are often said to unduly emphasize "biological factors" at the expense of "social factors," but such complaints are groundless. Every theory of human action necessarily implies a psychological theory (Homans 1964), and every psychological theory necessarily assumes that some mental mechanisms characterize *Homo sapiens* as a species, in the sense that having arms and not wings does (Fodor 1980). Any conceivable theory of human habitat preferences, including one employing such concepts as "learning," "socialization," or "capacity-for-culture," necessarily implies that some mental mechanisms are simply given: nothing comes from nothing. The savannah hypothesis differs from many psychological hypotheses primarily in its implication that the mental mechanisms, which collectively comprise human nature, are numerous, specific, and complex. Most "learning" theories, for example, imply that human beings possess only a few, simple, general mental mechanisms which underpin many kinds of action and are similar or identical across a wide array of species. If these mechanisms are made explicit, however, they will be seen to be not a whit more or less "biological" or "genetic" or "species-typical" than the mechanism Orians postulates. Elsewhere (Symons, forthcoming) I discuss these matters in detail, and argue that there are powerful logical, theoretical, and empirical reasons to believe that the human mind actually does comprise many complex, specific mechanisms, and that theories in which human action is conceived to be underpinned merely by a few, general "learning" or "capacity-for-culture" mechanisms are spectacularly inadequate.

I have deliberately presented the savannah hypothesis a bit differently from the way Orians himself did because I want to emphasize that the core of the hypothesis is not about the nature of past events but about the nature of the human mind: do human beings possess a species-typical emotional mechanism of such-and-such a sort or do they not? It happens that Orians is an evolutionary biologist, and an expert in habitat selection theory, not a psychologist. Orians argues that most animal species possess mechanisms designed by selection to detect and prefer habitats optimal for reproductive success, that the majority of human evolution occurred on the savannahs of Africa, and that human beings require certain habitat features for optimal survival and reproduction. "Our responses are exactly as would be predicted from [an] analysis of habitat quality combined with the assumption that positive responses to habitats are a major proximate factor in making decisions about settling" (Orians 1980, p. 61).

For most social and behavioral scientists the most significant aspect of the savannah hypothesis is not *why* this emotional mechanism exists but rather *that* such a mechanism exists at all. Even if it were to turn out that human beings evolved from polar bears in the Arctic, Orians could nonetheless be right about the emotions of human landscape preferences; he would simply be wrong about the evolutionary "why" of these preferences. Conversely, even if Orians is correct about human evolutionary origins and about the power of habitat selection theory, he could still turn out to be wrong about human psychology.

The savannah hypothesis could have been formalized without any reference to or knowledge of nonhuman animals, human evolution, or natural selection. But surely it is no accident that the scientist who actually did formalize it is an evolutionary biologist, trained to think in comparative, evolutionary, and selectional terms. From the perspectives of the most influential scientific psychologies, the existence of *any* psychological mechanism as specific as the one Orians postulates is inherently unlikely; but from the perspective of Darwinian psychology, that such a mechanism should exist is no surprise at all.

Darwinian Psychology and Marriage

What special contribution could the Darwinist conceivably make to the study of contemporary marriage? He has no access to privileged information about marriage. He may know more about nonhuman animal behavior and human evolution than most students of marriage do, but, since human beings are neither nonhuman animals nor early hominids, this knowledge, in and of itself, cannot provide privileged insight into the depths of the human psyche. What the Darwinist does bring to the study of marriage is a special point of view, a disposition to look at marriage in particular ways, to ask certain sorts of questions, to doubt some explanations, to favor others.

To summarize the argument of the previous section, every theory of human action necessarily implies a psychological theory, and every psychological theory necessarily implies that some brain/mind mechanisms are species-typical givens. Natural selection must have created these mechanisms; there is no other known candidate. While debates among evolutionists about the adaptive significance and evolutionary history of species-typical psychological mechanisms are not likely to be of general interest, what may be of general interest is the contribution that the evolutionist can make to the fundamental problem of identifying and describing these mechanisms.

If the Darwinist takes sides in a controversy among students of marriage, his primary contribution probably will be to provide a new and perhaps compelling reason for accepting one view and rejecting the other. For example, in attempting to explain polygyny Becker (1974) writes that "total output ["productivity"] over all marriages could be greater if a second wife to an able man added more to output than she would add as a first wife to a less able one" (p. 333). Goode (1974) notes in his comments on Becker's paper that "this hypothetical result, an increase in total output over all marriages, is essentially empty as a motivating personal or social force in marital decisions . . . the individual who decides does not ordinarily concern himself very much with his or her effects on the total output, or society as a whole. Thus, whether total output over all marriages is greater does not motivate people to enter polygyny" (p. 348). Goode's criticism of Becker is based essentially on common sense and everyday experience; the Darwinist can provide Goode with an additional argument: there is no known evolutionary force that designs the members of a species to maximize the total group's output of anything. Thus, should Becker counter Goode's criticism by saying that people need not *consciously choose* to maximize total output, the Darwinist will rejoin that it does not matter. Even if the hypothetical mechanism responsible for maximizing total output is assumed to operate unconsciously, no such mechanism could have evolved by natural selection.

Like many social and behavioral scientists (for example, Becker et al. 1977; Scanzoni 1979) Darwinists view marriage from the standpoint of individuals pursuing their own interests, interests that can be expected often to be in conflict. Darwinists can help to focus attention on the mental mechanisms that underpin these "interests" and determine what is a cost and what is a benefit. For example, in their economic analysis of marital instability, Becker et al. (1977) find it useful to assume children to be "capital specific to a particular marriage," that is, they treat children as a benefit to their natural parents and as a cost to stepparents. What is required to nudge this economic analysis away from tautology is an explicit statement about human nature: human beings tend to feel one way about their own children and another way about other people's children. The literature on animal behavior, the ethnographic record, and, especially, the theory of evolution by natural selection all provide strong grounds for suspecting the existence of some such species-typical psychological mechanism(s). As people have been known to abuse their own children and to cherish adopted children, the mechanisms involved obviously are not going to turn out to be simple and straightforward.

Since marriage involves relatively long-term relationships, perhaps in considering the motives for marrying, staying married, or divorcing, one should not treat any aspect of the human psyche as completely irrelevant. It seems to me that a reasonable way to begin to sort matters out is to list the basic reasons why people marry and stay married. I assume that each "reason" corresponds to an emotional or feeling state: no such thing as a psychological goal exists that is not, in the final analysis, emotional.

In various times and places, the following seem to have been common motives for getting or staying married: recognition in the community; material well-being; status, or power; children; companionship, or friendship; "attachment" (see Weiss 1979 for discussion); the state of being in love, or romantic love; sexual desire, or eros; love, or agape; sexual jealousy.

There are a number of points to be made about this list. First, it is obviously crude and preliminary. "Material well-being," for example, does not refer to a single goal but to many: the desire to be well-fed, to be warm, and so on. Second, some of the goals—material well-being and status, for example—are clearly interrelated. Third, people have feelings about and interests in not just their own marriages but other people's marriages as well. It is unlikely that I will look at my son's marriage in the same light that he looks at it: I am likely to emphasize, say, material well-being and status—both his, my own, and that of my other kin—more than he does, and to be less concerned than he is about the fact that he is in love. Furthermore, my feelings about marriage in general probably will differ from my feelings about either my own or my son's marriage. To the extent that I have the power to make and enforce the rules that govern marriages, the rules will reflect these various interests and feelings.

Human beings are, of course, rule-bearing creatures. Everyone is born into a setting with a preexisting set of rules with which he or she must cope. But these rules were made by individual human beings for human reasons, and it is human beings who perpetuate, break, and change them. Goode's statement that the individual making a personal marital decision "does not ordinarily concern himself very much with his or her effects on . . . society as a whole" is equally true of the individual making a decision about marital rules. To begin to understand the origin and change of marital rules one must consider human psychology and the distribution of power. Understanding polygyny, for example, entails understanding certain aspects of male sexual psychology (see below). "Monogamous" societies simply constitute societies where polygyny is outlawed. No societies outlaw monogamy, just as no societies outlaw the eating of rocks. The real challenge is to account for the development of antipolygyny laws, given male sexual psychology as a constant.

In summary, because "marriage" is not a characteristic of individuals at all, it is not a "useful" trait, in the sense discussed in the previous section: it is not the sort of thing that could conceivably have been shaped by selection. The question to which the Darwinist can address himself is: What species-typical mental mechanisms underpin marriage and divorce? The Darwinist provides his special contribution to the study of marriage by focusing on psychological mechanisms, by thinking about these mechanisms in selectional terms, and by using evolutionary, cross-cultural, and cross-specific data to develop hypotheses about the nature of these mechanisms. In the following section I shall consider, from a Darwinian perspective, just one of the possible motives for marriage: sexual desire.

Marriage and Sexuality

In *The Making of the Modern Family*, Edward Shorter (1975) writes: "Because sexual attachment is notoriously unstable, couples rest-ing atop such a base may easily be blown apart. To the extent that erotic gratification is becoming a major element in the couple's collective existence, the risk of marital dissolution increases" (p. 278). Shorter's observation, I shall argue, applies not just to the West or to modern times: it is a consequence of the very structure of human sexuality. The central Darwinian insight that informs my discussion is that the psychological mechanisms underpinning human sexual feeling, thought, and action were designed not to promote marriage but rather to promote reproductive success. This fact alone, of course, proves nothing: the stomach was designed to promote reproductive success; its method of doing so is digestion and absorption. Human sexuality might conceivably have been designed to promote reproductive success via its tendency to cement marriage. My argument, however, is that in a number of respects human sexual psychology undermines marriage; therefore, in the absence of nonsexual reasons for staying married, divorce is likely.

Marriage

The nature and origin of marriage and the family have always been central concerns of anthropology (see, for example, Gough 1971 and Stephens 1963). For most of humanity, and possibly for all of it before modern times, marriage is less an alliance of two people than of two networks of kin. In most traditional societies elders negotiate and arrange marriages although the principals often have a say in the matter. Obligations and rights entailed by marriage vary, but marriage is fundamentally a political, economic, and child-raising institution based on a division of labor by sex and economic cooperation between the spouses and among larger networks of kin. Marriage always entails sexual rights and duties, the most important of which, in cross-cultural perspective, probably is the husband's rights over his wife or wives. The great majority of known societies permit polygyny, allowing successful men to have more than one wife. Polyandry, on the other hand, is extremely rare.

This brief characterization of marriage should make clear that it is very misleading to equate "marriage" with "pair bond," as many evolutionists do. I have written at length on this matter (Symons 1979, 1980), as has Fox (1980):

It . . . does not help, and is positively misleading, to pose the problem as the origin of the pair bond in hominids. This is simply a bad analogy with an instinctive process in lower animals. Humans do not pair bond in this sense at all. *Marriage* is a legal, rule-governed institution, not a direct expression of instinctive drives. . . . Kinship systems then are not about nuclear families and pair bonds, they are about special relationships set up between people who exchange spouses according to a set of rules. The human formula for breeding success . . . was: Get control of the exchange system. And it is this element of *control* that is important. The young males say, "Give us females"; the females say, "Give us males who will provision us"; the old males say, "Sorry, the rules restrict all our choices here, and we must all obey the rules." The beautiful catch is that the rules are rigged to the benefit of the older males anyway [pp. 140–141].

Contemporary marriages, however, are unlikely to result from "special relationships set up between people who exchange spouses according to a set of rules." Marriages in the modern world typically are arranged by the principals, are not usually alliances among networks of kin, rarely have important political consequences, and may not even involve a significant division of labor between the spouses. Sexual rights and duties tend to be symmetrical between the spouses, and polygamy is illegal. Marriage is not normally a requisite to economic survival, nor does it necessarily enhance sexual opportunities. Nevertheless, people continue to marry and to live in marriagelike arrangements.

Since the circumstances of modern life differ so much from those in which the overwhelming majority of human evolution occurred—especially with respect to individual freedom and contraceptive technology—it is unreasonable to expect human beings in the modern world to act in ways likely to maximize their reproductive success. If it is to shed light on why people marry, stay married, or divorce, Darwinism will have to help in identifying the psychological mechanisms that underpin marital decision making. Undoubtedly it will be a very long time before any of these mechanisms are as clearly identified as is, say, the rise of the larynx during swallowing; however, it is reasonable to begin the task with the expectations that these mechanisms will turn out to be numerous, specific, and complex, that hypothetical mechanisms such as a "pair bonding instinct" are, therefore, likely to be hopelessly vague, and that a Darwinian perspective can help in deciding what questions to ask, what research to pursue, and what observations to emphasize.

Sexuality

I have argued (Symons 1979, 1980, forthcoming) that underlying the diversity of human sexual practices are two quite different sexual psychologies: female and male. Indeed, the designs of these psychologies are more obvious than are the designs of most mental mechanisms precisely because sexuality is one of the few aspects of the mind in which there appear to be substantial sex differences: it is the comparison of male and female that illuminates design. These sexualities are the coherent, integrated systems that a Darwinian perspective leads us to anticipate: one would expect the ideal design for, say, an eye (the relation between the curvature of the lens and the distance to the retina, and so forth) to be the same for men and women; but, because the sexes have always encountered very different reproductive opportunities and constraints, one would expect the ideal designs for male and female sexualities to differ markedly in specific sorts of ways. Men and women differ in the brain/mind mechanisms underpinning sexuality for the same evolutionary reason that they differ in the more obvious features of reproductive anatomy: they have been designed by selection to pursue different reproductive strategies.

There is room here for only the briefest possible sketch of these differences and their evolutionary rationales; the reader is referred to Symons (1979, 1980, and forthcoming) for detailed argumentation and references to the enormous literature on male–female differences in sexuality. Men and women typically differ in the circumstances leading to sexual arousal, in some of the criteria that determine sexual attractiveness, and in the occurrence of sexual jealousy.

Men are far more likely than women to be aroused by the visual stimulus of a member of the opposite sex. Because a human male could potentially impregnate a female at almost no cost to himself, as long as the risks were low, selection favored the basic male tendency to be aroused sexually by the sight of females. A human female, on the other hand, incurred an immense risk, in terms of time and energy, by becoming pregnant, hence selection favored the basic female tendency to discriminate with respect both to sexual partners and to the circumstances in which copulation occurred; females thus are aroused primarily by tactual rather than by visual stimulation, and then only when stimulated by selected males. (A man unknown to a woman cannot arouse her by touching her until at least a minimal relationship has been established; if he attempts to do so, his touch probably will frighten or annoy rather than arouse. But an attractive woman unknown to a man can arouse him immediately, simply by her presence.) A propensity to be sexually aroused merely by the sight of males would promote random mating from which a female would have nothing to gain, reproductively, and a great deal to lose.

Several interacting psychological mechanisms, not all of which are identical in men and women, underpin sexual attractiveness. Natural selection has designed these mechanisms to detect "mate value" (in the sense that the mechanisms underpinning taste were designed to detect "food value"). At least two "absolute" criteria of sexual attractiveness exist. First, observable signs of good health, especially as evidenced in skin condition, are always perceived as attractive. The association between signs of good health and mate value I take to be obvious. Second, attractiveness—especially female attractiveness—is universally a function of observable signs of age. Attractiveness diminishes in old age for both sexes, but before old age female attractiveness declines much more rapidly and predictably than male attractiveness does. Other things being equal, female sexual attractiveness peaks about the time of nubility. The evolutionary explanation is that a male who acquired a wife of this age stood the best chance of tying up her most fertile years. Male sexual attractiveness, on the other hand, depends much less on observable signs of age because in natural environments male mate value varied substantially with status and prowess, which often increased with age. More generally, a woman's sexual attractiveness depends more on her physical appearance than a man's sexual attractiveness does on his because female mate value was more accurately assessed from observable physical attributes than was male mate value.

With respect to relative criteria of sexual attractiveness (a relative criterion is a rule that specifies a standard of attractiveness by comparing individuals in the population with one another) there seem to be three rules. First, for some physical characteristics humans perceive the population mean, or other measure of central tendency, to be most attractive. The probable relation between mean-detection and mate value is that natural selection has produced the population mean, either directly by favoring it or indirectly by eliminating the tails of the distribution. With respect to many (not all) physical characteristics, individuals near the mid-point of the population can be expected to be the fittest. Second, high-status individuals, and characteristics reliably associated with such individuals, are perceived as attractive. This criterion is a much more important determinant of male than of female attractiveness because, as mentioned above, in a state of nature male mate value was much more a function of status than was female mate value. And third, human males tend to view variety as sexually attractive. Finding new women especially sexually attractive motivated attempts to accumulate wives, to arrange extramarital sexual opportunities, and to take advantage of the odd low-risk sexual opportunity when it presented itself.

Finally, the sexes appear to differ in the psychological mechanisms that underpin sexual jealousy. Sexual jealousy is a more ubiquitous aspect of male than of female psychology. Men tend to perceive their wives' sexual relations with other men—real or imagined—as undesirable, whereas women tend to discriminate those of their husbands' sexual relations that constitute a risk from those that do not. During the course of evolutionary history, the possibility of a man's wife engaging in sexual relations with other men jeopardized a husband's fitness. A husband risked having his wife's limited reproductive capacity tied up by other men and, since he could never be completely confident of paternity, investing in other men's offspring. A wife incurred little risk to fitness from her husband's sexual relations with other women per se because, even if these relations resulted in pregnancies, her husband's ability to impregnate her would not thereby be significantly diminished. What she did risk, however, was that her husband's attention to other women and his investment in their children might diminish his investment in her and her children.

Of what value is this Darwinian view of human sexuality? To me, at least, it is immensely satisfying intellectually because it accounts for so much with such a simple and compelling premise: the mind is an aspect of the brain, and the brain is the product of natural selection. I do not expect the question "What is mind?" to be answered satisfactorily in my lifetime, nor do I expect that we will know whether it is answerable at all, or even whether it is meaningful. But Darwinism can at least suggest satisfying answers to the lesser question, "What is mind for?"

This view of sexuality may even be useful to scientists who do not find evolutionary explanations satisfying. The hypothesis that many specific, adaptive psychological mechanisms underpin human action provides a guide for research. For example, in common parlance we describe both our feelings about landscapes and our feelings about the physical attributes of members of the opposite sex as "aesthetic." Does this mean that they share a common underlying mechanism? Someone who viewed the mind as the product of selection would surely tend to doubt it, since the criteria that determine "landscape value" manifestly have little in common with the criteria that determine "mate value." To take another example, when confronted with evidence that thinness is sexually attractive in one society and fatness in another, tanned skin here and pale skin there, a Darwinist would ask whether body shape and skin tone vary systematically with status, rather than sit back and marvel at the whimsical capriciousness of "culture" in setting standards of attractiveness. Similarly, the hypothesis that human males are designed to detect and prefer newly nubile females suggests many research questions: Can this hypothesis survive closer cross-cultural scrutiny? What are the specific cues used to detect age? Does female attractiveness decline smoothly with female age or are there dips in the curve, say, at menopause? Does perception of female attractiveness change systematically with the age or the status of the male doing the evaluating? This hypothesis also raises suspicions of certain explanations of well-known phenomena. For example, a distinguished student of marriage writes: "the very fact that more men than women remarry after divorce suggests that they need marriage more and benefit more from it" (Bernard 1979). A Darwin-inspired alternative explanation is that divorced men are more marriageable because there are more older women than men (since women tend to outlive men), that men tend to be reluctant to raise other men's children, and that men tend to find younger women most sexually attractive (see Chapter 1).

Does Sex Promote Marriage?

Many sexually reproducing species presumably experience sexual pleasure. The question I want to address is whether selection has designed any features of human sexuality to promote marriage, in the sense of encouraging a long-term relationship between sexual partners.

What would constitute an ideal, or even an effective, design for a marriage-promoting sexual mechanism is not completely clear. Nonhuman animals provide little help in this matter not merely because they do not marry but because no species appear to cement enduring relationships with enduring sexual activity. Indeed, pair-bonded "monogamous" mammals are characteristically hyposexual (Kleiman, 1977). When individuals gain advantages from remaining for long periods of time in one another's company, selection apparently has produced brain/mind mechanisms making this company per se satisfying, a seemingly far cheaper solution than would be enduring, intense sexual activity, with its concomitant high cost in terms of time, energy, and risk.

Unlike other animal species, adult human beings are more or less perennially sexual and, at least in a state of nature, more or less perennially married, but these attributes by no means constitute evidence that human sexual psychologies are designed to promote marriage. It seems to me that psychological mechanisms effectively designed for this purpose would make the central criterion for both sexual arousal and sexual attractiveness that of being someone's mate. In other words, even if such criteria as health, youth, central tendencies, and status were important during courtship, they would be replaced as determinants of sexual arousal and attractiveness by the single criterion of whether the individual being evaluated is or is not one's mate. Sex differences in tendencies to be aroused visually might possibly exist, but for a husband the most (perhaps the *only*) sexually arousing stimulus would be the sight of his wife. Furthermore, the excitement of marital sexual activity would tend to increase with time, so that real or imagined extramarital sex would pale by comparison. Husbands would be uninterested in the nubile women of pictorial pornography and wives would be bored by the gray-eyed counts of romance fiction. Indeed, these genres surely would not exist at all.

Needless to say, human sexuality appears not to be so designed. I know of no evidence that such criteria of sexual attractiveness as health, youth, and status tend to diminish in importance among married people, and the male taste for sexual variety—which seems to be the opposite of a marriage-maintaining mechanism—appears to depend in large part on visual arousal.

Even when marital sex is satisfying, familiarity probably reduces a wife's effectiveness as a visual stimulus; the seven-year itch seems to owe much to the roving eye (Symons 1979, forthcoming).[1] Furthermore, marital sexuality typically becomes less, not more, exciting with the passage of time; as sex therapist Avodah Offit (1981) remarks, "We experience less excitement with a mate to whom we are accustomed. That is the way of the world" (p. 239).

Even if sex itself does not normally cement marriage, however, sexual relations at the beginning of marriage could tend to foster enduring affection. This possibility seems worthy of systematic investigation; but certainly there is little evidence that sexual relations *necessarily* have this effect, and, again, there are intimations of sex differences: "Women grow attached to men through the favors they grant them," wrote Jean de La Bruyère, "but men, through the same favors, are cured of their love." Even this assessment may be a bit too hopeful. While striking exceptions do occur, the ethnographic record generally suggests that widespread male ignorance of female sexuality combined with the male tendency to focus primarily on the genitals in sexual interactions seldom results in the sort of sexual relations that warm the female heart. Davenport (1977) summarizes the ethnographic record:

> In most of the societies for which there are data, it is reported that men take the initiative and, without extended foreplay, proceed vigorously toward climax without much regard for achieving synchrony with the woman's orgasm. Again and again, there are reports that coitus is primarily completed in terms of the man's passions and pleasures, with scant attention paid to the woman's response. If women do experience orgasm, they do so passively (p. 149).

The situation is not necessarily better in modern, complex societies. Nirad Chaudhuri writes of marital sexual relations in traditional Hindu India as follows:

> Even as a boy I could detect in ageing women, who had not been released from the mood by widowhood, not only indifference to the life's partner, but almost passive hatred. . . . Yet in their nightly bed the two, who felt almost a loathing for each other, would oblige the respective bodies from the prickings of the most desiccated lust, and hate each other all the more for it. Throughout married life the drying up of the lust without its atrophy, and the growth of the repulsion marched step in step [quoted in Lannoy 1971:121].

Chaudhuri describes this state of affairs not as general but as widespread (see also Khanna and Varghese 1978).

Based on his thirty years as an endocrinologist and sex therapist in the Soviet Union, Stern (1980) characterizes marital intercourse in the U.S.S.R as follows:

> the man is selfishly concerned with his own pleasure, and the woman, totally submissive, consoles herself with outrageous overacting in what is, after all, a purely secondary role. For the man, the conjugal bed is simply a proving-ground for his virility, and for the couple the act of love itself becomes no more than a furious, painful paroxysm which momentarily draws them together though they are perhaps more unaware of each other than at any other time [p. 78].

In his opus on the history of love, sex, and marriage in England, Stone (1977) notes that by the late eighteenth century,

> sexual passion was an essential ingredient of many marriages among the squirarchy and professional bourgeois classes, and it was the frequent waning of this passion which led to the rise of extra-marital liaisons during this period [p. 543] . . . when that attraction eventually dried up, as it often did, many husbands sought sexual variety elsewhere, and the double standard continued to apply. Some women certainly sought sexual satisfaction in the arms of other men, but the majority of disappointed wives probably found compensatory psychic satisfaction in immersing themselves in the upbringing of their children [p. 544].

For further evidence along these lines, see Symons (1979).

In summary, human sexuality, especially male sexuality, is by its very nature ill-designed to promote marriage, and gender differences in sexuality do not seem to be complementary. This is precisely what a Darwinian perspective should lead us to expect. Females who did not discriminate between the poor and the great hunter or the fool and the headman, and males who did not discriminate between a familiar and new partner or between wrinkled and smooth skin were unlikely to become our ancestors.

This is not to deny that most men most of the time had only one wife, or that selection may tailor desires and dispositions to suit specific circumstances; perhaps, for example, males whose options are limited by physical unattractiveness or low status are more likely to pursue less attractive women and to be content with one woman (Trivers [1972] hints at such a possibility). The central question is: What psychological mechanisms are involved? Fox (1980) writes: "If older and more powerful men have not always had access to multiple wives, they have tried to monopolize access to the best; that is, the young and nubile" (p. 206). One wonders whether all men perceive the young and nubile to be the "best" (other things being equal), or whether men with lesser competitive abilities actually *perceive* attractiveness differently. Since studies of physical attractiveness uniformly find very high interjudge agreement, probably all men perceive signs of youth as sexually attractive. But perhaps men with lesser competitive abilities typically find female physical attractiveness somewhat less important for sexual arousal than do males with greater competitive abilities. If this were discovered to be so, the next question would be whether the underlying psychological mechanism is specific to sexual attraction or is the result of a more general (adaptive) tendency for our reach (desires) always to exceed our grasp, *but not by too much.*

Marriage and Human Malleability

Shorter's (1975) observation that marriages based on erotic gratification are likely to dissolve is not new. Even after marriage in England had become primarily a relationship between two people rather than a way for two families to aggrandize their political and economic fortunes, the ideal emotional basis for marriage was, according to Stone (1977), "personal affection, companionship and friendship, a well-balanced and calculated assessment of the chances of long-term compatibility" (p. 271). "Almost everyone agreed . . . that both physical desire and romantic love were unsafe bases for an enduring marriage, since both were violent mental disturbances which would inevitably be of only short duration" (p. 272).[2]

I have tried to show that in analyzing the psychological underpinning of marriage it can be useful to keep in mind that *Homo sapiens* is the product of evolution by natural selection; we are designed to promote gene, not individual, survival; reproductive, not marital success. Darwin's view of life gives us reason to suspect that Shorter and Stone have simply described the human condition.

A final point. We human beings can read, write, play bridge, raise cats or Cain instead of children, and do an infinite number of other things that natural selection did not design us to do. Although sexuality is in many ways ill-designed to cement marriages, we may nonetheless be able to use it for this purpose. Brauer and Brauer (1983) describe a technique by which orgasm can be extended for very long periods of time; it entails each partner's stimulating the other's genitals manually (not sexual intercourse), turn-taking, high-tech lubricants, special daily exercises, and months of diligent practice, first alone and then with one's partner. The perfection of this technique can enhance marriages, the Brauers say, not because it can overcome any of the limitation of human sexuality discussed in this essay, but rather because once the technique is mastered, neither partner can experience extended orgasm without the other. This is the sexual equivalent of the economic interdependence that has traditionally been the basis of marriage.

Nothing in the Brauers' technique is likely, so to speak, to come naturally. And so what? Long ago, Margaret Mead argued that the point is not to develop the most natural bread—wheat itself is artificial, a recent invention—but to develop the most nutritious bread. The more we know of our physiological nature, the better the bread we can invent. All our choices are to some extent limited by our nature; we cannot choose to grow wings and fly, and we cannot choose to find ringworm sexually attractive. But, perhaps paradoxically, the better we come to understand our nature the greater will be our freedom from it.

NOTES

1.   One test of this hypothesis would be to study marital sexuality among the blind. I would expect blind husbands to typically have less interest in sexual variety than sighted husbands do, and, in general, blind men and women to be more alike sexually than sighted men and women are.

2.   Romantic love appears to be as unlikely a candidate for marital cement as erotic gratification is. The emotion of being in love thrives only

in conditions of uncertainty about whether one's love is reciprocated (Tennov 1979) and is, therefore, almost always of limited duration (also see Blood and Wolfe 1960:222–223). If any sexual emotion underpins marriage, the most likely is sexual jealousy. The desire to acquire exclusive sexual rights to a woman has always been an important motive for marriage, and jealousy is durable; as La Rochefoucauld put it, "Jealousy is always born with love, but does not always die with it."

REFERENCES

Alexander, R. D. *Darwinism and Human Affairs.* Seattle: University of Washington Press, 1979.

Becker, G. S. "A Theory of Marriage." in T. W. Schultz (ed.), *Economics of the Family.* Chicago: University of Chicago Press, 1974.

Becker, G.S.; Landes, E. M.; and Michael, R. T. "An Economic Analysis of Marital Instability." *Journal of Political Economy* 85(1977):1141–1187.

Bernard, J. Foreword to G. Levinger and O. C. Moles (eds.), *Divorce and Separation.* New York: Basic Books, 1979.

Blood, R. O., Jr., and Wolfe, D. M. *Husbands and Wives: The Dynamics of Married Living.* New York: Free Press, 1960.

Brauer, A. P., and Brauer, D. *ESO.* New York: Warner Books, 1983.

Daly, M., and Wilson, M. *Sex, Evolution, and Behavior,* 2nd ed. Boston: Willard Grant Press, 1983.

Davenport, W. H. "Sex in Cross-Cultural Perspective." In F. A. Beach (ed.), *Human Sexuality in Four Perspectives.* Baltimore: Johns Hopkins University Press, 1977.

Fodor, J. "Reply to Putnum." In M. Piatelli-Palmarini (ed.), *Language and Learning: The Debate Between Jean Piaget and Noam Chomsky.* Cambridge, Mass.: Harvard University Press, 1980.

Fox, R. *The Red Lamp of Incest.* New York: E. P. Dutton, 1980.

Ghiselin, M. T. "Darwin and Evolutionary Psychology." *Science* 179(1973): 964–968.

Ghiselin, M. T. *The Economy of Nature and the Evolution of Sex.* Berkeley: University of California Press, 1974.

Goode, W. J. "Comment on G. S. Becker's A Theory of Marriage." In T. W. Schultz (ed.), *Economics of the Family: Marriage and Human Capital.* Chicago: University of Chicago Press, 1974.

Gough, K. "The Origin of the Family." *Journal of Marriage and the Family* 33(1971):760–771.

Hames, R. B. "Relatedness and Interaction Among the Ye'kwana: A Preliminary analysis." In N. A. Chagnon and W. Irons (eds.), *Evolutionary Biology and Human Social Behavior: An Anthropological Perspective.* North Scituate, Mass.: Duxbury Press, 1979.

Hamilton, W. D. "The Genetical Evolution of Social Behavior." *Journal of Theoretical Biology* 7(1964):1–52.

Homans, G. C. "Contemporary Theory in Sociology." In R. E. L. Faris (ed.), *Handbook of Modern Sociology*. Chicago: Rand-McNally, 1964.

Khanna, G., and Varghese, M. A. *Indian Women Today*. New Delhi: Vikas, 1978.

Kleiman, D. G. "Monogamy in Mammals." *The Quarterly Review of Biology* 52(1977):39–69.

Lannoy, R. *The Speaking Tree: A Study of Indian Culture and Society*. New York: Oxford University Press, 1971.

Lloyd, J. E. "Mating Behavior and Natural Selection." *The Florida Entomologist* 62(1979):17–34.

Offit, A. K. *Night Thoughts: Reflections of a Sex Therapist*. New York: Congdon & Lattes, 1981.

Orians, G. H. "Habitat Selection: General Theory and Applications to Human Behavior." In J. S. Lockard (ed.), *The Evolution of Human Social Behavior*. New York: Elsevier, 1980.

Scanzoni, J. "A Historical Perspective on Husband–Wife Bargaining Power and Marital Dissolution." In G. Levinger and O. C. Moles (eds.), *Divorce and Separation*. New York: Basic Books, 1979.

Shorter, E. *The Making of the Modern Family*. New York: Basic Books, 1975.

Stephens, W. N. *The Family in Cross-Cultural Perspective*. New York: Holt, Rinehart & Winston, 1963.

Stern, M., with Stern A. *Sex in the U.S.S.R.* New York: Times Books, 1980.

Stone, L. *The Family, Sex and Marriage in England 1500–1800*. London: Weidenfeld & Nicolson, 1977.

Symons, D. *The Evolution of Human Sexuality*. New York: Oxford University Press, 1979.

Symons, D. "The Evolution of Human Sexuality Revisited." *The Behavioral and Brain Sciences* 3(1980):203–211.

Symons, D. "Another Woman That Never Evolved." *The Quarterly Review of Biology* 57(1982):297–300.

Symons, D. "The Evolutionary Approach: Can Darwin's view of Life Shed Light on Human Sexuality?" In J. Geer and W. O'Donohue (eds.), *Approaches and Paradigms of Human Sexuality*. New York: Plenum, forthcoming.

Tennov, D. *Love and Limerence: The Experience of Being in Love*. New York: Stein & Day, 1979.

Trivers, R. L. "Parental Investment and Sexual Selection." In B. Campbell (ed.), *Sexual Selection and the Descent of Man 1871–1971*. Chicago: Aldine, 1972.

Trivers, R. L. "Parent–Offspring Conflict." *American Zoologist* 14(1974):249–264.

Weiss, R. S. "The Emotional Impact of Marital Separation." In G. Levinger, and O. C. Moles (eds.), *Divorce and Separation*, pp. 201–210. New York: Basic Books, 1979.

6 The Importance of Marriage for Socialization

A Comparison of Achievements and Social Adjustment Between Offspring of One- and Two-Parent Families in Israel

YOCHANAN PERES and RACHEL PASTERNACK

SOCIOLOGICAL INTEREST IN ISRAELI MARRIAGE focused for a long time on the kibbutz family. However, 90 percent of Israel's Jewish population reside in urban areas and maintain a rather conventional family life. As shown elsewhere (Peres and Katz

NOTE: *We are grateful to Dr. Amyra Grossbard-Shechtman for many helpful suggestions, and in particular for insisting on multiple regression analysis, which added credibility to our findings. Yasmin Alcaly's faithful and efficient assistance in programming is highly appreciated.*

1981), marriage in Israel is relatively stable; Israeli divorce rates fall below those of European countries (except Italy) and much below those of the Soviet Union or the United States. About 95 percent of all men and 97 percent of all women marry at least once before they reach age 40.

While the birth rates of Israelis of Asian or African descent have declined both from year to year and from generation to generation, Israelis of European background have tended to keep their birth rates steady. Since the late 1970s the medium-sized family has become the dominant pattern. The total fertility rate of all Jewish ethnicities is about 3.00 (2.7 for Europeans, 3.1 for Orientals; Israel Statistical Abstracts 1980, p. 90). Several behavior patterns show the centrality of marriage and the family in Israeli social life. Parents are anxious to see their offspring (particularly daughters!) marry, and are willing to bear a severe economic burden to provide housing for the young couple.[1] Weddings are major social events, usually celebrated in rented halls with several hundred guests present. Bar-Mitzvah and circumcisions are often celebrated in similar (though more modest) style.

In a society as modern as Israel according to political, technological, and economic criteria, one would expect the institution of marriage to be undergoing a serious crisis. Therefore the stability and centrality of marriage calls for an explanation.

Three features of Israeli society might serve as explanations:

- the prolonged external tension between Israel and its neighbors; marriage and birth rates rose after the outbreaks of hostilities in 1967 and 1973
- the familistic emphasis of the Jewish religion
- the traditional background of about 55 percent of the Israeli-Jewish population; the stability of marriage in townships with a religious and/or Oriental majority significantly eclipses that in European or secular regions.

The very existence of marriage as a stable and binding institution depends on its contribution to the socialization of the young, particularly in modern societies where other functions are being transferred to extramarital alternatives.

Questions at Issue

Is a continuous and socially sanctioned pair-bond an imperative precondition for successful socialization? This is certainly one of the major problems confronting any theory of marriage. Lately it has also become a social and even political issue. Should matrifocal (and sometimes patrifocal) arrangements for child-rearing be considered as alternative lifestyles, functionally equal to the conventional marital arrangement? Or should they be discouraged as less effective frameworks for socialization? Does the answer depend on the particular society or not? Is the "price" of fatherlessness (in terms of children's achievements) high in some societies and low or even nonexistent in others?

This study explores the impact of matrifocality on the academic achievements and social adjustment of Israeli children at school.

An institution's function can be operationalized by measuring the discrepancy between relevant outcomes obtained when that institution exists and when it does not. Reasonable people may differ about the best way to represent the "absence" of a marital arrangement. One might argue that children of married couples should be compared to offspring of unwed mothers who *deliberately* refrained from marriage. Otherwise, either negative selection or the stigma assigned to those whose marriage "failed" could explain results unfavorable for children of one-parent families. Voluntarily unwed mothers, however, are a very small and highly selected group in Israel. Only 0.6 percent of all Jewish women giving birth in 1980 were unwed. The behavior of such a tiny group is probably not indicative of what large segments of the population would do in a similar situation. In view of this, we decided to adopt the most widespread alternative to the two-parent marital arrangement, namely, the secondary one-parent family, secondary in the sense of having been founded as a two-parent family but becoming a one-parent family because of death or separation. It may also be argued that our data do not bear on marriage per se but on father's absence. Even if it was shown that one adult is less effective in raising offspring than two, it would not follow that the two parents have to be married to each other. While this argument sounds logically valid, it ignores the well-known fact that cohabiting adults (whether of the same or of opposite genders) tend not to stay together long enough to cooperate in raising children. Being married is viewed here in terms of actual behavior, rather than a legal situation. Thus we are not necessarily comparing marriage to its best imaginable alternative but rather to the framework in which most children of unmarried parents in Israel (or elsewhere) grow up.

In addition to investigating the overall impact of marriage on children's scholastic success and social adjustment, we shall examine several related questions. To what extent does the cause of matrifocality affect children's development independently of the matrifocality itself? In the case of severe conflict between the spouses, is divorce (from the offspring's point of view) preferable to continuation? Are children more affected by the absence of a parent of the same sex than by the absence of one of the opposite sex? Is the effect of matrifocality dependent on cultural context? Do mothers of traditional background, where sex roles are more rigid, face greater difficulties than more modern mothers in adjusting to the single-parent situation?

Procedure

Six elementary schools located in two small Israeli towns near Tel Aviv served as our laboratory. They had about 7,000 students. Among these all pupils from one-parent families from the fourth to the eighth grade formed the study group (N = 203), selected from the schools' records. Only two of these one-parent families were headed by a man. Eliminating these reduced the sample to 201. Of these, the mother was widowed in 68 cases, divorced in 100, separated in 33.

An additional group of 78 children whose parents were involved in severe conflict was also compared to a pair-matched control group. Since these children did not live in one-parent families they are not included in the overall analysis. The reader is also advised to consider the findings based on this specific group with extra caution: conflictual marriages were identified by school records (as were all other groups). Children's achievements and/or behavior could have been one of the reasons to file information about conflicts between their parents. In that case findings about this group might be negatively biased. Obviously these cautions do not affect the findings based on other subgroups.

The control groups were pair-matched to the study groups

by sex, age, country of origin, number of siblings, and level of mother's schooling.

The effects on children were judged by a variety of criteria, as follows:

1.   Scholastic achievements measured by standardized grades[2] in the three major subjects: arithmetic, English, and Hebrew.

2.   Teachers' evaluation of overall standing in class work.

3.   Intelligence, measured with the aid of M.I.L.T.A., an I.Q. test specifically designed for the Israeli school system (Ortar 1969). This test is admittedly "culture-bound": its purpose is to measure the ability of native Hebrew speakers. In accordance with the test's limitation, four subjects (two members of the study group and two controls) who immigrated within the last four years were excluded.

4.   Popularity among peers, measured by a sociometric test. Each pupil in the six schools' population was asked to name his "best friend" (from his class only) and the pupil he would least like to befriend. On the basis of the responses each subject in the study and control groups was assigned three sociometric scores. One was for social attraction[3]; another for social rejection[4]; and the third for relative divergence between attraction and rejection.[5]

5.   Adaptation to school norms. We assumed that the ability to adjust to norms of discipline and sociable conduct is part of a child's normal development. Information about this variable was attained from official school records (routinely kept for every pupil); teachers' evaluations of pupils' adjustment to school norms—evaluations made specifically for this study; and special treatment for pupils having difficulties in either studies or discipline, as recorded in the pupil's files and ranked for the purpose of this study in the following way:
    no special treatment
    private lessons
    treatment by school consultant[6]
    transferred to special class for nonadjusted children
    psychiatric treatment

Rachel Pasternack, in her capacity as supervisor at the six elementary schools, collected the data. She supervised the administration of a sociometric test and a short information sheet to the entire school population, but gave the M.I.L.T.A. I.Q. test to the study and pair-matched control groups only. She obtained the remaining data (grades, teachers' evaluation, discipline records, and, most important, information about the present marital status of parents) from the schools' official files. Neither pupils nor teachers

needed to know the study's purpose. Data were collected from entire classes, eventually forming one large sample that was sub-
divided into study and control groups only during data processing.
In that way, the study did not single out children of one-parent
households and did not give them special attention. Since their
cooperation was vital, school headmasters and school psychologists
were informed about the study's aims, but they were the only ones.

A crucial methodological issue is whether the study and control groups are really homogeneous for all relevant background
factors. If one-parent families, for example, are of lower socioeconomic status than intact families, the discrepancies in achievements, popularity, or adjustment may be caused by that fact rather
than by the breakdown of the parents' marriage. Table 6.1 compares study and control group families with respect to ethnic origin, occupation, schooling of both spouses, and number of children.

However, the groups are not matched for income, because all
data about the parents were taken from school records in which income is not included. Fortunately, parental schooling and father's
occupation are major determinants of income. Also, it is not necessary to control income when such determinants of income (schooling, occupation) are already controlled, because remaining gaps in
income are likely to be a result of father absence. Thus if income
were controlled (in addition to schooling and occupational prestige), we would have excluded a part of the very phenomenon
under study.

Table 6.1 indicates some minor discrepancies in socioeconomic background between the study and control groups, which
implies that multivariate methods are desirable to separate the
combined influence of parental status and socioeconomic background. Comparisons between each of the subgroups in the one-
parent sample (widowed, divorced, separated) and the respective
controls show only minor and mostly insignificant discrepancies in
background factors.

Findings: Scholastic Achievement

Table 6.2 shows that in all three subject matters, children of matrifocal families have significantly lower scholastic achievement
than children raised in two-parent families. Almost all study group

Table 6.1

Socioeconomic Background of Study Groups and Control Groups, and Israeli Population

Demographic Characteristics	Study Group N = 201	Control Group N = 201	χ^2 (Study vs. Control)	Israeli Population
Gender of child				
Male	58.9	58.1	0.0	51.2
Female	41.4	41.9	$p \leqslant .10$	48.8
Child's continent of birth				
Israel	82.6	86.3	2.97	90.5
Asia-Africa	7.2	6.9	$p \leqslant .56$	2.6
Europe-America	23.9	28.0		
Father's continent of birth				
Israel	26.3	21.8	3.05	56.3
Asia-Africa	49.1	41.9	$p \leqslant .58$	20.2
Europe-America	27.0	28.0		26.3
Father's occupation				
Academic workers	20.7	15.0		22.5
Clerical workers	22.7	21.6	2.40	20.1
Service workers	7.3	9.1	$p \leqslant .66$	7.4
Skilled industry workers	39.3	44.7		43.8
Unskilled workers	10.0	9.1		6.2
Father's years of schooling				
0	0.5	0.5		3.6
8	34.6	29.8	3.25	26.9
9–12	44.4	53.0	$p \leqslant .35$	50.9
13+	20.6	16.7		17.5
Average years of schooling	10.1	10.1		
Mother's years of schooling				
0	2.3	1.9		9.4
8	34.1	28.4	4.30	25.8
9–12	43.5	53.5	$p \leqslant .23$	46.2
13+	20.2	16.3		18.6
Average years of schooling	9.9	10.1		
Children in household				
1	24.6	11.4		
2	41.4	40.8	14.16	
3–5	33.0	46.8	$p \leqslant .001$	
6+	1.0	1.0		
Average number of children	2.5	2.8	2.3	

SOURCE: Statistical Abstracts, Central Bureau of Statistics, 1980.

Table 6.2

Scholastic Achievements (Standardized Z Scores)* by Groups

Groups	Arithmetic				English				Hebrew			
	N	Z	t	p	N	Z	t	p	N	Z	t	p
All one-parent families (study group)	201	−.26	−8.40	.001	135	−.36	−5.82	.001	201	−.05	−5.89	.001
All intact families (control)	201	.50			135	.34			201	.47		
Widowed	68	−.20	−5.10	.001	45	−.42	−3.83	.00	68	−.03	−2.60	.010
Intact families	68	.51			45	.43			68	.36		
Divorcees	100	−.18	−5.42	.001	60	−.29	−4.11	.001	100	−.09	−4.64	.001
Intact families	100	.51			60	.39			100	.65		
Separated	33	−.32	−3.31	.002	23	−.20	−1.98	.050	33	−.18	−2.15	.030
Intact families	33	.35			23	.28			33	.29		
Severe conflict	78	−.54	−4.79	.00	48	−.48	−3.87	.001	78	−.40	−6.56	.001
Intact families	78	.19			50	.34			78	.53		

*Class averages were used as bases for standardization.

scores are below class average (negative Z scores), while all control groups are above average. This is not self-evident since the Z scores were calculated from the relevant class means and only a small part of the school population was included in the actual comparison.

To make sure that these differences in achievement are not due to background factors, we applied a multivariate regression analysis to the data. Table 6.3 indicates that when many relevant background factors are controlled, children of intact families performed significantly better in arithmetic than children from matrifocal families. Most background variables did not add significantly to the explained variance, the exceptions being father's schooling and father's continent of birth, factors that had not been used in the matching of the control groups. Similar regressions run on English and Hebrew scores also showed a highly significant net effect of parental marital status on achievement. In addition, regressions run on a sample from which children of hostile families and their controls were excluded (thus allowing us to assess the ef-

Table 6.3

Multiple Regression
Dependent Variable: Standardized Grades in Arithmetic
Last Independent Variable: Intact Families Versus All Other Families
Last Independent Variable Forced; Other Independent Variables:
Stepwise

Variable	Simple r	β	R^2 Change
Father's schooling			
(years)	.22[a]	.15[a]	.048[a]
Mother's schooling	.19[a]	.09	.008
Father's continent of birth[c]			
(Asia-Africa)	− .15[b]	− .08[b]	.004
Number of siblings	− .05	.07	.01
Child's continent of birth[c]			
(Israel)	− .03	.03	.001
Father's continent of birth[c]			
(Europe-America)	.07[b]	.03	.001
One parent vs. intact families			
(study vs. control)	.38[a]	.37[a]	.13[b]

[a] $p \leq .01$.
[b] $p \leq .05$.
[c] Dummy variable.

fect of "pure" matrifocality) demonstrated that matrifocality has highly significant (negative) influence on all three measures of children's scholastic achievements. A similar overall detriment from father absence has been reported by several investigators over the last two decades (Deutsch and Brown 1964; Schelton 1969).

Does It Matter How the Marriage Was Broken?

The data in Table 6.2 imply that the exact circumstances under which the parents' marriage broke down are not the crucial cause of lower scholastic achievement. Admittedly any development that leads to the matrifocal situation is potentially traumatic to the child (Sugar 1970; Toomin 1974; Wallerstein and Kelly 1980). Either father's death or parents' divorce or separation may create feelings of guilt, self-doubt, mistrust, and so on, but the psychodynamic mechanisms involved are, nevertheless, quite different. It thus seems that the situation of single parenthood, rather than the process that led to it, brought about the discrepancy in scholastic achievement. In other words, we are dealing here with a function of marriage, not merely with the outcome of crisis in families.

The image of a deceased father is likely to be positive, in some cases even idealized, while the resentment the mother may feel toward the man who divorced her is often deliberately or subconsciously transferred to the child. Nevertheless, when children of widows are compared with children of divorced parents, these psychological factors are not reflected in scholastic achievement. The two groups do not differ significantly in any of the spheres under comparison. The t values for arithmetic, English, and Hebrew were, respectively, $-.17$ ($p < .86$), $.6$ ($p < .54$), and $.88$ ($p < .38$). Multivariate regression analysis led to the same general conclusion.

A related question is whether marriage preserves its educational function even when there is severe conflict between the spouses. Is the idea that divorce should be avoided "for the children's sake" empirically defensible? When we compared children whose parents were divorced with those whose parents were severely antagonistic but still married, we found that severe conflict breeds even worse scholastic achievement than divorce. However, this radical conclusion did not survive the multivariate regression analysis. When background factors were controlled, no significant difference between children of divorced and those of conflictual parents was found. We conclude, cautiously, that for parents involved in severe conflict, neither staying married nor getting divorced is advantageous for their children.

Are Boys More Affected by Father-Absence than Girls?

Identification with the parent of the same sex is an important idea in developmental psychology (Mowrer 1950; Biller 1976). Accordingly, the disadvantage of father absence should be greater for boys than for girls. Several studies have supported this hypothesis (Wasserman 1968; Herzog and Sudia 1973; Steinzor 1969). Unfortunately, neither these studies nor the present one have tested the hypothesis by examining the impact of mother absence as well. The main reason for this omission is practical: patrifocal families are hard to come by. Given this obstacle, we have pursued another track: Are the differences between the achievement of one-parent boys and their control samples significantly greater than the differences between one-parent girls and their controls? Table 6.4 presents analyses of variance in the three scholastic fields. The hypothesis about the greater effect of father absence on boys (in comparison to girls) is not substantiated by the data.

Does Ethnic Background Affect the Impact of Father Absence?

There are two grounds for expecting that a traditional background amplifies the impact of father absence. First, since the division of labor between husband and wife is more rigid in traditional cultures, it should be harder for the mother to substitute for the absent or nonfunctioning father. The increasing similarity between the genders in modern societies should make the father more dispensable. Radin (1976, p. 266) proposes that "cultures in which fathers are very powerful are most adversely affected by their absence," while Shepher (1980) observes that in highly modernized societies, such as Sweden, families seem "not to need" an adult male member. Second, the amount of prejudice and preventive so-

Table 6.4

Main and Interaction Effects of Family Patterns and Gender on Achievements (Standardized Grades) in Arithmetic, English, and Hebrew (ANOVA)

Source of Variation	Arithmetic (N = 402)				English (N = 368)				Hebrew (N = 402)			
	Sum of Squares	D.F.	F	Sig	Sum of Squares	D.F.	F	Sig.	Sum of Squares	D.F.	F	Sig.
Main effects	63.39	2	35.42	.001	33.75	2	17.10	.001	31.78	2	19.17	.001
Family pattern (F.P.)	63.02	1	70.42	.001	33.25	1	33.70	.001	28.93	1	34.90	.001
Gender (G.)	.42	1	.47	.490	.44	1	.44	.507	2.76	1	3.35	.070
Interaction effects	.08	1	.09	.770	.46	1	.47	.494	1.61	1	1.95	.160
(F.P.) × (G.)	.08	1	.09	.770	.46	1	.47	.494	1.61	1	1.95	.160
Explained	63.47	3	23.64	.001	34.21	3	11.56	.001	33.39	3	13.43	.001
Residual	381.24	426			262.51	266			353.11	426		
Total	444.72	429			296.72	269			386.50	429		

cial control against matrifocality in traditional societies exceeds by far similar controls in modern societies.

To test this hypothesis we used the same statistical method (ANOVA) that was used in testing the previous hypothesis (that fatherlessness has a stronger impact on boys than on girls). We found significant main effects of family patterns and of ethnicity on achievement in all three subjects (arithmetic, English, and Hebrew) but no interaction effects. Thus, in spite of plausible theory, we found no empirical support for the notion that single parenthood leads to more adverse effects in traditional than in modern societies.

Intelligence

Does the impact of fatherlessness on achievement operate through the intellectual or through the motivational sphere? In other words, does matrifocality affect the very potential to learn or only the propensity to apply this potential? Table 6.5 compares mean I.Q. scores of study and control groups. While all I.Q.s of study

Table 6.5

I.Q. by Group (Study and Control)

		I.Q.		
Groups	N	$\bar{X}$	t	p
All one-parent families (study group)	166	101.2		
			−2.67	.01
All intact families (control)	166	107.7		
Widowed	54	103.05		
			−1.78	.08
Intact families	54	111.28		
Divorcees	84	102.32		
			−1.85	.06
Intact families	84	108.23		
Separated	28	96.85		
			−1.05	.30
Intact families	28	104.67		
Severe conflict	67	97.38		
			−2.17	.03
Intact families	67	110.33		

groups fell below their respective controls, only one of the four comparisons yielded a significant difference (the cumulative effect for the entire study versus entire control groups was also significant). Comparing these results with those reported in Table 6.2 (as the group sizes are approximately equal, t values are comparable), we find that the child's potential (or "capacity to learn") is much less affected by the parents' conjugal situation than the child's actual achievements.[7]

Popularity Among Peers

Is marriage as functional for social acceptability of the offspring as it is for their scholastic achievement? Biller (1971, 1974) contends that father's absence interferes with peer relationships. To test this, we used three indices of pupils' social standing in their respective classes: acceptance, rejection, and relative divergence between acceptance and rejection, as described above. We then asked whether by these criteria children reared in one-parent families are less popular (less often selected positively) or whether they are more often actually resented. Finally, we asked if the answer is different for the various kinds of matrifocality (widowed, divorced, separated). The data presented in Table 6.6 as well as in multiple regression (not presented here) show that children of intact families are significantly more popular (more accepted as well as less rejected) than children of matrifocal and conflictual families. Also, children of parents involved in severe conflict are more frequently rejected by their peers, but this finding is not sustained when background factors are controlled by multiple regression. From Table 6.6 and even more so from multiple regression, no major differences among the various study groups could be inferred. Thus the major impact on the social development of children stems from the absence of a functioning father rather than from the circumstances that caused that absence.

If father absence had a stronger impact on boys than on girls, a significant interaction effect should have appeared. This, however, was not the case; neither gender nor ethnicity had a significant main effect or a significant interaction effect.

Table 6.6

Popularity among Peers by Group

Groups	Acceptance [A/(C − 1)]				Rejection [B/(D − 1)]				A − R [(A − B)/(E − 1)]			
	N	x	t	p	N	x	t	p	N	x	t	p
All one-parent families (study group)	201	.03			201	.05			201	−.02		
All intact families (control)	201	.07	−6.78	.001	201	.02	3.04	.001	201	.05	−7.02	.001
Widowed	67	.02			65	.03			65	−.008		
Intact families	68	.08	−2.10	.030	66	.01	1.23	.210	66	.06	−3.61	.001
Divorcees	99	.03			100	.04			99	−.008		
Intact families	93	.07	−2.66	.009	93	.02	2.48	.014	88	.05	−4.05	.001
Separated	33	.02			33	.06			33	−.02		
Intact families	30	.08	−1.85	.074	30	.04	.55	.580	29	.04	−1.70	.090
Severe conflict	78	.03			77	.06			77	−.02		
Intact families	73	.06	−1.39	.160	70	.01	4.83	.001	68	.04	−4.34	.001

Behavior at School

Beyond scholastic achievement and popularity, a third facet is adjustment to the school as an institution. Using personal files of students in which the pupil's conduct is recorded and evaluated, we tried to determine whether the various groups under study differ not only in the number but also in the type and pattern of behavioral problems. We classified the patterns as follows: (1) active deviations (disturbing class work, aggressive behavior toward peers or teachers, destruction of property); (2) passive deviations (tardiness, failure to fulfill required tasks, social isolation, low level of cooperation with peers and teachers); (3) no deviations (no special comments were made about this pupil); (4) distinction (excellence in scholastic work, special services to the school or class).

Table 6.7 presents the distribution of the various groups among these four patterns. The results reconfirm our former hypotheses. All study groups obtained from their teachers much less praise (distinction) and more criticism. But the data also add a qualitative dimension that comes into focus when we compare the conflictual to the other study groups. While the offspring of widowed, divorced, and separated parents have active and passive deviations with about equal frequency, the offspring of parents involved in severe conflict have active deviations from school norms exceeding passive deviations by more than 29 percent. The extra irritation caused by the struggle between the spouses is unequivocally revealed in this finding (Felner et al. 1975 report similar findings and offer the same explanation).

Discussion

The cardinal question of this study was whether parents who attempt to raise children in a nonmarital framework pay a "price" in terms of their children's development. The accumulation of findings presented above indicate clearly and systematically that such a price is in fact paid. Beyond this is another question: How exactly does marriage perform its socializing function? What are the mechanisms that make a harmonious marriage a superior framework for raising children? On a broad level two answers may be suggested. First, on the average more resources are invested in a

Table 6.7

Active and Passive School-Related Behavior by Group; χ^2 and Cramer's V

Groups	Active Deviation	Passive Deviation	No Deviation	Distinction	Total Percent	N	χ^2	Cramer's V
All one-parent families (study group)	35.8	29.8	28.4	6.0	100	279		
All intact families (control)	4.7	5.0	66.5	23.8	100	279	147.4[a]	.62
Widowed	32.4	33.8	27.9	5.9	100	68		
Intact families	7.4	4.4	64.7	23.5	100	68	43.2[a]	.56
Divorcees	35.0	26.0	31.0	8.0	100	100		
Intact families	3.0	6.0	66.0	25.0	100	100	60.8[a]	.55
Separated	36.4	30.3	30.3	3.0	100	33		
Intact families	0.0	3.0	69.7	27.3	100	33	30.8[a]	.69
Severe conflict	51.3	29.5	19.2	0.0	100	78		
Intact families	6.4	3.8	59.0	30.8	100	78	82.3[a]	.72

[a] $p \leq .05$.

child when his parents are married. Single parenthood as well as severe conflict between spouses deprive the child of vital inputs such as material or emotional support, know-how, social guidance, educational supervision. All these and many other forms of parental investment are more abundant in the case of a cooperating pair of parents. Second, the child's gradual development into a full-fledged member of society is motivated and guided by a process of identification with his parents, particularly the parent of the same gender.

Since these two explanations—the "resource" and the "identification" postulates—derive from different views of parent-child relationships, it is important to trace the critical points of differentiation between them. The comparison between boys and girls is such a critical point. The resource postulate applies to both genders in an almost symmetrical fashion. Married parents are likely to invest more in their offspring than unmarried parents do, irrespective of the child's gender. On the other hand, even if both parents function as models for their children, most developmental psychologists will agree that the parent of the same gender is a more direct and potent model; hence boys raised in a matrifocal family will have lower achievement and more behavioral or social problems than girls (each gender's record being compared to children of the same gender in intact families). The fact that our data fail to show a significant difference between the genders lends support, in our view, to the "resource approach" by eliminating one of its most plausible alternatives.

A further question is whether the superiority of marriage as a framework for socializing the young is culture specific. Although an international comparative study would be necessary to answer this question, our data do address it. Perhaps the negative effect of father absence is a function of conservative adherence to conventional gender roles. In a traditional cultural atmosphere, fatherless children may be stigmatized; eventually the popular belief in their "impaired" upbringing may become a self-fulfilling prophecy. If the *belief* in the harm caused by father absence, rather than real impairment, is the crucial factor, the divergence between the offspring of one-parent families and those of intact families should be greater in traditional than in modern subpopulations. Our data do not support this hypothesis. While children of European ethnic background show better overall achievement and are more popular (a finding well established in Israeli educational research; see Min-kowich, Davis, and Bashi 1977), the effects of father absence are equally severe for both groups.

A consistent finding is that it is the absence of father per se, and not the reasons why it came about, that is responsible for the child's deficits. In other words, the situation, not the reasons for it, is the main cause. There is, however, one important exception. When reports about children's conduct in school are examined, it becomes clear that active deviations from school norms (commission) were much more frequent among children of parents in conflict than among children of one-parent families.

Thus the cumulative weight of the evidence supports the "resource approach." The major importance of marriage for socialization stems from its ability to channel vast resources from generation to generation.

The policy implications of this conclusion are by no means self-evident. On the one hand, resources, unlike identification, can be forwarded to the young by public means and efforts. Thus it is sometimes argued that if one-parent families had per capita income equal to those at the disposal of intact families, all educational problems could be surmounted. But the resources transferred via marriage from parents to offspring are of a great variety. Money and other material goods are a major component of these resources, but they by no means exhaust them. Experience, knowledge, time, and emotional support are just a few examples of parental contributions to offspring socialization that cannot be replaced by money. Also, the total resources passed by marital couples to their children are so vast that an alternative tax-based scheme would go bankrupt trying to match them. In other words, it probably will never be possible to equal in taxes what married people are willing to contribute to their children's welfare.

The last issue we wish to discuss is one of evaluation and policy. Since marriage is defined in formal or even legal terms, the dilemma confronting unhappy spouses, who are also parents, is phrased: "Should the legal fiction of a marital relationship be preserved even if the relationship has degenerated to one of conflict?" If the answer to this problem is negative (as our own comparisons between the "conflict" and the "one-parent" groups indicate), then marital stability at any cost is not necessarily in the best interest of the spouses or even their offspring. One-parent families seem to be rather competent socialization agents when compared to married parents engaged in severe conflict. But the assumption underlying this reasoning is that legal dissolution is the sole policy issue. In other words, to divorce or stay legally married is assumed to be a matter of free will and rational decision, while level and intensity of conflict and struggle in marriage are determined by luck, fate, basic personality traits, intervention of third parties, or any other forces beyond human control. On the public policy level, these assumptions lead to legal innovations designed to make divorce easier and less harmful, while educational, economic, and legal attempts to facilitate harmony in marriage are relatively neglected.

A social scientist may adopt a different approach to marriage, emphasizing the content rather than the shell. He may perceive marriage as a socially sanctioned pair-bond in which common goals and interests prevail over centrifugal ones. The preservation of such a relationship is partially a voluntary matter, but it has also numerous and potent involuntary determinants. In terms of the children's chances of scholastic and educational success, a rather severe price is paid if the pair-bond breaks down. It makes relatively little difference how precisely this breakdown happens and who (if anyone) is "guilty." It also is not very consequential whether the actual breakdown of the marital relationship is followed by a legal divorce or not. To be sure, the educational damage caused by marital failure can be aggravated by intensive fighting, but that does not mean that marriage as a socializing institution can, at the present stage of social and educational knowledge, be replaced.

NOTES

1. Rental housing is extremely scarce in Israel; most newlywed couples purchase a small apartment for an equivalent of 5–7 average yearly earnings. The bulk of the purchase money is obtained from the couple's parents.

2. Grades in terms of standard deviations from the relevant class mean.

Thus a pupil who has a standardized grade of -0.5 is one-half S.D. below the average of his class.

3. $[a/(A - 1)] \times 100$ where a is the number of positive votes the child received and A is the total number of positive votes in his class.

4. $[r/(R - 1)] \times 100$ where r is the number of negative votes the individual pupil got and R the total number of rejections emitted in the relevant class.

5. $[(a - r)/(A + R)] \times 100$.

6. In Israeli schools, specially trained teachers are responsible for consultation with pupils' parents and teachers in cases of minor problems in scholarship as well as conduct.

7. To draw this conclusion one must not assume that I.Q. tests do not contain components of achievement; rather, it is assumed that I.Q. tests are more indicative of overall intellectual potential than scores earned in any specific discipline (for example, arithmetic, English).

REFERENCES

Biller, H. B. *Father, Child and Sex Role*. Lexington, Mass.: Heath, 1971.

Biller, H. B. *Parental Deprivation*. Lexington, Mass.: Heath, 1974.

Biller, H. B. "The Father and Personality Development: Parental Deprivation and Sex-Role Development." In M. Lamb (ed.), *The Role of the Father in Child Development*. New York: John Wiley, 1976.

Blalock, H. M. *Social Statistics*. New York: McGraw-Hill, 1960.

Deutsch, M., and Brown, B. "Social Influences in Negro–White Intelligence Differences," *Journal of Social Issues* 20(1964):24–35.

Felner, R. D.; Stolberg, A.; and Cowen, E. L. "Crisis Events and School Mental Health Referral Patterns of Young Children." *Journal of Consulting Psychology* 43(1975):305–310.

Herzog, E., and Sudia, C. "Children in Fatherless Homes." In B. M. Cladwell and Riccinti (eds.), *Review of Child Development Research*. Chicago: University of Chicago Press, 1973.

Israel Statistical Abstracts. Jerusalem: Central Bureau of Statistics, 1980.

Minkowich, A.; Davis, D.; and Bashi, J. *Success and Failure in Israeli Elementary Education*. New Brunswick, N.J.: Transaction Books, 1982.

Mowrer, O. H. *Learning Theory and Personality Dynamics*. New York: Ronald Press, 1950.

Ortar, G. *Achievement Tests*. Jerusalem: Hebrew University, 1969 (in Hebrew).

Peres, Y., and Katz, R. "Stability and Centrality: The Nuclear Family in Modern Israel." *Social Forces* 59(1981):687–704.

Radin, N. "The Role of Father in Cognitive Development." In Lamb, M. E. (ed.), *The Role of Father in Child Development.* New York: Wiley, 1976.

Schelton, L. A. "A Comparative Study of Educational Achievements in One-Parent Families and Two-Parent Families." *Dissertation Abstracts* 29(1969):8A.

Shepher, J. "The Dimension of Matrifocality." In *Sweden Research Report.* Haifa, Israel: University of Haifa, 1980.

Steinzor, B. *"When Parents Divorce: A New Approach to a New Relationship.* New York: Pantheon Books, 1969.

Sugar, M. "Children of Divorce." *Pediatrics* 46(1970):588–595.

Toomin, M. K. "Counseling Needs of the Child of Divorce." In J. G. Cull and R. E. Hardy (eds.), *Deciding on Divorce.* Springfield, Ill.: C. L. Thomas, 1974.

Wallerstein, J. S., and Kelly, J. B. *Surviving the Breakup.* New York: Basic Books, 1980.

Wasserman, H. L. *Father Absent and Father Present Lower Class Negro Families: A Comparative Study of Family Functioning.* Waltham, Mass.: Brandeis University, 1968.

PART III

Comparative Studies of Marital Change

7 *Historical Reflections on American Marriage*

JOHN MODELL

THIS CHAPTER TREATS in a broad fashion a number of issues in the history of American marriage with emphasis on certain qualities of the American institution. American marriage has long seemed to be a precarious institution. Rooted in, and apparently supporting, the state and the social order more generally, it has rested upon heterosexual love and thereby upon more or less transformed libidinal energies between two parties commonly held disparate in both appetite and capacity. The argument of this chapter will be to point to the historical resilience of this flexible institution, and to call attention to the operation of an essentially feminist dynamic, now and again galvanizing change within the institution. So important and yet so subject to interpersonal experimenta-

---

NOTE: Amyra Grossbard-Shechtman's thoughtful readings helped me greatly to recast my essay in the spirit of the volume, and stimulated my thinking about the marriage process.

tion, American marriage almost of necessity has been a focus of public concern, often feminist in outlook because of gender asymmetries in American life. The record, however, is one of resilience and persistence. Marriage has been admired, "worked at," an institution widely and repeatedly utilized.

The American setting, this chapter maintains, has made a difference. Like American institutions generally, marriage has represented an adaptation of the European basis. A plethora of material resources, a paucity of available labor, and an individualist strain of Protestant ideology gave the institution nearly from its outset a more voluntaristic cast, including an emphasis upon self-fulfillment and a somewhat lesser reliance on prudence in handling family assets.

The idea of "love" paradoxically not only enables the imprudent to understand their behavior but also describes the satisfaction often gradually achieved within a prudent marriage. It thus encompasses primal concerns for material security, family continuity, and sexual expression; and it suggests the possibility of bypassing or challenging received gender-role assignments, for love is seen to be the joint product of two individuals. The conflict between the emphasis on a warm and loving conjugal relationship and the performance of tasks of a more prosaic nature has constantly been and must remain a point of tension in American marriages. Conflicts are likely to arise between spouses in their performance for one another of mundane tasks. Such conflict provides a glaring contrast to expectations of "love."

The idea that marriage should be more than a conventional social arrangement has long produced a surface instability in the American institution, alarming many observers. Also, a feature inherited from Europe imposed a basic tension, by normatively prescribing monogamy and consecrating sexuality to marriage but requiring a number of years to intervene between sexual maturation and marriage. Thus, parental and lineage authority and its control of economic resources demanded prudence, while sexuality urged otherwise. There were, of course, substantial national variants in Western Europe, as well as regional variants in America (Wrigley 1982; Hajnal 1965; Laslett 1972; Flandrin 1979; D. S. Smith 1972, 1977; Levine 1977).

New World conditions modified this pattern in emphasis and degree, in the earliest days of European settlement. Men considerably outnumbered women, while newly encountered racial groups not sharing the Western European pattern lived nearby. Further, the structure of economic opportunity was radically different (Dunn 1969; Menard 1977; Menard and Walsh 1981; Greven 1970). New World marriages tended to be earlier than in Western Europe, more universal (within limits set by sex ratios), and more often economically independent or largely independent of ascendant kin. Contracted younger, American marriages tended to last longer than in Europe, the more so because of the relatively salubrious conditions in many American regions.

To a greater degree than European marriages, American marriages were seen as *de novo* productions, valued in no small part for their emotional benefits rather than for their contribution to generational continuity. American marriages within a generation or two after initial settlement revealed qualities congruent with the emerging American liberalism: an optimism, a sense of expansiveness of individual purpose, a feeling that corporate entities existed to assist individual purposes more so than individual purposes existed to serve corporate goals (Henretta 1978; D. B. Smith 1982). Romantically styled conjugal love initially comprised no great part of the ideology of American marriage. Nevertheless, relatively many American couples developed close attachments to each other. Americans looked first at emotional benefits when assessing or contracting a marriage. Reasonable hopes of economic betterment and, by this period, hopes of visible means of signifying this betterment to others, lent to the marital entrance a tone of warm expectancy (D. S. Smith 1973b; Cott 1976, 1977; Rothman 1981).

Foreign travelers often remarked about the emphasis that Americans placed on love for mate selection, although gender-role differentiation within marriage remained quite marked (de Tocqueville 1945 [1835, 1840]; Bremer 1853; Furstenberg 1966). Role asymmetries between men and women provoked occasional controversy (Faragher 1979; Degler 1980). On a grander level, social change encouraged a considerable variety of revised prescriptions for married life, sometimes feminist (Kern 1981). Historians of the United States have long characterized the 1820s and 1830s as a period of great perturbation within the young nation, amounting in large areas to a surprisingly broad public reconsideration of just what constituted right behavior. A loosely connected series of Protestant revivals seems to have focused interest on perfectionist goals that took in much of the private lives of individuals (Johnson 1978; Wallace 1978). One found utopian and separatist communities, abolitionist challenges to Negro slavery, temperance movements of considerable variety, and efforts to prevent the United States government from delivering the mail on Sunday (Thomas 1965).

According to Mary P. Ryan's examination of family change in upstate New York, the revivalist attack on besotted male conviviality initiated but did not itself produce a change in the meaning of marriage. Contributing more directly were aspirations to material success within the rapidly commercializing and industrializing economic order. People wanted to construct a domestic setting that would promote success for themselves and for their children. To accomplish this, marriage assumed "such social functions as a new method of childrearing, new standards of self-control, new bourgeois virtues such as temperance and sexual restraint." Self-conscious actions of wives *qua* wives in a society with asymmetrical gender roles were the prime agency in what ensued (Ryan 1981, pp. 153–155; see also Cott 1977; Smith-Rosenberg 1975; D. S. Smith 1973a; Jeffrey 1972).

A new bourgeois prudence in entering marriage dictated a revised marital love that urged wives to use "allure as . . . marital and sexual partner[s]" to elicit propriety and self-control from their husbands, to develop a warm and supportive home life, and to teach their children the same spirit. Such prudence focused upon character, not property, as the source of success in a commercial society. Accordingly, its emotional tone and the "love" it held in check were different (Ryan 1981, p. 180). Ryan reports that even the Mercantile Agency, when assessing credit risks, looked so closely at family life that it remarked with disfavor on men who had had, *by their wives*, an imprudently large number of children. Marriage, initially for the middle class and eventually beyond, had been turned to new purposes, and had a correspondingly new tone. Marriage and the courtship that led to it felt different, demanding more, redefining love, and leading more often to divorce. As with subsequent changes, the early-nineteenth-century alteration in the spirit of middle class marriage aroused public debate on the role of the state. Feminists tried to modify, but not to efface, gender asymmetries within marriage.

As the redefined marriage diffused through society, age at first marriage rose. A second reevaluation of marriage, taking place early in the twentieth century, came as economic developments began to promote a turnabout in this trend. Increased productivity led to an overall increase in disposable income, while the nature of that increased productivity encouraged the establishment of social mechanisms that began to buffer the radical uncertainty with which many individuals lived in industrial America (Modell 1979). With more individual and social resources available to them, with a bit more of a cushion against failure (and also less hope of rising through entrepreneurship), individuals could somewhat relax the moralized prudence that dominated middle-class-inspired family ideology. At this time, too, "women's sphere" at home was being supplemented by women's gainful employment outside the home, and women's satisfactions were more openly sought. Rapidly expanding educational opportunities provided an arena for youth subculture. A view of fixed character came to be supplanted by a more developmental view. Emotional growth was now explictly encouraged, to be achieved not by following adults' precepts but in expanding one's affective ties. In the faster-paced nuptial pattern of this period, a new courtship institution—dating—emerged. It involved a search for self-determination and gratification in the process of finding a mate (Modell 1983; Fass 1977).

In the early twentieth century, public debate over the marital institution grew from an initial concern for control of sexuality to a far broader movement to have the state promote marital soundness by offering sex education, prohibiting child marriages, and ridding the home of boarders. Public debate also centered on divorce reform (Pivar 1973, chap. 3; Connelly 1980; Modell and Hareven 1973; Richmond 1925; May 1980). In William L. O'Neill's analysis, a quarter-century of active debate over divorce reform was a genuine moral conflict. The heart of the issue was that increasing numbers saw the family as voluntaristic and not responsible for the continuance of the social order, while opponents saw the sanctity of marriage as the very basis for that social order (O'Neill 1967; Mohr 1978; Reed 1978). The new sense of unfolding human capacities encouraged an outlook that saw marriage as an act of relatively young people, and therefore sometimes in need of revision. Such notions at the extreme suggested "trial marriage" (which indeed was advocated in the debate without gaining any solid support). Marriage so conceived seemed to some a license to fornicate, a betrayal of the ideology of love. Most strands of divorce reform, however, in fact reflected a basically conservative faith in the capacity of the institution of marriage to contain and give value to the sexual motive and to human happiness in the here and now (Hale 1971, chap. 10; Herman 1973; Patten 1968 [1907]).

At some point in the 1960s another new phase in the history of American marriage began. Marked increases in the age at marriage, reversing the sharp downturn following World War II, went along with increased premarital sexuality among women and an increased public acceptance of gender symmetry within marriage (Modell, Furstenberg, and Strong 1978; Miller and Simon 1975; Duncan 1979; Thornton and Freedman 1979; Mason and Bumpass 1975). Dennis Hogan finds an increased variety of paths to adulthood under the impact of modernity, economic growth, military demands, and a changing age structure, and he finds that this variety affected the likelihood of divorce (Hogan 1981, pp. 56–61, 84, 206). To an extent formerly unimaginable, young people since World War II have been permitted to do as they please in contracting marriage. The upward climb in disposable income has enabled them to marry very nearly when they please, and to divorce when they please. A widened sense of what is appropriate cannot be easily documented, but surely a new "personal politics" promoting revision in gender roles and a new sexual liberty in courtship have occurred (Evans 1979; Modell 1980).

Public debate has reflected, dramatized, and publicized these modifications to the institution of marriage. Yet a consensus still prevails that marriages should constitute an independent unit wherein childbearing and child-rearing take place—warm, affectionate, and spontaneously intimate units, yet communally celebrated and even overseen. Despite enormous changes in the content of religion and in the composition of the population, most marriages in the United States have long been solemnized in religious ceremonies. Obviously, the meaning of the religious marriage sanction has changed over the past century: many marrying with a religious ceremony do not marry for eternity in the eyes of God, but the clergy are the officiants of choice, offering the preferred setting for the participation of family members and friends. The ceremony marks marriage as an institution worthy of communal celebration and communal oversight. This probably explains why marriages celebrated religiously are less likely to end in divorce (Schroeder 1939; Locke 1951).

Data on Philadelphia marriages from 1860 indicate a slow, gradual decline in secularly conducted weddings there, from an initial figure of about 10 percent in 1860 to a low of about 2 percent around the turn of the century, followed by a slow, gradual increase to about 8 percent in the early 1920s, followed by another decline to about 5 percent in 1937, when the data lapse. Jacobsen's national estimates show about 75 percent religious weddings in 1939, his earliest data point, and about the same proportion in 1948. By the time the U.S. Vital Statistics began to publish this figure in the early 1960s, the proportion was closer to 80 percent, from which it has declined only slightly since (Philadelphia, Board of Health Annual Reports, various dates; Jacobsen 1959, p. 55; U.S. Public Health Service, 1964–1979). The narrow range of variation of this aspect of marriage is itself worthy of note.

As always, an exclusive conjugal love, eroticized and more symmetrical than before, seems crucial to Americans, in ideology if not always in practice. The revealing analysis of the subjective side of marriage by Veroff, Douvan, and Kulka (1981, chap. 4) indicates that between a national survey in 1957 and its replication in 1976, the following four trends emerged.

1.   There was a lessening of the negative sanctions against those who do not or will not marry.
2.   There was an increase in the proportion of Americans who, when asked, cited drawbacks to marriage.
3.   There was an increase in the proportion who reported that their own marriages have rough spots. The increase was greater among men than among women.
4.   There was an overall increase in reported marital happiness.

Essentially, the authors conclude that marriage was and remains an institution central to Americans' well-being, even if it is less obligatory than it once was. Americans in recent decades, however, have demanded satisfaction in marriage. Their search has both enriched the matrimonial experience and placed upon it a burden that it sometimes fails to support.

Historical evidence of considerable depth and variety points to the resilience of the institution of marriage in the United States. This may seem surprising in light of the phenomenal changes that have occurred and the past expectations of scholars. The concern for the vitality of the institution has had many precedents. Analyses during the Great Depression lamented the failure of American marriage to promote fertility in the face of economic reversals, expressing anxiety that a permanent onset of individualism would defeat both the altruism inherent in Americans' view of parenthood and the commitment to childbearing sufficient for society to reproduce itself. Kingsley Davis, for instance, speculated in 1937 that the long-term fertility decline suggested that

> the family is not indefinitely adaptable to modern society. . . . Only two logical alternatives appear feasible for governments wishing to induce births. They can go back to a rural-stable regime, or they can invent a new system of reproductive institutions. In the nature of the case, they are not likely to pursue either alternative deliberately. But they may adopt some policy which in the end will have the effect of creating a new procreative system [Davis, 1937, pp. 305–306].

Americans proved ready to modify marriage without, however, promoting a new procreative system. If anything, the ability of most American families to adapt to Depression conditions emphasized the durability of the marital institution. Marriages, initially postponed in the Depression, quickly came close to catching up, even during the Depression itself (Stouffer and Spencer 1936). On the one hand, couples relaxed their economic standards for marriage and modified their emotional and economic interdependency within newly formed families and between them and their parents. The already somewhat amorphous institution of engagement became more so, as the economic prudence it embodied ceased to make sense (Brooks 1941; Stouffer and Lazarsfeld 1937; Rockwood and Ford 1945; McConaghy 1938).

Flexibility in marital arrangements had much to do with how well couples rode out Depression strains (Cavan and Ranck 1938; Bakke 1940). Typically, families that successfully adapted their role structures to cope with the Depression emerged even more committed to the values of marriage. The Lynds put it eloquently: "These homes seem to give the lie to the ricocheting process of social change outside. Actually, they serve as a reminder of the basic sources of human conservatism and resistance to change" (Lynd and Lynd 1937, p. 145; Elder 1974).

To keep marriage, people were even willing to support radical governmental intervention. In September 1937, Roper inquired of a national sample: "Should the government give financial aid to young people to help them get married and establish homes?" About eleven in twelve had an opinion, and almost half of these favored this extraordinary proposal (see Table 7.1). Those for whom prompt marriage was particularly salient (younger people and women) and those for whom it was particularly difficult under current conditions (the unemployed and the less prosperous and secure) were most in favor, but the proposition found substantial support in all groups. Commitment to prompt marriage clearly outweighed the norm of economic self-sufficiency.

Postwar developments revealed the depth of American commitment to marriage. Parental sponsorship of young marriages, the product of the Depression, remained. The state self-consciously promoted conventional nuclear family-building through massive subsidies to home ownership and to suburbanization. The "baby boom" of the 1950s reaffirmed the institution of marriage.

The long-term growth of divorce is commonly regarded as a sign of the weakness of marriage. The brilliantly executed decomposition of divorce by marriage cohorts carried out by Preston and

Table 7.1

Proportions Approving of Government Subsidies to Permit Marriage, by Sex and Age, and by Sex and "Economic Level," 1937

	Men	Women
Age		
17–20	43.2%	47.5%
21–24	42.5%	37.5%
25–34	42.5%	42.6%
35–44	37.7%	41.6%
45–54	33.3%	41.6%
55+	28.5%	37.3%
Economic Level*		
Above Average	21.5%	23.3%
Average	31.1%	34.7%
Not poor	41.4%	44.4%
Poor	43.7%	48.8%
On relief	50.7%	58.2%

*Economic Level is an interviewer rating.
Percentages are of all respondents, including those expressing no opinion.

SOURCE: AIPO 99, September 16, 1937, special tabulation by Roper Center Archive, University of Connecticut, Storrs.

McDonald (1979), while explaining a fair amount of divorce by the weaknesses of marriages entered in times of economic and other public crises, discerns a powerful upward secular trend in divorce extending back for a century. Are we to see here a steady erosion of the institution of marriage, with divorce an indicator of reduced commitment to it? Does this trend, like the no less strong tendency toward reduced marital fertility, indicate that American marriage has progressively lost its purpose as well as its compulsory nature? The historical record suggests the contrary. The institution is uneasy but flexible, subject to repeated revision. A bridge between an expanding inner life and a demanding public one, marriage has been "worked at" in different ways by each generation, creating new forms but leaving at least one element alive, the ideology of conjugal love as justifying rather than undermining one's antecedents and material estate.

A most powerful insight into this question is provided by William Goode's early postwar study. Here, he explores in considerable detail some of the personal and structural consequences of a single macrosocial observation: "divorce is not as yet fully institutionalized in our own cultural structure [although it is elsewhere]. . . . It is equally certain that this attitude is changing" (1956, p. 10, italics removed). As Goode observed, divorce was not then quite a part of the marriage system because it ran up against assumptions about love, a notion that then served to explain to participants the nature of the American marital union. "Divorce is an official recognition of unhappiness, and it denies one basic premise of the romantic complex, that a couple married because both are deeply in love and the love will, of course, continue" (1956, p. 4). Goode, in a snapshot, has caught a core dynamic element of marriage as an American institution.

We must ask whether the American notion of being in love has been modified so that love can be both real and impermanent. Can it be that the long-term growth of divorce constitutes no weakening of the institution of marriage but rather a modification of it under changing assumptions about the nature of the sources and spirit of the marital bond? Love, of course, is hard to measure—surely historically—and we are perhaps on safer ground by returning to Goode once again and asking whether institutionalized mechanisms conducive to remarriage of divorced people have come to exist, so that divorce has become part of a process of becoming free to love again and thus marry again (Goode, 1956, chap. 19; see also Cherlin 1981 for a balanced contemporary view reflecting this perspective).

Remarrying divorced people have often been denied or have themselves eschewed religious weddings. This is entirely in keeping with a sense that prior divorce dishonors the new marriage. Table 7.2 shows age-specific proportions with religious weddings of single people and of divorced people who married or remarried in 1963, the first year for which such data are available, and for 1978. The table is an intriguing one, offering three findings.

1. Single people marrying at the conventional ages for first marriage are the most likely of all to marry in a religious setting. The proportion religiously married at 20–24 exceeds not only those older, shown, but those marrying younger, not here tabulated.
2. In 1963, divorced people were far less likely than single people at the same ages to marry in religious ceremonies.
3. By 1978, the propensity for religious settings of those who remarried much more closely resembled those of the single people, especially at lower ages. A religious ceremony was especially less frequently sought by single people marrying late, but no less so by the divorced.

In other words, how one came to the altar—whether directly or via a previous nuptial event—has rapidly become less important to the ceremonial, communal display of the event. One's marital

Table 7.2

Proportions of Marriages with Religious Officiant, by Age, Sex, and Previous Marital Status, 1963 and 1978

	Men				Women			
	1963		1978		1963		1978	
Age	Sing.	Div.	Sing.	Div.	Sing.	Div.	Sing.	Div.
20–24	85.9%	63.6%	83.4%	63.6%	88.5%	60.9%	84.8%	58.3%
25–34	83.4%	59.9%	76.8%	62.1%	79.4%	58.4%	73.8%	58.6%
35–44	69.1%	59.2%	59.0%	56.8%	67.3%	56.6%	57.3%	57.2%
45–54	66.3%	55.6%	55.0%	56.7%	69.7%	55.6%	53.9%	58.0%
55–64	65.6%	56.8%	56.8%	55.1%	81.6%	60.6%	61.1%	58.9%

SOURCE: Calculated from U.S. Department of Health, Education, and Welfare, Public Health Service, National Center for Health Statistics, *Vital Statistics of the United States* (1964, 1979).

history was mattering less, one's attitudes and bearing more. As Goode suggested, divorce has become institutionalized, as a part of the marriage system. Marriage has been modified in the postwar era to allow a wider range of individual choice, a lessened difference in the emotional demand made upon marriage by the two sexes, and a widened definition of "love."

Table 7.3 answers whether in recent years divorced people who remarried were becoming more or less prone to marry one another. Was divorce a lifetime marker selective or limiting when one came to marry again? Because the composition of the legally marriageable pool varies markedly by age (as the single are married off), proportions vary greatly by age. The presentation here focuses on an age span (25 to 34) in which there were relatively many single as well as divorced people in the marriage pool. The ratio of "endogamous" (divorce/divorcee or single/single) marriages to "exogamous" marriages (divorced person/single person) is the critical figure here. We ask of the data whether for divorced young men and women remarrying at these ages there was a tendency to marry other divorced people, and if so, whether this tendency decreased over time. Quite clearly "endogamy" of the divorced is the dominant pattern; but there is also a strong downward trend in this ratio, for both men and women. Acceptance of the legitimacy of divorce as a necessary component of a marriage system incorporating large volitional elements and a wider definition of "love" has, with some lag, encouraged acceptance of divorced people as

Table 7.3

Proportions of Single and Divorced Men and Women Marrying Divorced Persons Aged 25–34—Selected Years Between 1961 and 1978

	Men			Women		
	Divorced	Single	Ratio D/S	Divorced	Single	Ratio D/S
1961	46.9%	13.3%	3.53	50.1%	17.2%	2.92
1962	48.6%	12.8%	3.80	56.9%	18.6%	3.06
1977	52.6%	18.9%	2.78	63.2%	26.9%	2.35
1978	52.4%	18.9%	2.77	64.1%	26.9%	2.38

SOURCE: Calculated from U.S. Department of Health, Education, and Welfare, Public Health Service, National Center for Health Statistics, *Vital Statistics of the United States*, Volumes 3 on Marriage and Divorce (1962, 1963, 1978, 1979).

legitimate reentrants to a total marriage pool. The stigma is not gone, but it has weakened considerably. The operation of the marriage market, of course, is not explained entirely by such normative factors, but surely divorce no longer seems, as once it did, to dishonor marriage, which is still an honored institution and a desired state. Rules of entry have changed somewhat, patterns of entry more so. Yet love is still its central ideology, a love that now can be both real and impermanent.

REFERENCES

Bakke, E. Wight. *Citizens Without Work.* New Haven, Conn.: Yale University Press, 1940.

Bremer, Frederika. *The Homes of the New World*, 3 vols., trans. Mary Howitt. London: Arthur Hall, Virtue & Co., 1853.

Brooks, Melvin Schubert. "Wisconsin Birth and Marriage Rate Trends by Occupations, 1920–1930." Unpublished Ph.D. thesis, University of Wisconsin, 1941.

Cavan, Ruth Shonle, and Ranck, Katherine Howland. *The Family and the Depression.* Chicago: University of Chicago Press, 1938.

Cherlin, Andrew. *Marriage, Divorce, Remarriage.* Cambridge, Mass.: Harvard University Press, 1981.

Connelly, Mark Thomas. *The Response to Prostitution in the Progressive Era.* Chapel Hill: University of North Carolina Press, 1980.

Cott, Nancy. "Eighteenth-Century Family and Social Life Revealed in Massachusetts Divorce Records." *Journal of Social History* 10 (1976):20–43.

Cott, Nancy. *Bonds of Womanhood: Woman's Sphere in New England, 1780–1835.* New Haven, Conn.: Yale University Press, 1977.

Davis, Kingsley. "Reproductive Institutions and the Pressure for Population." *Sociological Review* 29(1937):289–306.

Degler, Carl. *At Odds.* New York: Oxford University Press, 1980.

Duncan, Otis Dudley. "Indicators of Social Typing: Traditional and Egalitarian Situation and Ideological Responses." *American Journal of Sociology* 85(1979):251–260.

Dunn, Richard S. "The Barbados Census of 1680: Profile of the Richest Colony in English America." *William and Mary Quarterly* 26(1969): 3–30.

Elder, Glen H., Jr. *Children of the Great Depression.* Chicago: University of Chicago Press, 1974.

Evans, Sara. *Personal Politics.* New York: Knopf, 1979.

Faragher, John Mack. *Women and Men on the Overland Trail.* New Haven, Conn.: Yale University Press, 1979.

Fass, Paula. *The Beautiful and the Damned.* New York: Oxford University Press, 1977.

Flandrin, Jean-Louis. *Families in Former Times,* trans. Richard Southern. Cambridge: At the University Press, 1979.

Furstenberg, Frank F., Jr., "Industrialization and the American Family: A Look Backward." *American Sociological Review* 31(1966):326–337.

Goode, William J. *After Divorce.* New York: Free Press, 1956.

Greven, Philip J., Jr. *Four Generations.* Ithaca, N.Y.: Cornell University Press, 1970.

Hajnal, John. "European Marriage Patterns in Perspective." In D. V. Glass and D. E. C. Eversley (eds.), *Population in History.* Chicago: Aldine, 1965.

Hale, Nathan G., Jr. *Freud and the Americans.* New York: Oxford University Press, 1971.

Henretta, James A. "Families and Farms: *Mentalité* in Pre-Industrial America." *William and Mary Quarterly* 35(1978):3–32.

Herman, Sondra R. "Loving Courtship or the Marriage Market? The Ideal and Its Critics 1871–1911." *American Quarterly* 25(1973):235–252.

Hogan, Dennis P. *Transitions and Social Change.* New York: Academic Press, 1981.

Jacobson, Paul H. *American Marriage and Divorce.* New York: Rinehart & Co., 1959.

Jeffrey, Kirk. "The Family as Utopian Retreat from the City." In Sallie Teselle (ed.), *The Family, Communes and Utopian Societies.* New York: Harper & Row, 1972.

Johnson, Paul E. *A Shopkeeper's Millennium.* New York: Hill & Wang, 1978.

Kern, Louis J. *An Ordered Love: Sex Roles and Sexuality in Victorian Utopias.* Chapel Hill: University of North Carolina Press, 1981.

Laslett, Peter. "Introduction: The History of the Family." In Peter Laslett and Richard Wall (eds.), *Household and Family in Past Time.* Cambridge: At the University Press, 1972.

Levine, David. *Family Formation in an Age of Nascent Capitalism.* New York: Academic Press, 1977.

Locke, Harvey J. *Predicting Adjustment in Marriage.* New York: Henry Holt & Co., 1951.

Lynd, Robert S., and Lynd, Helen Merrell. *Middletown in Transition.* New York: Harcourt Brace, 1937.

Mason, Karen Oppenheim, and Bumpass, Larry L. "U.S. Women's Sex-Role Ideology, 1970." *American Journal of Sociology* 80(1975):1212–1219.

May, Elaine Tyler. *Great Expectations: Marriage and Divorce in Post-Victorian America.* Chicago: University of Chicago Press, 1980.

McConaghy, James L. "Now That You Are Engaged." In William Frederick Bigelow (ed.), *The Good Housekeeping Marriage Book.* New York: Prentice-Hall, 1938.

Menard, Russell R. "Immigrants and Their Increase: The Process of Population Growth in Early Colonial Maryland." In Aubrey C. Land and Edward Papenfuse (eds.), *Law, Society, and Politics in Maryland*. Baltimore: Johns Hopkins University Press, 1977.

Menard, Russell R., and Walsh, Lorena S. "The Demography of Somerset County, Maryland: A Progress Report." *Newberry Papers in Family and Community History*, Number 81-2. Chicago: Newberry Library, 1981.

Miller, Patricia Y., and Simon, William. "Adolescent Sexual Behavior: Context and Change." *Social Problems* 22(1975):58–76.

Modell, John. "Changing Risks, Changing Adaptations: American Families in the Nineteenth and Twentieth Centuries." In Joan Challinor and Allen Lichtman (eds.), *Kin and Communities*. Washington, D.C.: Smithsonian Institution Press, 1979.

Modell, John. "Normative Aspects of American Marriage Timing Since World War II." *Journal of Family History* 5(1980):210–243.

Modell, John. "Dating Becomes the Way of American Youth." In Leslie Page Moch and Gary Stark (eds.), *Essays on the Family and Historical Change*. College Station: Texas A & M Press, 1983.

Modell, John; Furstenberg, Frank F.; and Strong, Douglas. "The Timing of Marriage in the Transition to Adulthood: Continuity and Change, 1860–1975." In John Demos and Sarane Spence Boocock (eds.), *Turning Points*. (Supplement to *American Journal of Sociology*, Volume 84.) Chicago: University of Chicago Press, 1978.

Modell, John, and Hareven, Tamara K. "Urbanization and the Malleable Household: An Examination of Boarding and Lodging in American Families." *Journal of Marriage and the Family* 35(1973):467–479.

Mohr, James. *Abortion in America: The Origins and Evolution of a National Policy, 1800–1900*. New York: Oxford University Press, 1978.

O'Neill, William L. *Divorce in the Progressive Era*. New Haven, Conn.: Yale University Press, 1967.

Patten, Simon N. *The New Basis of Civilization*. Cambridge, Mass.: Belknap Press of Harvard University Press, 1968(1907).

Philadelphia, Board of Health. *Annual Reports*, various dates.

Pivar, David J. *Purity Crusade: Sexual Morality and Social Control, 1868–1900*. Westport, Conn.: Greenwood Press, 1973.

Preston, Samuel H., and McDonald, John. "The Incidence of Divorce Within Cohorts of American Marriages Contracted Since the Civil War." *Demography* 16(1979):1–25.

Reed, James. *From Private Vice to Public Virtue*. New York: Basic Books, 1978.

Richmond, Mary E. *Child Marriages*. New York: Russell Sage Foundation, 1925.

Rockwood, Lemo D., and Ford, Mary E. *Youth, Marriage, and Parenthood*. New York: John Wiley, 1945.

Rothman, Ellen K. "Sex and Self-Control: Middle-Class Courtship in America, 1770–1870." *Journal of Social History* 15(1981):409–426.

Ryan, Mary P. *Cradle of the Middle Class*. New York: Cambridge University Press, 1981.

Schroeder, Clarence Wesley. *Divorce in a City of 100,000 Population.* Printed Ph.D. thesis, University of Chicago, 1939.

Smith, Daniel Blake. "The Study of the Family in Early America: Trends, Problems, and Prospects." *William and Mary Quarterly* 39(1982):3–28.

Smith, Daniel Scott. "A Demographic History of Colonial New England." *Journal of Economic History* 32(1972):165–183.

Smith, Daniel Scott. "Family Limitation, Sexual Control, and Domestic Feminism in Victorian America." *Feminist Studies* 1(1973a):40–57.

Smith, Daniel Scott. "Parental Power and Marriage Patterns: An Analysis of Trends in Hingham, Massachusetts." *Journal of Marriage and the Family* 35 (1973b):419–428.

Smith, Daniel Scott. "A Homeostatic Demographic Regime: Patterns in West European Family Reconstitution Studies." In Ronald Demos Lee (ed.), *Population Patterns in the Past.* New York: Academic Press, 1977.

Smith-Rosenberg, Carroll. "The Female World of Love and Ritual: Relations Between Women in Nineteenth-Century America." *Signs* 1(1975): 1–29.

Stouffer, Samuel A., and Lazarsfeld, Paul F. *Research Memorandum on the Family in the Depression.* Social Science Research Council Bulletin, Number 29, 1937.

Stouffer, Samuel A., and Spencer, Lyle M. "Marriage and Divorce in Recent Years." *Annals of the American Academy of Political and Social Science* 188(1936):56–69.

Thomas, John, L. "Antislavery and Utopia." In Martin Duberman (ed.), *The Antislavery Vanguard.* Princeton, N.J.: Princeton University Press, 1965.

Thornton, Arland, and Freedman, Deborah. "Changes in Sex Role Attitudes of Women: Evidence from a Panel Study." *American Sociological Review* 44(1979):831–842.

Tocqueville, Alexis de. *Democracy in America*, trans. Phillips Bradley. New York: Knopf, 1945(1835, 1840).

U.S. Department of Health, Education, and Welfare, Public Health Service, National Center for Health Statistics. *Vital Statistics of the United States.* Volumes 3 on Marriage and Divorce, 1964–1979.

Veroff, Joseph; Douvan, Elizabeth; and Kulka, Richard, A. *The Inner American.* New York: Basic Books, 1981.

Wallace, Anthony F. C. *Rockdale.* New York: Knopf, 1978.

Wrigley, E. A. "Marriage, Fertility, and Population Growth in Eighteenth-Century England." In R. B. Outhwaite (ed.), *Marriage and Society.* New York: St. Martin's Press, 1982.

8 *Japan: Culture Versus Industrialization as Determinant of Marital Patterns*

JOY HENDRY

JAPAN PROVIDES AN INTERESTING CASE in the examination
of changes in the institution of marriage. Although an industrialized nation, it has an indigenous tradition completely different
from the West. With only just over 100 years to accomplish several
centuries of development elsewhere, it is now rivaling even the
most advanced nations in technological achievements. Some of the
other chapters of this volume suggest that striking similarities exist in trends associated with marriage in all industrialized
societies, and I would like to consider here the extent to which the
Japanese case does or does not now approximate that of other nations. Kingsley Davis suggests that marriage in Japan is some
thirty years behind that of the United States, but evidence based
on field research indicates that the situation may be more complex.
The Japanese have for more than a millennium been very skillful
at borrowing beneficial aspects of other societies. The last 100
years have witnessed an enormous amount of Western influence,
but the Japanese have also been selective. I hope to argue that
while in many ways marriage in Japan may resemble that of other

197

industrialized nations, it is characterized by persistent basic differences as well. Moreover, some of the new trends in Western countries have quite strong precedents in traditional Japan which until now were absent in Judeo-Christian history.

Statistics from Japan and other industrialized nations that relate directly to technological development are similar and may be dispensed with at once. Medical advances, having greatly increased life expectancy and having provided the means for safe birth control, have made possible a decline in fertility and a later age at first marriage. Similarly, the increasing numbers of housewives in the labor force can no doubt be related to the use of mechanical aids and increasing efficiency in the home. The requirements of industry for a relatively mobile population have caused the decline in the proportion of three- and four-generation families in favor of nuclear families consisting merely of parents and their children.

As for the ideology of marriage, various notions concerning the selection of spouses and expectations of behavior between them have been consciously adopted from Europe and the United States, propagated in the press and in school curricula, and even codified in laws arising from the post-World War II Constitution, written during the Allied Occupation. Nevertheless, at a practical level it is precisely in these areas of spouse selection and of marital behavior that great differences remain. As a Japanese social scientist recently commented about the attitude of most Japanese toward the present Constitution, "They simply do not care much about its applicability to reality" (Kumon 1982). The Constitution rests on the Western ideology of individualism and defines marriage as an institution of equal rights and the concern of only the two parties involved. In practice, however, the direction and sometimes the arrangements of marriage are still very much a family matter. The ideals of individualism often give way to strong obligations to the preceding and following generations. The Japanese word for individualism hardly escapes the connotations of the word for selfishness. Thus the Japanese situation contrasts strongly with Modell's description of historical developments in the United States when there was a rapid move to seeing marriages as *"de novo* productions, valued for the emotional resources they might provide for their members rather than for their contribution to generational continuity" (p. 183).

The Japanese now seek emotional benefits from marriage, although earlier in this century a marriage based on emotional attachment was regarded as foolish, if not bestial, and such a union still often remains an ideal, heavily qualified in practice. To understand the present situation and to make an estimate about where marriage in Japan might go in the future, it seems essential to incorporate a historical dimension.

Let us, then, sketch briefly the changes in the Japanese family and marriage from the latter half of the last century, when Japan was first reopened to Western influence, through one or two reactionary periods, to the present day. This will give some idea of the depth of the influence of industrialization and the likelihood of Japan's further convergence with the Western situation. In particular, an examination of modern Western features of marriage that now exist in Japan will enable us to say whether these features have altered or modified indigenous arrangements, perhaps as necessarily following industrialization, or whether they have themselves been modified by the peculiarly Japanese situation.

The Household

Until 1945, the legal family unit was the "household" or the *ie*.[1] It was usually a residential unit, although members temporarily resident elsewhere were not excluded. It was also often an economic unit, each member contributing labor insofar as he or she could and receiving a share of the common benefits. The household's most important characteristic, however, was its element of continuity. It included not only the living members at any one time, but also the ancestors remembered at the Buddist altar found in most established houses, and the expected descendants. If a house died out, it was considered a great tragedy, and therefore living-members bore the important duty of providing the descendants. Ideally, the eldest son inherited the headship of the house and brought in a wife to bear the descendants, while the other siblings left to set up new houses or to marry into other established ones. If the house produced no male offspring, it could adopt a daughter's husband, or a more distant relative, or even a stranger, as the heir to ensure the continuity. Once such an adoption took place, the new heir assumed the name of the house and forfeited any previous allegiances in order to preside over the adopted household. Similarly, a wife who married in would take leave of her own ancestors and her duty would be to attend full-time to the needs of the house of her husband. She would come under the tutelage of her mother-in-law to learn the ways of this new home, and if she failed to meet the requirements, she could be returned to her original home. Thus, her relationship with her mother-in-law may well have been more important than the one she had with her husband.

The word commonly used for "wife" has the literal meaning of "woman of the house," suggesting the important role she played in the *ie*. It was her duty to take care of her parents-in-law when they grew old, to attend to the ancestral memorials for the well-being of previous members of the family in the after-life, and to bear and rear the children for future generations. If she failed in these duties, or even if she fell ill and could no longer carry them out, it was customary to return her to her natal house and to bring in a new wife to look after the needs of the *ie*, including the rearing of the first wife's children.

Thus the general principle that underlay the *ie* system was that individual members were expected to subordinate their own personal needs and desires to those of the household. Early child-rearing enforced this important idea, and my own recent research suggests that the principles of considering others and placing the needs of the collectivity before one's own personal desires are still inculcated very early in childhood. Nowadays an employee may apply the same principles in serving a company or other place of work, although a housewife's allegiances still remain in the home.

With industrialization, the economic role of the *ie* has been gradually replaced by outside bodies such as factories and companies, although many of these, including the large concerns such as Mitsubishi and Mitsukoshi, were originally established along family lines. In towns and cities where work was available, nuclear families have mushroomed. These were often set up by younger brothers of a successor, who were always expected to leave the *ie* on marriage. In the years preceding World War II, when the mortality rate was decreasing and large families were favored (in fact, encouraged by the authorities for the sake of imperial expansion), there were many noninheriting sons available to take up work away from home in the developing industries. Much has been written by Japanese and Western observers alike about the increase in these new families and an expected decline in the *ie* system, but in fact, despite the abolition of the *ie* as a legal unit during the Allied Occupation, the ideology of the continuing family is far from dead. Although the percentage of nuclear families increased from 59.6 percent of all families in 1955 to 63.9 percent in 1975, the total number of families, which include a parent or parents of the married couple as well as their children, has also increased over this period (*Japan Statistical Yearbook* 1980, p. 32, Table 17). National Census figures show no change in the percentage of nuclear families from 1970 to 1980. Most heads of continuing families hope that they will be able to persuade one of the new generation to carry on the line, possibly also the family business if they have one, and they expect at least to be taken care of in their old age. They also apply pressure on newly married offspring from an early stage to bear descendants.

Of course, there has been a definite shift in residence patterns associated with industrialism. For example, when no children are left in an ancestral home, the grandparents may eventually be brought to the new residence of one of their children. The postwar laws of succession stipulate that all children must be considered equally, rather than the eldest son having sole rights and responsibilities. Apparently it is becoming quite common for elderly people to move to a daughter's home instead of always remaining in or moving to that of the eldest son.[2] Of elderly people aged 65 and over, 75.5 percent live with relatives, and of married couples living with parents, 84 percent live with the husband's parents and 13 percent with those of the wife (Economic Welfare Bureau 1980, p. 17). The three-generation families generally predominate in rural areas, whereas urban areas are more likely to be mixed, with a greater number of nuclear families.[3] However, there is also a tendency for elderly people to maintain living quarters near their children's families, particularly in cities where houses are small. Despite considerable interaction between the generations, each family in this case would be recorded as nuclear. Unlike the Chinese situation, where a shortage of housing may be maintaining intergenerational living, in Japan a lack of space in city houses and apartments is cited as a reason why families that might ideally live together are actually living separately.

The Formation of Marriage

In the traditional family system marriage was clearly a very important step in the process of maintaining the household. For the sake of domestic harmony, the Japanese regarded it as essential that the bride, or adopted husband, be equipped to fit into the particular ways of the house, and there were various means to try to ensure this. In preindustrial Japan there was little mobility among the common people, most of whom lived in rural communities based on particular occupations. Village endogamy was usual so that spouses were likely to share values and expectations about family life. Youth groups, found in many areas, provided opportunities for young people to spend time together, especially when a youth lodge also made it possible for them to pass the night in each other's company. Marriages were usually based on free choice and mutual attraction, but within the limits of the community, subject to the approval of the youth groups, and eventually requiring the final agreement of the parents. Elsewhere, young men would visit the girls of their choice at home. If the parents approved of the match, they would allow their daughter to sleep near the door to receive her lover; if not, they would hide her inside. The girl also had the option of consenting to or refusing such a relationship. Samurai houses, on the other hand, had to look farther afield to find spouses of similar social status. Alliances created between houses on marriage were often important politically. Sometimes a go-between would be necessary to make the arrangements between two relatively distant families.

The first great influx of Western influence in Japan in the nineteenth century helped to abolish strict social divisions as well as the rules against much movement for commoners. Improved roads and an extensive railway network, made possible by the new capitalist economy, enlarged the sphere of choice for marriage partners generally, and some households began to confirm aspirations to higher economic status by arranging marriages with prestigious families in other communities. The youth groups tarnished their traditional image of responsibility with respect to marriages by harassing families involved in these new exogamous unions. Gradually marriages arranged between communities became more common than the endogamous ones.[4] In some areas, cousin marriage was popular because it was said that a related family would be of a similar type. However, as knowledge spread about the genetic problems associated with such a union, marriages arranged through a go-between became the norm.

At the end of the nineteenth century, a strong reaction occurred against the Western influence that had been incorporated into Japanese society. Samurai values were now propagated through the new comprehensive education system. Although there were discussions at an ideological level throughout the period about the advantages of marriages based on pure love of a Christian type,[5] in practice the old samurai family system was strengthened at this time. Marriages were often arranged by elders with only a minimum of discussion with the young people concerned, and old people now report that they were happy to leave a decision of such importance in the hands of their parents. However, it should perhaps be noted that there were also old people in the area of southern Japan where I carried out research whose marriages were based on mutual attraction. They were the lucky ones in that their parents were able to make a reasonably respectable match of their love affairs. Others, however, had experienced exploits such as the night visits, which were common earlier, to no avail, for when it came to marriage, they were forced to put the family first and forget these lovers. The "night visit" had lost its legitimacy as a means to form a union.

At the time when the family system, regarded as the very foundation of Japanese society, was supposedly threatened, there was much propaganda against marriages based on mutual attraction. The reason was that love matches could ignore the needs of the *ie* (for example, Mochizuki 1976, p. 157). The words used for "love" were loaded with connotations of weakness and bestiality, connotations that seemed more appropriate for extramarital affairs than for the serious business of maintaining and allying households. When Japan was attempting to expand as a world power in the period preceding World War II, officials circulated a good deal of propaganda supporting traditional values. The propaganda maintained that filial piety was second only to loyalty to the Emperor, and since all households were regarded as ultimately related to the Imperial Line, loyalty to the Emperor became somewhat of an extension of filial piety.

After Japan's defeat in World War II, it experienced a renewed interest in the ideology of an apparently superior system. The hopes of the previous idealists were now codified in the new Constitution, which stipulated: "Marriage shall be based only on the mutual consent of both sexes and it shall be maintained through mutual cooperation with the equal rights of husband and wife as a basis."[6] Love could now be sought between partners, and mutual attraction became a relatively respectable element of marriage again.

Today, partners no longer need their parents' permission to marry once they are over the age of majority (20), whereas previously a man had to be 30 and a woman 25 before they were legally free to make their own decisions. Many young people express the hope that they will meet their own partner. A lengthening courtship pattern seems to have evolved, including "dating," "going steady," and a stage of "private understanding" of the other's intentions before the couple will initiate plans to marry (Mochizuki 1976, pp. 165–167). In the area of my research, such marriages seem to succeed quite well as long as the lovers come from reasonably compatible households, especially when they are setting up a new house of their own. An inheriting son, however, must select a wife who will be able to maintain good relations with his mother. It is still not unusual for a love affair to be curtailed in the interests of the household.

The arranged marriage has been altered, but it has by no means disappeared, nor does it look likely to do so. At first arranged entirely by elders, it has gradually been softened, first by the exchange of photographs and then by the inclusion of a meeting at which the prospective partners can see and eventually talk to each other. Nowadays, such a meeting is often followed by "dates," *odeto* in the Japanese terminology, and either side may terminate negotiations if it experiences doubts about the suitability of the match. Some people participate in a large number of such meetings until they finally arrange a marriage. One of the chief advantages of the system is that the go-between possesses a number of institutionalized ways to retreat without loss of face for either side. Thus, young people are presented with a variety of possible partners from the right social background, the ideal being that eventually they will fall in love with one, although this is by no means always necessary.[7] Unlike the situation in the United States, where, as John Modell has pointed out, the verbal and behavioral vocabulary of dating spreads rapidly, dating in Japan still seems to be rather limited. The arranged meeting is thus extremely practical and convenient.

Parents continue to express concern for the welfare of their descendants and so take pains to investigate the family of a prospective son-in-law or daughter-in-law for hereditary diseases or propensities toward madness or criminality. An outcaste class, now officially abolished, is also avoided. The go-between also proves useful for these investigations. A love match may be investigated in the same way. Young people are advised to ask their lovers whether they have had German measles and mumps before they agree to marry them. Also, people begin to suspect character defects or family problems if a person does not announce an engagement after the optimal age of marriage, about 24 for a woman and 27 for a man. Thus, in practice, young people may start out by seeking a love match of their own initiation but wind up, as they approach the optimum age, being less and less averse to participating in the meetings arranged by well-meaning uncles, aunts, or bosses.

In other ways, too, marriage in Japan is still more than a desired state between two people who happen to fall in love. It is an occasion that causes families to incur enormous expense. The gifts exchanged before the marriage ceremony, the trousseau taken by the bride to her new home, and the reception itself, when neighbors and workmates as well as the family and relatives are usually feasted in style, all provide opportunities for conspicuous displays of wealth, which in turn lead to years of saving for the future marriages of one's offspring. A marriage ceremony provides families with an opportunity to demonstrate tangible evidence of their social and economic status and with one of the few ways to confirm aspirations to a higher status.[8]

Marriage also allows young people to confirm their adult status and to make a statement to society about their future plans. Although at age 20 there is a ceremony to celebrate the attainment of adulthood, in a rural community at least, a man is not really eligible to become a household head until he marries (Hendry 1981a, pp. 206–207). Many young men leave the community for a while, with the result that until they do actually marry, their families are uncertain about whether their sons will settle in the family home or not. Similarly, second and other sons who work nearby remain in their natal home until they marry and set up a new house. A girl who has no brother to inherit her family home may be noncommittal about receiving a husband as the adopted heir until a concrete situation suggests itself. In companies, too, labor mobility is much more unlikely once an employee has settled down and found himself a wife (Clark 1979, p. 187). Employers often become go-betweens for their employees, a practice that perhaps expresses a permanent long-term interest. Japanese society views marriage as an important and serious step in the life cycle; only a tiny minority of Japanese people fail to marry eventually.[9]

Marital Relations

Despite the recent emphasis on "love" as an important element in the formation of marriage, couples of some years' conjugal standing rarely describe their relationship as one of "love" and instead describe it as one of "sympathy" or "fellow feeling" (dōjō), or just "endurance" or "tolerance" (gaman). While modern couples, who tend to emphasize the emotional bond, may be creating a new kind of relationship, Japanese scholars still claim that the natural bond parents share through their children is more important than the contractual one they have created between themselves. The linguist Takao Suzuki, for example, suggests that the underlying definition of their relationship gives Japanese couples no need to reconfirm and strengthen their contractual state as Americans do by using "saccharine terms" such as "honey" and "darling" and by exchanging gifts on wedding aniversaries and birthdays (Suzuki 1978, pp. 136–137). Indeed, many Japanese regard kissing and hugging as inappropriate behavior in front of the children.

On the whole, expectations for a marital relationship are lower in Japan than in the West. In the country and in family businesses couples may work together, but company employees and other men who work outside the home often return so late in the evening that they see little of their wives and children. The ideal images of the home as a "haven of support, love, comfort, and moral order," as cited in the chapter by Alan Stone, or of families as "comfortable young homeowning commuter families" do exist in Japan; indeed, the invented Japanese word myhomism captures these images well. In practice, however, a man is expected to put company demands before those of his family, so that even a previous arrangement for a birthday party or a wedding anniversary would have to be shelved if unexpected work came up. A man who complained in such circumstances would be considered selfish. The Japanese situation exhibits parallels with the Chinese. Margery Wolf points out that the encouragement of a strong relationship between husband and wife should not go so far as to turn them into self-indulgent lovers (p. 229). Here, too, the previous loyalty to the family should now be turned to the demands of the workplace.

Recreation is more often taken with peers of the same sex or with workmates. In Tokyo and other large cities, the huge number of bars and other entertainments with attendant women provide plenty of opportunity for men to enjoy themselves without their wives. Although young families may be seen out together with children, and summer holidays by the sea have become rather popular, these holidays usually last only a couple of days, and groups of men or older women away from home together are probably just as common. Parties of Japanese men certainly abound in well-known resorts in other Eastern countries. Younger women, who may be very involved with child-rearing, tend to spend time with other mothers, often with those who live in the same neighborhood or who participate in the same P.T.A. group. Newly married couples may continue to go out together after the now rather statutory honeymoon, and groups of older couples are sometimes seen at resorts or on foreign trips, but baby-sitting arrangements for the sake of parental entertainment are virtually nonexistent.

The putative subordinate role of Japanese women receives much publicity in the West, but Western assumptions may somewhat confuse the actual situation for Japanese women. In an extended family, the young wife is initially regarded as subordinate to the senior wife, but she gradually gains status within the house, and is eventually regarded as its mistress. This changing of status is not unlike the way men rise with age and experience through the ranks of a company, although it is true that the same cannot be said for women in that milieu. With regard to male/female interaction, strictly distinguished roles exist, including that of women to serve their menfolk with meals and other refreshments, but a woman may also have the responsibility of administering the house's finances.

The wife's role in the nuclear family evolved in the early part of this century from a Japanese interpretation of the European concept of "better-half,"[10] a concept that perhaps offers less prestige than women possessed when they reached their ultimate position in the extended household. Japanese women today, however, are often rather proud and defiant about the value of their domestic role. Women supervise the care and education of the children and value this responsibility highly, reflecting a different view of children from the one that prevails in the West.[11] It is said, for example, that since the soul of the three-year-old lasts till 100, much time and attention should be devoted to molding the child's character in the early years. Housewives in middle class families also now concern themselves to no small degree with the education of their children, often taking pains to keep up with everything the class is studying to make sure that their child does not fall behind the expected standards. Many women also go out to work when their children reach school age, but it is regarded as selfish to neglect them in the early period. Substantial aid from men remains rare, although some husbands help in the home or bathe the children if they are home from work in time.

The Wider Position of Women in Japanese Society

The majority of women in Japan also participate in economically productive activities during at least part of their lifetimes (see Table 8.1). In a traditional household with its own enterprise, the younger wife may concentrate on the business and leave child-rearing to a less physically able grandparent. The same system enables a young wife to go out to work. Most women also work before they marry. Although it is still reported that some companies expect their female employees to leave upon marrying (Clark 1979, pp. 118, 194), an increasingly popular leave scheme is available for public and some other employees, consisting of a year's leave after the birth of a child, with return to the job guaranteed. By law, women can have maternity leave six weeks before and six weeks after birth, and when they are back on the job they must be allowed feeding time of 30 minutes twice a day until the baby is a year old.[12] In fact, many mothers in nuclear families prefer the leave scheme, since they wish to continue working but also believe that they should care for the baby at home at least until it is one

Table 8.1

Work Force Participation of Japanese Women

Year	Percentage of the Labor Force Comprised of Women	Percentage of Women Aged over 15 Who Are Gainfully Employed	Percentage of Women Aged over 15 and Not In School Who Are Gainfully Employed
1960	40.7	54.5	58.3
1965	39.8	50.6	55.7
1970	39.3	49.9	52.9
1975	37.3	45.7	49.6
1980	38.7	47.6	51.8

SOURCE: Rōdō Shō Fujin Shōnen Kyoko, 1981, pp. 43–47.

year old. It is reported that only 1.7 percent of babies under one year are taken to day nurseries or other facilities, while the remaining 98.3 percent are taken care of in their own homes (Japan, Economic Welfare Bureau 1980, p. 23).

As Table 8.2 illustrates, the proportion of women in the labor force who are married has increased considerably over the past twenty years. This increase has been correlated with the rise in women's educational level and an increase in disposable time resulting from a lightening of the burdens of housekeeping and childcare (Japan, Ministry of Labor 1981, p. 3). The average number of children per family is now only two, whereas before World War II

Table 8.2

Marital-Status Distribution of Women Employees

Year	Total Number of Women Employees (in Millions)	Percentage		
		Unmarried	Married	Widowed
1955	5.07	64.7	20.9	14.4
1960	7.10	62.4	25.0	12.6
1965	9.20	54.1	34.3	11.6
1970	10.92	48.6	40.1	11.2
1975	11.59	37.9	51.3	10.9

SOURCE: "Women of Japan." *About Japan Series 5.* Foreign Press Center, Japan, 1977.

it was five.[13] Nevertheless, a recent survey indicates that some 50 percent of women want to give up work when their children are born (Japan, Economic Welfare Bureau 1980, p. 23), and the recent major increase in the number of married women going out to work seems to be for those in their thirties and forties (Japan, Ministry of Labor 1981, p.1). In fact, Table 8.1 shows a decrease in the percentage of all women in the labor force from 1960 to 1975, although the figures began to rise again in 1980.

The educational level of women has improved considerably in the last twenty years. The number of female graduates of four-year universities increased from 16,448 in 1960 to 93,698 in 1980, and the ratio of female to all university graduates in employment increased from 10.6 percent in 1960 to 21.6 percent in 1980 (Japan, Ministry of Labor 1981, p. 3). In 1976, 93.5 percent of girls were entering high school, as opposed to 91.7 percent of boys, and as many as 33.6 percent were continuing their education beyond that by entering a university or junior college (Japan, Foreign Press Center 1977, p. 4). It is becoming possible for women to be highly successful in careers such as medicine and teaching, for example, and to maintain marriages and families simultaneously. Women who work and care for a family often take advantage of the traditional childcare role of the grandmother. However, the day-care facilities have also increased enormously since World War II.[14]

Outside marriage, possibilities for women also exist in the service industries and in the world of entertainment. In traditional Japan, daughters were often leased for a period of ten to twelve years to undergo training to become accomplished entertainers of the *geisha* variety. The hostesses of today usually enter the trade by choice, to work either for a period before marriage or to avoid poverty caused by the dissolution of their previous marriages. Not all such women are prostitutes; some are respectable entrepreneurs; some stay in such activities for only a short time to make money quickly, while others devote their lives to pursuing and teaching the traditional arts of entertainment (see, for example, Lebra et al. 1976, chaps. 6 and 7).

Feminism exists in Japan, indeed an international journal is published there in English by an organization called Feminist, Inc. Addressing itself to the problems of women seeking independence, the movement is still very marginal. As Pharr has pointed out, the views consonant with the radical feminist perspective in other countries are "very much at odds with dominant thinking" in Japan (Pharr 1981, p. 71). The continuing strength of marriage and the high value placed on the rearing and education of children erode the strength of the feminist movement. In addition, as Davis and van den Oever have suggested, feminism has a connection with the lack of family commitments in later life (Davis and Van den Oever 1982, p. 21), whereas in Japan older women may maintain useful roles by rearing their grandchildren. Otherwise, middle-aged women who have reared their children and who find no vital role left to play, may express an interest in a less radical type of feminism. The increasing trend for married women to return to work may solve this empty-nest problem. If so, their situation would recall that of the preindustrial period, when most women participated in economic activities, at that time usually activities of the household.

Divorce and Remarriage

The Japanese view divorce as highly undesirable, a position consistent with the importance they attach to marriage. The divorce rate is considerably lower than that for other industrial nations (see Table 8.3), and the chance for remarriage remains far below that of the United States, for example. Nevertheless, the divorce rate is increasing and the circumstances surrounding divorce appear to be changing quite rapidly. In the latter part of the last century, the divorce rate was actually much higher than published figures be-

Table 8.3

Recent Changes in the Divorce Rate in Several Countries
(per 1,000 persons)

Country	1966	1970	1975
Japan	0.80	0.93	1.07
West Germany	0.98	1.26	1.73
Hungary	2.02	2.21	2.46
England and Wales	0.78	1.18	2.43
U.S.A.	2.54	3.46	4.82
Sweden	1.32	1.61	3.14

SOURCE: Ministry of Welfare, Japan, White Paper 1979, p. 28 (translation).

cause of the practice of delaying the registration of marriage until
the union appeared to be successful. One estimate put the number
of divorces per 1,000 population at 3.39 for 1883 (Kawashima and
Steiner 1960, p. 214). In those days the usual explanation for divorce was that the wife (or adopted husband) did not fit in with
the ways of the house and that a new spouse had therefore to be
sought. In such cases the outsider returned to his or her original
household and usually remarried. Any children of the first union
remained in the house of their birth and maintained little subsequent contact with the natural parent who had left. Since the patrilocal situation was more common than the matrilocal one, it was
more often the woman who returned, and, indeed, the law in the
early part of the period made it much easier for a man to divorce
his wife than vice versa.[15]

At the beginning of the twentieth century, the divorce rate began a steady decline. This has been attributed to increased Western
influence, which championed the rights of the individual, brought
in almost universal education for boys and girls alike, and increased employment opportunities for unmarried women. The net
result caused a delay in the average age at marriage and more freedom of choice for women selecting a marital partner. The increase
in nuclear families also was responsible for the decrease in the divorce rate since it reduced the likelihood of conflict between a
mother-in-law and her son's wife (Kawashima and Steiner 1960;
Iwasaki 1930, 1931). Despite a law passed in 1898 that designated
mutual consent as sufficient grounds for divorce, the decrease in
the divorce rate persisted throughout the reactionary period, although perhaps the continuing practice of delaying registration
had some effect on the decrease. In 1942 the divorce rate reached a
low of only 0.64 per 1,000 persons, as compared with 0.94 in 1921
(Japan, Bureau of Statistics 1980, p. 38). After World War II, the
rate jumped to 1.02 in 1947, after which it declined again until
1960. Since 1960, however, the divorce rate has been increasing
(Japan, Bureau of Statistics 1980).

Japanese analysts associate the recent increase with factors
similar to those used previously to account for the decrease, such
as the increasing economic independence of women and the
mounting expectation of an emotional bond between husband and
wife (Japan, Economic Welfare Bureau 1980, p. 10). Indeed, an earlier scholar predicted that these same factors would eventually

lead to an increase (Iwasaki 1983, p. 583). Divorce certainly seems to have increased rather than decreased as the courtship period has been extended, but the two factors may not necessarily be correlated. Today, divorce seems to be a different phenomenon from what it was in the earlier part of the industrializing period. In the community of mostly extended households where I carried out research, the divorce rate has declined so dramatically that no recent cases of divorce had occurred, although the family records had numerous examples at the end of the nineteenth century (Hendry 1981a, p. 102). Recent cases known to my informants were almost always in urban areas and involved households limited to a nuclear family. In the event of divorce, children are increasingly more likely to stay with their mothers (see Table 8.4), although divorced women rarely receive financial compensation of any worth and are much less likely than men to remarry (Japan, Economic Welfare Bureau 1980, pp. 10–11; Japan, Foreign Press Center 1977, p. 16). Indeed, according to a 1972 opinion poll, 83 percent of divorced women said that they had no desire to remarry (Japan, Foreign Press Center 1977, p. 16; Mochizuki 1976, p. 164), suggesting a general disillusionment with marriage altogether. Men, on the other hand, are more keen to remarry, some seeking divorce for this purpose (Japan, Economic Welfare Bureau 1980, pp. 10–11) and thus reflecting a situation different from the previous one in which a man could easily maintain a mistress outside the home. Adultery used to be a crime if committed by a woman but was not even grounds for divorce if committed by a man. Today, however, the law supports the expectation of mutual fidelity (Tamura 1976, pp. 145–149). The increasing divorce rate partially results from a change in behavior in accordance with the law, and partly from a shift to registering marriage earlier (Ota 1981, p. 14). An investigation of the current factors associated with divorce in Japan could be a fruitful area of future research. Court cases account for only 1 percent of divorces, while 90 percent are based on mutual consent and the rest are arranged by arbitration (Japan, Foreign Press Center, p. 16). The go-between who arranged the marriage is often called in when problems arise.

Despite the influence of Western ideas, one aspect of divorce that seems to have remained intact from earlier times is the way children are isolated from the estranged parent. The Japanese expressed surprise when the biological mother of Lady Diana

Table 8.4

Changes in the Partner with Whom Children Stay in Cases of Divorce (in percent)

	One Child		Two Children			Three Children		
Year	With Father	With Mother	Both with Father	Both with Mother	One Each	All with Father	All with Mother	Other
1955	53.3	46.7	40.8	35.2	23.9	36.4	33.2	30.5
1965	47.6	52.4	43.1	37.1	19.8	40.7	34.1	25.2
1975	34.9	65.1	32.9	51.1	15.5	30.6	46.3	23.1
1978	28.2	71.8	27.0	60.9	12.1	24.6	55.4	20.0

SOURCE: Ministry of Welfare, Japan, White Paper 1979, p. 28 (translation).

Spencer attended her daughter's wedding to Prince Charles while Lady Diana's stepmother did not attend. Their surprise reflects the high value that the Japanese place on rearing a child, a role that the stepparent assumes. Thus, the old concepts of the *ie* system, stressing continuity rather than genetic ties, and the general importance that Japanese accord to child-rearing still maintain a strong hold on Japanese divorce behavior.

Living Together

Living together is another custom found in modern Japan which reflects Western influence but also has historical precedents. A wide variety of unmarried couples take up residence together. At one extreme are pairs of young people who reject the traditional values of marriage, who state that they have no intention of ever formalizing their union, and who base their relationship on mutual attraction and a sharing of ideas. In her recent book, *Political Women in Japan*, Susan Pharr described a relation of this sort between political activists of a left-wing group known as Radical Egalitarians (Pharr 1981, p. 67). Other couples, however, live together for the purpose of having a period of relative freedom from social constraints, perhaps while they are studying or working away from their families. They marry later, sometimes to the person with whom they cohabited, sometimes to quite different people, perhaps introduced through the arranged meeting system.

Although Western influence has made its mark, attitudes concerning extramarital sex usually have been freer in Japan than in the West, especially for men. Some young couples nowadays seem to make it a condition of their informal union that each partner be free to engage in outside liaisons if they desire, but the attitude that a man is freer than his wife or mistress to engage in outside exploits seems to persist. Concubinage was common in the past; indeed, the number of concubines a man could support was a measure of his status. At the beginning of the modern period, the concubine had legal status, and her children could be recognized as legitimate offspring.[16] It was Western influence that led Japan in 1882 to do away with this legal support (Aoyama 1976, p. 140), but some examples of concubinage may still be compared with the *casa chica* or second wife of Latin American countries.

Illegitimacy declined from 9 percent of all births at the beginning of the century to 1 percent in 1964, but this is probably due to the increasing availability of contraceptives and safe ways of terminating pregnancy rather than to the decline of concubinage (Hartley 1970, pp. 78–91). There is still little stigma attached to being illegitimate. As Seward has pointed out in his "unorthodox approach to Japanese," it is useless to try to use the Japanese word for illegitimate child as an insult in Japan. The fact that the previous emperor was illegitimate seems to perturb the average Japanese not at all (Seward 1968, p. 167).

The modern Japanese practice of living together recalls similar situations from the past. The Japanese often recall an ancient practice known as foot-in marriage (*ashiire-kon*), whereby a couple divided its time between its two families before settling together, perhaps working for the man's parents and spending the night at the woman's house, or even spending a period sleeping together at a youth lodge. If the union appeared successful, the couple eventually assumed control over the man's house when his parents retired. This practice has also been called "trial marriage," but the Japanese folklorist Omachi Tokuzo has interpreted it rather as a form of transition from a matrilocal to a patrilocal system.[17] Bride stealing, another traditional practice, sometimes took place when the parents disapproved of a prospective union. The couple would run away, perhaps aided by other members of a youth group, and once they had cohabited for some time, the parents would often give their approval. Such a situation may still arise, providing another explanation why unmarried couples may live together.[18]

A final form of cohabitation is a long-established, unregistered union which the community nevertheless regards as a marriage. These unions crystallize for various reasons, including the reasons mentioned above or just plain ignorance about the need for registration. This type of union falls into the category of "common-law marriage" (*naien* in Japanese) rather than in the category of living together (*dōsei*), a more temporary arrangement that lacks the intention to marry. Legally, despite the lack of registration, the union is often treated as a quasi-marriage, with rights of compensation for one-sided dissolution, widow's pension in case of accident at work, inheritance on death, and the right of a wife and children to take the family name after years of customary usage (Ota 1981). However, if the couple does not register because one of the partners is already married, then the situation of the third party must be taken into consideration before the union can be regarded legally as a quasi-marriage. Social recognition of the union as a quasi-marriage seems to increase if the union is long-standing while the old marriage is virtually defunct (Ota 1981, pp. 7–10). In the final analysis, however, the act of marriage seems necessary for legal protection (Ota 1981, p. 6), and people who overtly reject the marriage system probably put themselves in a questionable legal situation.

Conclusion

It can be seen, then, that many aspects of Western marriage, including its newer developments, also exist in Japan. There is no denying the enormous influence from Europe and the United States in the Japanese family system. Nevertheless, after over 100 years of contact with the Western world, a hard core remains that is basically Japanese in origin. As a Japanese analyst wrote a few years ago, reflecting on a survey of young people's views, in marriage there is an inner part that seems not to have changed at all and an outer layer that seems to have changed a lot (Mochizuki 1976, p. 161). Marriage may not always emphasize the continuity of the household, though it still has a function in this respect, but it has by no means lost its association with status, with the completion of a transition to adulthood, and with the permanent and proper way to create a family. An emotional bond in marriage based on mutual attraction is gaining importance, even if it is not quite the same as "love" in the Christian sense. As it turns out, this concept is not entirely new in Japan, for it was a common basis for marriage in the preindustrial period. Nor is the trial marriage, which has shocked the older generation in the West, without precedent in Japan. The freer attitudes toward sex, characteristic of our new "permissive" generations, have long been accepted in certain quarters of Japanese society. Perhaps one could point to the new roles of women as a part of Japanese society that has evolved according to Western dictates without retaining its core of Japanese tradition. However, given a historical span, it would be possible to show that women previously had considerable power and status in Japan. The novels by Murasaki Shikibu (*The Tale of Genji*) and (*The Pillowbook of*) *Sei Shonagon*, written nearly a thousand years ago, are well-known in the West, and the picture painted in the recent best-seller *Shogun* is by no means entirely false. The ultimate Imperial Ancestress is a woman, and considerable evidence exists that women had very powerful religious roles in ancient times (see, for instance, Wada 1978, pp. 15–18). Indeed, the writer of the foreword to the 1978 edition of "Feminist International" writes, "While women in the West seek to create a women's culture, Japanese women seek to revive the women's culture that has always been an important, if sometimes unrecognized, source of their civilization."

I have perhaps exaggerated some of the similarities between modern practices and those found in preindustrial times in order to make a point, but when one considers how rapidly and completely the inculcation of samurai values was accomplished during the first major reaction to Western influence, and how quickly and efficiently the mechanics of industrialization have been made successful, one can only conclude that other Western values are being rejected at a very basic level. For example, there has for long been talk about individualism in Japan, but the detailed examination of early child-rearing practices I carried out in 1981 seems to suggest that individualism is far from being accepted as an appropriate value to inculcate in young children.[19] Rather, they are trained early in consideration for others, the need to avoid causing trouble, and the requirements of the wider group, be it family, school class, or, later, company, before fulfilling their personal desires. The emphasis in the new Constitution on individual rights and freedom is taught at an ideological level in schools, however, and young people between school age and marriage may be very individualistic. They may live away from home and pursue their own interests, even to the extent of cohabiting with a boyfriend or girlfriend. Certainly in the anonymity of urban areas it is possible to evade social pressures from the family and community, and Japanese society is complex enough to allow some members to continue to live in such a free way. For most young people, it is precisely marriage that brings them into responsible adult life, and that causes them to place personal desires in the context of community needs, whether they be company loyalty, care of the elderly, or the rearing of the next generation.

Japanese people realize that many of the strengths of their industrial system lie in traditional values. They are now reconsidering some of the Western values they have attempted to adopt during the past century. As has been the case in the past, a period of great receptivity to outside influence is being followed by a period of consolidation. In fact, in many other ways, Japan seems to be going through another reversion to tradition. Festivals that had virtually died out in the immediate postwar period have recently been revived and have grown in size in the last few years. Similarly, the activities of traditional groups such as "children's clubs," "youth groups," and "old peoples associations" have increased.[20] The organization of Japanese companies, far from adopting Western ways in furthering their international activities, is, on the contrary, apparently influencing Western practice.[21] With respect to marriage, the Japanese are already practising ideas advocated elsewhere in this volume for improvement of marriage in the West, such as a more practical and calculating approach (Stone) and a greater concern with the welfare of children (Peres and Pasternack).

The traditional family system in Japan worked well. It will not disappear overnight. Of course, modifications have occurred, but I suggest that these changes remain less drastic than those that accompanied industrialization in Europe, despite the speed of industrialization in Japan's case. The system of arranged meetings for marriage, the role of the go-between, and the maintenance of close relations with the extended family, benefiting mothers who wish to work outside the home and parents who eventually cannot care for themselves, all possess considerable advantages. And if divorce proceedings in the United States appear fairer, at least for women, consider the ultimate advantages for children of being reared in a new stable home rather than being shunted to and fro between their natural parents. Some of the drawbacks of individual rights have been noticed and are as yet largely avoided by the Japanese.

In sum, then, it seems that marriage in Japan is showing little sign of weakening. True, as elsewhere, people live together, marry later, and have fewer children. Indeed, the period before marriage probably plays an important role in resolving the conflict between a nationally prevailing ideology of individualism and the difficulty of its application in everyday life. Even the low fertility is seen as a national need to curb population growth. The children that one does have, though, must be carefully prepared for their own contribution to society. The importance of this is witnessed in a book on pre-kindergarten child-rearing, written by no less a figure than the head of the Sony Corporation. The emotional bond between spouses is important, but an excess of attention with this concern can diminish it to mere self-indulgence.

NOTES

1.   A more detailed discussion of the *ie* is to be found in many works, some of which are referred to in Hendry (1981a, p. 15). Notable are Ariga (1954) and Dore (1971, p. 9ff).

2.   See Japan, Economic Welfare Bureau (1980, p. 17); cf. Dore (1971, pp. 131–133) and Koyama (1966, p. 109).

3.   During research carried out in 1981 in a provincial city in Chiba prefecture, I obtained the following figures for the families of children enrolled in three kindergartens: in a predominantly farming area, only 12.4 percent of the children lived in nuclear families; in a predominantly urban area, 67.6 percent of the children lived in nuclear families; and in a private kindergarten, drawing on the better-off families in both areas, 54.4 percent lived in nuclear families.

4.   Detailed discussion of previous practices for the formation of marriage, and their change during the Meiji period may be found in Kamishima (1969), Ariga (1948), and Yanagida (1948), among others, and less comprehensively, but in English, in Hendry (1981a, pp. 23–26), where more references are available; Varner (1977, pp. 459–483); and Yanagida (1957, pp. 161ff).

5. Tamaki (1976, pp. 132–135) and Takamure (1963, pp. 243–255). An excellent summary in English of the debate at an intellectual level is to be found in Dore (1971, pp. 92–94).

6. U.S. Department of State Publication, No. 2836. Discussion of the provisions for the family in the new Civil Code are to be found in Steiner (1950, pp. 169–184).

7. More detailed discussion of arranged meetings and the role of the go-between is to be found in Hendry (1981a, chap. 4).

8. Hendry (1981a, p. 191); cf. Nakane (1967, pp. 158–159) and Dore (1953, pp. 67–68).

9. According to figures published in 1970, 98 percent of men and 96 percent of women had experienced marriage by the time they reached the age of 50, but, as the author of the paper in which they are published points out, these figures would be even higher if they included unregistered unions (Mochizuki 1976, pp. 160–161).

10. The content and influence of this ideal is discussed in Kamishima (1969, pp. 150–155) and in Takamure (1963, pp. 148–154).

11. This is a topic I discuss briefly in Hendry 1984, and in some detail in a book to be published in 1986 by Manchester University Press.

12. Labor Standards Law (*Rōdōkijunhō*), Numbers 65 and 66.

13. Japan, Foreign Press Center (1977, p. 4). More detail is available in an article published by Japan, Ministry of Foreign Affairs (1976).

14. The total number of day nurseries in Japan has increased from less than 2,000 in 1947 to 20,604 in 1978 (Early Childhood Education Association of Japan 1979, p. 98).

15. More detail about these laws, including further references to other sources, are to be found in Hendry (1981a, pp. 21–22).

16. Aoyama (1976, pp. 139–140). Other sources are referred to in Hendry (1981a), pp. 19–20.

17. This practice has been discussed in English by Omachi (1973, pp. 251–266) and Yanagida (1957, pp. 162–163). The practice of "trial marriage" is also described in a study of Okinawa by Maretzki and Maretzki (1963, p. 89).

18. I have given a couple of examples in Hendry (1981a, pp. 120–121), where there are also a number of references to Japanese discussions of the practice.

19. I presented a paper on the topic "Individualism and Individuality in Modern Japan" at the 1982 conference of the British Association of Japanese Studies, which is being published in the 1982 proceedings of the plenary session. Other papers in the session were on the topic of individualism in modern Japan.

20. For a discussion of these groups and other references to works on them, see Hendry (1981b).

21. See, for example, Dore (1973, chaps. 13 and 15).

REFERENCES

Aoyama, Michio. *Meiji Kon'inhō no Keisei to Sono Tokushitsu* (The Shape and Characteristics of Meiji Marriage Law). In Itsuo Emori (ed.), *Nihon no Kon'in* (Japanese Marriage). Tokyo: Gendai no Esupuri, No. 104, 1976.

Ariga, Kizaemon. *Nihon Kon'in Shiron* (A Study of the History of Marriage in Japan). Tokyo: Nikko Shoin, 1948.

Ariga, Kizaemon. "The Family in Japan." *Marriage and Family Living* 16(1954):362–373.

Clark, Rodney. *The Japanese Company.* New Haven, Conn.: Yale University Press, 1979.

Davis, Kingsley, and Van den Oever, Pietronella. "Demographic Foundations of New Sex Roles." *Population and Development Review* (September 1982).

Dore, Ronald P. "Japanese Rural Fertility: Some Social and Economic Factors." *Population Studies* 7(1953):67–68.

Dore, Ronald P. *City Life in Japan.* Berkeley: University of California Press, 1971.

Dore, Ronald P. *British Factory–Japanese Factory.* Berkeley: University of California Press, 1973.

Early Childhood Education Association of Japan. *Early Childhood Education and Care in Japan.* Tokyo: Child Honsha, 1979.

Hartley, S. F. "The Decline of Illegitimacy in Japan." *Social Problems* 18(1970):78–91.

Hendry, Joy. *Marriage in Changing Japan.* London: Croom Helm, 1981a.

Hendry, Joy. "Tomodachi-kō: Age-Mate Groups in Northern Kyushu." *Proceedings of the British Association for Japanese Studies* 6 (1981b).

Hendry, Joy. "Becoming Japanese: A Social Anthropological View of Child-Rearing." *Journal of the Anthropological Society of Oxford* 15(1984): 101–118.

Iwasaki, Yasu. "Divorce in Japan." *American Journal of Sociology* 36(1930):435–446.

Iwasaki, Yasu. "Why the Divorce Rate Has Declined in Japan." *American Journal of Sociology* 36(1931):568–583.

Japan, Bureau of Statistics. *Japan Statistical Yearbook,* 1980.

Japan, Economic Welfare Bureau (Economic Planning Agency). *Current State and Future Problems of the Japanese Household—Outline,* 1980.

Japan, Foreign Press Center. *The Women of Japan. About Japan Series,* No. 5, 1977.

Japan, Ministry of Foreign Affairs. *Report from the Japanese Side in the World Fertility Survey. Information Bulletin* 1(1976).

Japan, Ministry of Labor. *Actual Situation of Female Labor—Outline.* Japan: Foreign Press Center, 1981.

Kamishima, Jirō. *Nihonjin no Kekkonkan* (The Japanese View of Marriage). Tokyo: Chikuma Sosho, 1969.

Kawashima, Takeyoshi, and Steiner, Kurt. "Modernization and Divorce

Rate Trends in Japan." *Economic Development and Cultural Change* 9(1960):213–240.

Koyama, Takashi. "The Significance of Relatives at the Turning Point of the Family System in Japan." *The Sociological Review, Monograph 10*, "Japanese Sociological Studies." Keele University, 1966.

Kumon, Shumpei. "Some Principles Governing the Thought and Behavior of Japanists (Contextualists)." *Journal of Japanese Studies* 8(1982): 5–28.

Lebra, Joyce; Paulson, Joy; and Powers, Elizabeth. *Women in Changing Japan.* Boulder, Colo.: Westview Press, 1976.

Maretzki, Thomas W., and Maretzki, Hatsumi. "Taira. An Okinawan Village." In Beatrice Whiting (ed.), *Six Cultures.* New York: John Wiley, 1963.

Mochizuki, Takashi. *Gendai Nihon no Kekkon no Keitai* (The Shape of Marriage in Modern Japan). In Itsuo Emori (ed.), *Nihon no Kon'in* (Japanese Marriage). Tokyo: Gendai no Esupuri, No. 104, 1976.

Nakane, Chie. *Kinship and Economic Organization in Rural Japan. L.S.E. Monographs in Social Anthropology*, University of London. The Athlone Press, 1967.

Omachi, Tokuzō. "Ashiire-kon." In Richard M. Dorson (ed.), *Studies in Japanese Folklore.* Port Washington, N.Y.: Kennikat Press, 1973.

Ota, Takeo. "Die jetzige Lage des Rechtsschutzes für 'Naien' Beziehung und künftige Probleme." *Zinbun* 17(1981):1–15.

Pharr, Susan J. *Political Women in Japan.* Berkeley: University of California Press, 1981.

Seward, Jack. *Japanese in Action.* New York: Weatherhill, 1968.

Steiner, Kurt. "Revisions of the Civil Code of Japan: Provisions Affecting the Family." *Far Eastern Quarterly* 9(1950):169–184.

Suzuki, Takao. *Japanese and the Japanese.* (Translated by Miura Akira). Tokyo: Kodansha International, 1978.

Takamure, Itsue. *Nihon Kon'inshi* (A History of Marriage in Japan). Tokyo: Nihon Rekishi Shinsho, 1963.

Tamaki, Hajime. "Kindai no Kekkonkan" (Modern Views of Marriage). In Itsuo Emori (ed.), *Nihon no Kon'in* (Japanese Marriage). Tokyo: Gendai no Esupuri, No. 104, 1976.

Tamura, Goro. "Otto no Teisō Gimu." In Itsuo Emori (ed.), *Nihon no Kon'in.* (Japanese Marriage). Tokyo: Gendai no Esupuri, No. 104, 1976.

U.S. Department of State. *Constitution of Japan (translation). Publication No. 2836, Far Eastern Series 22.*

Varner, Richard E. "The Organized Peasant: The Wakamonogumi in the Edo Period." *Monumenta Nipponica* 32(1977):459–483.

Wada, Yoshiko. "Woman and Her Power in the Japanese Emperor System." *Feminist Japan* 4(1978):15–18.

Yanagida, Kunio. *Kon'in no Hanashi* (On Marriage). Tokyo: Iwanami Shoten, 1948.

Yanagida, Kunio. *Japanese Manners and Customs in the Meiji Era*, trans. Charles S. Terry. Tokyo: Centenary Culture Council Series Obunsha, 1957.

9 Marriage, Family, and the State in Contemporary China

MARGERY WOLF

IN MOST, IF NOT ALL, peasant societies the development of the state as a political force has meant conflict with the family. China has not been an exception. The state in traditional China strongly supported the values of the old family system, even when those values on occasion required that family needs take priority over state needs.[1] The ideology of the family system and the ideology of the state were mutually supporting, both being based on a Confucian morality that held sacred a system of generation, age, and gender hierarchies. As Maurice Freedman explained:

NOTE: *Although I must bear full responsibility for this chapter's failings, it strengths come from the careful readings given it by Carol A. Smith, Emily Honig, William L. Parish, Martin King Whyte, Muriel Bell, and Arthur Wolf. This chapter was originally printed in* Pacific Affairs, *vol. 57, no. 2 (Summer 1984), pp. 213–236. It is reprinted here with the kind permission of that journal.*

From the point of view of the state, a man's obligations to it were in fact both qualified and mediated by his kinship relations. They were qualified in the sense that obligations springing from filial piety and mourning duties were held to modify duties owed to the state. An official who lost a parent was supposed to retire during his mourning. People related to one another in close bonds of kinship were so far regarded by the written law to require solidarity among them that the Code provided that certain relatives might legitimately conceal the offenses of one another (except in cases of high treason and rebellion), either escaping punishment altogether or suffering a penalty reduced in accordance with the closeness of the relationship; and that it was an offence generally for close kinsmen to lay even just accusations against one another. There was built into the system the principle that close patrilineal kinship set up special rights and duties standing apart from the rights and duties between men and the state [Freedman 1979, pp. 241–242].

The imperial state came into conflict with the family system when families were joined together in lineages, and lineages were strong enough to control territory. In the years before Liberation, both anticommunist Westerners and the ruling Guomindang warned that the Chinese Communist Party was intent upon "destroying the family." In truth, the communists were bent on destroying the *ideology* of the old family system; they recognized, as did their imperial predecessors, that it was this ideology that led to the organization of ever larger and more powerful groups of kin—the lineages that might be a threat to the new state's political organization. The Communists had no intention of destroying the family as a domestic unit, for it was as essential to their society as to the one they displaced.

In the thirty-some years since Liberation, the new state has been in quiet contest with the old family system for the loyalty of its citizens. In the cities, the state has manipulated everything from ideology to housing in order to break the old bonds of moral debt and filial duty to patrilineal kinsmen. Its success has been impressive, perhaps because much of the urban population—in particular, that majority to whom the revolution was addressed—had already begun to question the old truths. In the countryside, those old truths were the only truths until a rival ideology was brought in by the revolution. The Chinese countryside has undergone massive social transformation, but the Communists learned early on that family reform is a touchy issue—that landlords and organized lineages might be destroyed, but the bonds of kinship are a force to be used, not attacked.

This chapter will look closely at the struggle between family and state as it affects marriage formation. Again and again, the reader will find me qualifying statements by stating whether they are applicable to the city or to the countryside. The gulf that now exists between rural and urban society is a fairly new feature in China's social landscape. F. W. Mote expresses the old relations between country and city elegantly when he explains:

> The rural component of Chinese civilization was more or less uniform, and it extended everywhere that Chinese civilization penetrated. It, and not the cities, defined the Chinese way of life. It was like the net in which the cities and towns of China were suspended. The fabric of this net was the stuff of Chinese civilization, sustaining it and giving it its fundamental character. To extend this metaphor, China's cities were but knots of the same material, of one piece with the net [Mote 1977, p. 105].

Unlike Europeans, Chinese did not see their cities as "beleaguered islands in a sea of barbarism" (again quoting Mote), but as part of a whole with considerable movement on the part of the intellectual and elite population between rural family homes and their urban branches. This continuity began to erode in the late nineteenth century when the break-up of the civil service drained the vitality out of the rural elite. One might have expected Mao's peasant revolution to rebuild the ties between country and city, but in his efforts to destroy the class system, Mao destroyed the rural elite; and in his need to control urban unemployment, he put an end to the migration of rural people to the cities, in effect ending meaningful social interaction between the two populations. Over the last thirty years, the rural people in China have become second-class citizens in all but the rhetoric of the state. This has had, as we shall see, considerable influence on their willingness to conform to state policy.

The Meaning of Marriage

In traditional China, marriage was but a building block in the basic institution of society, the family. One of the most sacred duties of a son was to provide descendants for his and his father's ancestors. To do so, he must marry. Wealthy families and land-owning peasants used marriages to form ties with other families that might be useful in times of trouble or advantageous in commercial or political arenas. Poor families saw the marriages of their children as a necessary step in providing for their old age. The wedding itself was a major social event in the life of a family and, even though a proper wedding might bring parents to the verge of bankruptcy, the brideprice, dowry, gifts, and feasting could not be foregone if the family wished to remain a part of the moral community. The pair who were being wed were minor actors. Ordinarily they were not consulted about whom they would marry or when, but were presented with a mate at the time deemed appropriate by the senior generations. Some parents, out of poverty or callousness, gave their daughter to whichever family offered the most for her; many others tried to avoid marriages that would cause their daughters grief. Parents of sons chose brides who would meet the needs of the family first and of their sons second. Even the young people accepted this as the parents' and their own filial duty.

Except for a highly Westernized, highly politicized urban elite, the traditional attitudes toward marriage were not seriously questioned until the Communists' victory in 1949. In the first half of this century, family reform was an issue among the articulate minority who had contact with foreigners, but it did not extend into the countryside until the revolutionaries were forced out of the cities in the late 1920s. Even then, the pressure for change was weak, circumscribed by the need for political support from a conservative male peasantry. Nonetheless, the first law the Communists promulgated after the revolution was the Marriage Law of 1950, and it was designed to intervene at a basic level in the intimate affairs of the family. The opening paragraph states that the "supremacy of man over woman . . . is abolished"—a political commitment many women in the West have yet to win. Subsequent paragraphs ban polygyny, child betrothal, brideprices and dowries, and the coercion of either party to the union.

The immediate impact of this law has been described elsewhere (Stacey 1983; Johnson 1983; Davin 1976; Croll 1978; Meijer 1971). Suffice it to say here that when the campaign to enforce the law was launched in 1953, it quickly became clear that the Communists would have to temper their efforts to "liberate" women and the younger generation, if they were to retain their support in the rural areas. Local cadres perceived the law as a threat to their patriarchal powers, and grew suspicious of a government that was giving with one hand and taking away with the other. The campaign was abandoned, but the law was not. In the cities, workplace study groups continued to discuss the various aspects of the law, and the state slowly began to implement them; but minimal pressure for compliance was exerted on rural people.

Mao's policy regarding the family had multiple purposes. He sought to free women from their subjugation to men and from the oppression resulting from their lowly status within the family. He also wished to release the younger generation from the tyranny of their elders. Mao spoke to this point long before Liberation in his celebrated *Report on an Investigation into the Peasant Movement in Hunan*, written in 1927:

> A man in China is usually subjected to the domination of three systems of authority: (1) the system of the state (political authority) . . . (2) the system of the clan (clan authority) . . . and (3) the system of gods and spirits (theocratic authority). . . . As to women, apart from being dominated by the three systems mentioned above, they are further dominated by men (the authority of the husband). These four kinds of authority—political authority, clan authority, theocratic authority, and the authority of the husband—represent the whole ideology and institution of feudalism and patriarchy, and are the four enormous cords that have bound the Chinese people and particularly the peasants [Mao Tse-tung 1953, p. 40].

The rural class structure depended on the patriarchal power of the lineage (translated "clan" in the above quotation). To destroy it and consolidate the power of the Communists, Mao encouraged those most oppressed by the system to speak out and take power. He also recognized the economic potential of women, referring to it in speeches on several occasions:

> Women comprise half of the population. The economic status of working women and the fact of their being specially oppressed prove not only that women urgently need revolution but also that they are a decisive force in the success or failure of the revolution [Hsu Kwang 1974, p. 17].

And, less idealistically: "China's women are a vast reserve of labor power. This reserve should be tapped and used in the struggle to build a mighty socialist country" (Dorros 1976, p. 351).

Communist policies were aimed at destroying the old family system and the patriarchal ideology that supported it, not at destroying the family as a domestic unit. Nor were the Communists intent on degrading the domestic unit in favor of the marital bond. A handbook about marriage registration put out by the civil office of the Ministry of Interior states:

> Through the work of marriage registration we help to build and strengthen new democratic and united families and further develop the cause of socialist construction. We all know that once a couple becomes man and wife through marriage, they will build a family. After they build a family, not only will they bear children, but they may also have to live with other relatives and take care of elderly parents and younger brothers and sisters. *This kind of family relationship is much broader and more pervasive than the relationship between husband and wife* [Civil Office of the Ministry of Interior 1968, p. 14; emphasis added].

The family has been one of the few sources of welfare services available in a poor country determined (at least until recently) to develop itself without foreign assistance. To retain the Chinese family without the old Chinese family system, and to maintain the ideology of mutual obligation yet shed the patriarchal ideology of the old system, required restructuring—and marriage reform was a critical first step.

In normative terms, marriages are still formed to serve the interests of a larger group. Formerly that group was the family and the lineage; now it is the collective or society. A carefully defined and controlled marriage registration system was set up to place the formation of marriages firmly under the control of the Party. The Party, not the family, has the final word on who may marry whom, when they may marry, how their union will be celebrated, and so forth. Those in charge of marriage registration are instructed to make sure not only that each marriage meets the requirements of the Marriage Law but that the principals to each marriage understand the rights granted them by virtue of that law (Dorros 1976, p. 371). The orientation of both parties to a marriage is expected to be toward the larger group—the collective—and the

content of that relationship should be one of unswerving selfless-
ness. In a guide for young people issued in 1964, *The Correct Handling of Love, Marriage and Family Problems*, the writer cautions
young people "consciously [to] put the revolutionary cause in first
place" (Lu Yang 1969, p. 8). Lu Yang tells them:

> Marriage problems, when compared to the revolutionary cause, are
> minor matters and should be put in second place; but speaking in
> terms of the life of an individual, love, marriage, and the organiza-
> tion of a new family are, after all, serious matters. Whether they are
> treated well or not will concern not only an individual's progress and
> the happiness of family life, but also all of society [Lu Yang 1969,
> p. 11].

In reading the various guides and handbooks relating to issues
of marriage and divorce, one detects tension regarding expressions
of individualism.[2] Freed from the oppression of the "feudal" family, people were expected to transfer their loyalties from that collective to one organized by the state. Young people were to choose
their own mates, and the young bride was no longer subject to her
mother-in-law's rule. Therein lies a contradiction and an anxiety. If
society encourages a strong relationship between husband and
wife, one by its very nature likely to be emotionally charged, there
is a risk of comrades in socialist nation-building turning into self-
indulgent lovers. The guidebooks insist that love is shared labor,
mutual support in studying, mutual criticism, and comradely solidarity—a companionate marriage without the romance.

These are the official formulations, but what in fact does marriage mean to the post-Liberation generations getting married? In
1980–1981, some thirty years after the Marriage Law was promulgated, I interviewed 300 women in two cities and four rural communes about their work lives, their domestic lives, and their social
lives. Because of the restraints Chinese officialdom placed on me
and my informants, these were often formal and stiff interview ses-
sions. But from them, and from informal interactions not sanctioned by my hosts, I was able to get some sense of what marriage
means now in China. Women in the two cities, Beijing and Shaoxing, willingly gave me the official version of the purpose of marriage. They told me that a good marriage was one in which both
parties were willing to work for the good of the country, studied
hard to increase their knowledge so they could contribute more to

their work units, and were not afraid of hard work. When I agreed that this was the official definition and asked for more personal opinions, many added that a spouse should "show concern" for his or her mate, be even-tempered and get along with other people. However, before the interview drew to a close, I also asked how they had chosen their own husbands, who did various kinds of household chores, etcetera, and their amused answers to these questions revealed more about the content of the new marriages. Love was an ideal occasionally mentioned, but few could define it. Certainly, they had little opportunity to develop it or any other intimate feelings before marriage. Even in the cities, Chinese "courtships," that is, the events that lead up to an engagement, are often short and embarrassing. When choosing a spouse, a woman looks to see if the man she is attracted to or has been introduced to has a good class background (no landlords or intellectuals), good family conditions (for example, few dependents), good earning-power, and good looks. Some women told me, laughingly, that the last two factors were most important, and quoted a saying to the effect that men only care about a woman's looks and women only care about a man's earnings.

The sad thing about many of the new marriages is that the young couples often seem as mismatched as they were in the old days, when marriages were arbitrary matches arranged by the parents. The young person who is taught that his or her spouse will be a best friend and lifelong companion often finds, "after the rice is cooked," that they have very little in common. Even though marriage is delayed until both parties are in their mid- or late twenties, both are usually sexually inexperienced, and, from all reports, many women wish they had stayed that way (Hershatter and Honig 1982). The urban housing situation is very tight, so couples must either delay their marriages until housing is available (sometimes for years) or move into the already cramped quarters of the husband's (less commonly the wife's) family. In the latter case, as one woman told me, if you want to have an argument, you either take a walk or resign yourself to involving the whole family. In a society where until recently any inessential interaction between husband and wife in front of others was considered the ultimate in poor taste, a young couple living cheek by jowl with parents and siblings has limited opportunity to form that private culture most Western couples consider intrinsic to marriage.

Young people who do manage to get a room of their own often find it less a love-nest than a staging ground for separate lives centered on their workplaces. The workplace (or unit, as the more literal translation of the Chinese reads) is one of several means by which the state achieves control over its citizenry. Until you have a unit, that is, have been assigned a job, you cannot marry because your unit, not your family, gives you permission to marry. It is also your unit that gives you permission to get on a list at the Housing Bureau for living space, that gives you the chits allowing you to buy furniture for it, and that gives you the ration cards for everything from rice to cotton cloth. It is at your unit that you participate in political-study classes, learn of changes in policy, are given your contraceptives, and are told when you are eligible to become pregnant. I do not know if there is a conscious effort by the Party to transfer the center of a person's life from her home to the unit where she works, but the end result is just that.

In short, marriage for urban women is a necessary step in the passage from one stage of life to another. The two stages are often described as "before you have children" and "after you have children," and for both economic and social reasons one must marry in order to have children. When I asked why people have children at all in view of the population problem so often invoked in China now, I was told that the state needs another generation of workers (just as the family once needed another generation of worshippers). When I pressed further, I was told, often with giggles, that everyone wants a baby to play with. As in the past, a child is the only individual toward whom one can openly display affection. I think women clearly hope (or, in the case of the women I interviewed, hoped) to find in their husbands someone with whom they can share their innermost feelings: the study-group documents, editorials, and advice manuals have told them this is the inevitable result of free-choice marriages. Most women indicated in one way or another that they had been disappointed in this hope. To my initial surprise, more of the older women—women married to men chosen by their parents—described to me relationships that were clearly warm and close. I suspect that, once the initial disappointments are past, many of these young marriages will also mellow into affectionate companionship. Unlike North Americans, they do not have the option of the quick divorce and new search for a more satisfactory mate that also precludes the possibility of learned happiness.

Both happily and unhappily married Chinese farm women in

Taiwan in the "old days" gave the impression of being submissive to the strictures and patriarchal ideology of the traditional family system. Their behavior, nonetheless, revealed their recognition that the male social structure was not in their best interests, and that it was up to them to provide for their own future security (Wolf 1972). It took me a good many years of relaxed field work in Taiwan to reach this revisionist view of the Chinese family system, and it is highly unlikely that I shall ever have the opportunity to do that kind of field work in China. However, it does seem to me that rural women in China take many of the Party promises less seriously than do men. Certainly they are aware that the decree that women are no longer subordinate to men is parroted and ignored like many other slogans. A woman in Shaanxi whom I asked about the 1953 Marriage Law campaign told me that she had young children in those years and was not able to go to meetings. She could not remember anything about it. At another commune, I attended the final award-giving session of a campaign to improve mother-in-law/daughter-in-law relations. There was a big turnout (a cadre told me later the women would "get in trouble" if they failed to show up), but few paid much attention to the speakers: the audience chatted among themselves, mended clothes, and attended to their children. A young woman from Beijing who was traveling with me thought they were inattentive because they were too ignorant to understand. It was painfully obvious to me that they were bored to tears, and expressing it in the direct way that rural people have.

Farm women are fun to interview. In China they were, if anything, more nervous about the Beijing cadres than about the foreign interviewer. If I asked a question they were afraid to answer, they simply refused to respond, whereas the urban women tried to placate me and the cadres with any slogans they could think of that might come somewhere near the topic. When I asked rural women about marriage in new China, they were sincere in their appreciation of their new power to veto marriages suggested by their parents. Even though many of them had met their husbands only once or twice before marrying them, they insisted in their conversations with me that their marriages were quite different from the old *baoban* (arranged) marriages. Somehow their nod of agreement put them and their marriages in a category different from that of their parents. It created slightly different expectations about the relationship between husband and wife. No one could quite articulate for me what that difference was, but it seemed to follow from the fiction that they had chosen each other and hence must already have some emotional tie or commitment.

In the main, marriage in rural China is still viewed primarily as an event in the life of the family, much as it was in pre-Liberation China. The state has laid out a new set of rules to be worked around, but the needs of the family can usually be met within those regulations or by bending them to fit. If marriage in the city is the process that makes adults out of children, in the country it is still the means by which a woman is transferred from one family to another. City women, married or unmarried, are paid by the state at their place of employment; rural women earn workpoints that are entered in the accounts of their fathers before marriage or of their fathers-in-law after marriage. The majority of the guests at an urban wedding are friends and fellow workers; the "master of ceremonies" is likely to be the head of the man's unit. In a country wedding, kinsmen outnumber friends, and the important guests are representatives not of the state but of the families and their affines.

China's urban marriages have a misleading similarity in form to Western marriages. However, for women in China marriage is the necessary transitional act in achieving adulthood. It is inevitable, and it is recognized by both the participants and their parents as the end of the easy years. Choosing a husband is a serious affair and has little resemblance to the sentimental romance that Westerners associate with courtship. Rural marriages are less easily confused with the Western model. Through the Marriage Law, the state has placed more emphasis on relations between the two people who are marrying; but, by and large, rural marriage is still a matter of families, not lovers.

Since Liberation, then, marriage has taken on different meanings in rural and urban China, a state of affairs that I believe was neither conscious nor desired on the part of the present government. The state's successes have been in the cities. It is there that the new ideology about the content of a proper marriage found fertile or at least friable soil in which to take root. In the countryside, to continue the metaphor, the state's teachings fell on hard ground. In competing for their loyalties, the state has thus far not managed to provide rural people with that which they most value—security. Men and women, old and young, have found much for which they are grateful to the new government; but matters of the family have always been matters for the family. As we shall see in the pages ahead, rural people have managed at nearly every turn to modify or outwait the state's attempts at interference.

Age at Marriage

Article Four of the 1950 Marriage Law set a minimum marriage age of 18 for women and 20 for men. By 1956, at the outset of the first birth-limitation campaign, these minimum ages were being described as a compromise with "the masses' level of consciousness." The ages that were considered "appropriate" were then 23–28 for women (now 26–28) and 25–30 for men (now 28–30). The Party recognized that it would be impossible to enforce such a dramatic shift nationwide without losing support, so they did not press these standards. Their early goal was merely to prevent marriages between children or by children to older men (or in some places older women), in order to ensure that the marrying parties were old enough to make the decision the new law insisted was their right. In traditional China, young people were married early for a variety of reasons, ranging from a need for labor in a farm household to a need for offspring in all Chinese households. From the perspective of the people arranging the marriages, the sooner their children married the sooner they could reap the benefits of having a daughter-in-law to help in the kitchen and grandchildren who could add to the comforts (and the security) of their old age. From the perspective of the Party, these were the very feudal ideas that the revolution hoped to overturn.

Table 9.1 indicates the degree of Party success in enforcing this article of the law in country and city.[3] The women who are

Table 9.1

Mean Age at First Marriage for Women

	Age in 1980–1981								
	20–29	(n)	30–39	(n)	40–49	(n)	50–59	(n)	60+	(n)
Urban	25.3	(15)	23.7	(25)	21.6	(22)	19.9	(15)	19.8	(22)
Rural	22.9	(40)	20.3	(57)	18.7	(40)	18.0	(39)	18.3	(39)

now between the ages of 40 and 49 were the first cohort to marry after the promulgation of the Marriage Law. In the cities, this cohort married a good year and a half later than did the cohort who married before Liberation. It would appear that city residents were both aware of and willing to abide by the Marriage Law early on. Moreover, as the years went by, city women's ages at marriage continued to coincide with the new guidelines set down by the Party. Rural women were another matter. Even the oldest women had married, on the average, by the minimum age later established in the new law, but the women in my sample did not display a change in the traditional age at marriage until the 1960s (the cohort now between age 30 and 39). Only those who have married in the last ten years have averaged anywhere near the minimum "appropriate" age set by the Party during the 1960s. They are still well below the current minimum "appropriate" age.

The earlier age at marriage for rural women among the older cohorts of these samples reflects the greater degree of parental or, in its absence, extended-kin control over the marriages of young people. In the economically disastrous decades before Liberation, many urban youths came from families who were powerless to help or hinder them; for lack of means and lack of parental authority to force the early marriages, they married later than their rural counterparts. The pre-Liberation weakening of parental authority in the cities was very definitely a factor in the state's success in usurping parental prerogatives in the cities after Liberation, but the state's control over vital resources was determining.

In the cities, couples who marry must obtain permission from their work unit—which means, of course, the Party secretary of the unit. Circumventing the age restrictions would be both difficult to accomplish and likely to cause an entry in one's dossier that might have unpleasant ramifications later. Couples seeking to marry in the rural areas have only to register the act with their brigade office; any discrepancies between age and law might be handled through the intervention of relatives who worked in that office or had other relatives who did. Failing that, registration is simply delayed. Upon noting a rash of early marriages in a brigade, I was told that some couples held the social marriage whenever they chose, and then registered it after they came of age—when, for example, they registered the birth of their first child. In the urban areas where the wherewithal even to make a marriage, let alone maintain a family, is under the control of the state bureaucracy, such maneuvers would be nearly impossible.

More effective state controls and heavier doses of propaganda may account for the urban acceptance of late marriages, but neither control nor propaganda is entirely absent in the rural areas. One might have expected that the state after thirty years would be somewhat more successful than these figures indicate. In no small part, the campaign has fallen short because state values (late marriage reduces the birth rate and keeps workers focused on socialist construction) and the old family-system values (early marriage means more grandchildren, which enhances the status of the family and produces more income earlier for the senior generations) come in conflict over this issue.

Other state interventions may also have created situations for the women in my tables that made late marriage less likely. All the collectives I studied were in "model brigades." This means that through some bit of good fortune—a relative in the right place or a decision to change the course of a river—these collectives were designated as models for others to emulate. It is pretty clear that their high income results as much from state subvention at some point in their development as it does from the inhabitants' efforts or talents, but no cadre could publicly admit this. The effect of these cases of prosperity—people in model collectives eat better, dress better, and are housed better—on the marriage market must be taken into consideration. Although the state has made some half-hearted attempts to encourage endogamy, nearly all Chinese marry their daughters out to other villages and their daughters-in-law in from other villages. Unmarried women earn more than any other category of women, so parents with marriageable daughters might see it to their advantage to delay their marriages as long as possible. But marrying a daughter into a model brigade is next best to marrying her to someone with an urban registration. Such a marriage not only promises a better life for the girl, it might mean a more comfortable old age for the parents. One assumes that the economic advantages are also apparent to the model brigade family looking for a wife for their son. The younger the woman they marry to their son, the longer they, rather than her parents, will have the benefit of her workpoints. Unfortunately, I did not think to ask the age of out-marrying women in the model brigades who, if my reasoning is correct, would marry later. Still,

Table 9.2

Average Difference in Age Between Husband and Wife

	Wife's Age in 1980–1981			
	20–49	(n)	50+	(n)
Urban	3.89	(61)	5.19	(36)
Rural	2.92	(137)	5.41	(81)

from the amount of concern expressed in newspaper editorials and unofficial chats with cadres, I suspect that the model status of the collectives I studied plays a very minor role in maintaining rural women's lower age at marriage. The problem of early marriage appears to be more widespread. In fact, Parish and Whyte found that women marrying between 1968 and 1974 in nonmodel collectives in Guangdong were on the average 21.1 years of age—about halfway between the average ages of my overlapping cohorts (Parish and Whyte 1978, p. 163).

The data in Table 9.2 show another interesting difference between the rural and urban couples. Nothing in the Marriage Law says that husband and wife should be the same age or nearly the same age. Yet in the years since Liberation the discrepancy in ages of mates has narrowed markedly. Of particular interest to me here is that the difference has narrowed more among rural couples than among urban couples. I would have predicted that urban couples, who have somewhat more autonomy to choose their spouses, would select age mates; and that rural women, who are still governed by their parents, would be married to the latter's choice of older and more established men. What the data, in fact, reveal are adjustments to the different economic realities of rural and urban life. Both the income figures gathered by Whyte and Parish and my own data reveal a positive relationship between wage level and age among male workers (Whyte and Parish 1984). The better marriage for a calculating young city woman (or her parents) is to the man who has been on the job longer than she and is further up the pay/status hierarchy. He may retire earlier than her age-mates, but until he does his income will be higher under the current incentive system. Women in rural areas exist under a different set of conditions. In the old days, kind parents as well as avaricious ones sometimes married their daughters to much older men who offered material advantages. Yet, if the men fell prey to the illness or early death common to peasant China, instead of being well off, these young women might be burdened with several children and a decrepit husband who could do little to support them. Now health, strength, and long-term earning potential are far more attractive to rural women (who earn dramatically less than men). There are no pensions in rural China to compensate for the shorter peak-earning-years of older husbands. The only dependable support in old age comes by way of children, and the sooner they are born, the sooner one can begin to reap the benefits. Perhaps more important, under the current restrictions on the number of children a woman may bear, families want those children born early in a woman's fertile years rather than later, so that in the event of changes in policy, or tragedy, she will be able to produce more.

In the struggle to retain the loyalty of the rural male population just after Liberation, the state made a series of compromises with family-reform efforts, expecting to return to the issues when more groundwork had been laid. Rather than insisting that the rural population meet the "appropriate" age standards for marriage, they tolerated the lower standard written into the Marriage Law. In its turn, the rural population has on the average met the legal marriage-age requirements, but has been slow in moving toward the higher ages now considered "appropriate." (In some collectives, women stubbornly told me the best age to marry was around 20, and in others they told me the best age was around 26, innocently describing later in the same interview the weddings of their 20-year-old daughters.) In conjunction with the birth-limitation program, increased pressure is being applied to cadres to encourage later marriage, but the families of young people seem to be reluctant, at least those of the women with whom I talked. They may be willing to limit the number of births they have—the pressure is enormous in model communes—but they seem less willing to comply with the state's schedule for births (Wolf 1985).

Urban people accommodated themselves soon after Liberation to the demands of the state rather than to those of the old family system, and have tended to respond positively to each change in state policy regarding desirable marriage age. In no small part, this response has reflected the degree to which China's urban residents have understood and accepted the goals of the state. But the line between ideology and coercion on a less abstract level is difficult to establish in a society with such tight controls. Insufficient and ramshackle housing provides confirming evidence to the individual citizen who doubts the state's assertion that China is a struggling nation whose young people must delay their marriages in order to devote their energies to developing their impoverished country; low wages confirm the state's assertion that neither nations nor families can afford extra children. The state, of course, determines how many housing units will be built and establishes the wage structure. At the time of Liberation, urban residents, because of the weakening of parental authority, may have had less capacity to resist state expropriation of family prerogatives; now, some thirty years after Liberation, urban residents may have no defensible ideology with which to foster resistance.

Free-Choice Marriage

The freedom to choose the person with whom one will live out one's adult life is the core of the Marriage Law and, for many Chinese, may be all they know about it. Many words have been devoted to the hows and whys of it, and much propaganda has been distributed to the outside world about the success of it. Not surprisingly, when I asked women in my two urban samples, Beijing and Shaoxing, who had arranged their marriages, the younger women all denied vehemently that anyone had. They had made "free-choice marriages." To say otherwise, of course, would have been to say they had broken the law. Less direct questioning indicated that in the cities, the program has been fairly effective. By and large, urban senior generations do not present their offspring with spouses, although they may arrange for someone to introduce them to a few prospective mates. A Beijing mother told me that most young people met someone on their own or through work or school, but "well-behaved" girls or "shy" boys might need their relatives' help to locate someone suitable. In Shaoxing, a city less dominated by politics, women were divided over questions designed to elicit how much influence parents should have in their daughters' marriages. Twenty-three out of forty-one women said they felt the girls should find their own mates, but eighteen said that they should have some parental help or at least parental approval before taking any final steps. Probably the mothers of many

Table 9.3

Husband Selection: Rural

	Age in 1980–1981				
	20–29	30–39	40–49	50–59	60+
(n)	(60)	(48)	(29)	(20)	(21)
Selected by self (%)	27	26	25	5	9
Selected by parents (%)	55	65	68	95	90
Selected by both (%)	17	10	7	0	0

young women are very much involved in the final decision, but it is not something they are willing to discuss with a foreign interviewer in the presence of local officials.

As usual, the rural interviews were not the same. Women answered more frankly, and also very differently. The data presented in Table 9.3 tell the story. Just after Liberation, the number of women who said they decided for themselves whom they would marry jumped to around a quarter of the women in the cohort marrying in the 1950s (now aged 40–49). There has been little change since. Only a fourth of the country women who married in the last decade claimed to have found husbands on their own. In a social setting that still suspects sexual involvement between any two people of the opposite sex seen in casual conversation or walking alone together, to meet, get to know, and decide to marry without disqualifying oneself as a decent and acceptable mate takes a lot of ingenuity.

Since who influences decisions is difficult to judge even for the people making the decisions, in three of the rural sites I also asked a simpler question, one designed to give me some sense of how much autonomy women actually exercised in selecting their mates: "When did you first meet your husband?" Of the 112 rural women who married under the protection of the Marriage Law, 38 percent (43) knew their husbands before they became engaged to them; 29 percent (32) met them only after they were engaged (an act nearly as binding as marriage); and 33 percent (37) did not meet them until the day of their marriage.

These data serve to indicate perhaps more strongly than what has gone before how much the family still controls marriage in the rural areas. In the cities, parents still serve in an advisory capacity, but the larger family—the uncles, grandfathers, and cousins who make up a local lineage—is irrelevant to marriage unless called upon by a worried parent to "introduce" someone. In the rural areas, the extended kin are important actors in what will be a major social event, and from an individual woman's perspective they are determining agents in the quality of her adult life.

The Cost of Marriage

Foreign visitors to pre-Liberation China and Taiwan were often shocked at the enormous expense to which the Chinese went to marry their young and bury their dead. A decent wedding in Taiwan cost somewhat more than an adult farmer could expect to earn in a year. From an economic perspective, it was a horrendous waste of money, but money was not all that was involved. Marriages could be had, and were had, considerably cheaper. What was being bought was not a bride, as the Communists have insisted, but status for two families. The bigger the show, the more status for the groom's family; the bigger the dowry, the more status for the bride's family. The relatives of both shared in the reflected glory and in the good food. The entire village shared in the excitement of strangers coming and going, the worth of dowries to estimate, the number of guests and the quality of the food to be evaluated, and a helpless bride to be teased and examined. To be the center of this excitement and gain the face of having done it properly, families who could ill afford it competed with each other in almost potlatch proportions. Many a family has impoverished itself with the marriage of an eldest son.

The Communists sought to do away with this in Article Two of the Marriage Law, which prohibited "the exaction of money or gifts in connection with marriage." Their success was both brief and limited. During the Cultural Revolution, when all "feudal" practices came under the close scrutiny of the Chinese Moral Majority, the austere tea-and-speeches weddings of the cities were sometimes found in the country; but, even then, many families managed to have inconspicuous banquets, secretly exchange brideprices, and smuggle dowries. Parish and Whyte were told that the gifts (including but not limited to money) given to the parents of the bride had increased in value since Liberation, whereas the dowry taken by the bride to her new home had decreased substantially (Parish and Whyte 1978, pp. 180–192). They felt that this was a direct consequence of the new earning power of young women, which made them an asset to their own families as well as to their husbands'. The hypothesis is a good one, but my informants insist that the size and cost of the dowries expected have gone *up*, not down. When I asked country people why they thought the cost of marriages had gone up, they said it was because times were better so people could afford more. When I asked city people, they said that people in the countryside spent much more than did those in the city, and it was because this was the only time a country girl would be able to get new clothes, quilts, and a wristwatch, since she did not have a job like city girls. The explanations for the high costs of city weddings ranged anywhere from a shortage of girls to a shortage of boys, from interference by feudal parents to greedy young women, from the taste for bourgeois luxuries learned from the Gang of Four to the natural desire of the young couple to celebrate.

My data again show differences in the rural and urban settings. The stronger influence of the family in rural China is clearly exhibited in the way marriages are currently celebrated. Times are good, comparatively, and rural families are back to demonstrating rank and status. Weddings are a traditional way of doing so. But the rules have changed. Women are no longer valued for their reproductive capacity alone, so their side has another counter in the bargaining process, thereby inflating the requirements on both sides. Moreover, young people are more likely to be aware of the degree to which they are being exploited by their fathers: the patriarchal family system remains in place and their earnings go to support it. They may with good reason see this as an opportunity to take out their share.

Urban young people are less likely than their rural counterparts to be advertising their family's rank and status with fancy wedding parties, but they are nonetheless having elaborate, expensive marriage celebrations. The foreign press in China has had great fun documenting the cynicism and malaise under which urban youths now labor. In one decade, young people have seen their life-sacrificing idealism hailed by the country's leaders and then condemned as a national disaster. The more articulate tell one another (and some foreigners) that they believe in nothing, certainly not in Party propaganda. The less articulate say little and indulge themselves when opportunities arise. Their eyes have dropped from the horizon of China's potential greatness to their personal prospects. Having worked for the glory of the Party and found that, for many, its rewards were hard labor in a distant border region, they have now turned to working for their own security in a not very secure social world. Material possessions and the enjoyment of one day at a time are becoming the Beijing style, and that style includes lavish wedding parties and as many gifts as the young couple's marketability can command. In the cities, the state has managed to invalidate the belief system behind the elaborate traditional marriage, but the frequent vacillations within the ideology that was intended to replace the old beliefs have caused many to lose faith. I do not think the return of the old marriage customs says much about old family ideology, but it does say a great deal about the current strength of the state's hold on the urban youths' imagination.

Household Composition After Marriage

Ideally, in traditional China, families searched out wives for their sons and brought them home to live with them. The more married sons and the more generations under one roof, the greater the prestige of the family. Inevitably, friction developed between married brothers or married sons of brothers, and the extended family divided, creating two or more smaller units. Among the common people, extended households rarely lasted beyond the marriage of the second son—if they formed at all. Among the poor (the great majority in traditional China), one or more brothers often had to leave the family home in search of work elsewhere, returning once a year, and sometimes returning to find that other family members had also gone their separate ways in search of a living.

Since the Chinese Communists wished to end the domination of the old family system, I would not have been unduly surprised had my informants assured me that they, like most Westerners, formed upon marriage a separate domestic unit or neolocal family. Such was not the case, as the data in Table 9.4 indicate. In the urban sample, a larger number of women in the cohorts marrying under the Marriage Law formed neolocal families by their mar-

Table 9.4

Percentage of Women Forming Neolocal Households at Marriage

	Age in 1980–1981						
						Total	
	20–29	30–39	40–49	50–59	60+	20–49	50+
	% (n)	% (n)	% (n)	% (n)	% (n)	% (n)	% (n)
Urban	38 (16)	31 (26)	57 (21)	33 (15)	27 (22)	42 (63)	30 (37)
Rural	0 (40)	11 (57)	5 (40)	13 (40)	13 (38)	5 (137)	13 (78)

riages (42 percent) than did those who married before its protection (30 percent). It would appear from a look at the cohort-by-cohort increase that this was a gradual rather than an abrupt change. The larger number (57 percent) in the cohort marrying just after Liberation undoubtedly results from the fact that during this period large numbers of soldiers flocked to the cities in search of work and then married there. In the last decade, one of the constraints on marrying couples has been poor housing. According to the young people, even though they would prefer to live alone, if they are to marry before they are middle-aged, they must resign themselves to squeezing into an apartment with the husband's family—unless one or the other of them has influential relatives or factory housing. It seems likely that the percentage of urban couples forming new families in the cohort aged 20–29 would be considerably higher were the housing available.

The rural samples show a startling *decrease* in the number of marrying couples forming neolocal families, dropping from 13 percent of those marrying before Liberation to only 5 percent of those marrying afterward. Not one of the forty rural women marrying in the last decade formed a separate household with her spouse. The urban officials who traveled with me to China's countryside were genuinely impressed by the luxury of space that rural living provided when compared to the cities. Teams and families were building houses in every commune I visited, and we were told that at some point in their lives every married couple, save a youngest or only son and his wife, could count on having a house of their own. (The youngest or only son is expected to live with and take care of the aging parents.) It is not insufficient housing but controlled migration and prosperity that accounts for the decrease in neolocal families. In the old days, a fair number of men found themselves bereft of family, either because of early deaths or delayed marriages or because they or the other members of their families had taken to the roads in search of work. Of necessity, when they married they formed neolocal families. With better times and the stiff regulation controlling migration, rural families have reverted to the traditional pattern of a successful family, that is, housing its married young under the roof and authority of the patriarch.

Ironically, in not building more urban workers' housing, the state is forcing young people who would prefer to break with the old family system either to delay marriage or to live under the (reduced) authority of their parents. Yet in the country, the collectives (often a group of relatives) are helping people build new houses to shelter a modernized version of the traditional family.

The New Marriage Law of 1980

The Third Session of the Fifth National People's Congress, which met in 1980, passed a new marriage law, raising the minimum age for marriage by two years, making family planning mandatory, and, among other things, rendering into law some of the customary family obligations of the traditional society. When I asked officials why the minimum age for marriage had not been raised to the current "appropriate" age for marriage, I was told that it was kept low out of consideration for the national minorities who have no population problem, hence need not delay marriage. I suspect it was also not raised beyond a level the state knew it could enforce. The requirement to practice family planning appears in two separate articles, one saying it will be practiced and the other saying it is mandatory for both men and women. Again, the precise requirements are not spelled out, because the family-limitation program operates with different rules in different areas, with the biggest differences occurring between country and city.

Of particular interest to us in terms of the topic of this chapter are the new statements of obligation among family members. In traditional China, the duties of children to parents and grandparents were heavy and binding. Lifelong support was basic, and the inculcation of filial piety—the encompassing concept—was so thorough that parents of adopted children tried to keep from them the identity of their biological parents, because it was assumed they would feel dual obligations, even if they had not seen the parents since infancy. In contemporary rural China, sons are expected to support their parents, grandparents, and younger siblings if the need exists. These obligations are not incumbent on daughters, for the woman transfers her filial duties to her husband's family at marriage. A widow who does not remarry assumes her former husband's debt to his parents. When I asked what a production team might do if a man refused to support his parents, the cadres told me that they would garnishee his workpoint account. They would not garnishee that of a married daughter, however, because she "belongs to another family." In contemporary urban China, the rules are less clear. The first response to my question was usually that the old people have pensions now (many do), but a review of the household budgets I collected shows that contributions to the support of the separate-living elderly are made by the sons, with lesser amounts contributed by a few daughters with particularly good jobs. When urban parents were living with adult children, the children were their sons, not their daughters, although I was struck by the warm relations and frequent contact between mothers and daughters, a rarity in the old society.

The new Marriage Law not only places children under the same financial obligations as in the traditional society, it also adds a generation omitted from the Marriage Law of 1950. Grandchildren "who have the capacity to bear the relevant costs have the duty to support and assist their grandparents." But it breaks with traditional customary law in that it extends this obligation of the younger generation to the maternal grandparents as well. The Marriage Law of 1950 referred only to the parents and was interpreted by everyone with whom I spoke as the obligation of sons and their wives. However, the new birth-limitation program creates serious problems for couples whose single allowed child is a girl. Unless the girl and her husband are obliged to support her parents as well as his, her parents face an uncertain old age. If daughters can (and must) fulfill the same functions as sons, the disaster of bearing a female child will be at least partially alleviated.

In sum, in the cities the new law serves to restore one aspect of the old family ideology in order to support the government's desperate attempt to control population growth. At the same time, it strikes a blow at the patrilineal orientation of the Chinese family by equating the rights of the maternal relatives with those of the paternal. In the cities it may work; I doubt that it will in the countryside. Extending the range of obligation to the generation of grandparents involves no real change in rural China, but extending the economic responsibility of a couple to the parents of the wife seems unenforceable. The women's parents live in another brigade and belong to another surname group. To obtain contributions from an unwilling couple, two power blocs must be confronted: the bureaucracy of the collective and another kin group. Those who have tried to work in any capacity in China will shudder at the prospect of having to cross from one bureaucracy to another in any kind of negotiation. When these two bureaucracies are peopled by different kinsmen—by definition in opposition—the negotiations will be long and tedious at best. When the content of the negotiation is a threat by the state to traditional family ideology, success seems a most unlikely prospect.

Conclusions

In a 1937 essay titled "On Contradiction," Mao Zedong wrote:

> When the superstructure (politics, culture, etc.) obstructs the development of the economic base, political and cultural changes become principal and decisive. Are we going against materialism when we say this? No. The reason is that while we recognize that in the general development of history the material determines the mental and social being determines social consciousness, we also—and indeed must—recognize the reaction of mental on material things, of social consciousness on social being and of the superstructure on the economic base [Mao Tse-tung 1967, p. 336].

After Liberation, while Mao was struggling to develop the economic base of a country impoverished by wars and mismanagement, he made full use of the organization and communication skills he and his army had learned in the Jiangxi soviets and in the Yanan base-camps to turn the class structure upside down. However, in the conservative northern border regions, he must have made a decision, perhaps an essential one, about priorities. One might "recognize" the salutary action of a transformed superstructure on the economic base under some circumstances, but in regard to women, the traditional Marxist approach must suffice. As Kay Ann Johnson so ably sums it up:

> The dominant Chinese view of the status of women asserts that after the political victory of the revolutionary movement, once women are brought in to remunerative social (i.e., non-domestic) production, interrelated and liberating changes in all other areas of society and family life will naturally occur: women's traditional dependence on men will be broken, they will become both more socially valuable and valued for their economic contribution to family and society, they will wield more authority in their communities and family, and eventually the entire cultural superstructure of male superiority and female subordination will give way to new norms of equality and female worth which realistically reflect women's new relationship to production [Johnson 1976, p. 105; see also Johnson 1983].

When discontent among rural cadres over the "liberation" of their womenfolk expressed itself in ways similar to those Mao had witnessed in Yanan, the campaign of 1953 to implement the Marriage Law was allowed to die. Instead of pressing for family reform, he for once did follow the lead of the masses and allowed the "restoration" of the old family system that many an impoverished peasant had, in fact, barely experienced. As a result, changes in marriage in the rural areas have been limited, at most giving the young some say in their marriages and giving women some presence in the family decision-making processes. The patrilineal family remains strong. The state, in a sense, has been preempted by the family both in authority over individuals and even in economic organization—rural collectives often were superimposed over existing villages that were also likely to be single-surname villages (Diamond 1975, pp. 25ff.). Lineage structure, insofar as it was controlled by the landlord class, was destroyed; but the social and kin relationships persist to this day, retarding and sometimes deflecting ideological change. Many of the changes that have occurred in the countryside seem to have come about through coercion and fear of the consequences of noncompliance for both the collective and the individual. This is a slow way to alter the superstructure, and a good way to change vague distrust of the unknown into conscious opposition to a perceived threat.

Urban changes have been greater and less superficial. Ideological education has been more persuasive and more pervasive.

Study groups in the workplace, textbooks in the schools, and editorials in the newspapers can make whatever reform is underway uppermost (or at least unavoidable) in the minds of an urban citizenry in ways impossible in the countryside. Moreover, the young in the cities receive from the hands of the state what they used to receive (and in the country still do receive) from the family. Permission to marry comes from the work unit; the job that makes marriage and adulthood possible comes from the state, not by way of father's land or uncle's rice shop. Where the rural patriarchs have, for the time being at least, kept much of their authority over women and younger generations, among city-dwellers paternal authority has been thoroughly undermined by the state's taking to itself many of the sanctions and indulgences the patriarchy once had exclusive rights to dispense.

To be sure, such structural factors as low incomes, inadequate housing, increased educational opportunities, and a serious unemployment problem have a strong influence, as they do in other developing countries, on the various changes occurring in urban marriages I have addressed in the pages above. However, these factors are manipulated by the government just as surely as are propaganda campaigns. A conscious decision on the part of the state could provide more housing, less education, higher wages, or more jobs, although obviously other economic and social considerations must be and have been taken into consideration. The fact remains that the state's control in the urban areas over things material as well as things ideological has allowed it to prevail in its struggle with the family in a way that has not yet been possible in the countryside.

NOTES

1.   By "family system," I mean the group of men who shared or assumed they shared a common ancestor, and because of this relationship were bound together by rights, duties, and ideology. In some areas of China, these groups were both large and well-organized, forming patrilineal descent groups that controlled whole villages or even groups of villages.

2. Two years after the essay quoted above was published, it came under Party attack for being "revisionist" and, worse yet, for suggesting that, in the matter of marriage, individual concerns might be ranked as high as society's needs.

3. The reader should bear in mind that, although unique and, I believe, accurate, these data come from a sample of women selected for me from "model" collectives. Those selecting the people I interviewed had no reason to select them for the age at which they married.

REFERENCES

Civil Office of the Ministry of Interior, China. "How to Manage Marriage Registration Work Well." *Chinese Sociology and Anthropology* 1(1968):14.

Croll, Elisabeth. *Feminism and Socialism in China.* New York: Schocken Books, 1978.

Davin, Delia. *Woman-Work: Women and the Party in Revolutionary China.* Oxford: Oxford University Press, 1976.

Diamond, Norma. "Collectivization, Kinship, and the Status of Women in Rural China." *Bulletin of Concerned Asian Scholars* (1975).

Dorros, Sybilla Green. "Marriage Reform in the People's Republic of China." *Philippine Law Journal* 51(1976):351.

Freedman, Maurice. "The Family in China, Past and Present." In *The Study of Chinese Society: Essays by Maurice Freedman.* Stanford, Calif.: Stanford University Press, 1979.

Hershatter, Gail. "Making a Friend: Changing Patterns of Courtship in Urban China." *Pacific Affairs* 57 (1984): 237.

Hershatter, Gail, and Honig, Emily. "Chinese Women." Unpublished paper delivered at National Women's Studies Association Meetings, June 1982.

Honig, Emily. "The Life and Times of Yu Luojing." *Pacific Affairs* 57 (1984):252.

Hsu Kwang. "Women's Liberation Is a Component Part of Proletarian Revolution." *Peking Review* 17(1974):12.

Johnson, Kay Ann. "The Politics of Women's Rights and Family Reform in China." Ph.D. Dissertation, University of Wisconsin, 1976.

Johnson, Kay Ann. *Women, the Family, and Peasant Revolution in China.* Chicago: University of Chicago Press, 1983.

Lu Yang. *The Correct Handling of Love, Marriage, and Family Problems.* Chi Nan: Shantung People's Publishing House, 1964.

Mao Tse-Tung. *Report of an Investigation into the Peasant Movement in Hunan.* Beijing: Foreign Languages Press, 1953.

Mao Tse-tung. "On Contradiction." In *Selected Works of Mao Tse-tung* (trans.). Beijing: Foreign Languages Press, 1967.

Meijer, M. J. *Marriage Law and Policy in the Chinese People's Republic.* Hong Kong: Hong Kong University Press, 1971.

Mote, F. W. "The Transformation of Nanking, 1350–1400." In G. William Skinner (ed.), *The City in Late Imperial China.* Stanford, Calif.: Stanford University Press, 1977.

Parish, William L., and Whyte, Martin King. *Village and Family in Contemporary China.* Chicago: University of Chicago Press, 1978.

Stacey, Judith. *Patriarchy and Socialist Revolution in China.* Berkeley: University of California Press, 1983.

Whyte, Martin King, and Parish, William L. *Urban Life in Contemporary China.* Chicago: University of Chicago Press, 1984.

Wolf, Margery. *Women and the Family in Rural Taiwan.* Stanford, Calif.: Stanford University Press, 1972.

Wolf, Margery. *Revolution Postponed: Women in Contemporary China.* Stanford, Calif.: Stanford University Press, 1985.

10 African Marriage in an Impinging World
The Case of Southern Africa

ADAM KUPER

READING MODERN STUDIES OF AFRICAN MARRIAGE, one is struck immediately by the diversity of contemporary developments. For Southern Africa—on most measures the least "traditional" region of the continent—recent trends are extremely difficult to summarize. Indeed, scholarly findings often seem mutually irreconcilable. In certain areas, including relatively isolated rural districts, reports describe the break-up of the traditional household, the emergence of independent female household heads, and the marginalization of the husband and father. A recent study shows that in parts of Botswana, for example, the courts experience difficulty in distinguishing "marriage" from casual forms of cohabitation (Comaroff and Roberts 1981). And yet traditional marriage forms, including bridewealth payments and polygyny, apparently still persist in some areas, even in a few urban districts.

These variations are mainly the consequences of contact with industrial societies. Such contact has brought a high level of labor migration by men. It has also dissolved traditional political arrangements at the rural base. However, external forces are filtered through local structures, producing different consequences in different areas. In my view, the state of the local rural economy rather than local variation in traditional culture is the critical factor. Labor migration is caused by poverty, and it produces a flow of income to the rural areas which is, in part, used for investment. But different kinds of local poverty exist, and, accordingly, different rational strategies of investment occur. Marriage institutions respond to these circumstances, producing a variety of local developments in marriage, bridewealth, and domestic organization.

This chapter presents two contrasting case studies to convey the range of developments in marriage in Southern Africa and to illuminate the reasons behind these developments. I use two countries to develop my argument, Botswana and Lesotho, both independent, small, poor countries embedded in the economy of South Africa, the dominant economic power in the region. The people of both countries speak closely related languages of the Sotho-Tswana family.

Traditional Systems

In the past the Bantu societies in eastern and southern Africa relied upon a combination of pastoralism and agriculture. Men worked with cattle and goats and hunted, while women provided the largest part of the agricultural work force.[1] Women were thought to be dangerous to cattle and could not participate in pastoral activities. Men did, however, help with heavy seasonal work in the fields. With the introduction of ploughing (with ox-drawn ploughs) in some areas at the turn of the century, the male contribution became critically important although still limited to a short part of the agricultural season.

A combination of pastoralism and agriculture, using a simple technology, reduced the risks inherent in the practice of traditional husbandry. Seasonal shortages and occasional crises could be insured against to some extent by maintaining a dual economy. However, not every individual family had to achieve this delicate balancing act. In some places a division of labor occurred between ethnic groups in the community or between social classes. Typically, in eastern and southern Africa, a small elite of rich and politically influential men had a disproportionate number of cattle, while a large number of poorer men, dependent on agriculture and vying for the favors of the cattle-owning elite, borrowed cattle in return for political support.

A man made bridewealth payments in cattle. These payments gave him certain rights in his wife, especially in her children and in her labor. If a marriage ceremony has been completed, and *a fortiori* if bridewealth has been paid, then a child "belongs" inalienably to his father. Since, in any case, a boy can expect little from his mother's kin in the way of capital or support after childhood, young men will try to attach themselves to their fathers, even in extreme instances (as I saw in the Kalahari) paying bridewealth on behalf of a deceased father in order to make a claim on his estate. Claims to a child's labor are of minor importance, since agriculture is marginal and pastoralism is not labor-intensive. Adults only cooperate in work if it is mutually beneficial to do so. Polygyny was prestigious, and a rich and powerful man might have several wives. Each wife with her children formed a semi-independent unit (a "house") within the household, with its own resources.

Goody (1973) has suggested that bridewealth payments and polygyny (with which bridewealth generally is associated in Africa) tend to reduce economic differentiation. As men grow richer in cattle so they are inclined to spend some of their wealth. They spend it on wives, the wives give birth to a large number of children, the children divide the cattle that remain, and the African pastoralist evolves from cowhand back to cowhand in three generations. Marriage, and above all polygyny, redistributes resources.

In my view this is a misinterpretation. The rich man who invests cattle in bridewealth reduces his economic risks by balancing his investments in pastoralism with an investment in agriculture. He relies precisely on an efficient balance between these two economic activities to maintain his wealth and privileged position. In return for cattle he obtains, in the first instance, additional wives who provide extra agricultural labor. He can use the resulting agricultural surplus either to pay casual labor (traditionally paid in beer) or to exchange for goats and cattle. Livestock increase very rapidly even under simple technological conditions, but a certain number must always be retained in order to carry the cattle owner over years of drought or disease (see Dahl and Hjort 1976). Marriage payments and polygyny therefore are not equalizing mechanisms. On the contrary, they maintain an unequal distribution of resources.

A consequence of this basic calculation is initially paradoxical but actually economically rational. Where, for environmental reasons, agriculture is significantly more important than pastoralism, female labor is especially valuable. The absolute level of bridewealth is higher in such communities. In societies where cattle are more productive and more plentiful, agriculture, and therefore female labor, is less highly valued (see Turton 1980). The bridewealth price is accordingly depressed.

A second consequence of the situation is that when new economic opportunities develop—above all the opportunity to go on migrant labor—men in those families and communities where pastoralism is least important embrace the opportunity more enthusiastically. Migrant labor soon becomes a functional alternative to pastoralism. Some implications of these relationships will be dealt with later in the chapter.

Politics and Preferential Marriage

Marriage and bridewealth in Southern Africa were never simply economic matters but always had a strong political component. Traditionally, although land was not a scarce resource, access to land and to grazing and hunting privileges was a function of membership in a political community. One had to be accepted by a local chief. The status of citizenship then implied access to land for agricultural purposes, and for grazing and hunting. Gaining membership in a political community often involved forging links of clientage, either directly with the chief or with an important man in the area. These links typically hinged on exchanges of women and of cattle. The clients had the use of cattle and a share in any increase. The sister of a client was often married to a chief. The politically more important people therefore accumulated wives, in part as a function of the multiplicity of their political links with different clients. And in return they lent out cattle which bound the clients further to them. If these links continued from generation to generation—as was usually the case—they found expression

Table 10.1

First-Kin Marriages in Botswana and Lesotho: Categories of
Marriages with First-Kin as a Percentage of All First-Kin Marriages[a]

	FBD	BD	MBD	Other	Total
Botswana					
Nobles	43	11	23	23	100
Commoners	13	7	48	32	100
Lesotho					
Nobles	44	—	19	37	100
Commoners	28	—	44	38	100

[a]First-kin = same grandparent or more closely related.
FBD = father's brother's daughter; BD = brother's daughter; MBD = mother's brother's daughter.
SOURCES: Schapera 1957, pp. 149, 151; Ashton 1952, pp. 327–337.

in marriages that repeated each other in pattern. Such repetitive marriages were often conceptualized in terms of a preference for marriage with a mother's brother's daughter, traditionally a common form of kinship marriage among the Sotho-speakers in Southern Africa.

Among the small aristocracy, however, other factors were significant. People competed for influence, attempting to maintain close links to the ruling circle. For the royals this meant links with a man's own father's brothers, father's brother's sons, brothers and brother's sons. A large proportion of marriages of men in such positions therefore occurred with father's brother's daughters, or even with brother's daughters.

Schapera's studies in the 1940s showed that marriage with close kin occurred fairly often in Botswana, particularly among tribal aristocrats (Table 10.1). ("Close kin" were people who shared at least a common great-grandfather.) Thirty-two percent of the wives of aristocrats were close kin, as against 18 percent of the wives of commoners.[2] Ashton (1952) published roughly comparable figures for Lesotho,[3] but unfortunately he established the kinship relationship between spouses in only about 60 percent of the marriages surveyed. This obviously biased sample had 77 percent of aristocrats and 41 percent of commoners marrying close kin. Both samples, however, revealed a similar bias in the type of close-kinswoman preferred as a spouse. Commoners preferred mother's brother's daughters, while aristocrats preferred father's brother's daughters.

Over the past fifty years, the power of local chiefs and headmen to dispose of land and citizenship privileges in the traditional fashion has steadily declined. These rights were diffused first to colonial officers and later especially to elected politicians, land boards, district councils, and so forth. The weakening or even the disintegration of the traditional bonds of clientage has been a consequence of these developments. The traditional leader today often cannot influence the disposal of resources that are politically defined, such as rights to citizenship and land. He also is less inclined to assume a traditional view of the value of dispersing his cattle. Cattle have an immediate monetary value, for they can be sold to slaughterhouses. In many areas milk may be sold commercially. The wealthier and more influential men therefore frequently rationalize their cattle holdings and buy ranches or have commercially organized cattle posts.

Another modern development, at least in Botswana, is the dispersal of population from the small village capitals to the fields. People now live less directly and immediately under the control of political leaders.[4] With the disappearance of its political rationale, preferential marriage on kinship lines is rapidly becoming a thing of the past, although it is still practiced more than people themselves recognize.

Polygyny

Plural marriage, or polygyny, has also declined. In Botswana, nobles initiated between 1830 and 1860 married an average of 3.3 women each. The following generation married an average of 1.8 women, the third generation an average of 1.4 women and the fourth generation, which began initiation in 1920, married an average of 1.1 women each. Among commoners the generation initiated between 1830 and 1860 were marrying an average of 1.9 women per man, and by the fourth generation, this figure had decreased to 1.1 women per man.[5] A comparable decline occurred in Lesotho.

What caused this decline? One cannot exclude the influence of Christianity, for right from the first the missionaries warned very strongly against polygyny. However, the missionaries equally opposed bridewealth, and in Botswana, where bridewealth was relatively less important, they achieved a number of successes; but in Lesotho, where local people placed a higher value on bridewealth, the missionaries made practically no impact on the practice, although they were at least as powerful as in Botswana. By analogy, then, the missionary factor is not sufficient to account for the decline of polygyny.

Another explanation has already been touched upon. The breakdown of relations of clientship meant that the political figures who were accumulating a number of wives as a consequence, or as an expression, or a means, of maintaining their political ties, no longer had either the opportunity or the motivation to do so. Plural marriages therefore became less common because they lost their political rationale.

Special local reasons also contributed to the decline of polygyny. The citizens of Lesotho began to experience land shortages around the 1930s. Increasingly, men received land for one wife only, a policy that reduced the attractions of polygyny. In Botswana, as I shall show, agriculture in general became less significant, making investment in any marriage less economically rational.

Botswana and Lesotho: Contrasting Economies

The populations of Botswana and Lesotho were virtually indistinguishable in the precolonial period. The differentiation of these populations occurred largely as a consequence of the colonial history of the last 150 years.

The colonial misadventures of Lesotho—to sum up very quickly—produced a concentration of the populations in a small mountainous area that had traditionally been on the margin of their agricultural heartland. White settlers also robbed the local people of their large pastoral areas. As a consequence, by the late nineteenth century the population of Lesotho overwhelmingly depended on agriculture. Lesotho was consequently among the first regions to send large numbers of men to the diamond diggings in Kimberley and then to the gold mines of the Witwatersrand; and it remains among the countries most strongly oriented to migrant labor.

In Botswana the situation was somewhat different. The Tswana tribes, who occupied what is today Botswana, were living on the western semidesert margins of the main Tswana settlement area, on the edge of vast grazing lands. These lands suited the dispersed grazing of cattle (comparable perhaps to areas in New Mexico and Texas), but not the traditional agricultural methods. The Boer farmers who took so much of the outlying land of the Basotho did not find the land particularly attractive; accordingly, the western Tswana were left with enormous areas of land suitable for pastoralism and relatively unsuitable for agriculture. In this area, residents regarded pastoralism as far more important and agriculture as less important than in Lesotho. Although migrant labor became significant particularly in areas of relative poverty in Botswana, it never reached a level comparable to that in Lesotho. Paradoxically, however, in Botswana marriage and the family have changed radically, while in Lesotho, otherwise so dramatically transformed by colonialism, domestic institutions present a more traditional aspect.

Recently, as Table 10.2 shows, the national cattle-herd of Botswana has been five to six times as large as that of Lesotho. In both countries cattle are very unevenly distributed among the population. Also, in both countries agriculture is almost wholly in the hands of small peasant producers. The relatively greater productivity and reliability of Lesotho farming is evident.

In considering developments in Botswana and Lesotho, I use a series of modern anthropological studies. Students from Leiden University, who were repeating local community studies carried out by Schapera in the 1930s and 1940s, compiled one set of studies in Botswana. Other independent studies, notably Kooijman (1978) and Gulbrandson (1980), support the students' results. (See also Brown 1983.)

Professor Isaac Schapera kindly placed at our disposal unpublished reports of local censuses and community studies that he had completed before and during World War II. From Leiden we therefore were able to organize two re-studies in the late 1970s.[6]

Botswana

Marja Molenaar (1980) repeated a study made by Schapera of a ward in the Kwena capital, an area that continues to draw much

Table 10.2

Botswana and Lesotho: Basic Statistics

	Botswana	Lesotho
Population and paid employment (in thousands)		
1978 population	726	1,279
Migrant laborers in South Africa	50	150–200
Cattle ownership (in thousands)		
1977	3,000	520
1798	3,000	550
Agricultural production, major crops (in 1,000 metric tons)		
Corn		
1977	35	126
1978	52	143
1979	8	129
Sorghum		
1977	33	62
1978	45	59
1979	13	86
Millet (Botswana), wheat (Lesotho)		
1977	5	61
1978	5	58
1979	1	30

labor migration. The second study, by Els Kocken and G. C. Uhlenbeck, was of a village called Tlokweng, which Schapera had also studied before World War II. Originally an area of very high labor migration, it found itself in the 1960s next door to the new capital city, Gaborone, Botswana's Brasilia, which now provides adequate work opportunities an hour's walk from home.

Marja Molenaar found that the ward which Schapera had studied in 1938 and in 1943 had grown enormously by the time of her study in 1978. The population had increased from just under 200 persons to 640. Moreover, the population of children had increased disproportionately. In 1938, children constituted roughly one-third of the population of the ward; in 1978 almost half of the population of the ward were children.

A second development was the substantial increase in the number of unmarried women and in the number of children born out of wedlock. The decline in polygyny only partially accounts for these changes. In 1938, 8 percent of women in the ward over the age of 16 never had been married; in 1978, 60 percent had never been married. A large majority of these unmarried women were now mothers. Moreover, while in 1938 the average unmarried mother had one child, in 1978, she had two or three children.

The number of unmarried men also increased. In 1938, 23 percent of the adult men were unmarried; in 1978, 65 percent. The age of marriage had also changed. In the 1930s and 1940s, according to Schapera, women were marrying between 21 and 25 years of age, while men were marrying for the first time at the ages of 25 to 30. (This differential in age of marriage generated the extra women who made the plural marriage system possible.) In 1978, Molenaar found that men were marrying at around the age of 35, and women between the ages of 25 and 35.

Is the definition of marriage used here too strict? Gulbrandson, working in a neighboring district, came up with remarkably similar figures and rejected the possibility that they were based on a false view of marriage. On the contrary, "only 21 of the 90 unmarried mothers in this sample claimed that they received some support from the children's father" (1980, p. 30).

The dramatic changes in the incidence of marriage and in the incidence of illegitimacy were correlated with an unexpected change in household composition. Households grew in size. After 1938 the population of the ward increased more than three times, but the number of households had not even doubled because most of the unmarried men and women, and the children of unmarried mothers, remained in the households of their parents. Consequently, many more three-generation households existed than in traditional times.

Practically none of the unmarried mothers were able to form independent households. Although they considered the situation to be undesirable, they remained dependent on their brothers and fathers. They agreed that they were a burden on their brothers and fathers and complained that they and their children had only a secondary claim on the resources of the household. Yet a woman, particularly if she had young children, was unable to maintain herself independently. Moreover, since these children could not inherit from their mother's father or brother, they were obliged to depend upon older men to raise money, cattle, and labor for ploughing.

I turn now to the second study, by Kocken and Uhlenbeck (1980), of Tlokweng. The changes paralleled those reported for the Kweneng, but in addition another, less common change occurred from high dependence on migrant labor to low dependence on it. In 1943 Schapera found that more than half of the families in the village had members abroad as migrant laborers, but in 1978 very few migrant laborers were abroad, since they could commute easily to jobs in Gaborone.

In 1943 Schapera found that 73 percent of women in the village above the age of 16 were married; in 1978, only 35 percent were married while 45 percent were unmarried but had children. These unmarried women were usually attached to the households of father or brothers. As in the Kweneng ward, a shift in household composition produced more households containing three generations.

In 1943 about half the women aged 20 to 24 already had married, while in 1978 half the women were married only by the age of 35 to 39. Kocken and Uhlenbeck found that only about 30 percent of the unmarried mothers still expected to marry. The rest were resigned to bringing up their children alone, dependent on brothers and fathers. The unmarried mothers in Tlokweng were, however, in a better position than their unmarried counterparts in the Kweneng, because they had the opportunity of traveling daily to work in domestic or minor clerical positions in Gaborone. They therefore could contribute substantially to the resources of their households without neglecting or losing control of their children. Despite this advantage, very few of these unmarried mothers established their own homesteads, although most of them wished to do so. In fact, only 18 percent of the unmarried mothers had achieved an autonomous homestead. All of these women were over 38 years old and had mature, or almost mature, children. Moreover, they had abandoned any expectation of marriage.

Such homesteads require substantial, regular, and consistent cash incomes, earned usually by two people, to hire field labor and to pay for tractors. If a woman commands a very high income, she may buy food in shops, but very few are so fortunate. Women are very unlikely to own cattle, not only because of a traditional male bias against female cattle ownership and the exclusion of women from the inheritance of cattle, but also because control of cattle requires male labor, which is more expensive and more difficult to control for women than is female agricultural labor.

Other reports support the results of these careful case studies. Schapera and Roberts (1975) described similar changes over the last generation in a ward in Mochudi. Kooijman (1978) analyzed the economic dilemma of women in a middle-sized settlement who desperately attempted to mobilize the economic assistance of lovers. Gulbrandson (1980) has confirmed these findings in detail for the Southern District. (See also Curtis 1972.)

But has a complete revolution occurred in the position of women? A number of these unmarried mothers traditionally would have been junior wives in polygynous households. They would have been relatively disadvantaged compared to the first-married and politically more important wife, whose children would have received the lion's share of the inheritance. Yet these women would have enjoyed an element of security, getting some access to cattle resources and, with the development of migrant labor, receiving some cash income. In a polygynous household each wife and her children formed a distinct "house" with their own estate and a right to a major share in the earnings of its sons and the bridewealth of its daughters.

Today the women are in a rather similar position. They occupy a secondary, dependent, and disadvantaged position, though they are beholden not to a polygynous husband but to a brother or a father who concentrates his attention and resources on another woman dependent, his wife. The greatest disadvantage of children born in these households is that they have no claims to inheritance, because bridewealth has not been paid for their mothers and they are consequently not legitimate children and heirs of their fathers.

Men who have fairly stable liaisons postpone bridewealth payments, judging that they have little to gain from formalizing a marriage, certainly a second marriage. Men nowadays often pay bridewealth many years after a marriage, and the question of whether a man is "married" to a particular woman has become an ambiguous and controversial issue. The courts are continually called in to settle claims to maintenance and to decide controversies about the inheritance (Comaroff and Roberts 1981). However, bridewealth in Botswana is traditionally low, and one of the very interesting developments over the last generation (which I noticed in the field in the western Kalahari in the 1960s) is that young men reaching maturity sometimes pay bridewealth to their mother's family on behalf of their fathers, on whose estates they then can make certain claims for inheritance.

Lesotho

The situation in Lesotho is very different. Women continue to
marry young, very few independent women with children exist,
bridewealth payments are high, and litigation typically does not
concern the status of a union or a son's rights to inheritance as in
Botswana, but instead concerns the payment of bridewealth
(Kuper 1969; Poulter 1976). Young married couples still tend to
form households early, and the development of three-generation
households, so common in Botswana, occurs less frequently.

For Lesotho I rely on recent work by Judith Gay (1980) and by
Colin Murray (1982), who concentrated especially on marriage, domestic organization, migrant labor, and bridewealth. On the basis
of these reports it is possible to discuss the more specific questions
of age at marriage, household size, the status of children, and the
issue of unmarried mother and female-headed households. (See
also Spiegel 1980.)

Gay reported that 81 percent of women in her sample over the
age of 14 were married or had been married; 68 percent of household heads were men, and of female household heads over 80 percent were widows. Further, 46 percent of households contained a
simple nuclear family. Murray's figures, taken from one community, are less striking, though still forming a strong contrast to the
situation in Botswana (1982, especially pp. 54–55). Most telling of
all, perhaps, are the figures for bridewealth and for age at marriage. Poulter (1976) and Murray (1982) document the persistence
of the high traditional *bohali* (bridewealth) rate, roughly three
times the traditional Botswana average, which in any case the people of modern Botswana seldom realize in practice. The phenomenon of continuing bridewealth payment is paired with a low age at
marriage. Ian Timaeus of the Centre for Population Studies, London School of Hygiene and Tropical Medicine, provided me with
the following data on mean age at first marriage in Lesotho.

	Men	Women
1966 Census	26.0	20.4
1976 Census	24.8	20.1
1977 Fertility Survey	24.5	20.2

He cautions that such figures are not precise. "However, my best
guess would be that age at first marriage for men has declined

rather than that the 1966 figure is in error" (personal communication). The Botswana mean is about ten years higher.

To what must we ascribe this traditional pattern in an area of Southern Africa which on every other count is far more affected by political and economic changes than Botswana?

Murray has developed a persuasive and sophisticated analysis of the reasons for the maintenance of superficially traditional marriage arrangements in a very untraditional environment. Marriage in Lesotho, in fact, is traditional only with respect to age at marriage, the payment of bridewealth, and the establishment of new households. Van der Wiel (1977) found that 77 percent of men aged 20–39 were absent on migrant labor. The fact that in half of the households the male household head is absent reveals the very untraditional nature of what really is happening in Lesotho.

In what do these migrants invest their earnings? In Lesotho, migrant labor rather than cattle ownership provides the basis of rural subsistence. However, compared to Botswana, agriculture still constitutes an important resource. The migrant laborer goes to the city and remits funds regularly to his home base, in order to maintain a place to retire to and an enterprise that will support him in his old age. He accomplishes this goal by keeping a wife and children on a small farm to which he will retire. When he returns home in his forties, his sons begin their activities as migrant laborers and remit some cash to him. His daughters get married to young men who must pay him a portion of their migrant earnings in the form of bridewealth payments. Bridewealth payments in modern Lesotho, paid largely in cash, serve to link the industrial laborer with his rural base. Just as the traditional pastoralist invested a part of his capital in wives, who worked his fields, so the modern migrant laborer in Lesotho puts part of his earnings in an alternative economic resource, his family farm and his children (Spiegel 1980, pp. 117–121).

In Botswana, the labor migrant considers an agricultural base to be of little importance and instead accumulates another kind of resource for his retirement, namely, a cattle herd. He remits funds to his father or brother who remain behind, and to whose household he remains attached. They will buy cattle for him and tend it with their own herds, perhaps at a slight charge. The migrant laborer returns to claim his cattle upon retirement. A wife and children would merely provide a drain on his resources during his absence (see especially Kooijman 1978 and Gulbrandson 1980).

Women Migrants

Studies now are being made of an even more radical change, the development in some areas of migrant labor by women. In Lesotho, studies have shown that the women who go into the cities as migrant laborers are not unmarried but rather married women whose marriages have broken down (Van der Wiel 1977, p. 34; Gay 1980). Left with neither a husband nor a brother or father to look after them, they travel to the cities and set up Carribbean-type female-headed households, dependent entirely on their own labor. Preston-Whyte (1978, 1981) has studied Zulu women migrants and has found that they also were often victims of failed marriages, although circumstances sometimes obliged single mothers as well to move to the city. It is very difficult for women to gain rights in land on their own account, especially when they are squatters on white-owned land, because the farmer generally allocates land to the wives of his own field hands.

Review and Predictions

The ethnographic materials I have reviewed may be summed up in various ways, but I would stress three striking features.[7] First of all, despite the radical political, economic, religious, and social changes of the past three generations, the fundamental Southern Bantu formula of marriage (the exchange of women against the payment of bridewealth) has remained remarkably stable. Second, this formula, initially so closely attuned to the economic circumstances of a traditional society, has permitted remarkably flexible adjustment to various circumstances such as those found in different parts of Southern Africa in this century. Third, and partly as a consequence of the very flexibility of these institutions, the lines of modern development have been very diverse.

While it is unlikely that development will be any more uniform in the future, some changes may nevertheless be predicted. Certainly, the available land is decreasing in rural south Africa for the maintenance of even a marginal rural subsistence base by women, old men, and young children. These circumstances will oblige many more women to migrate into the cities. These women will be forced increasingly into activities that, although marginal and unproductive, probably are more attractive than the total hopelessness of the rural home. In the cities these women will find little advantage in a stable relationship with any particular man. They will, when young, have a variety of relationships yielding a certain amount of income. When older they will be obliged to rely on their daughters, in return for services in looking after children. I predict therefore a growth in what we call Carribbean-type families. Women with some education and higher earning capacities will have the opportunity to make more prestigious and more satisfying marriage arrangements. In such cases, a husband, who once again is taking on an income-earning wife, probably will continue to pay bridewealth for her.

Yet some of the fundamental constraints may change. So far only women with large salaries (mainly nurses and teachers) have achieved a genuine independence. They can choose whether or not to marry and they have no need of the protection of a brother or father. As for poorer unmarried women, if they were given an equal right to claim farms in "communal" areas, their position would be significantly eased. Other changes in the inheritance laws, granting them claims on the family cattle, would also aid them.[8] In the absence of such changes, however, the rural areas offer little to women on their own and condemn them to an indeterminate and uncertain life in the cities.

I have summarized the common features of a series of cases that appear irreconcilably diverse but actally exhibit two fundamental continuities. All the systems I have discussed rest, first, on the differentiation of male and female labor and, second, on the preferential allocation of capital resources to men. These are the basic conditions of African marriage systems. Local variants result from the differing value in particular circumstances of male labor, female labor, and male capital resources.

These fundamental continuities do not reflect material determinants. The basic conditions of these systems are not given by nature. In some parts of the world women inherit property, men receive dowry payments when they marry, and male and female labor is interchangeable. The African model—perhaps more specifically a Bantu model—rests in the end upon obstinate cultural premises.

NOTES

1.   The traditional systems are described in detail in Kuper (1982). See also Schneider (1964).

2.   The figures are taken from Schapera (1957, p. 145). See also Schapera (1940, 1950).

3.   Ashton (1952) devoted an appendix to Southern Sotho kinship marriages, as does Murray (1982).

4.   There are political and economic reasons for this dispersal of population, which both reflects and exacerbates the weakening of traditional political controls. See Kuper (1975a, pp. 144–146); Silitshena (1979).

5.   These statistics and their significance for preferential marriage are analyzed in Kuper (1975b).

6.   Another re-study of a Tswana ward is reported in Schapera and Roberts (1975). A fine account of these changes in a previously unstudied area of Botswana is provided in Kooijman (1978).

7.   One of the issues, which I have not touched upon for want of adequate data, is the question of birth rates. How many children do men and women want in the various Southern Africa situations that I have sketched? How many do they have? What is the economic, social, and psychological value attached to these children? This issue is of enormous significance and interest, and it waits a properly organized investigation.

8.   Legal reforms are being instituted, and it will be interesting to see their effect. Probably, however, women (with few exceptions) will not be in a position to manage cattle which they may now inherit, and will be obliged to sell them off.

REFERENCES

Africa South of the Sahara. London: Europa Publications, 1981–1982.
Ashton, Hugh. *The Basotho.* London: Oxford University Press, 1952.

Brown, Barbara. "The Impact of Male Labour Migration on Women in Botswana." *African Affairs* 82(1983):367–388.

Comaroff, J. L., and Roberts, S. *Rules and Processes: The Cultural Logic of Dispute in an African Context.* Chicago: Chicago University Press, 1981.

Curtis, Donald. "The Social Organisation of Ploughing." *Botswana Notes and Records* 4(1972):67–80.

Dahl, G., and Hjort, A. *Having Herds: Pastoral Herd Growth and Household Economy.* Stockholm Studies in Social Anthropology, Vol. 2, 1976.

Gay, Judith. *Basotho Women's Options: A Study of Marital Careers in Rural Lesotho.* Ph.D. dissertation, Cambridge University, 1980.

Goody, J., and Tambiah, S. *Bridewealth and Dowry.* Cambridge: At the University Press, 1973.

Gulbrandson, O. *Agro-Pastoral Production and Communal Land Use: A Socio-Economic Study of the Bangwaketse.* Gaborone: Rural Sociology Unit, Ministry of Agriculture, 1980.

Kocken, E. M., and Uhlenbeck, G. C. *Tlokweng, a Village Near Town.* Leiden, Netherlands: Institute of Cultural and Social Studies, University of Leiden, 1980.

Kooijman, K. F. M. *Social and Economic Change in a Tswana Village.* Leiden, Netherlands: Africa Study Centre, 1978.

Kuper, Adam. "The Work of Customary Courts." *African Studies* 28(1969):37–48.

Kuper, Adam. "The Kgalagari and the Jural Consequences of Marriage." *Man* 5(1970):355–381.

Kuper, Adam. "The Social Structure of the Sotho-Speaking Peoples of Southern Africa." *Africa* 54(1975a):67–81, 139–149.

Kuper, Adam. "Preferential Marriage and Polygyny Among the Tswana." In M. Fortes and S. Patteron (eds.), *Studies in African Social Anthropology.* London: Academic Press, 1975b.

Kuper, Adam. *Wives for Cattle.* London: Routledge & Kegan Paul, 1982.

Molenaar, Marja. *Social Change Within a Traditional Pattern.* Leiden, Netherlands: Private printing, 1980.

Murray, Colin. *Families Divided: The Impact of Migrant Labour in Lesotho.* Cambridge: At the University Press, 1982.

Poulter, Sebastian. *Family Law and Litigation in Basotho Society.* Oxford: Clarendon Press, 1976.

Preston-Whyte, E. "Families Without Marriage: A Zulu Case-Study." In John Argyle and Eleanor Preston-Whyte (eds.), *Social System and Tradition in Southern Africa.* Cape Town, South Africa: Oxford University Press, 1978.

Preston-Whyte, E. "Women Migrants and Marriage." In E. J. Krige and J. L. Comaroff (eds.), *Essays on African Marriage in Southern Africa.* Cape Town, South Africa: Juta, 1981.

Schapera, I. *Married Life in an African Tribe.* London: Faber, 1940.

Schapera, I. "Kinship and Marriage Among the Tswana." In A. R. Radcliffe-Brown and Daryll Forde (eds.), *African Systems of Kinship and Marrige.* London: Oxford University Press, 1950.

Schapera, I. "Marriage of Near Kin Among the Tswana." *Africa* 37(1957): 139–159.

Schapera, I. "Some Notes on Tswana Bogadi." *Journal of African Law* 22(1978):112–124.

Schapera, I., and Roberts, S. "Rampedi Revisited: Another Look at a Tswana Ward." *Africa* 45(1975):258–279.

Schneider, H. K. "A Model of African Indigenous Economy and Society." *Comparative Studies in Society and History* 7(1964):37–55.

Silitshena, Robson. *Changing Settlement Patterns in Botswana: The Case of Eastern Kweneng.* Ph.D. dissertation, University of Sussex, 1979.

Spiegel, A. "Rural Differentiation and the Diffusion of Migrant Labour Remittances in Lesotho." In P. Mayer (ed.), *Black Villagers in an Industrial Society.* Cape Town, South Africa: Oxford University Press, 1980.

Turton, D. "The Economics of Mursi Bridewealth: A Comparative Perspective." In J. L. Comaroff (ed.), *The Meaning of Marriage Payments.* New York: Academic Press, 1980.

Van der Wiel, A. C. A. *Migratory Wage Labour: Its Role in the Economy of Lesotho.* Mazenod, Lesotho: Mazenod Book Centre, 1977.

11 *A Familistic Religion in a Modern Society*

JAMES E. SMITH

TODAY MORE THAN 5 MILLION MORMONS live in more than 100 countries. While these members of the Church of Jesus Christ of Latter-day Saints[1]—also called the Mormon Church—form only a tiny part of the world's Christian population, the worldwide Mormon population is increasing at a rate that will double its size every fifteen years.

When Joseph Smith founded "The Church of Christ in these last days" in 1830, it had six official members. These revered Joseph as a prophet who had communed directly with God and other heavenly messengers. He had just published *The Book of Mormon*, which he claimed was a translation of ancient records concerning peoples on the American continent and of Christ's visit to them shortly after his resurrection. With tremendous missionary

NOTE: *The author wishes to thank Tim Heaton, Caroline Hoppe, Kristen Goodman, Howard Bahr, and Darwin Thomas, all of whom offered valuable insights and data for this chapter.*

Table 11.1

Mormon Church Membership and Growth Rate, by Decade

Year	Total Church Membership	Average Annual Percent Growth in Preceding Decade
1900	283,765	4.10
1910	398,478	3.35
1920	525,987	2.78
1930	670,017	2.46
1940	862,664	2.53
1950	1,111,314	2.53
1960	1,693,180	4.21
1970	2,930,810	5.49
1980	4,633,000	4.58
1981	4,919,909	—

zeal the first "Mormons" (as they were called by their detractors) set out to convince their families, friends, and countrymen that Joseph Smith had restored to the earth the pristine Gospel of Jesus Christ. By 1845 the Mormons numbered tens of thousands, the largest concentration being in the Mormon city of Nauvoo, Illinois. After a forced exodus from Nauvoo to the Territory of Utah, the church continued to grow rapidly, due partly to high fertility and partly to extensive immigration of European converts. By the time Utah was admitted as a state in 1896 the membership had risen to a fourth of a million, two-thirds of them living in Utah.

During the twentieth century the Mormon Church has grown at an average annual rate of 3.6 percent with rates well over 4 percent in recent decades (Table 11.1). At the same time the location of the Mormon population has shifted from a concentration in Utah, where less than one-fourth of all Mormons now reside, to other states where nearly half the church is found. An "internationalization" of the Mormon population has accompanied this "nationalization." In only ten years from 1970 to 1980, the Mormon community outside the United States increased 62 percent and the number of Mormons in Mexico, Argentina, Brazil, and Japan has tripled. In Mexico alone there are now over a quarter million Mormons, constituting the largest concentration outside the United States. In all, almost one-third of all Mormons now live outside the United States.[2]

Table 11.2

Concentration and Distribution of Mormon Church Membership,
by Year

Year	Concentration (percent) of Mormons in		Percent of Mormons in	
	U.S. Population	Utah Population	U.S.	Utah
1910	.38	60.6	88.8	57.5
1920	.36	59.6	73.2	51.0
1930	.47	64.2	86.4	48.5
1940	.57	63.5	86.3	40.5
1950	.67	67.9	90.5	42.1
1960	.83	72.3	87.9	38.0
1970	1.02	73.4	70.7	26.5
1980	1.55	70.2	71.2	20.9

SOURCE: Deseret News, *1983 Church Almanac*, p. 272.

In spite of its rapid growth, the Mormon population is still small in absolute numbers and a tiny part of the total population of most places where Mormons are found (Table 11.2). Only in Samoa, Tonga, and a few western states of the United States do Mormons comprise over 1 percent of the total population. In Utah, of course, about 70 percent of the population is Mormon, but even this is not far above the concentration of Roman Catholics in Rhode Island (63 percent). Although Mormons constitute over 1 percent of the population of every Mountain and Pacific State, this regional representation is less impressive than the concentration of Southern Baptists in the much more heavily populated southern region stretching from Delaware to Texas.

Although small in size when compared with the largest denominations, the Mormon Church, with roughly the same number of members as the Episcopal Church, is the fifth largest religious body in the United States. But the growth rate of Mormonism, far outstripping that of leading denominations and exceeding, with the exception of Christian Science, that of all the smaller indigenous American denominations as well, is the most impressive attribute of the church. However, it is probably its wealth, even more than its growth rate, that makes the Mormon Church so formidable among religious groups. Although church finances are not made public, a reasonable guess is that its members voluntarily contribute over $700 million per year to the church.[3] With a university enrolling 25,000 students, a church building program requiring $1 million a day, radio and television stations, ranches and farms, skyscrapers, publishing houses, retail stores, real estate, and cash investments, it is little wonder that the leadership of the Mormon Church includes men with substantial business and financial backgrounds.

Mormon Familism

Like any denomination, Mormonism can be viewed from several perspectives: as a theology, a formal organization, a social movement, a self-selected subpopulation, etc. Yet, viewed from any of these perspectives, Mormonism gives the observer the immediate sense that the family occupies a central place. Of course, the centrality of the family in Mormonism does not itself distinguish it from other religions. But what does cause Mormonism to stand out is that it "is not simply concerned with the family, as are so many other groups; the Mormon religion in the last analysis really is *about* the family" (Foster 1982, p. 7).

Practices within the Mormon Church provide evidence for the centrality of family life. One of the most often cited statements by a Mormon prophet is that "no other success can compensate for failure in the home." Faithful Mormons reserve one night each week for "family home evening," a time when religious discussion and family activities take place. All church members are supposed to receive monthly visits from "home teachers" who are assigned from among lay priesthood members in the local Mormon congregation. The "family preparedness" program encourages members to store food and otherwise prepare for economic self-sufficiency. Mormon media campaigns and the extensive missionary program of the church rely heavily upon the idea of "family togetherness" for their appeal. The most popular catch phrases of modern Mormonism virtually always include the terms "family" or "home": the most important work you do will be within the walls of your own home; happiness is family home evening; the happy family is a bit of heaven on earth; families are forever. The last phrase is particularly instructive. Mormons sincerely believe that families are, or at least can be, "forever" in the sense that familial relations will continue in the next life for those who are worthy. This belief, perhaps more than any other, underlies the Mormon emphasis on the family and explains why Mormons are so anxious to have "family" as their rallying banner.

The Eternal Family

In Mormon theology, men and women must be married for eternity to attain the highest degree of salvation in the hereafter. Since eternal marriage is an ordinance that must be performed by a duly constituted religious authority on earth, Mormons believe they must ensure in this life that they are eternally married.[4] Civil marriages "til death do you part" are performed by the Mormon priesthood, but it is the eternal marriage—marriage in a Mormon temple—that all faithful Mormons are supposed to seek. This temple marriage, or "sealing," is the official church dispensation that guarantees to a Mormon couple that they will be married in the next life provided they remain faithful.

Most Mormons assume that since the eventual resurrection will restore the physical body to each man and woman, those who are worthy of eternal marriages in the hereafter will continue in a physical as well as psychological bond of marriage throughout eternity. The offspring of such eternal unions will be children with spirit bodies, that is, bodies in human form but of finer or purer matter.[5] To Mormons this eternal, procreative family consists of much more than just another reward for the righteous; it is an essential part of the cosmic order itself. In Mormon theology God, literally an eternal father, lived in a mortal state, was married, proved faithful, and now procreates spirit children. Those children include the spirits of all people who have lived on the earth making the spirits of all people literally the offspring of God.

This Mormon view of the cosmos is distinctively nonmystical. God is anthropomorphic, although with attributes of mind and body beyond imperfect human imagination. Nevertheless, Mormons believe that "as God is, man may become"[6] so that to the Mormon this life is not only a time to prepare to meet God but also a time to prepare to become a God. Mormons interpret the

New Testament scripture—that "there are Gods many and Lords many"—to mean that many Gods live in eternal families in the heavens. However, Mormons owe allegiance only to one God, literally the father of all spirits of this earth's inhabitants.

Not only does the nuclear family of husband, wife, and children take on cosmic significance in Mormonism, but so does the extended family. Children born to parents during this life are "sealed" to their parents, presumably meaning that parents may exercise authority over their children in the next life as well. When a Mormon couple has been married for eternity, children born to the union are automatically considered to be sealed to their parents. When a couple is sealed following an earlier civil marriage, or when children are legally adopted, a brief ceremony is performed in a Mormon temple to seal the children to their parents.

Authority and the Family

In his influential analysis of the chief religious appeal of early Mormonism, Mario DePillis (1966) stressed that Mormonism provided an answer to a quest for religious authority in nineteenth-century America. In Mormonism the priesthood embodies religious authority, an authority that Mormons define simply as the right to act for God. A fundamental argument of Mormonism is that this authority must exist in the true Christian Church. The early Christian Church lost the authority through widespread spiritual corruption, and did not regain it until heavenly messengers appeared before the prophet Joseph Smith. Without true priestly authority a minister might solemnize a marriage "for eternity" but heaven would refuse to recognize it as such. Legitimate priestly authority is therefore essential to the Mormon practice of eternal marriage.

Priestly authority is not only necessary to seal husbands to wives and children to parents but also to legitimize church leadership. The Mormon priesthood is a lay priesthood, and all males over 12 years of age who conform to basic church teachings are eligible to hold some degree of priestly authority. A Mormon man must hold the rank of Elder in order to be sealed to his wife and children in a Mormon temple. Since this same priestly role entitles the man to function in various church leadership positions, a high correlation exists between making a commitment to religious activity and being married for eternity.

There can be no doubt that the ideal, eternal Mormon family is in important ways patriarchal. But in Mormonism the term "patriarch" is filled with positive connotations; it refers directly to the ancient Hebrew patriarchs, Abraham, Isaac, and Jacob, whom Mormons see as enlightened prophets who understood the Christian message by vision of the future, and who perpetuated religious covenants, including eternal marriage, which Mormons now subscribe to. Except for a small but sometimes vocal minority within the church, Mormons seem to be in complete sympathy with Paul's counsel that the man should be the head of the household just as Christ was the head of his Church.

The risks of the abuse of priestly authority were recognized by Joseph Smith himself in a warning that Mormons now accept as scripture:

> when we undertake to cover our sins, or to gratify our pride, our vain ambition, or to exercise control or dominion or compulsion upon the souls of the children of men, in any degree of unrighteousness, behold, the heavens withdraw themselves; the Spirit of the Lord is grieved; and when it is withdrawn, Amen to the priesthood or the authority of that man [Doctrine and Covenants, Section 121].

In recent years Mormon church leaders have spoken directly to the issue of spouse abuse, and members desiring to participate in the Mormon temple rites are specifically asked about this when interviewed by their local Mormon bishop (that is, pastor). Less extreme abuses of patriarchalism are, of course, more difficult to detect and regulate. Among Roman Catholics, Protestants, and Mormons in Utah, empirical data suggest that "anticipated differences in the relative power of wives and husbands reflecting the presumed patriarchalism of Mormon families did not appear" (Bahr 1982, p. 208). However, the data did demonstrate that Mormons differed significantly from others in their lack of tolerance for nontraditional role definitions (p. 216). The Mormon Church's official opposition to the Equal Rights Amendment was a clear institutional indicator that the church is sensitive to perceived threats to traditional female roles.

Mormon Polygyny

Probably the most widely known fact about Mormon marriage is that at one time (1852–1890) polygyny was practiced by Utah Mormons. Although this chapter is about modern Mormon marriage, some idea of Mormon polygyny should prove helpful, especially since it was in the revelation to Joseph Smith concerning polygyny that the idea of eternal family relations was first set forth. Given the combined importance of priesthood authority and the eternal family in Mormonism, it is not surprising that early in Mormon history Joseph Smith questioned whether the biblical patriarchs had authority to practice polygyny. The result of his queries was a revelation, probably in 1831, that led to rumor, internal dissension, external persecution, and ultimately contributed to the murder of Joseph Smith by a conspiracy of disaffected Mormons and others. This revelation condoned polygyny provided it was regulated by the priesthood. Within a few years Joseph Smith and at least one of his closest associates had entered polygynous unions. Within a decade polygyny was secretly practiced by a number of church leaders.

It was not until 1852, after having been exiled to the Territory of Utah, that the Mormons publicly announced their intention to practice polygyny on a wide scale. Subsequently, more than 20 percent of all married Mormon men may have had more than one wife at some time in their lives (Smith and Kunz 1976). But from 1852 onward the Mormons faced incessant conflicts with the federal government over the practice. Following an unfavorable Supreme Court decision, and threatened with disenfranchisement, the church finally capitulated. A carefully worded "Manifesto" announcing the abandonment of polygyny was approved by vote of the church. It is debatable whether the Manifesto was really meant to end the practice of polygyny, or was only a smokescreen to allow a more limited practice of polygyny to continue secretly. It is clear, however, that even the leading Quorum of the Twelve Apostles (second only to the President of the Church in authority) was not united behind total abandonment until more than a decade later (Cannon 1983). Moreover, official denunciations of polygyny were issued fairly regularly for decades after 1890 indicating some confusion and reluctance to abandon the practice among Mormons who had been taught earlier that this form of marriage was a religious obligation. Today, although Mormon doctrine condoning the *principle* of polygyny has not changed, the *practice* of polygyny has been entirely suspended. The church immediately excommunicates any Mormon entering a polygynous union, and, even in a country where civil law permits polygyny a polygynist may not become a Mormon.

On the surface, Mormonism's shift from tenacious adherence to polygyny in the nineteenth century to modern enthusiastic endorsement of traditional nuclear family values is an enigma. Attempts to explain the shift have produced polarized viewpoints. Some Mormon apologists have tried to explain away the possible theological problems caused by this change by proposing that polygyny was instituted strictly for demographic reasons—a surplus of single and widowed females—and that the practice was unnecessary once the demographic reasons no longer existed. Other observers see the abandonment of polygyny as a fundamental change in the very essence of Mormon doctrine.

Yet one finds that whatever the changes from the days of polygyny to today, certain basic aspects of Mormon family doctrine and practice have persisted from the beginning of the religion. These include condemnation of all sexual intercourse outside of marriage, encouragement of universal marriage at young ages, expectations of high fertility, reinforcement of male leadership in the home, definition of a woman's role as that of mother and homemaker, and strong sanctions against divorce. While Mormons have not perfectly embodied these norms in their behavior, they have in several aspects of familial behavior maintained an impressive distinctiveness from surrounding society. An empirical analysis of Mormon family patterns can demonstrate the degree to which the centrality of the family in Mormon ideology translates into a family experience different from that of other groups, and to what extent changes in the wider society have had an effect on Mormons.

Family Patterns

A thorough statistical overview of Mormon family patterns is not possible for a number of reasons. Many of the necessary data simply are not collected by the Mormon Church or anyone else, and many data that are collected are not made public by the church. Nevertheless, the following four main sources of information on the Mormon family can be used to construct a composite picture of family life: (1) statistics for the State of Utah where Mormons, especially in rural areas, constitute a majority of the population; (2) limited data published by the church; (3) results of general surveys that include Mormon respondents; and (4) currently unpublished data available in sources such as the 1981 L.D.S. Church Membership Survey. The reader should realize the distinction between "Utah data" and "Mormon data" and should also be aware that some published data from the Mormon Church are of dubious quality. Unless otherwise indicated, data used in this chapter are from standard U.S. statistical sources, such as the *Statistical Abstract of the U.S.*, Utah Vital Statistics annual reports, or unpublished research reports for the 1981 L.D.S. Church Membership Survey. All L.D.S. survey data are cited with permission.

Prevalence of Marriage and Age at Marriage

American Mormons are more likely to be married at any given age than are their American counterparts, as shown in Table 11.3. The "unmarried" category shows the net effect of five factors—permanent celibacy, delayed marriage, divorce, remarriage, and widowhood. One reason for the prevalence of marriage among Mormons is that they marry at a younger age than other Americans. In 1980 the mean ages at first marriage for Utah and U.S. brides and grooms were as follows:

Grooms		Brides	
Utah	U.S.	Utah	U.S.
22.5	23.2	20.5	21.4

Heaton and Goodman (forthcoming) have shown that earlier Mormon marriage is attributable to more marriages just below the mean age rather than significantly larger proportions at very young ages. The expectation that single Mormon males will serve as full-time missionaries for two years (reduced to 18 months in 1982 and raised again to 24 months in 1984) explains why Utah grooms are closer to the U.S. age at marriage than Utah brides.

Table 11.3

Percent of Population Unmarried, by Age and Sex, United States and North American Mormons, 1980[a]

	Males		Females	
Age	U.S.	Mormon	U.S.	Mormon
20–24	72.1	70.7	58.0	49.3
25–29	40.9	35.4	35.1	24.5
30–35	27.4	20.8	27.3	16.1
35–39	19.7	13.6	24.1	13.4

[a]North American Mormons include U.S. and Canadian Mormons, 97 percent of whom are estimated to be in the United States.

SOURCES: Deseret News, *1982 Church Almanac*, pp. 225–227, 1981; U.S. Bureau of the Census, "Marital Status and Living Arrangements, March 1977," *Current Population Reports*, Series P-20, No. 323 (April 1978), p. 7; ibid., No. 365 (October 1981), p. 7.

Since about 30 percent of all Mormon 19-year-olds enter missionary service (the proportion is probably higher in Utah), many Mormon males do not enter the marriage market until they are 21 years old. The norms for early marriage do, however, cause some of this lost time to be recaptured because many, if not most, missionaries marry within a year of their return home.

The combination of Mormon norms for high educational attainment, early marriage, and full-time missionary service has interesting consequences. Consider, for example, the data on educational attainment of brides and grooms at marriage (Table 11.4). Of the sixteen reporting states in 1976, Utah had the highest proportions of brides and grooms who had completed *some* college education prior to marriage. But of those Utah brides and grooms who had started college prior to marriage, smaller percentages completed four years of college than in most other states. The presence of Brigham Young University in Utah probably explains much of this pattern. Virtually all of the 25,000 full-time students at B.Y.U. are members of the Mormon Church. Nearly three-fourths are single, and jokes about B.Y.U.'s function as a Mormon marriage market only thinly disguise the very real and intentional function which the school serves in that regard. B.Y.U. men generally attend one year of college, serve a full-time mission for 18 or 24 months, then return to B.Y.U. and marry within a year to two.

Table 11.4

Educational Attainment of Brides and Grooms,
Utah and United States, 1976[a]

State	13 Years	16 Years
Percent of Brides Completing		
California	41.3	15.1
Utah	46.1	11.9
Wyoming	32.3	8.7
Illinois	38.9	10.3
Virginia	28.0	12.1
Tennessee	21.5	7.9
16 States	33.4	12.5
Percent of Grooms Completing		
California	48.1	22.0
Utah	52.9	15.3
Wyoming	36.6	14.4
Illinois	34.1	14.8
Virginia	31.3	15.8
Tennessee	26.5	12.2
16 States	38.5	17.2

[a]Percentages based on total numbers of brides and grooms reporting education. Selected states from the sixteen reporting states are presented.

SOURCE: National Center for Health Statistics, *Vital Statistics of the United States: 1976, Vol. 3: Marriage and Divorce*, 1980, Section 1, p. 71.

Women often marry a returned missionary during their college years and many of these young wives discontinue their education to bear children. The resulting financial burdens cause some husbands to discontinue college as well.

Fertility

Marriage at young ages implies the possibility of high fertility and in the case of the Mormons this possibility is realized. The Mormon Church reported a crude birthrate of 28.2 births per thousand members worldwide in 1980, well above the rate of 16.2 for the United States and the rates for other industrialized nations. Table 11.5 presents the Mormon Church, Utah, and U.S. crude birthrates at the turn of each decade since 1950. Mormon and Utah fertility have both followed a generally declining trend with Mormon fertility at a higher level. The upturn in Utah fertility from 1970 to 1980 is evident in both the crude birthrate and births per 1,000 women

Table 11.5

Mormon Fertility, Utah and United States, Selected Years

	Crude Birth Rate			Births per 1,000 Women Aged 15–44	
Year	Mormon Church	Utah	U.S.	Utah	U.S. White
1950	37.8	30.4	24.1	139.4	102.3
1960	34.6	29.2	23.7	146.5	113.2
1970	28.4	25.3	18.4	117.4	84.1
1980	28.2	28.3	16.2	123.0	68.5[a]

[a]Data for 1979.

SOURCES: Utah Department of Health, *1980 Utah Vital Statistics* p. 22, 26 (1982);
U.S. National Center for Health Statistics, *Vital Statistics of the United States, 1976,
Vol. 1: Natality*, PMS81-1100, Table 1-2 (1980).

of reproductive age. A closer look at changes in Utah age-specific fertility rates from 1970 to 1980 reveals the following percentage increases in fertility by age of mother:

Age of mother	15–19	20–24	25–29	30–34	35–39	40–44	15–44
Percent change	+15	−7	−8	+4	+5	−2	+5

Increasing teenage fertility obviously contributed the most to increasing Utah fertility during the 1970s, not only because of the large percentage increase in the rate for this age group but also because more women were in the 15–19 age group than in the older age groups. The increase in fertility of women in their thirties, although also significant, resembled the national increase for this age group more closely than did the teenage fertility increase in Utah.

It could be postulated that the increasing fertility of teenage Utahans in the 1970s occurred because their fertility was "catching up" to the Utah norm. In 1970 only the 15–19-year-old population in Utah possessed a fertility rate as low as the U.S. white fertility rate (see Table 11.6) but by 1980 the fertility of Utah's teens exceeded the fertility of U.S. teens significantly, although still not to the extent that the fertility of older Utah women exceeded that of older U.S. women. Of course, to outline how teenage fertility has reached the high Utah level does not provide an explanation for the teenage fertility behavior, for, after all, the rise has not occurred as the result of a conscious goal. In addition, the increase

Table 11.6

Age-Specific Fertility Rates, Utah and United States, 1970 and 1979

	Births per 1,000 Women of Age					
	15–19	20–24	25–29	30–34	35–39	39–44
1970 Utah	57.0	208.2	206.0	120.4	55.2	12.5
1970 U.S. White	57.4	163.4	145.9	71.9	30.0	7.5
Ratio Utah/U.S., 1970	.99	1.27	1.41	1.67	1.84	1.67
1979 Utah	64.4	196.8	196.3	126.7	57.8	12.2
1979 U.S. White	44.5	109.7	114.6	60.5	18.2	3.5
Ratio Utah/U.S., 1979	1.45	1.79	1.71	2.09	3.18	3.49

SOURCE: Utah Department of Health, *1980 Utah Vital Statistics* (1982), pp. 22, 26.

should not be overly interpreted; teenage fertility in Utah is no more extraordinary than Utah fertility in general.

Whatever its causes, Utah's sustained high fertility has had profound social and demographic consequences. The median age of Utah's population is nearly six years lower than the median of 30 years for the United States and Utah's average household size of 3.26 persons is higher than the 2.75 persons per household in the United States. While Utahans earn a mean household income that is about parallel with the national average, they have a lower per capita income due to the preponderance of large families. But despite their lower per capita income, Utahans, manage to educate their children so well that the proportion of Utah's population that graduates from college stands among the top five states. And while Utah per capita income is relatively low, Utah has been consistently lower than the nation and the other mountain states in the percent of its population receiving Supplemental Security Income, Aid to Families with Dependent Children, and Food Stamp benefits. Only 7.6 percent of all families fall below the poverty level, placing Utah in the lowest decile of the states in this statistic (Martin 1981).

Fertility Control

Although Utah Mormons could have been considered a natural fertility population in the nineteenth century, Mormon fertility today falls far short of natural fertility levels. In their analysis of Mormon respondents in the 1965, 1970, and 1975 National Fertility Studies, Heaton and Calkins (1983) report that Mormons were just as likely as other non-Catholics to have ever used birth control. Moreover, when using birth control, Mormons seem willing to adopt the most advanced methods. Interview data suggest that Mormon women do not have large families as a result of rejecting the use of birth control per se on theological or other ideological grounds (Bahr et al., 1982; Thornton 1979). Instead, it appears that Mormons want moderately large families. Although based on small N's, the following data on Mormons from the National Fertility Survey (Heaton and Calkins, 1983) illustrate the point:

	Mean Expected Number of Children per Family	Mean Children Ever Born per Family
1975 (N = 71)	3.15	3.06
1970 (N = 117)	3.89	2.57
1965 (N = 70)	4.11	3.47

It seems clear that in what is becoming the no-growth population of the United States, Mormons' reproductive expectations have also dropped but are still at a fairly high level.

Divorce

Statistics on Mormon divorce provide a surprising contrast to the family-oriented Mormon practices of marrying early and creating large families. Utah consistently has had a crude divorce rate above or at the national level (see Table 11.7). However, when county data are examined, a moderately high negative correlation (− .56) is found between the crude divorce rate and the percentage of the county population that is Mormon. In light of this the Utah crude divorce rate can be adjusted to yield something closer to a Mormon crude divorce rate by weighting the county divorce rates by the proportion of the Utah Mormon population residing in each county. As shown in Table 11.7, this procedure yields an adjusted state crude divorce rate of 4.99 instead of 5.3 for 1980. This rate is still very high. The conclusion is unavoidable that Mormons are more similar to non-Mormons in their divorce behavior than in their fertility behavior.

Table 11.7

Crude Divorce Rate, Utah and United States, by Year

Year	Utah	United States
1950	3.0	2.6
1960	2.4	2.2
1970	3.7	3.5
1980	5.3 (4.99)[a]	5.3

[a]Utah county crude divorce rates weighted by proportion of Utah Mormon population residing in county.

SOURCES: Utah Department of Health, *1980 Utah Vital Statistics* (1982), p. 5; National center for Health Statistics, *Monthly Vital Statistics Report*, "Annual Summary of Births, Deaths, Marriages, and Divorces: United States, 1980," Vol. 29, No. 13, p. 1 (Sept. 17, 1981); Deseret News, *1982 Church Almanac* (1981), p. 221.

The high fertility of Utahans causes the number of children involved per divorce in Utah (1.17 in 1978) to exceed the national average (1.01 in 1978). The shorter life-span of Utah marriages ending in dovrce—5.0 years compared to the 6.6-year average for twenty-nine reporting states in 1978—prevents an even larger number of children in Utah from being involved. The number of children whose parents divorce per 1,000 children under 18 years of age is lower (15.6 in 1978) in Utah than in the United States as a whole (18.1 in 1978). Nevertheless, the increase in child involvement in divorce has been as dramatic in Utah as it has been in the United States. From 1970 to 1978 the increases were 44.4 percent in Utah and 45 percent in the United States. Divorce is clearly a very real part of the Mormon family scene, both in terms of the number of spouses and the number of children involved.

Working Women

Another countercurrent to Mormon familism is the entry of women into the labor force, propelling the state of Utah from far below the national average in 1940 to about an equal level in 1970 (see Table 11.8). But in the same period the proportion of working women in full-time employment declined. It seems that female part-time work is popular in Utah because it is more compatible than full-time work with raising a large family. While this may explain why Utah women engage in more part-time work, it does not explain

Table 11.8

Percent of Women in the Labor Force, Utah and United States,
1940–1970

	1940		1950		1960		1970	
	Utah	U.S.	Utah	U.S.	Utah	U.S.	Utah	U.S.
Percent in labor force[a]	17.6	25.4	25.9	32.5	30.9	33.7	43.1	45.4
Percent working[b]								
1–14 hours	2.8	2.8	12.0	5.1	20.6	12.6	16.6	11.0
15–34 hours	12.7	15.2	15.5	13.2	19.5	16.0	26.2	22.0
35 hours or more	84.5	82.0	72.5	81.7	59.5	71.4	57.2	67.0

[a]Age 14 and over, 1940–1960, and 16 and over, 1970.
[b]Age 14 and over 1940; 14–29 years, 1950; 14–34 years, civilian labor force, 1960; 16–34 years, civilian labor force, 1970.
SOURCE: Bahr (1979).

the increasing percentage of women taking part-time jobs as opposed to no jobs at all. One possibility is the difficulty of supporting a large family in an increasingly urban and technologically advanced economy. Four- and five-bedroom houses have become more difficult to find and to afford, even in Utah. Inflation and educational expenses have a bigger impact on large families who, even in relatively prosperous times, live closer to the margin. Larger families generally must compensate for hard times by increasing their income rather than by substituting inferior goods in food, housing, and transportation, simply because they are often already using inferior goods.

In the United States about 42 percent of married Mormon women hold jobs outside the home (see Table 11.9), while more

Table 11.9

Percent of Mormon Ever-Married Women in Labor Force,
by Marital Status, 1981

Current Marital Status	Percent
First marriage intact	41.8
Remarriage	50.8
Divorced	67.6
Widowed	23.6

SOURCE: Goodman (1982), Table 3.

than two-thirds of the divorced do so. Among Mormons, this contrast between married and divorced women, while an expected result of economic needs, serves to reinforce the deviant status of Mormon divorced women who not only lack a husband but who also work outside the home. In reluctant and often implicit recognition of the rising divorce rates among church members, Mormon leaders often encourage young women to prepare for careers. Nevertheless, Utah women are only slightly above the median for school years completed by women over 25 in the U.S. (12.4 years for Utah, 12.1 years for the United States). And while Utah has consistently led the nation in the percentage of men and women who completed four or more years of college, the percent of bachelor's degrees earned by women in Utah (38.6 percent in 1975–1976) is the lowest of the mountain states and does not manifest the same upward trend that the mountain states exhibited from 1969–1970 to 1975–1976. By 1976 the percentages of master's and doctorate degrees granted in Utah to women were 23 and 16, respectively, compared to 46 and 23 for all mountain states (McDonald 1981).

In sum, Mormon women work in about the same proportions as other U.S. women, but much less often in full-time jobs. They complete college less often than women elsewhere, while their husbands complete college more often. They appear to avoid careers outside the home unless divorce or the need for supplemental family income make a job necessary.

Premarital Sex and Illegitimacy

While divorce and female labor force participation contradict the ideals of the Mormon family system, they are realities that are capable of gaining some acceptance without fundamentally threatening Mormon theology. This is surely true of female employment, less so of divorce. Church leaders are reluctant to cancel marriage "sealings" even when civil divorce has occurred. However, neither deviation is considered as bad as sexual sins, especially adultery. Adultery virtually always results in excommunication of those involved; sexual activity among the unmarried is usually treated less severely.

The following percentages of Mormons who disapprove of premarital intercourse demonstrate the conservative feelings of Mormon college students (Christensen 1982, p. 9):

	Mormons	N	Non-Mormons	N
Men	88.1	60	20.1	259
Women	92.2	182	27.6	370

The same survey showed that in 1978 nearly three-quarters of the Mormon respondents in Utah (male and female college students) reported that they were virgins compared with only 42 percent of midwestern non-Mormon respondents. Among the Mormons who reported premarital coital experience, between 40 percent of males and 50 percent of females reported that they disapproved of premarital coitus, as opposed to about 6 percent for the equivalent non-Mormon group (p. 11). Thus, Mormon sanctions against premarital sex not only prevent many young Mormons from participating but also elicit negative reactions from those who do participate.

The illegitimacy rate for Utah seems to pose an incongruity in the whole picture of Mormon chastity. In 1980 there were seventeen illegitimate births per 1,000 unmarried women (age 15–44) in Utah compared to 13.7 for unmarried white women in the United States. However, it is incorrect to infer from this that there is more nonmarital sexual activity in Utah than among white U.S. women. The relative level of Utah and U.S. illegitimacy rates is determined by three factors: the relative level of nonmarital sexual activity (RS) in the two populations, the relative usage of contraceptives among the unmarried (RC), and the relative use of abortion in terminating pregnancies of the unmarried (RA). These factors relate to the relative level of illegitimacy (RI) as follows:

$$RI = (RS)\,(1/RC)\,(1/RA)$$

Thus, a relatively high level of illegitimacy (RI over 1.0) is consistent with a relatively low level of nonmarital sexual activity (RS under 1.0) if the relative use of abortion and/or contraception is sufficiently low to compensate. In 1980 there were 1,082 abortions per 1,000 live births among the unmarried in Utah. In the United States the figure was about 3,000. Taking Utah as the numerator, the ratio RA was therefore about .36 yielding a value for 1/RA of about 2.8. Because we do not have adequate data on contraceptive usage among the unmarried in Utah, we will temporarily assume that their usage does not differ from women in the United States (making RC equal to 1.0). Our formula is now:

$$1.24 = (RS)(1.0)(2.8)$$

$$\text{or, } RS = .44$$

This is our rough estimate of the relative sexual activity of unmarried Utah women compared with unmarried U.S. white women. This value for RS, which implies that unmarried Utah women are less than half as sexually active as U.S. women, is also consistent with Christensen's (1982) survey data cited above in which three-fourths of Mormons reporting themselves to be virgins and about 40 percent of non-Mormons made that claim, implying a value for RS of .42 $(1.0-.75/1.0-.40)$. Thus the higher illegitimacy rate in Utah is consistent with much lower levels of nonmarital sexual activity when the differences between Utah and U.S. unmarried women in the use of nontherapeutic abortion is taken into account. These calculations were based on the assumption that the unmarried in Utah and in the United States as a whole share similar levels of contraceptive use; if we had considered the extra difficulty that unmarried Utahans experience in obtaining contraceptives, we would have calculated an even lower estimate of the Utahans' nonmarital sexual activity relative to white U.S. women.

Variations Within Mormonism

The analysis and discussion so far have treated Mormons as one homogeneous population thereby concealing significant internal variations within Mormonism. As the church continues to gain a larger part of its membership from outside the United States, family patterns will begin to reflect a combination of the cultural origins of the converts and Mormon culture. Ethnic, social class, geographic, and other more or less standard types of differentials could also be expected within Mormonism. But currently "degree of religiosity" distinguishes most clearly between different family patterns within Mormonism. Specifically, participation in Mormon

eternal marriage, usually referred to as temple marriage, divides
Mormons into different groups with regard to familial behavior.

About forty Mormon temples have been built or formally announced, the most famous being the large granite structure in Salt
Lake City. Mormon temples are never used for regular church
meetings, but are reserved for performing special religious rites,
the most important being temple marriage. A Mormon couple par-
ticipates only once in a temple marriage except in cases of remarriage and sometimes in a sealing of parents to children. In addition, a ceremony called "the endowment," roughly similar to
Masonic ritual, takes place in Mormon temples.

Those who are granted the entry to Mormon temples hold a
permit called a temple recommend, signed by two local Mormon
leaders certifying that the bearer is a member in good standing.
Worthiness is assessed in an annual interview in which questions
are asked about sexual morality, payment of contributions, obedience to the Mormon dietary code (abstinence from tobacco, al-
cohol, tea, coffee, and harmful drugs), and willingness to follow
church leaders' advice. Mormons who hold temple recommends are
generally more orthodox in their beliefs and more active in church
programs. Those who do not hold temple recommends are often active in church programs but do not have temple recommends because of some intervening factor. Some common intervening factors are failure to pay a tithe (tenth) of one's income to the church,
laxity in observing the dietary code, and marriage to a non-Mormon (which does not automatically preclude entry to a temple but
often makes it impractical because the spouse cannot attend). Recent converts must wait one year before they are eligible for a temple recommend. Finally, there are the so-called inactives, who participate little or not at all in church functions.

Many church programs are organized around the assumption
that these groups do in fact represent inner, middle, and outer
populations in terms of commitment to Mormon beliefs and participation in church activities. The church uses formal programs
for activating those who are inactive, for preparing new converts
and the recently activated for a temple recommend, and for maintaining participation of temple recommend holders. Mormon leaders usually interpret the failure of a member to renew a temple
recommend, or to participate actively in church programs, as a
form of spiritual slippage and as a move toward the periphery of

Table 11.10

Mean Number of Children Ever Born (CEB), by Age and Type of Marriage, Ever-Married U.S. Mormon Women, 1981

Age	Total		Not Married in Temple		Married in Temple	
	N	Mean CEB	N	Mean CEB	N	Mean CEB
20–24	210	1.32	102	1.39	108	1.25
25–29	322	2.23	133	1.88	189	2.47
30–34	315	2.89	139	2.19	175	3.42
35–39	247	3.31	116	2.50	130	4.02
40–44	174	3.59	82	3.16	93	4.00
45–49	172	3.98	94	3.52	78	4.54
50–54	168	4.03	88	3.68	81	4.42
55–59	133	3.85	72	3.57	60	4.18
60–64	136	3.63	76	3.40	60	3.92
65–69	112	3.69	45	3.31	68	3.93

SOURCE: Unpublished data, 1981 L.D.S. Church Membership Survey.

Mormonism. Conversely, to hold a temple recommend is a sign of "worthiness" and commitment.

Data relating the temple recommend status and activity levels of Mormons to other variables are scarce and are usually considered sensitive by the church. But we do have some data concerning the importance of these social divisions within Mormonism. Among Mormon college students, for example, a strong correlation exists between regular attendance at church and maintenance of premarital virginity (Christensen 1982). Interestingly, only about half of Mormon students who refrain from sexual relations before marriage report that religious and moral teachings were the most important reasons for refraining. For these Mormon students regular church activity held more significance than the particular content of church teachings.

Other survey data have shown that Mormons married in the temple have significantly higher fertility than Mormons married civilly. Table 11.10 shows an average of 3.42 children born to women of the first group compared to 2.71 for other Mormon women. Only among 20–24 year-olds does the difference disappear. Temple marriages are also more stable. In 1975, for various types of marriages in the intermountain states, the following percentages had been divorced (Bahr 1978):

Temple marriage (Mormons only)	5
Temple marriage following civil marriage (Mormons only)	11
Church marriage (Mormons and non-Mormons)	14
Civil marriage (Mormons and non-Mormons)	33

It is generally estimated that about 60 percent of all existing Mormon marriages are temple marriages. If temple marriages were not more stable than other marriages one would expect to find about 60 percent of the divorces in Utah occurring in temple marriages. But from 1971 to 1979 only between 7.5 and 8.5 percent of all Utah divorces were granted to couples married in a Mormon temple.

A final item of information on internal variations within Mormonism concerns female labor force participation. Table 11.11 presents the large differences between Mormons in their attitude to nontraditional family patterns that allow wives to work outside the home. Clearly, more active Mormons are less tolerant of arrangements that deviate from the wife-mother-housekeeper role for women. While these attitudes do not directly measure actual behaviors, the differences are great enough to warrant the conclusion

Table 11.11

Percent Disapproving of Dual Career Work Arrangements, by Church Attendance, Adult Utah Mormons, 1974

		Church Attendance	
Item	All Respondents	Weekly	Less Than Weekly
Each spouse works half-time outside the home and half-time at home with housekeeping and child-care tasks	53	61	39
Both husband and wife are employed full-time outside the home. Paid help is hired for household tasks and many meals are eaten outside the home.	68	76	55

NOTES: Total number of respondents over 1,000. Disapproval defined as "strongly disapprove" or "disapprove."

SOURCE: Bahr 1978, Table 9.

that more active Mormons are more likely to live in a household with a full-time wife-mother than are less active Mormons.

The foregoing data, sketchy though they are, demonstrate that Mormons vary significantly in familial norms and behavior. As the divorce data suggest, perhaps some types of Mormons share more similarities with non-Mormons than with other Mormons. In spite of this, a large enough segment of the Mormon population sufficiently differs from the non-Mormon population to make the overall Mormon family pattern stand out in bold relief. I have suggested a concentric zone view of the Mormon population built on two factors—Mormon temple rites and church activity—to divide Mormons into these groups that differ significantly on some items.

From this concentric zone view one could argue, albeit tentatively, that if anything seems to account for differences between Mormons and non-Mormons it is that Mormons have constructed a temple-centered culture in the midst of modern society. The modern temple is a bastion against the world in the sense that entry is limited, temple rites are kept secret, and even Mormons must prove worthiness to enter. All temple activities are interpreted in the context of the ultimate Mormon goal of preserving the family into eternity. A whole series of programs and a general but often unspoken goal of Mormonism are to cause all of its members to participate in the temple, for only there can they be sealed into family units for eternity. Whatever the psychological and sociological mechanisms may be that translate these efforts into family behavior, or that cause the selection of people with certain family behavior patterns from the general population of Mormons, those Mormons who have access to the temple provide the key to the maintenance of a distinctly Mormon family culture that differs from society at large.

NOTES

1. After 1844 several schismatic movements arose within Mormonism. The Church of Jesus Christ of Latter-day Saints refers to the church led by Brigham Young and today headquartered in Salt Lake City. A much

smaller body, the Reorganized Church of Jesus Christ of Latter Day Saints, is headquartered in Missouri. All references to Latter-day Saints or Mormons in this chapter refer to the Utah branch of the church.

2.   Basic data on the Mormon Church are available in reports of the April General Conference of the Church and in the annual *Church Almanac* published by the church-owned Deseret News. Errors can be found in the published data, but more important, the record-keeping system of local church units is staffed by frequently changing lay members. Nevertheless, for an organization of its size and geographic diversity the Mormon Church lives up to its reputation for having an obsession with accurate record-keeping. Taken as estimates, the Mormon membership data manifest an internal consistency that confirms their general reliability.

3.   This estimate assumes that all U.S. Mormons have the same per capita income as Utah Mormons and that approximately 3 percent of all income is in fact paid as tithing (the norm is 10 percent). Non-U.S. tithing income is not included in this estimate since it is known to be a small share of total church income.

4.   There is insufficient space to deal with the comprehensive Mormon doctrine of proxy ordinances work which makes it possible for many rites to be performed by the living for the dead. This doctrine effectively makes it possible for all people to experience, either in person or by proxy, the necessary rites of salvation.

5.   Mormon scripture states that "all spirit is matter, but it is more fine or pure, and can only be discerned by purer eyes; we cannot see it; but when our bodies are purified we shall see that it is all matter" (Doctrine and Covenants, section 131).

6.   The full expression, coined by an early Mormon leader, is "as man is, God once was; as God is, man may become." It was near the end of his career that Joseph Smith launched these radical ideas and was, not surprisingly, accused of blasphemy.

REFERENCES

Arrington, Leonard, and Britton, James. The Mormon Experience: A History of the Latter-day Saints. New York: Vintage Press, 1979.

Bahr, Howard. *"Mormon Families in Comparative Perspective: Denominational Contrasts in Divorce, Marital Satisfaction, and Other Characteristics."* Unpublished manuscript, Family and Demographic Research Institute, Brigham Young University, 1978.

Bahr, Howard. "The Declining Distinctiveness of Utah's Working Woman." *Brigham Young University Studies* 19(1979):525–543.

Bahr, Howard. "Religious Contrasts in Family Roles." *Journal for the Scientific Study of Religion* 21(1982):201–217.

Bahr, Howard; Condie, Spencer; and Goodman, Kristen. *Life in Large Families: Views of Mormon Women.* Washington, D.C.: University Press of America, 1982.

Cannon, Kenneth L., III. "After the Manifesto: Mormon Polygamy 1890–1906." *Sunstone* 8(1983):27–35.

Christensen, Harold T. "The Persistence of Chastity: A Built-in Resistance Within Mormon Culture to Secular Trends." *Sunstone* 8(1982):14–20.

DePillis, Mario G. "The Quest for Religious Authority and the Rise of Mormonism." *Dialogue Journal of Mormon Thought* 1(1966):68–88.

Foster, Lawrence. *Religion and Sexuality: Three American Communal Experiments of the Century.* New York: Oxford University Press, 1981.

Foster, Lawrence. "Between Heaven and Earth." *Sunstone* 7(1982):7–15.

Goodman, Kristen. "Divorce Among Latter-day Saints." Unpublished manuscript (1982).

Heaton, Tim, and Calkins, Sandra. "Family Size and Contraceptive Use Among Mormons: 1965–1975." *Review of Religious Research* 25(1983):103–114.

Heaton, Tim, and Goodman, Kristen. "Religion and Family Formation: The Case of Latter-day Saints." *Review of Religious Research*, forthcoming.

Leone, Mark P. *Roots of Modern Mormonism.* Cambridge, Mass.: Harvard University Press, 1979.

Martin, Thomas. "Welfare." In Howard Bahr (ed.), *Utah, in Demographic Perspective: Regional and National Contrasts.* Provo, Utah: Family and Demographic Research Institute, Brigham Young University, 1981.

May, Dean. "Mormons." In S. Thernstrom (ed.), *The Harvard Encyclopedia of American Ethnic Groups.* Cambridge, Mass.: Harvard University Press, 1982.

McDonald, Laura B. "Utah Educational Attainment in Regional and National Perspective." In Howard Bahr (ed.), *Utah in Perspective: Regional and National Contrasts.* Provo, Utah: Family and Demographic Research Institute, Brigham Young University, 1981.

Smith, James E., and Kunz, Phillip R. "Polygyny and Fertility in Nineteenth Century America." *Population Studies* 16(1976):465–480.

Stark, Rodney. *The Mormon Miracle: How New Religions Succeed.* Seattle: University of Washington, forthcoming.

Thomas, Darwin L. "Families in the Mormon Experience." In W. V. D'Antonio and J. Aldous (eds.), *Families and Religion: Conflict and Change in Modern Society.* Beverly Hills, Calif.: Sage Publications, 1983.

Thornton, Arland. "Religion and Fertility: The Case of Mormonism." *Journal of Marriage and the Family* 41(1979):131–142.

PART IV

Law and the Revolution of Sex Roles

12 The Divorce Law Revolution and the Transformation of Legal Marriage

LENORE J. WEITZMAN

IN 1970, CALIFORNIA LAUNCHED a legal revolution by instituting the first no-fault divorce law in the United States. This pioneering new law promised to free the legal process of divorce from the shackles of outmoded tradition. It embodied "modern" concepts of equity and equality, and was immediately heralded as the family law of the future.

Before 1970 all states in the United States required fault-based grounds for divorce. One party had to be judged guilty of

---

NOTE: *The issues and data discussed in this chapter are explored in greater depth in my book,* The Divorce Revolution: The Unexpected Social and Economic Consequences for Women and Children in America *(New York, Free Press, 1985).*

This work began in an interdisciplinary research project with Ruth B. Dixon and Herma Hill Kay, to whom I owe a great debt for collaboration and support. I was also aided by suggestions from William J. Goode, Kingsley Davis, Amyra Grossbard, Bernard Lewis, Lillian B. Rubin, and Arlene Skolnick.

some marital fault, such as adultery or cruelty, before a divorce could be granted. California rejected this traditional system by permitting parties to divorce when "irreconcilable differences" caused the breakdown of their marriage. This simple change transformed the legal process of divorce. By 1985, just fifteen years later, every state but South Dakota had adopted some form of no-fault divorce law (Weitzman 1985).

These no-fault divorce laws are unique in several respects. First, they eliminate the need for grounds in order to obtain a divorce. (In fact, in many no-fault states it is not even necessary to obtain a spouse's consent in order to obtain a divorce.) Second, they undercut the old system of alimony and property awards for "innocent" spouses. Third, no-fault laws seek to undermine the adversary process and to reduce the acrimony and trauma of the fault system. Finally, new norms for dividing property and awarding alimony eliminate the anachronistic assumptions in the traditional law and treat wives as full and equal partners in the marital partnership.

When I first read about California's new law I was fascinated by the reformers' attempt to alter the social and psychological effects of divorce by changing the legal process. I had just completed two years as a postdoctoral fellow at Yale Law School, with a focus on family law, and I saw California's law as an exciting experiment in legal reform.

I also shared the reformers' optimism and assumed that only good could come from an end to the old fault-based system of divorce. The sham testimony and vilification that were required to prove fault insulted the dignity of the law, the courts, and all the participants. How much better, I thought, to construct a legal procedure that would eliminate vicious scenes and reduce, rather than increase, the antagonism and hostility between divorcing spouses. How much better to lessen the trauma of divorce for both parents and children. And how much better to end a marriage in a nonadversarial process that would enable the parties to fashion fair and equitable financial arrangements. If I, as a researcher, had a personal or political goal beyond my stated aim of analyzing the effects of the new law, it was to help potential reformers in other states learn from the California experience.

In the early 1970s I joined with Herma Hill Kay and Ruth B. Dixon in an interdisciplinary effort to study the social and legal consequences of California's divorce law reforms.[1] We embarked on an analysis of court records, interviews with family law judges and lawyers, and in-depth interviews with recently divorced men and women.

As this research progressed, it became evident that the consequences of the legal reforms extended far beyond the original vision of the reformers. Without fault-based grounds for divorce, and without the need to prove adultery or mental cruelty, the reformers had not only recast the *psychological context* of divorce (and had in fact reduced some of the hostility and acrimony it generated), but they had also transformed the *economic consequences* of divorce and, in the process, had redefined the rights and responsibilities of husbands and wives in legal marriage.

Ends may influence beginnings. In a society where one-half of all first marriages are expected to end in divorce, a radical change in the rules for ending marriage inevitably affects the rules for marriage itself and the intentions and expectations of those who enter it.

The Unintended Consequences

One unanticipated and unintended result of the no-fault reforms has been widespread economic disruption for divorced women and their children. The new rules for alimony, property, and child support shape radically different economic futures for divorced men, on the one hand, and for divorced women and their children on the other. Women, and the minor children in their households—90 percent of the children live with their mothers after divorce[2]—experience a sharp decline in their standard of living after divorce. Men, in contrast, are usually much better off and have a higher standard of living as a result of a no-fault divorce.

How could these simple changes in the rules for divorce have such far-reaching effects? Why would a legal reform designed to create more equitable settlements end up impoverishing divorced women and their children?

In the pages that follow we will see how the new rules, rules designed to treat men and women "equally," have in practice served to deprive divorced women, especially mothers of young children and older homemakers, of the protections that the old law provided. These women have lost both the legitimacy and the financial rewards that the traditional divorce law provided for wives and mothers. Instead of recognition for their contributions as homemakers and mothers, and instead of compensation for the years of lost opportunities and impaired earning capacities, these women now face a divorce law that treats them "equally" and expects them to be equally capable of supporting themselves after divorce.

Since a woman's ability to support herself is likely to be impaired during marriage, especially if she has been homemaker and mother, she may not be equal to her former husband at the point of divorce. Rules that treat her as if she is equal simply serve to deprive her of the financial support she needs. In fact, marriage itself contributes to the economic inequalities between men and women and to the different structural opportunities that the two spouses face at divorce. While most married women give priority to their family roles, most married men give priority to their careers. She often forgoes further education and occupational gains for homemaking and child care, while he often acquires more education and on-the-job experience. As a result, her earning capacity is impaired while his earning capacity is enhanced. In both single-income and two-income families the couple, as a unit, are more likely to have given priority to the husband's career.

If the divorce rules do not allow her to share the fruits of her investment in his career (through alimony and child support awards); and if divorce rules expect her to enter the labor market as his equal—even though she may have fewer job skills, outdated experience, no seniority, and no time for retraining; and if she continues to have the major responsibility for their children after divorce, it is easy to understand why divorced women are likely to be much worse off than their former husbands. Confronted with expectations that they will be "equally" responsible for the financial support of their children and themselves, they have typically been unequally disadvantaged by marriage and have fewer resources to meet those expectations. In addition, rules that require an equal division of marital property often force the sale of the family home and compound the financial dislocations by forcing children to change schools, neighborhoods, and friends just when they most need continuity and stability.

The result is often hardship, impoverishment, and disillusionment for divorced women and their children. As we will see below, our research reveals that, on the average, divorced women and the minor children in their households experience a 73 percent decline in their standard of living in the first year after divorce. Their former husbands, in contrast, experience a 42 percent rise in their standard of living (Weitzman 1985).

The unintended economic consequences of no-fault divorce provide the first major theme of this paper. The second major theme traces the effects of no-fault divorce on the institution of marriage.

The Transformation of Marriage

No-fault divorce has not only redefined the rules for divorce. It has also transformed the legal rules for marriage. No-fault divorce has recast the legal rights and responsibilities of husbands and wives and the legal relationship between parents and children. As a result, it is creating new norms and new expectations for marriage and family commitments in our society.

A divorce provides an important opportunity for a society to enforce marital norms by rewarding the marital behavior it approves and by punishing transgression. It does this by handing out legal rewards and punishments, and by ordering people to pay for their transgressions in dollars and cents. Consider, for example, the issue of alimony. If a divorce court awards alimony to a fifty-year-old woman who has spent twenty-five years as a homemaker and mother, it is reinforcing the value of her domestic activities by rewarding the woman's devotion to her family. (It may also be punishing a husband for abandoning his wife in middle age.) But if, by contrast, the divorce court denies the housewife alimony, and tells her that she must instead get a job and support herself, it is undermining the value of her domestic activities and penalizing her for investing in her family at the expense of her own career. (The court is also releasing the husband from his traditional responsibility for his wife's support.) When divorce courts make these decisions, they are revealing and enforcing new expectations for husbands and wives. Although these expectations are being applied retroactively in divorce decrees, they necessarily suggest new expectations for marriage as well.

A change in the law of divorce, that is, a change in the rules for what is expected of husbands and wives at divorce, may also change the rules for legal marriage. The divorce law both creates and "institutionalizes" new marital norms. That is why marital rules and boundaries are often most clearly articulated (and enforced) at the point of divorce.

Consider next how rules for dividing property at divorce similarly reflect marital norms. When legislatures and courts decide that property acquired during marriage is "his" or "hers" or "theirs," they are defining the financial provisions of the marriage contract and the relative worth attributed to the contributions of husband and wife. If, for example, the divorce laws allow a husband to keep most of the property acquired during marriage, they imply that his work and his income were most important in building the family's wealth. But if, by contrast, the divorce laws assure the housewife one-half of the marital property upon divorce, they suggest that her contribution to the acquisition of family assets has been of equal worth. The second set of rules reflect norms that value homemaking and child care because they reward the homemaker's contribution with a guaranteed equal share of the family's property.

The rules for dividing property at divorce reveal an underlying philosophy of marriage itself: does the law assume that marriage is a temporary alliance of two separate individuals, or does it assume marriage is a complete partnership in which the parties' individual interests and identities are fully merged? If divorce laws allow each spouse to keep whatever income and property he or she acquires during marriage, it encourages both spouses to put their own self-interests first. But if the law treats all income as "joint property," it encourages the pooling of resources and sharing within the marital partnership.

In the past, most laws governing the allocation of family property focused on marriage and death. Rules regulating the transfer of property on these occasions, from bride price and dowry to primogeniture and widow's dower, are common to all societies and have developed over centuries. Since high divorce rates are relatively recent phenomena in our society, we are still uncertain about what rules are appropriate and what allocation of family property is fair when a marriage is dissolved. Throughout the Western world legislatures and policymakers are struggling with similar questions—fully cognizant of the broad implications of these rules and the ways in which they define, control, and shape the nature of marriage.

This is not to suggest that transfers of family property upon divorce have replaced those made at marriage or death. Both marriage and death are still important occasions for gifts and property transfers. But today, for the first time in our history, two people entering marriage are just as likely to be parted by divorce as by death (see Chapter 2), and the amount of money and property being transferred at divorce now rivals the amount passed by will or intestate succession (Glendon 1982). Thus the decisions of the divorce courts are central to the allocation of family property—and the shaping of marital norms.

In the pages that follow I will use the changing law of divorce as a vehicle for examining some of these larger social changes in both the legal and the social structure of marriage. After a note on research methods, I first review the traditional law of divorce. I then examine the innovations of the no-fault law along with some of its empirical effects. The final section of this chapter explores the larger implications of these results. I believe that this analysis will show that the law shapes—at the same time that it reflects—social changes in the nature of marriage.

The Research

This chapter draws on a decade of research on the social and economic effects of no-fault divorce in California.[3] The research involved the collection and analysis of five types of data: systematic random samples of 2,500 court dockets (records) over a ten-year period; in-depth, face-to-face interviews with 169 family law attorneys; in-depth, face-to-face interviews with forty-four family law judges; similar interviews with a comparative sample of English legal experts; and in-depth, face-to-face personal interviews with 228 divorced men and women about one year after their legal divorce. These sources encompass a vast amount and range of data to provide an integrated portrait of the law and its effects.

This research design is unusual in that it uses a variety of sources. It does not rely solely on judges or lawyers (as legal scholars tend to do) or solely on divorced men and women (as sociologists and psychologists tend to do). It also has the advantage of a systematic data base in the random samples of divorce decrees drawn from court records.

Although most of the data were collected in California, the findings are relevant to the entire United States because the major features of the California law have been adopted by most other states (see Weitzman 1985, pp. 40–51). The major sources of data referred to in this paper are as follows:

Court Records

A total of 2,500 divorce cases were drawn from court records between 1968 and 1977. Two samples were drawn in 1968, two years before the no-fault law was instituted. One systematic random sample of about 500 divorce decrees was drawn from San Francisco County court records. A second systematic sample of about 500 divorce cases was drawn from Los Angeles County, giving us a total of about 1,000 divorce cases in 1968.

The same procedure was used to draw two samples of divorce cases in 1972, two years after the no-fault law was instituted. Here again, systematic random samples of about 500 San Francisco and 500 Los Angeles cases were drawn.

A third sample of divorce cases was drawn from court dockets in 1977 to examine the extent of the change seven years after no-fault divorce was instituted. Since few significant differences were found between divorce cases in San Francisco and Los Angeles in 1968 and 1972, the 1977 sample was limited to 500 cases from the greater Los Angeles area (where one-third of all California divorces are granted).

Judges

Structured in-depth, face-to-face interviews with virtually all of the judges who were hearing family law cases in San Francisco and Los Angeles counties—forty-four judges and commissioners—were conducted in 1974 and 1975. These interviews, which enjoyed response rates of 90 to 96 percent of the judges in each county, averaged three hours each.

More informal interviews were obtained at local and statewide judicial conferences and judicial education courses between

1980 and 1985 when I presented and discussed the preliminary results of this research. In addition, twenty-six completed written questionnaires were obtained at a statewide conference of family court judges in 1981.

Attorneys

Structured in-depth, face-to-face interviews with 169 matrimonial attorneys were conducted in the San Francisco Bay Area and in the greater Los Angeles area in 1974 and 1975. The seventy-seven attorneys from the San Francisco Bay Area comprised most of the family law bar in the San Francisco-Oakland-Berkeley area.

In Los Angeles County, where more than 1,400 attorneys identified themselves as matrimonial attorneys, the interviews were restricted to a subsample of ninety-two "experts": those who had held an office in the Family Law Bar Association or who had been identified as one of the three most knowledgeable or most effective attorneys by their peers in the first group.

Although the 115-page interview schedule took an average of four hours to complete, there was an extraordinarily high response rate: 97 and 100 percent for San Francisco and Los Angeles, respectively. These structured interviews were supplemented by informal interviews at local, state, and national bar association meetings between 1980 and 1985 when I presented the preliminary results of this research.

Divorced Men and Women

In-depth, face-to-face interviews with 228 recently divorced men and women (114 men and 114 women) were conducted in the greater Los Angeles area. A stratified random sampling procedure was used to obtain respondents of all socioeconomic groups and all lengths of marital duration.

The interviews with divorced men and women, which lasted an average of nearly six hours each, were conducted in 1978, approximately one year after the respondents' legal divorce. Here too we benefited from a high response rate (83 percent of the respondents located agreed to be interviewed) and extraordinary cooperation. The respondents were willing to share vast amounts of personal information with us and attached great importance to the research.

The interview sample was stratified by length of marriage and socioeconomic status. We oversampled couples in longer marriages and couples with property so that we would have enough couples in these groups for analysis. To present an accurate portrait of the population of divorced persons, the interview responses reported below are weighted to reflect the proportion of each group of respondents in a normal sample of divorced persons.

American Divorce Law

American divorce law, with historical roots in the English common law,[4] was based on the underlying premise that marriage was a permanent and cherished union which the Church—and then the state—had to protect and preserve. It was assumed that the holy bond of matrimony would best be protected by restricting access to divorce. As Clark observed,

> [They believe] that marital happiness is best secured by making marriage indissoluble except for very few causes. When the parties know that they are bound together for life, the argument runs, they will resolve their differences and disagreements and make an effort to get along with each other. If they are able to separate legally upon less serious grounds, they will make no such effort, and immorality will result [Clark 1968, pp. 242–243].

Although there was some difference in the early divorce laws in the North and South, by 1900 most states had adopted what I shall refer to as the four major elements of nineteenth-century divorce law: fault-based grounds, one party's guilt, the continuation of marital responsibilities after divorce, and the linkage of financial awards to findings of fault.

Restrictive Law: Grounds
Required for Divorce

Since the aim of the law was to preserve marriage as a permanent, lifelong union, divorce was restricted to situations in which one party committed a serious marital offense such as adultery,

cruelty, or desertion, giving the other party the legal basis or
ground for the divorce (Kay 1970, p. 221).

The standards for judging appropriate grounds reflected the
gender-typed expectations of traditional legal marriage. While the
almost ritualistic "evidence" of misbehavior varied from state to
state, husbands charged with cruelty, the ground used most often,
were often alleged to have caused their wives bodily harm, while
wives charged with cruelty were more typically accused of neglecting their husbands, homes, or wifely duties (Clark 1968, p.
349). Along the same lines, desertion for women was typically supported by evidence of a wife's withdrawal of affection, refusal to do
housework, or attention to outside interests, but the same behavior
would not be considered as desertion by the husband unless he
also stopped supporting his wife financially.

Over time, in actual practice, many divorcing couples privately agreed to an uncontested divorce where one party, usually
the wife, would take the *pro forma* role of the innocent plaintiff.
Supported by witnesses, she would attest to her husband's cruel
conduct, and he would not challenge her allegations. But even if
the testimony was staged, it nevertheless reflected what the courts
considered "appropriate violations" of the marriage contract—and
thus reinforced the sex-appropriate obligations of marriage itself.
The husband, obligated to support and protect his wife, was sanctioned for nonsupport and physical abuse. The wife, responsible for
care for her home and husband, was sanctioned for neglecting her
domestic responsibilities.

The grounds required for divorce, even if agreed to in private
negotiations, had two important consequences. First, they set the
terms for the divorce, and those terms were set in the context of a
moral framework, discussed below. Second, the need for grounds
created practical, psychological, and moral disincentives to divorce. On the practical level, since only the innocent party could
file for the divorce, if one wanted a divorce and was not "innocent"
(because one was having an affair), one had to persuade or "buy" a
divorce from one's spouse. This might prove difficult, emotionally
trying, and expensive, especially if one's spouse genuinely wanted
to stay married.

On the psychological level the need for grounds meant that
one had to face allegations of one's adultery, desertion, or cruelty
in court. Divorce hearings could be embarrassing, and sometimes

humiliating, with public revelations of one's adultery, battering, sexual inadequacy, personal failures, or bad moral character. Because the procedure required sufficient evidence of misconduct to establish fault, private detectives, witnesses, and photographs might be brought into court to attest to a spouse's misconduct and/ or to reveal the details of an adulterous affair. Even though many divorcing couples privately agreed to grounds in an uncontested divorce, if any accusatory spouse wanted to be difficult or to embarrass his or her spouse, the legal procedure provided an open forum for malicious allegations.

Finally, the testimony required to prove grounds was morally offensive to many participants and created an ethical barrier for some. In order to prove one had grounds for a divorce one spouse might have to commit perjury and provide false testimony about his or her spouse's conduct. Many participants felt that this was distasteful, demeaning, and morally offensive.

A Moral Framework: Guilt and Innocence

A closely related feature of the old divorce law was that it created a moral framework for divorce. Since a divorce could be granted only to an innocent party who was harmed by his or her spouse's violations of the marriage contract, the law required that one party be "guilty," the other "innocent." As the Tennessee Supreme Court stated, "divorce is conceived as a remedy for the innocent against the guilty" (*Brown* v. *Brown*, 1955).

The need to have a guilty party in order to get a divorce had two consequences. First, it required adversary proceedings. The plaintiff's success in obtaining a divorce depended on his or her ability to prove the defendant's fault. Second, the law forced the parties to label their behavior in moral terms. One party was designated as guilty or responsible for the divorce, the other party was labeled an "innocent victim."

Perpetuation of Gender-Based Roles and Responsibilities

Third, divorce law perpetuated the gender-based division of roles and responsibilities enshrined in the traditional marriage contract.

In this state-dictated contract, the woman presumably agreed to devote herself to being a wife, homemaker, and mother in return for her husband's promise of lifelong support (Weitzman 1981b, pp. 1–97). Although traditional family law assumed that the husband's support would be provided in a lifelong marriage, if the marriage did not endure, and if the wife was virtuous, she was nevertheless promised alimony—a means of continued support. Alimony thus perpetuated the husband's responsibilities for economic support and the wife's right to be supported in return for her domestic services. It thus maintained at least part of the basic reciprocity in the legal marriage contract.

Traditional divorce laws also perpetuated the gender-based division of roles with respect to children: the husband remained responsible for their economic support, the wife for their care. All states, by statute or by case law tradition, gave preference to the wife as the appropriate custodial parent after the divorce, and all states gave the husband the primary responsibility for his children's economic support.

Financial Awards Linked to Fault

Finally, the old divorce law linked the financial terms of the divorce to the determination of fault. Being found "guilty"or "innocent" in a divorce action had important financial consequences.

Alimony, for example, could be awarded only to the innocent spouse "as a judgment *against* the guilty spouse" (California Civil Code 139, repealed by Stats. 1969, C. 1608, p. 3313, Section 3, operative January 1, 1970). Thus, when the court found a woman guilty of adultery she was typically barred from receiving alimony. On the other hand, if the husband was found guilty of adultery or cruelty, he might have to pay for his transgressions with alimony. As Eli Bronstein, a New York matrimonial lawyer, justified these rules, "If a woman has been a tramp, why reward her? By the same token, if the man is alley-catting around town, shouldn't his wife get all the benefits she had as a married woman?" (Wheeler 1974, p. 57).

The law also linked property awards to fault. In most states the courts had the power to award property held by either spouse upon divorce and could therefore use property as a reward for virtue and a punishment for sin. In California, for example, the judge was required to award *more than half of the property to the innocent spouse*. This rule provided strong financial incentives for husbands and wives to fight about who was innocent and who was guilty.

Linking financial awards to fault had three important consequences. The first, as we just noted, was the incentive it created for spouses to accuse each other of being responsible for the divorce. As Judge William Hogoboom observed, the lure of substantial property awards encouraged heated charges and countercharges between spouses (Hogoboom 1971, p. 687). Thus, proving a spouse's guilt might not only make one feel morally superior, it could also pay off in a better property settlement. The legal requirements thus fostered an adversarial climate of escalating accusations, acrimony, and hostility because successful accusations were rewarded with money and property.

A second consequence of linking financial awards to fault was that it gave the innocent or injured spouse a great deal of power and a decided economic advantage. Since the innocent party had to file for the divorce, and had the option of choosing the grounds, she (but sometimes he) had the de facto power to shape the nature of the divorce suit, and, even more important, to prevent it. And, since both the granting of the divorce and the financial settlements were linked to fault, the "innocent" party had a powerful lever to use in property and alimony negotiations.

A third consequence of the linkage of financial awards and fault was that it created financial disincentives to divorce because it made the prospect of divorce a costly one for men. Since it was most commonly the man who wanted the divorce, in practice men, especially middle and upper class men, often "bought" their divorces by agreeing in advance to give their wives more property (such as the family home), or alimony, or child support, or all of these. As we will see below, alimony awards were less common than generally assumed, but the innocent wife typically received a larger share of the property—especially if her husband's adultery or cruelty was flagrant and/or the only family asset was the family home. Thus a man contemplating divorce faced the expensive prospect of providing alimony for his ex-wife, child support until his children reached twenty-one, and losing his home and some of his other assets.

The Legal Reform: No-Fault Divorce

The 1970 California reform was the first law in the Western world to abolish completely any requirement of fault as the basis for marital dissolution. The no-fault law provided for a divorce upon *one* party's assertion that "irreconcilable differences have caused the irremediable breakdown of the marriage." In establishing this new standard for marital dissolution, the California State Legislature sought to eliminate the adversarial nature of divorce and thereby to reduce the hostility, acrimony, and trauma characteristic of fault-oriented divorce.

The discussion that follows focuses on the "pure" no-fault divorce law instituted in California. This type of legal regime is in effect in about half of the states in the United States (see Weitzman, 1985 for a detailed review of the laws in other states).

No-fault divorce changed each of the basic elements in the traditional divorce law. As exemplified by the California statute, the new legislation reflects six major innovations. First, no-fault eliminates the need for grounds in order to obtain a divorce. This permissive standard facilitates divorce and represents a dramatic departure from the restrictive norms of the previous law. Second, no-fault law eliminates the need to prove one party's guilt in order to obtain a divorce. This, too, was a radical change for it signaled a rejection of the moral framework of the old law. Third, the pure no-fault law in California allows one person to make a unilateral decision to get a divorce. It is no longer necessary to obtain the consent or agreement of an "innocent" spouse.

A fourth feature of the no-fault law is that it seeks to treat men and women "equally," thereby repudiating the gender-based assumptions of the traditional law. Fifth, no-fault law establishes new standards for financial awards, standards based on the parties' current financial needs and resources. These norms negate the concept of compensation for past behavior, whether guilt or innocence. Finally, the new law seeks to create a new social-psychological climate that fosters amicable divorce by abolishing the adversarial process.

This section examines each of these new legal standards and highlights some of their empirical effects using data from our California research. More detailed reports of these findings (and our research methods) are found in Weitzman and Dixon 1979 and 1980, and in Weitzman 1981a and 1985.

Permissive Law: The Abolition of Grounds

The basic premise of no-fault divorce "is that the nineteenth century concept of divorce, based only upon a matrimonial offense committed by one or both of the parties, is essentially outmoded and irrelevant often producing cruel and unworkable results" (Krom 1970, p. 156). The new law substitutes "marital breakdown" as the only justification for divorce. In rejecting the restrictive posture of the old regime, the reformers sought to facilitate divorce when one party no longer wished to remain married. They argued that fault-based grounds were inappropriate in two respects: first, they were artificial and often had little relationship to the cause of the marital breakdown; second, they led to perjury, hypocrisy, and collusion—insulting the dignity of the court and the parties involved.

The new law therefore abolished the need to have *any* grounds in order to obtain a divorce. Now the divorce could begin with a neutral "petition for dissolution," with no specification of the grounds or reasons for the divorce. Because the parties do not have to give the court any justification for the divorce, they no longer have to offer—and prove—allegations of misconduct. All that is required is one party's claim that "irreconcilable differences" have caused a marital breakdown.

The abolition of grounds eliminates many of the practical, psychological, and moral disincentives that resulted from the fault-based requirements of the old law. In addition, since there is no longer any need to bargain about grounds and fault-based accusations, *the "innocent" spouse no longer has the power* to prevent or delay a divorce or to bargain for a better financial settlement in return for an agreement to divorce.

It is interesting to note that many of the divorced men and women we interviewed reported that they were both surprised and disturbed by the freedom the new law gives spouses to simply terminate a marriage. As one woman explained:

> It's just too easy. You shouldn't be able to just walk out on your family. I think there has to be some reason—some real ground for someone to be able to divorce his wife. . . . He made a commitment and I believe that the vows we took were not empty vows. . . . I think no-fault divorce robs me of my right to keep my family.

A man echoed these sentiments:

> I was outraged when I found that my wife had been having an affair
> and she still had the right to get a divorce without any—and I mean
> any—grounds. That divorce law legalizes adultery.

Another woman complained that the no-fault law violated her marriage contract:

> I thought we had a contract and I lived up to it. . . . For thirty years
> I was a good wife and a good mother. . . . Then my husband decided
> he wanted a younger woman and he left me. . . . He didn't need a
> reason, my lawyer said . . . it didn't matter if I didn't do anything
> wrong . . . it didn't matter that he was the one to commit adultery.
> He broke our contract. . . . But I'm the one who is being punished.

No Fault: Eliminating the Moral Framework

When the new law abolished the concept of fault, it also eliminated
the moral framework of guilt and innocence and the notion of interpersonal justice in divorce. With this seemingly simple move,
the California legislature eliminated the punitive element of moral
condemnation that had pervaded Western thought for centuries,
and dramatically altered the legal definition of the reciprocal obligations of husbands and wives during marriage.

There were two rationales for rejecting the traditional concept
of fault. First, it was based on the artificial conception that *one person*
was "at fault" and responsible for the marital breakup. Second, it
assumed that the court could determine who that person was. The
reformers argued that even if the court could determine who de-
served the greater blame, which they thought rather unlikely, this
question entailed an inappropriate invasion of marital privacy. The
focus of the new law was to be on the present and future, that is,
on fashioning an equitable settlement, rather than on the past, that
is, on trying to reconstruct who did what dreadful thing to whom.

Our interviews with California judges and lawyers who handled divorce cases before and after the legal reform reveal that the
abolition of fault has had a major impact on the legal process
(Weitzman and Dixon 1980). These experts reported that fault-
based accusations were much more than a ritualistic charade.

Under the old law the parties' guilt and innocence were important factors in both negotiations and trial outcomes and influenced property and alimony awards. As one attorney remarked,

> Fault made a big difference; if the old man was an S. O. B. or was running around with a twenty-year-old girl, or beating his wife or stealing money from her trust account, you knew you were going to clean him out.

Not so under the new law. The influence of fault is vastly diminished, if not nonexistent. One indication of this is provided by the judges' and attorneys' responses to a series of hypothetical divorce cases. When asked to predict the outcome of a case in which the wife was portrayed as strongly at fault ("she was promiscuous and openly having affairs with other men"), only 18 percent of the experts predicted she would receive alimony under the old law. When asked about the identical case in 1975, under the new law, 70 percent predicted she would be awarded alimony.

The abolition of fault has dramatically changed the economics of divorce settlements. In removing fault-linked financial sanctions, the new laws have not only undermined the moral authority of the traditional norms (by lowering the rewards for virtue), they have also changed the other side of the cost–benefit equation and lowered the cost of violating the marriage contract.

Many men and women were distressed to discover that fault no longer matters. The lack of penalties for adultery, for example, and the absence of rewards for "good marital behavior" violated their common-sense understanding of the terms of their "marriage contract."

Consider, first, the question of the economic sanctions for adultery. Under the old law the adulterous husband or wife typically had to pay for his or her infidelity with a disadvantageous property or alimony award. Today, in contrast, there are no penalties for adultery and no rewards for marital fidelity. One divorced woman expressed the outrage she felt when she found out that her husband would no longer have to "pay" for betraying her:

> You may want to kill the bastard, humiliate him and make him pay through his nose, but go try and find a lawyer that will help you do it. All they know how to say is "it's not relevant." "It's not relevant." I've heard it 100 times like a broken record. Why the hell isn't it rele-

vant? He screws my best friend—all of my best friends, to be more precise—and they say "you have to learn to forget it. . . ." What did I get? Not one red cent.

It is evident that this woman believed (as did over 90 percent of the men and women we interviewed) that marital fidelity was part of the moral (and legal) contract she had with her husband and that he should have to "pay" if he violated the norm. Although not all of our respondents would agree that the payment should be financial (some would have settled for an admission of guilt and an apology; others wanted public humiliation), and some might feel mollified if there were appropriate mitigating circumstances, most of them expressed at least some discomfort with the no-fault norm that no consequences whatsoever—neither financial awards of alimony or property or child support nor the traditional retribution of courtroom embarrassment—are to be imposed on an adulterous spouse.

The attorneys and judges we interviewed generally approved of the principles of the no-fault law. Since most of them had practiced under the fault system, they were aware of its abuses, and few of them wanted to return to the sham testimony, mudslinging, and vilification of the old law.

Their one dissatisfaction with the no-fault regime concerned one of its unanticipated side effects: the no-fault rules eliminated the lever that lawyers used under the old law to get decent economic settlements for wives. As attorney Riane Eisler notes, under the fault system, if a woman made marriage her full-time job, and if a judge thought she had done her job well, and if her husband had the means, she could expect a good settlement (Eisler 1977, pp. 14–15). But the elimination of guilt and innocence under no-fault took away the weapons lawyers traditionally used to get her that economic settlement. If she isn't innocent, and he isn't guilty, there is no lever to get her more property or spousal support (Eisler 1977).

No Consent

Perhaps as radical as the elimination of grounds and fault is the new law's abolition of the need to obtain a spouse's agreement to divorce. Under the no-fault law all that is needed is *one* party's assertion of marital breakdown. The second party does not have to agree to the assertion and does not have to agree to the divorce. The no-fault law thereby permits one spouse to decide unilaterally to get divorced, and there is virtually nothing his or her spouse can do to stop it.

The no-consent standard is another reflection of the shift from restrictive law to permissive law. It places the decision about the divorce in the hands of either party in contrast to the old-law norm of predetermined, state-defined grounds for divorce. In addition, in contrast to the old-law assumption that one had "a right" to remain married if one adhered to one's marriage contract, the new law permits divorce just because one spouse wants it, whether or not the other spouse did anything "wrong," and whether or not the "innocent" spouse agrees to the divorce.

Obviously, the possibility of unilateral divorce undermines the power of the reluctant spouse because it eliminates the need for behind-the-scenes negotiations—in fact, it eliminates the need to communicate at all—in order to secure his or her consent. Once again, many of the divorced men and women we interviewed were surprised to learn that their spouse could divorce them without their consent. As one man said,

> I really could not believe it! I felt totally powerless. She didn't ask me what I wanted . . . she didn't even tell me she was going to file. . . . One day I got home from work and found the papers in the mail.

The unanticipated and probably unintended consequences of the no consent rule have fallen most heavily on the older and economically weaker wife. As attorney Fran Leonard, an attorney for the Older Women's League, notes:

> Under the fault system, if one spouse opposed the divorce, the other had to "bargain" in order to get it. For example, if a man wished a divorce in order to remarry, either he would have to prove, over her opposing testimony, that his wife was an adulteress, or insane, or some such; or he would "bargain" with her. The bargain often was a property settlement in exchange for her "giving" him the divorce. (She would file, accusing him of one of the traditional grounds, and he would offer no opposition.)
>
>   With the advent of no-fault, older wives lost this tool. No longer is there an "innocent" party to be awarded extra property and support. No longer can she unilaterally hang on to the marriage until

the terms offered secure her future apart from the marriage [Leonard 1980, p. 2].

As Leonard concludes, superficially, this appears fair: few people favor perpetuating dead marriages on something very close to economic blackmail. But the practical result of this apparently fair rule has been a drastically diminished settlement for the economically dependent homemaker.

Since most of the divorced men and women we interviewed had not experienced a divorce under the old law, they had no standard of comparison for evaluating the no-consent rule. In general, they approved of its underlying principle—the freedom to leave a marriage that was no longer satisfying. For example, in response to the following statement, "No-fault also means that you can't stop your wife/husband from getting a divorce even if you don't want to be divorced. Do you think that is fair?" Over 85 percent of the divorced men and women we interviewed said yes.* In addition, in response to the question, "If one person is responsible for the failure of the marriage do you think he or she should be able to get a divorce if his or her husband or wife doesn't want to be divorced?" Over 85 percent of the interview sample said yes.

No Compensation/No Retribution in Financial Awards

Because the prior divorce law linked both the granting of the divorce and the financial settlement to the determination of fault, it created powerful incentives for spouses to escalate their accusations of fault. Charges of fault, if substantiated, paid off for the aggrieved or "innocent" spouse.

No-fault laws, in contrast, provide no punishment for the guilty and no reward for the innocent because there is no guilty party and no innocent party. The reformers argued that justice for both wife and husband is better served by considering the parties' economic situations rather than their guilt or innocence.

Attorneys play a critical role in explaining and "socializing" their clients to these new no-fault norms: they "educate" their

---

*Those in marriages of more than eighteen years were less likely to agree, but even in this subgroup a majority agreed with the statement.

clients about what "counts" (economically) under the current law. A woman who comes into her attorney's office expecting a generous financial settlement because her husband is at fault, or a man who has threatened to cut his wife off because she has betrayed him will soon learn, under the new law, that the court (and their attorneys) will not give them any legal (or moral) support for their financial requests. An attorney is instead likely to counsel them to "forget the past," to "realize you are better off without her or him," and to "build your own life." As hollow as these phrases may sound to many of the newly separated, they accurately reflect the "new economic reality" of no-fault divorce.

The new economic reality also means that there are no financial rewards for "good behavior" during marriage. In most areas of life people believe that good conduct and virtue ought to be rewarded. Traditional family law promised these rewards for those who had fulfilled their marital obligations: the housewife who devoted herself to her husband, home, and children, and the husband who devoted himself to providing them with life's necessities. Both the dutiful wife and dutiful husband were to be rewarded at divorce, especially if they were betrayed or were subjected to physical or mental cruelty. The absence of any "economic" rewards for virtue often comes as a shock to the newly separated spouse.

Most distressed are those who have conformed to the received norms during a long-term, traditional marriage. For example, a 55-year-old Los Angeles surgeon complained that he never took the time off to go to the symphony or to spend a carefree summer at the beach with his wife and children because he thought his job was to "be there to earn the money so that my kids and wife could have everything they wanted." He expressed his outrage at the lack of financial rewards for his exemplary behavior as follows:

> Now, *she* walked out on me and what do *I* get? Nothing. Nothing. And what does *she* get? She gets half of my house, half of my pension . . . [etc.]. For what I ask you? For running off with a jerk psychologist. That's my reward?

It is not surprising that many of the older men and women feel that "they've changed the rules in the middle of the game." No-fault laws have changed the rules. Once again, it is typically the attorneys who must inform the unrewarded "innocent" spouse that the no-fault law provides neither compensation nor retribution.

The economic message of the new law is clear: investing in the marital partnership by being a faithful breadwinner or a devoted homemaker no longer pays. One's economic "take" from the marriage will be the same no matter what one has done.

The reformers probably did not foresee this result because they were so entrenched in the old framework. Their major concern was the removal of the financial incentives that the old system provided for spouses to blame each other. Their vision extended only as far as the abolition of fault, acrimony, and bitterness and the more realistic financial awards they hoped that would bring.

Consider, for example, the new standards they established for the division of property. To remove the incentives for fault-based accusations, and to remove the possibility of courts considering who did what to whom, the new California law specifies that the court *must* divide the marital property equally: half to the husband, half to the wife.

The California reformers first considered but then rejected the "equitable division" standard for dividing property because they preferred a fixed standard that limited judicial discretion. They also wanted to affirm the community property presumption that marriage is an equal partnership in which the financial and nonfinancial contributions of the two spouses are of equal worth. The equal division standard was seen as fair—and "protective" of wives—because it guaranteed each spouse one-half of the jointly accumulated property.

A final aim of the new standard is to allow the parties to make a clean break. Once the property is divided equally at divorce, each spouse is free from continuing financial entanglements with the other.

Our research suggests that these changes in the rules for the division of property have had a major impact. Before 1970, under the old law, the wife, who was usually the innocent plaintiff, was typically awarded a significantly larger share of the marital assets. In 1968 wives were awarded more than half (60 percent or more) of the property in both San Francisco and Los Angeles cases. Most of these awards allowed the wife to keep the family home and furnishings, which were often the single most valuable family asset.

No-fault brought a dramatic shift in property awards: between 1968 and 1977 the percentage of cases in which the property was divided equally rose from 26 percent to 64 percent of the cases in Los Angeles.

One important result of the equal division norm is the increase in the number of family homes being sold upon divorce. The legal tradition was to award the family house to the wife, both because it was assumed to be hers in the sense that she organized, decorated, and maintained it and because she was usually adjudged to be the innocent plaintiff and thus deserving of more than half the community property. In addition, if the wife had custody of the children, she needed the home to maintain a stable environment for them.

But today more homes are being sold so that the property can be divided equally. The number of cases in which there was an explicit court order to sell the home rose from about one in ten in 1968 to about one in three in 1977. (Those wives who manage to keep the home are those who have other property they can trade—such as an interest in a pension—for their husband's share of the home.)

Surprisingly, the presence of minor children in the home has not deterred judges from ordering it sold. Our data reveal that 66 percent of the couples who were forced to sell their homes had minor children. The disruptive effects of these forced sales on minor children are explored further in Weitzman (1985).

Gender-Neutral Expectations: No Sex-Based Assumptions

A fourth feature of the no-fault law is its attempt to treat men and women equally by abolishing the sex-based assumptions of the traditional law. Thus it no longer assumes that husbands will be responsible for the financial support of their former wives. Nor does it seek to maintain the dependency of homemakers and mothers after divorce.

In rejecting the old law's norm of male support, the legislators pointed to the difficulty that men face in supporting two households if they remarry, and argued that the old law had converted "a host of physically and mentally competent young women into an army of alimony drones who neither toil nor spin and become a drain on society and a menace to themselves" (Hofstadter and Levittan 1967, p. 55).

Similarly, in rejecting the traditional assumption of a wife's continued dependency after divorce, the reformers pointed to the changing position of women in general and to their increased participation in the labor force in particular, and assumed that women were now equally capable of supporting themselves—and their children—after divorce. While the reformers recognized the need to support the older housewife, they did not believe that the younger woman, whether a housewife or employed, required support; they portrayed her as a potential "alimony drone" who ought to be self-supporting.

Changes in Alimony Awards: The New Standard of Self-Sufficiency.

Our California data reveal several changes in the patterns of alimony awards that reflect these new standards (Weitzman and Dixon 1980; Weitzman 1981).

First, in accord with the new law's goal of making the wife self-sufficient after divorce, there has been a shift from permanent alimony awards, awards based on the premise of the wife's continued dependency, to time-limited transitional awards. Between 1968 and 1972, permanent alimony—awards labeled permanent, until death, or until remarriage—dropped from 62 to 32 percent of the alimony awards in Los Angeles County. By 1972 (and in subsequent years) two-thirds of the alimony awards were transitional awards for a limited and specified duration. The median duration of these fixed-time awards was twenty-five months, or about two years. Thus the average award carries an expectation of a short transition from marriage to self-sufficiency.

Second, the standards of the new law have dictated a greater reliance on the wife's ability to support herself. Economic criteria, such as the wife's occupation and predivorce income, are therefore more important than the old standards of fault and innocence. However, we were surprised to find that wives with rather low predivorce incomes (those of $10,000 a year) and wives with rather limited and marginal employment histories were being denied alimony because the courts presumed they were capable of supporting themselves. While a woman's chance of being awarded alimony also depends on her age, husband's income, and the length of the marriage (see Weitzman and Dixon 1980, pp. 166–172), our general conclusion is that the California courts are applying minimalist and unrealistic standards of self-sufficiency and denying alimony to most divorced women.

The result of these standards is that the vast majority of divorced women, roughly five out of six, are not awarded alimony. Only 17 percent were awarded alimony in 1978. (These awards averaged 350 a month in 1984 dollars.) This does not represent a decline from the percentage of alimony awards under the old law (in 1968 only 19 percent of the divorced women were awarded alimony), because alimony has always been confined to the wives of middle class and upper class men, and these couples have always comprised a small minority of the divorcing population. But the patterns of alimony awards within this group have been drastically altered by no-fault.

Thus the major impact of no-fault divorce on alimony awards lies in new expectations for middle class and upper class women. Instead of the old law's expectation that divorced women will remain dependent and its provision for permanent alimony, no-fault has brought an expectation that divorced women will become independent and self-sufficient after divorce. Thus middle class women who could count on alimony under the old law are now expected to be—or to become—capable of supporting themselves after divorce. These women are increasingly being denied alimony altogether, especially if they have worked or have earned even minimal incomes before the divorce, or they are being awarded small amounts of alimony for short periods of time to "ease the transition." An award of $350 a month in 1984 dollars for a period of two years must convey a clear message to the newly divorced middle class woman: she will now have to earn enough money to support herself (and her children, as we will see below).

It is interesting to note that the new law guarantees, in theory, support for three groups of women who are exempted from the new standards of self-sufficiency: women with custody of young children, women in need of transitional support, and older homemakers incapable of self-sufficiency. Despite the law's guarantees, we found that the new legal norms are being applied to these women as well, and few of them are awarded support.

Mothers of Preschool Children.   Consider first the case of women with custody of preschool children. We found that alimony awards to mothers of children under six dropped more than for any other group under the new law. By 1978, only 13 percent of this group were awarded alimony (now called spousal support).

Why do young children appear to have so little effect on alimony awards? One possible explanation might be that courts are awarding child support instead of "wife support." This is unlikely because tax incentives encourage a husband to call "child support" "alimony" rather than vice versa, and because most child support awards are so low that they cannot include extra support for the wife. Median child support awards in Los Angeles in 1978 were $100 per month per child, typically not enough to cover even half of the cost of raising a child.

A better explanation for the decline in awards to mothers of young children is that the goal of making the wife self-sufficient has taken priority over the goal of supporting the custodial parent. Two-thirds of the Superior Court judges who hear family law cases in Los Angeles espoused this new ideology: they said it was "good" for a divorced woman to earn money instead of being dependent on her former husband, work was a healthy form of rehabilitation that would help her build a new life, and combining work and motherhood were now normal in our society. Although the sex-neutral standards of the new law give priority to the needs of custodial parents caring for minor children, the judges' responses suggest that they are always balancing the interests of children against the father's interest in keeping his income for himself. When they are able to rationalize work as healthy and good for the newly divorced woman, they conclude that it is better for "the family as a whole" for her to work. They thereby solve the problem of the husband's limited financial resources by allowing him to keep most of his income.

Despite judges' reports of how they think they divide the husband's income, our empirical analysis of the awards reveals that the husband is rarely ordered to part with more than one-third of his income to support his wife and children. He is therefore allowed to retain two-thirds of his income for himself while his former wife and children, typically three people, are expected to live on the remaining one-third. Since this proves impossible, most divorced women must work or seek other sources of support, such as Aid to Families with Dependent Children (AFDC).

Women in Transition.   We found a similar combination of social and economic justifications for the low level of alimony awards to women in transition and to older homemakers.

With respect to the women in transition—women who have worked (even at part-time marginal jobs) before the divorce and those who earned $10,000 a year—are simply presumed to be capable of supporting themselves after divorce. Thus many women who could have benefited from the education and retraining that transitional awards are supposed to provide are denied these opportunities because they have been defined as already self-sufficient. The small group of women who are awarded transitional support are typically given short-term awards—a year or two—which may not be sufficient in the turmoil and aftermath of a divorce. Nevertheless, judges are clearly reluctant to "require" a husband to "finance" his ex-wife's retraining.

Consider, for example, the judges' responses to the following hypothetical divorce case. A nurse supported her doctor husband through college, medical school, an internship, and a residency. After eleven years of marriage, they decided to divorce. The wife, now 29, wants to go to medical school. Would you, we asked judges, award her four years of support to allow her to do that? Less than one-third (31 percent) of the judges said they would. They did not think it was fair to saddle her husband with her "optional" expenses since she was clearly capable of supporting herself. If this is the judicial response to a "strong case" in which a woman had supported her husband for eight years, it is not surprising to learn that few judges take seriously awards for education and retraining.

Older Homemakers.   The third group of women who were supposed to be exempted from the new law's standards of self-sufficiency are the older homemakers who have been housewives and mothers throughout marriages of long duration. Although many more women in this category are awarded spousal support, one out of three is not. Once again the judges approach these cases mindful of the husband's need for "his income" and his limited capacity to support two families. Thus, despite the law's theoretical assurance of protection for displaced homemakers, in reality one out of three long-term homemakers is not awarded alimony.

This examination of alimony awards under no-fault illustrates the strength of the new legal norms of gender neutrality and gender equality most poignantly. No-fault legislation attempts to treat men and women equally—or as if they were equal—at the point of divorce. The problem with this standard is that it ignores the *structural inequality* between men and women in the larger society. Divorced women and divorced men do not have the same opportunities: the women are more likely to face job and salary discrimination and more likely to be restricted by custodial responsibilities.

A second problem with the reformers' attempt to institute equality at the point of divorce is that women have typically been unequally disadvantaged by the marriage itself. If one thinks of one common marital pattern in which a housewife and mother supports her husband's career as a doctor, lawyer, or businessman, it is evident that marriage can vastly alter the employment prospects of the two spouses in different directions. His career prospects may be enhanced while hers may be impaired; his earning capacity may grow while hers may decline. Thus marriage itself can be partly responsible for the dramatically different prospects that men and women face after divorce. They are, in fact, not equal.

In light of these structural impediments to postdivorce equality for men and women, it is not surprising that we found that in just one year after the legal divorce, women and the minor children in their household experience a 73 percent decline in their standard of living when income is compared to needs (Weitzman 1985). In contrast, men experience a 42 percent rise in their standard of living one year after the divorce. This vast discrepancy between former husbands and wives is partially a result of the fact that men are typically not ordered to pay alimony and are asked to pay very meager amounts of child support. This leaves them with much more money—absolutely and relatively—to spend on themselves. Women, on the other hand, who typically earn much less money, have custody of their children and are expected to support the children and themselves with meager if any financial aid from their ex-husbands. As we noted above, it is not just the wage and employment gap between men and women in the larger society but also the different opportunities and responsibilities that marriage imposes on men and women that leads to the rapid downward mobility of divorced women (and children) after divorce.

Sex-Neutral Responsibilities for Children.

The final rejection of traditional marital roles in the new law involves the responsibility for children after divorce. In the new standards for child custody the preference for the mother (for children of tender years) was replaced by a sex-neutral standard that instructs judges to award custody in the "best interests of the child." Similarly, the new equality between the spouses is reflected in child support standards: the new law makes both husbands and wives responsible for child support.

In contrast to the financial effects of no-fault, the new standards for child custody have not, as yet, changed the pattern of child custody awards. Despite the sex-neutral standards, women requested and received custody in the overwhelming majority of divorce cases in 1968, 1972, and 1978 (an average of 90 percent). Men who seek custody are fairly successful in obtaining it, but on the whole, both mothers and fathers seem to prefer maternal custody.

Similarly, the sex-neutral standards for child support have not had any noticeable empirical effect, but that is probably because child support awards were so low under the old law that mothers were already providing half—if not more than half—of the support for their children after divorce. Child support awards for two children average $350 a month in 1984 dollars.

Nonadversarial Divorce: The New Social-Psychological Climate

The final aim of the no-fault law was to alter the social-psychological climate of divorce by eliminating the adversarial process. As we have seen, the reformers believed that at least some of the acrimony of a fault-based divorce resulted from the legal process itself, rather than from the inherent difficulties of dissolving a marriage. They believed that husbands and wives who were dissolving their marriage were potentially "amicable," but the legal process forced them to be antagonists. The need to prove fault, and the financial benefits to be gained from exaggerated accusations, were the villains: they encouraged legal wrangling, generated hostility, and exacerbated personal acrimony.

The reformers hoped that a no-fault law would create a different climate for divorce. By eliminating fault they sought to eliminate the hypocrisy, perjury, and collusion "required by courtroom practice under the fault system"; to reduce the adversity, acrimony, and bitterness surrounding divorce proceedings; to lessen the personal stigma attached to the divorce; and to foster more rational and equitable support and property awards (Hogoboom 1971, p. 687).

Although it is difficult to measure hostility and acrimony in the legal process, our research suggests that the no-fault law has in fact served to undermine litigiousness. For example, the random samples of divorce cases drawn from court records reveal that the introduction of the no-fault law led to a sharp reduction in legal activity between filing and the interlocutory decree, and a shorter time between the filing and final decree, both suggesting a less acrimonious process.

A decline in the amount of litigiousness is also suggested by the reduction in the number of pages in case files. The percentage of thin files (under twenty pages) increased significantly between 1968 and 1972 while the percentage of extremely litigious ones (fifty pages or more) declined. At its minimum, a no-fault divorce in California takes only five pages of paper and about two minutes of court time. (In fact, some childless couples can now file for and obtain their divorce by mail.)

Since few of the divorced men and women we interviewed had obtained a divorce under the old law, they had no basis for comparing their experience with a fault-based system.

The greater antagonism and bitterness under a fault system is, however, suggested by data from a "comparative" sample. Sociologists Graham Spanier and Linda Thompson interviewed divorced men and women under a traditional fault law in the state of Pennsylvania in 1977, just one year before our California interviews (Spanier and Thompson 1984). They reported that the majority of their respondents expressed a strong dislike of the legal system because it forced them to accuse and blame their partners. Typical comments were: "It was just terrible, all the listing of indignities, and placing blame and fault" and "You have to make him look rotten. I didn't like making him look worse than he really was (ibid.)."

Spanier and Thompson note that the fault-based legal system encouraged the parties to become adversaries to a greater degree than they already were, aggravated their already fragile relationship, fostered antagonism between them, and upset and humiliated them by forcing public discussion of their intimate problems. Their respondents reported they were urged to lie about each other and to use "dirty tricks." As one women stated:

> I just couldn't do the lying, so he did. It really got to me—all the dirty little games you have to play. Having to tell all those twisted half-truths [Spanier and Thompson 1984, p. 92].

As this quote suggests, the Pennsylvania men and women were also disturbed by the dishonesty and perjury in the fault system.

A final complaint of respondents in the fault system concerned the tactics attorneys used to prolong the divorce, increase fees, and make the parties behave like enemies. As one woman said:

> His lawyer tried to make me crack. I don't know how they live with their conscience. . . . [H]e broke me down in stages. I just gave up for peace and serenity. After we started the court case he [husband] wouldn't let me charge anything and would let checks bounce that I wrote. We never finished the case. He told lies. I felt deflated. It was all part of his lawyer's tactics. They work. . . . He [attorney] knew it was tearing me up. I know [it was the lawyer] because other people who have used him told me [Spanier and Thompson 1984, p. 93].

Fortunately the Pennsylvania interviews included several of the same questions we asked in California so that some direct comparisons are possible. Overall, respondents express much less satisfaction with the legal process under the fault system: 55 percent of the Pennsylvania respondents indicated they were dissatisfied with the entire divorce process (including the law, judges, and lawyers), compared to 18 percent of our California respondents.

Under the fault system in Pennsylvania, respondents were more likely to report that their lawyers advised them to do things that might anger their spouses (29 percent versus 8 percent in

California), and were more likely to say that they had to lie or make up statements in order to obtain a divorce (26 percent compared to less than 3 percent in our California sample).

Further, although only a minority of the Pennsylvania respondents were advised by their attorneys to engage in "dirty tricks," such as not paying bills (13 percent) and taking money out of savings (13 percent), even fewer California respondents were so advised (respectively 6 percent, 8 percent). Finally, only 6 percent of those under the fault system said that the attorneys *decreased* the conflict and hostility between the spouses, compared to 23 percent of the California men and women.

Overall, these responses reveal that the no-fault system is much less likely to stimulate and encourage antagonistic and hostile divorces.

Interviews with the attorneys and judges also suggest that there is less acrimony and hostility under the new law. One anecdotal example is indicative. When asked how they would "build a case" under the adversarial system, attorneys told of asking clients, "What are the most terrible mean things he (or she) ever did," encouraging their clients to add to these accusations by asking "what else can you think of," or "can you think of anything worse than that?" Under no-fault, in contrast, since the spouse's behavior is irrelevant to both the divorce and the financial settlement, attorneys rarely mention asking their clients "personal questions" about their marriage or their spouses' behavior. Instead they expressed impatience with clients who wanted to "waste their time" with these "irrelevant" emotional concerns. What do you do, we asked, when you have a client who wants to talk about the marriage and *wants you to know* about the terrible things his or her spouse did? One attorney's technique for handling these clients suggests how different the no-fault climate is:

> I tell her that I am always willing to listen to her concerns but I'm not trained to do counseling. Then I look at my watch and remind her that my time is costing her $175 an hour.

A summary of the changes in the divorce law is provided in Table 12.1.

Table 12.1

Summary of Changes in Divorce Law

Traditional Divorce	No-Fault Divorce
Restrictive law	Permissive law
To protect marriage	To facilitate divorce
Specific grounds	No grounds
Adultery, cruelty, etc.	Marital breakdown
Moral framework	Administrative framework
Guilt vs. innocence	
Fault	No-fault
One party caused divorce	Cause of divorce irrelevant
Consent of innocent spouse needed	No consent
Innocent spouse has "power"	Unilateral divorce
Can prevent/delay divorce	No consent/agreement necessary
Gender-based responsibilities	Gender-neutral responsibilities
Husband responsible for alimony	Both responsible for self-support
Wife responsible for custody	Both eligible for custody
Husband responsible for child support	Both responsible for child support
Financial awards linked to fault	Financial awards based on need and equality
Alimony for "innocent" wife	Alimony based on need
Greater share of property to "innocent" spouse	Property divided equally
Adversarial	Nonadversarial
One party guilty, one innocent	No guilty or innocent party
Financial gain inproving fault	No financial gain in charges
	Amicable resolution encouraged

The Transformation of Marriage

The divorce law revolution transformed more than the prior legal assumptions about divorce. It transformed the legal norms for marriage by articulating, codifying, and legitimating a new understanding of the marital partnership and marital commitment in our society. The new laws reflect, among other things, changing social realities, emerging social norms, and everyday legal practice. Ideally, that is as it should be: if law is to be effective, it must accord with social and practical reality. But the new divorce laws do not adequately or accurately reflect social reality, and they therefore exacerbate some of the grossest inequities in our society.

Traditional family law established a clear moral framework for both marriage and divorce: marriage was a partnership, a lifelong commitment to join together "forsaking all others," for better or for worse. Husbands and wives were assigned specific roles and responsibilities, and these obligations were reinforced by law. The moral obligations of marriage were, in theory, reinforced by alimony and property awards so that spouses who lived up to their marriage contract were rewarded, and those who had not were punished.

Of course, we now know that the reality of divorce settlements often diverged from this theoretical ideal. Alimony was the exception rather than the rule, and fathers often breached their responsibility for child support. But the old structure did give the spouse who wanted to remain married considerable bargaining power, and to that extent it reinforced marriage as against the alternative of divorce. The required grounds and the need to prove fault created barriers to divorce. In addition, because the old structure linked fault to the terms of the economic settlement, divorce was expensive for men of means. If she was "innocent," the wife of a man with money and property could expect to be awarded a lifetime alimony, the family home, and other property to meet her needs. In addition, her husband would remain responsible for her financial support. (So, too, could the guilty wife expect to be punished and be denied alimony and property.)

The new reforms altered each of the major provisions of the traditional law, and in the process, they redefined the norms of legal marriage. No-fault laws abolished the need for grounds and the need to prove fault in order to obtain a divorce. They abandoned the gender-based assumptions of the traditional law in favor of standards for treating men and women "equally" in alimony and property awards. They negated the traditional role that fault played in financial awards and instead decreed that awards should be based on the divorcing parties' current financial needs and resources. And finally, the new rules shifted the legal criteria for divorce—and thus for viable marriage—from fidelity to the marriage contract to individual standards of personal satisfaction. The rules are thereby redefining marriage as a time-limited, contingent arrangement rather than a lifelong commitment.

From State Protection of Marriage to
Facilitation of Divorce

The divorce law reforms have moved the state from a position of protecting marriage (by restricting marital dissolution) to one of facilitating divorce.

They adopt a laissez-faire attitude toward both marriage and divorce, leaving both the terms of the marriage contract—and the option to terminate it—squarely in the hands of the individual parties. The pure no-fault states also eliminate any moral dimension from the divorce: guilt and innocence, fidelity and faithlessness, no longer affect the granting of the decree or its financial consequences (Weitzman 1985).

The individual's freedom to end the marriage is further bolstered in some states by no-consent rules that give either party the right to obtain a divorce without the other's agreement. Since pure no-fault–no-consent rules allow one spouse to make a unilateral decision to terminate the marriage, they transfer the economic leverage from the spouse who wants to remain married to the spouse who wants to get divorced. It is an important difference. Under the prior law the party who wanted a divorce might well have to make economic concessions or "buy" a spouse's agreement. But under the no-consent rule it is the one who hopes to preserve the marriage who must do the bargaining. Apart from the economic implications, which are considerable, these laws strengthen the hand of the party who seeks the divorce, increasing the likelihood that divorce will in fact occur.

From a Lifetime Contract to an Optional,
Time-Limited Commitment

The new divorce laws no longer view marriage as a lifelong partnership, but as a union that remains only so long as it proves satisfying to both partners. In addition, the traditional obligations of marriage, like the institution itself, are increasingly being redefined by the new divorce laws as optional, time-limited, contingent, open to individual definition, and, most important, terminable upon divorce.

In contrast to the traditional marriage contract whereby a

husband undertook lifelong responsibility for his wife's support, the new divorce laws suggest that this and other family responsibilities can—and may—be terminated upon divorce, or soon after divorce, as evident in the new rules for alimony, property, child support, and custody. Short-term alimony awards, discussed above, are evident throughout the United States as courts define women as "dependents" for shorter and shorter periods of time (Freed and Walker 1985). Current awards in California average two years.

Similar in its effect is the emphasis on a speedy resolution of the spouses' property claims. My research reveals many more forced sales of family homes than in the past, to hasten the day when each spouse can "take his (or her) money and leave." Arrangements that delay the sale of the home so that minor children do not have to move are viewed with disfavor by the courts because they "tie up the father's money." The judges we interviewed asserted that each spouse is entitled to his or her share of the property and should not have to wait for it. There is also a tendency to "cash out" other shared investments such as pensions and retirement benefits to provide a "clean break" between the parties at the time of the divorce.

Even parenting is becoming increasing optional and terminable upon divorce. Indeed, a de facto effect of the current laws is to deprive children of the care, companionship, and support of their fathers. This is evident in the courts' treatment of postdivorce visitation and child support. Furstenberg et al. (1983) found that 52 percent of the children of divorce in a nationally representative sample had not seen their fathers at all in the past year, and only 17 percent of the children had seen their fathers at least once a week. These data indicate that a majority of divorced fathers are abandoning their parental roles after divorce and are being allowed to do so without legal sanction.

In fact, one of the strongest supports for the assertion that fathers—who are 90 percent of the noncustodial parents—are legally allowed to abandon their children is the lack of a legal course of action to compel a parent to see his or her children. The implicit message is that joint parenting—and even parenting itself—is an "optional" responsibility for divorced fathers.

This message is also reflected by the law's tolerance for fathers who abandon their children financially and in the meager amounts of court-ordered child support. The courts award little child support to begin with, thereby allowing fathers to rid themselves of much of their financial responsibility for their children, and then fail to enforce child support awards once they are made (Cassity 1978, 1983; Chambers 1979, 1985; U.S. Bureau of the Census 1979, 1981).

The inadequacy of child support awards has been well documented. A 1978 U.S. Census survey found that divorced fathers paid an average of $1,951 per year per child (U.S. Bureau of the Census 1981, p. 5, Table B). In 1981 they paid an average of $2,220 (ibid., p. 3, Table B), which represents a 16 percent decline in real dollars between 1978 and 1981 (ibid., p. 7). In California we found that the average child support award was typically less than the cost of day care alone—it did not approach half of the cost of actually raising children (Weitzman and Dixon 1979; Weitzman 1985).

Past research has also more than amply documented the widespread noncompliance with child support awards (Chambers 1979). The 1981 Census survey, for example, showed that more than half (53 percent) of the millions of women who are due child support do not receive it (U.S. Bureau of the Census 1983, p. 1).

While child support awards have always been inadequate and poorly enforced, what appears to be unique about the current situation is the willful disregard of court orders among middle class and upper middle class fathers. For example, our California data reveal that fathers with incomes of $30,000 to $50,000 a year are just as likely to avoid child support payments as men with incomes of under $10,000 a year. The explanation for this lies in the legal system's lax enforcement, which has given fathers tacit approval (and financial incentives) for evading court orders. (This is discussed at length in Weitzman 1985, pp. 283–318).

Although 1984 federal legislation to strengthen the enforcement of child support may alter the present pattern, thus far family law judges and lawyers have been reluctant to bother with enforcement. When we collected our data the California law already contained many of the strict enforcement provisions of the 1984 federal law, but the judges we interviewed preferred not to use them (Weitzman 1985, pp. 292–295, 300–306).

Preston contends that the financial and social "disappearing act of fathers" after divorce is part of a larger trend: the conjugal family is gradually divesting itself of care for children in much the same way that it did earlier for the elderly (Preston 1984). To date, indications of parental abandonment have focused on fathers. Thus far, most analysts have seen mothers as firmly committed to their children. But as the norms of the new divorce laws permeate popular awareness, this picture also may change.

The import of the new custody laws, especially those that change the maternal presumption to a joint custody preference, undermine women's incentives to invest in their children. As women increasingly recognize that they will be treated "equally" in child custody decisions, that caretaking and nurturance of children find no protection in the law and are punished by the job market, and that joint custody awards may push them into difficult, restrictive, and unrewarding postdivorce custodial arrangements, they may increasingly take to heart the new laws' implied warning that motherhood does not pay.

The optional and time-limited marital commitments embodied in the new divorce laws have a differential effect on men and women. While they free men from the responsibilities they retained under the old system, they "free" women from the security that system provided. Since women's investments in home, family, and children have typically meant lost opportunities in the paid labor force, they are more dependent on the long-term protection and security that the traditional law promised them. It is not surprising that our research finds women "suffering" more under the new laws, for these laws remove the financial safeguards of the old law—with a decline in alimony awards and a decrease in women's share of the community property—at the same time that they increase the financial burdens imposed on women after divorce.

For men, by contrast, the new legal assumption of time-limited commitments means a new freedom from family financial obligations. In fact, the new laws actually give men an incentive to divorce by offering them a release from the financial burdens of marriage. In fact, the wealthier a man is, and the longer he has been married, the more he has to gain financially from divorce (Weitzman 1985).

From Protection for Housewives and Mothers to Gender-Neutral Rules

If the new legal assumptions were accompanied by provisions that enabled both spouses to choose the extent to which they would assume breadwinning and homemaking roles, and if they then gave each spouse "credit" for the roles they in fact assumed during marriage, then the law would accurately reflect the complexity and variety of marital roles in these years of "transition." But the present legal system seems to leave no room for such flexibility.

Rather, it suggests that a woman (or a man) who chooses homemaking and parenting risks a great penalty because she (or he) will pay heavily for that choice in the event of a divorce. Even if two parties agree to form an equal partnership in which they give priority to his career while she assumes the larger share of the housework and child care, and even if they agree that he will share his earnings and career assets with her, their agreement may have no legal standing. The woman will still be expected to be self-sufficient after divorce, and the man's promise of continued support and a share of his earnings—the promise that is implied in most marriages with a traditional division of labor—will be ignored in most courts.

The penalty can be equally severe for the woman who works during marriage, or who works part-time, but who nevertheless gives priority to her family over her work. Her claims to share her husband's income through spousal support fall on deaf ears in courts, which are concerned only with her "ability to engage in gainful employment" (Weitzman 1985).

Under the new legal assumptions the average divorced woman in California will be awarded no alimony, only minimal child support (which she probably will not be able to collect), exactly half of the joint tangible assets (an average of less than $10,000 worth of property), and an explicit directive to become immediately self-supporting. Even if she had married under the old law, and lived her life by the letter of the traditional marriage contract, and is 45 or 55 at the time of divorce, chances are that the courts will apply the new standards of self-sufficiency to her as well. Especially disadvantaged by these new assumptions are mothers of young children and older homemakers.

Thus one implication of the present allocation of family resources at divorce is that women had better not forgo any of their own education, training, and career development to devote themselves fully or even partially to domesticity. The law assures that they will not be much rewarded for their devotion, and they will suffer greatly if their marriage dissolves.

The concept of marital roles embodied in the new divorce laws carries an equally sobering message about motherhood. Divorcing mothers of preschool children have experienced a greater decline in alimony awards than any other group of women since the no-fault laws were instituted and the vast majority of these mothers—87 percent—are awarded no alimony at all. They are expected to find jobs immediately, to support themselves completely and, for the most part, to support their children as well.

In addition, since the age of majority children has dropped from age 21 to age 18, the divorced mother of teenage children confronts the fact that her former husband is not legally required to support their children once they reach age 18 even if they are still in their senior year of high school, much less through college. However, both high school and college students in these post–child-support years usually remain financially dependent on their parents. It is their mothers who are much more likely to respond to their needs and to support them, even though they are typically financially less able to do so.

Finally, the woman who has raised her children to maturity and who, as a result of the priority she has given to motherhood, finds herself with no marketable skills when she is divorced at 45 or 55, typically faces the harshest deprivations after divorce. The courts rarely reward her for the job she has done. Rather, the new assumptions imply that her motherhood years were wasted and worthless, for she, too, is measured against the all-important new criterion of earning capacity.

Thus the new divorce laws are institutionalizing a set of norms that may be as inappropriate in one direction as the old norms were in another. The old law assumed that all married women were first and foremost housewives and mothers. The new law assumes that all married women are employable and equally capable of self-sufficiency after divorce. Both views are overly simplistic, impede women's options, and exert a rigidifying influence on future possibilities.

For most women in our society, marriage and career are no longer either/or choices. Most women do not expect to choose between work and marriage, or between a career and motherhood. The vast majority of American women want all three. But, as Shirley Johnson has observed, when "women who have both worked full time and carried the lioness's share of the household management and child rearing responsibilities, find out that their dual role is not recognized or rewarded in divorce settlements, the effect of the new divorce laws is to encourage women to . . . shift their energies into the labor market" (Johnson 1985). Johnson argues that the economic message in the new divorce laws is that it no longer pays for a woman to "invest in marriage-specific skills" since such investments have a relatively low payoff in a society with a high risk of marital dissolution.

From Partnership to Individualism

The new divorce laws alter the traditional legal view of marriage as a partnership by rewarding individual achievement rather than investment in the family partnership. Instead of the traditional vision of a common financial future within marriage, the no-fault and no-consent standards for divorce, and the new rules for alimony, property, custody, and child support, all convey a new vision of independence for husbands and wives in marriage. In addition, the new laws confer economic advantages on spouses who invest in themselves at the expense of the marital partnership.

This focus on the individual underlies many of the changes discussed above. It reflects not only a shift in the legal relationships between the family and its adult members but also a shift in the courts' attitudes and practices in meting out rewards at divorce.

The traditional law embodied the partnership concept of marriage by rewarding sharing and mutual investments in the marital community. Implicit in the new laws, in contrast, are incentives for investing in oneself, maintaining one's separate identity, and being self-sufficient. The new stress is on individual responsibility for one's future, rather than on joint or reciprocal responsibilities.

Once again, it is easy to see how these new assumptions reflect larger cultural themes: the rise of individualism, the emphasis on personal fulfillment, the belief in personal responsibility, and the importance we attach to individual "rights." These trends have at once been applauded for the freedom they offer and criticized as selfish, narcissistic, and amoral (Lasch 1979). Whether this change represents a decline or an advance depends on one's personal values: are we concerned with the security and stability that the old order provided or with the misery it caused for those who were forced to remain in unhappy marriages?

Our evaluation will also depend on how we see the past. The belief that the rise of individualism has fostered a decline in the family rests on the assumption that the family was stable and harmonious in the past. But historians have not yet identified an era in which families were stable and harmonious and all family members behaved unselfishly and devoted their efforts to the collective good (Skolnick 1983). That "classical family of western nostalgia," to use William J. Goode's term for the stereotype (Goode 1968), has been one of the major casualties of recent research in family history (Skolnick 1983).

But historical research does suggest a change in the psychological quality of family life and a rise in what Lawrence Stone calls "affective individualism"—a growing focus on individuals as unique personalities and a political emphasis on individual rights (Stone 1977). The rise of affective individualism has brought emotional closeness between nuclear family members and a greater appreciation for the individuality of each person in the family. Historically, this trend strengthened the husband–wife unit at the expense of the larger family and the kinship network in which it was embedded. More recently, as rising divorce rates demonstrate, the strength of the husband–wife unit has declined and values of "pure" individualism are emerging. The new divorce laws reflect this evolution in that they encourage notions of personal primacy for both husband and wife. They imply that neither spouse should invest too much in marriage or place marriage above self-interest.

Both the new rules for spousal support and the new rules for property undermine the marital partnership. Despite the partnership principles that underlie the division of property, that is, the idea that property accumulated during marriage is to be shared equally at divorce—the current bases for dividing property belie such principles.

If the major breadwinner is allowed to retain most of the new property or career assets he (or she) has acquired during marriage—assets such as a professional education or good will, or health benefits, or enhanced earning capacity—the law's implicit message is that one's own career is the only safe investment. This encourages both spouses to invest in themselves before investing in each other, or their marriage, or their children.

This is one area in which the new legal assumptions are not congruent with the attitudes and assumptions of the divorced men and women we interviewed. Our interviewees rejected the limited definition of alimony as based on "need" and minimal self-sufficiency, and instead saw alimony as a means of sharing their partnership assets—the income and earning capacity in which they had both invested, and the standard of living they expected to share. These "sharing principles" for alimony were seen as an essential element in their implicit partnership "contract."

One implication of these changes is that marriage is likely to become increasingly less central to the lives of individual men and women. The privileged status of marriage in traditional family law, as well as the protections and restrictions placed on its inception and dissolution, reinforced its importance and encouraged husbands and wives to invest in it and to make it the center of their lives. The new laws, in contrast, discourage shared investments in marriage and thereby encourage both husbands and wives to dissociate from investments in the partnership. As more men and women follow the apparent mandate of the new laws, it seems reasonable to predict that marriage will lose further ground.

Indeed, William J. Goode persuasively argues that the trend is already well in progress. He observes that for both men and women marriage is simply less important today than it was in the past, and he foresees the further "decline of individual investments in family relationships over the coming decade" because investments in one's individual life and career pay off better in modern society (Goode 1984). As more women seek to follow men in the path of acquiring status, self-esteem, and a sense of individual accomplishment from their jobs, the importance of marriage will rest increasingly on its ability to provide individuals with psychic and emotional sustenance. This, Goode observes, is a difficult and fragile bond. In these trends he sees profound implications for the future of intimate relationships and the bearing and rearing of children in Western nations.

The Clouded Status of Children

A final feature of the new divorce laws is their ambiguous message about parental responsibility for children. In the past, the sustained well-being of the children of divorce was assumed to be the state's primary concern in any legal proceedings involving children. Indeed, it was this concern that dictated most of the traditional divorce law protections for women: women were recognized as the primary custodians of children, and in that capacity were to be accorded preferences and support to ensure the fulfillment of their responsibilities. Similarly, women who had devoted the productive years of their lives to child-rearing were to be rewarded for that appropriate and honorable effort.

Under the new laws, the state's concern for the welfare of children is far less in evidence. Rather, it appears that in the law's practical application, at least, the children have been all but forgotten in the courts' preoccupation with parental "equality."

The same rules that facilitate divorce facilitate the disruption of children's lives. The gender-neutral rules that encourage or force mothers to work also deprive children of the care and attention they might otherwise have. (Effectively, the fate of divorcing mothers is still the fate of the children of divorce because, sex-neutral custody standards notwithstanding, mothers still are the primary caretakers of children after divorce.) Also, the actual effects of the current laws deprive children of both the care and the support of their fathers.

In sum, under the present laws divorced fathers *may* participate more in the lives of their children if they choose to do so, but they need not so choose; and mothers *must* work outside the home whether they wish it or not, and thus *must* divide their energies between jobs and children. One might well ask what legal protections remain to insure parenting for children after divorce.

Even as the law over time evolves to reflect social reality, it also serves as a powerful force in creating social reality. Although the divorce law reformers knew that equality between the sexes was not yet a reality when they codified assumptions about equality in the law, they had seen trends in that direction and believed the new law would accelerate those trends. My research shows however, that the law actually slowed any trend toward economic equality that may have been developing. It worsened women's condition, improved men's condition, and widened the income gap between the sexes. The law has moved us toward a new reality, to be sure, but it is not, in the economic sphere at least, the hoped-for reality.

So long as the laws remain in force in their present form and their present application, postdivorce equality between the sexes will remain an illusion.

NOTES

1. Prior publications of the results of this research include Weitzman and Dixon 1979; Weitzman and Dixon 1980; Dixon and Weitzman 1980; Weitzman 1981a; Dixon and Weitzman 1982; and Weitzman 1985.

2. Although thirty states have adopted some form of joint custody laws, mother custody awards are still the norm and mothers have the primary responsibility for their children after divorce in the vast majority of the cases. The legal trends and the empirical data on child custody are reviewed in Weitzman 1985, pp. 215–261.

3. I am indebted to Ruth B. Dixon for being my partner in the collection of the American data. More detailed information on these samples and research methods is provided in Weitzman 1985, pp. 403–412.

4. "Divorce, in the modern sense of a judicial decree dissolving a valid marriage, and allowing one or both partners to remarry during the life of the other, did not exist in England until 1857" (Kay 1970). Since marriage was regarded as an indissoluble union, it could be ended only by the death of one of the parties (Rheinstein 1972). A rare exception, originating in the late seventeenth century, allowed divorce on the sole ground of adultery by special acts of Parliament. As a practical matter, however, few of these divorces were granted (Clark 1968, p. 281). The Church permitted divorce *a mensa et thoro*, literally a divorce from bed and board, which allowed the parties to live apart. But this legal separation did not end the financial obligations of marriage.

REFERENCES

Babcock, Barbara; Friedman, Ann; Norton, Eleanor Holmes; and Ross, Susan Deller. *Sex-Based Discrimination.* Boston: Little, Brown & Co., 1974.

Brown v. Brown, 198 Tenn. 600, 281 S.W. 2d:492 (1955).

Cassity, Judith. *Child Support and Public Policy.* Lexington, Mass.: D. C. Heath, 1978.

Cassity, Judith. *The Parental Child Support Obligation.* Lexington, Mass.: D. C. Heath, 1983.

Chambers, David. *Making Fathers Pay.* Chicago: University of Chicago Press, 1979.

Chambers, David. "The Coming Curtailment of Compulsory Child Support." *Michigan Law Review,* forthcoming, 1986.

Clark, Homer. *Domestic Relations.* St. Paul, Minn.: West Publishing Co., 1968.

Davis, Kingsley. "The Future of Marriage." Chapter 2 in Kingsley Davis and Amyra Grossbard-Shechtman (eds.), *Essays on Contemporary Marriage.* New York: Russell Sage Foundation, 1986.

Dixon, Ruth B., and Weitzman, Lenore J. "Evaluating the Impact of No-Fault Divorce in California." *Family Relations* 29 (1980):297–307.

Dixon, Ruth B., and Weitzman, Lenore J. "When Husbands File for Divorce." *Journal of Marriage and the Family* 44 (1982):103–114.

Ehrenreich, Barbara. *The Hearts of Men: American Dreams and the Flight from Commitment.* Garden City, N.Y.: Doubleday, 1983.

Eisler, Riane Tennenhaus. *Dissolution: No-Fault Divorce, Marriage and the Future of Women* (New York: McGraw-Hill, 1977).

Freed, Doris Jonas, and Foster, Henry H. "Family Law in the Fifty States: An Overview." *Family Law Quarterly* 17 (1984):364–447.

Freed, Doris Jonas, and Walker, Timothy. "Family Law in the Fifty States: An Overview." *Family Law Quarterly* 18 (1985):369–471.

Furstenberg, Frank F.; Nord, Christine W.; Peterson, James L.; and Zil, Nicholas. "The Life Course of Children of Divorce: Marital Disruption and Parental Contact." *American Sociological Review* 48 (1983):656–668.

Glendon, Mary Ann. *State, Law and Family: Family Law in Transition in the United States and Western Europe.* New York: Elsevier, 1977.

Glendon, Mary Ann. *The New Family and the New Property.* Toronto: Butterworths, 1981.

Glendon, Mary Ann. "Property Rights upon Dissolution of Marriage and Informal Unions." *The Cambridge Lectures 1981,* Nancy E. Eastham and Boris Krivy (eds.). Toronto: Butterworths, 1982:245–267.

Glendon, Mary Ann. "Family Law Reform in the 1980s." *Louisiana Law Review* 44 (1984):1553–1573.

Goode, William J. *World Revolution in Family Patterns.* New York: Free Press, 1968.

Goode, William J. "Individual Investments in Family Relationships Over the Coming Decades." *The Tocqueville Review* 6 (1984):51–84.

Hofstadter, S., and Levittan, S. "Alimony—A Reformation." *Journal of Family Law* 7 (1967):55.

Hogoboom, William. "The California Family Law Act of 1979: 18 Months' Experience." *Journal of the Missouri Bar* 27 (1971):687.

Johnson, Shirley Lans. "The Economic Position of Divorced Women." *Fairshare,* 1985, forthcoming.

Kay, Herma Hill. "A Family Court: The California Proposal." In Paul Bohannon (ed.), *Divorce and After.* Garden City, N.Y.: Doubleday, 1970.

Kay, Herma Hill. *Sex-Based Discrimination,* 2nd ed. St. Paul, Minn.: West Publishing Co., 1981.

Krom, Howard. "California's Divorce Law Reform: An Historical Analysis. *Pacific Law Journal* 1 (1970):156–181.

Lasch, Christopher. *The Culture of Narcissism.* New York: Norton, 1979.

Leonard, Frances. "The Disillusionment of Divorce for Older Women." Washington, D.C.: Older Women's League, 1980.

Preston, Samuel. "Children and the Elderly: Divergent Paths for America's Dependents." *Demography* 21 (1984):435–457.

Rheinstein, Max. *Marriage Stability, Divorce and the Law.* Chicago: University of Chicago Press, 1972.

Skolnick, Arlene. *The Intimate Environment.* Boston: Little Brown, 1983.

Spanier, Graham B., and Thompson, Linda. *Parting: The Aftermath of Separation and Divorce.* Beverly Hills, Calif.: Sage Publications, 1984.

Stone, Lawrence. *The Family, Sex and Marriage in England 1500–1800.* New York: Harper & Row, 1977.

Thornton, Arland, and Freedman, Deborah. "The Changing American Family." *Population Bulletin* 38 (1983):1–43.

U.S. Bureau of the Census. "Divorce, Child Custody and Child Support." *Current Population Reports.* Series P-23, No. 84 (1979), p. 7, Table 1.

U.S. Bureau of the Census. "Child Support and Alimony: 1978," Series P-23, No. 112 (1981).

U.S. Bureau of the Census. "Child Support and Alimony: 1981," Series P-23, No. 124 (1983).

Weitzman, Lenore J. *The Marriage Contract: Spouses, Lovers, and the Law.* New York: Free Press, 1981a.

Weitzman, Lenore J. "The Economics of Divorce: Social and Economic Consequences of Property, Alimony and Child Support Awards." *U.C.L.A. Law Review* 28 (1981b):1181–1268.

Weitzman, Lenore J. *The Divorce Revolution: The Unexpected Social and Economic Consequences for Women and Children in America.* New York: Free Press, 1985.

Weitzman, Lenore J., and Dixon, Ruth B. "Child Custody Awards: Legal Standards and Empirical Patterns for Child Custody, Support and Visitation Rights after Divorce." *University of California Davis Law Review* 12 (1979):473–521.

Weitzman, Lenore J., and Dixon, Ruth B. "The Alimony Myth: Does No-Fault Divorce Make a Difference?" *Family Law Quarterly* 14 (1980):141–185.

Wheeler, Michael. *No-Fault Divorce.* Boston: Beacon Press, 1974.

13 New Models of Marriage and Divorce

Significant Legal Developments in the Last Decade

GRACE GANZ BLUMBERG

IN RECENT YEARS some scholars have suggested that the legal institution of marriage is withering away, that is, that the state is receding from the role of marriage regulation and is increasingly leaving the parties to their own devices. This interpretation is generally supported by reference to no-fault divorce, the doctrinal decline of alimony, and recent developments in the legal treatment of cohabitation in lieu of marriage (Glendon 1976, 1977; Blumstein and Schwartz 1983). Glendon, for example, argues that marriage and cohabitation tend toward convergence. As marriage experiences legal diminution via no-fault divorce and the decline of alimony, cohabitation, its shadow institution, is gaining legal recognition and has reached the point where it is, from a legal perspective, analogous to marriage (Glendon 1976).

In this chapter I argue that this is a misleading portrayal of significant recent legal developments in the United States, and I propose an alternative view of the direction that law has taken. I believe that significant recent legal developments coherently express a new view of marriage and divorce. This view accepts the fragility of the conjugal aspect of marriage but asserts that the economic and coparental incidents of marriage are much more durable. They survive divorce and are entitled to legal solicitude and protection. The persistence of the economic and coparental incidents is registered in the rapid recent development of marital property and joint custody doctrine. Recognizing that the divorcing parties cannot truly go their independent ways, a processual handmaiden to divorce has been developed to assure that the parties can work together with respect to the residual aspects of their relationship. This procedural development is often characterized as "mediation," although strictly speaking, it may include as well other nonjudicial forms of divorce settlement. Its purpose is to avoid adversary process that would escalate hostility and to help the divorcing spouses to work together in the future. This chapter will discuss these three recent developments: marital property law expansion, joint custody, and mediation, and will relate them to a coherent view of marriage and its dissolution. I will not attempt to critically evaluate any of these developments. It is generally accepted that marital property law is an appropriate area for legal development.[1] The wisdom of joint custody is, in contrast, vigorously disputed (Adler and Chambers 1978; "Further Observations" 1983; Steinman 1983). Commentators have generally viewed mediation favorably, but there are grounds for serious reservations (Folberg 1982; Crouch 1982; Silberman 1981). My purpose is not to evaluate the wisdom of each development but rather to point out how far each has progressed and what each contributes to a coherent legal philosophy of marriage and divorce.

For purposes of this chapter, I divide marriage into three incidents: the conjugal, the economic, and the coparental. It is my thesis that modern divorce law, while it freely terminates the conjugal relation, increasingly recognizes and regulates the economic product and coparental aspects of the defunct conjugal relation. What we have, in effect, is a dramatic increase in state ordering at the breakdown of marriage.[2]

First, in order to avoid the appearance of selectively and arbitrarily choosing the details of my landscape, I will explain why I think the adoption of no-fault divorce and the doctrinal decline of alimony are relatively insignificant, or lesser-order, legal developments. I will also discuss the American legal treatment of cohabitation in order to demonstrate that it has had relatively little bearing on the legal institution of marriage.

No-fault divorce and the doctrinal decline of alimony loom large only if one reads these doctrinal shifts literally, without reference to legal practice and lay understanding of such practice. On a literal level, fault-based divorce doctrine embodied the concept of life-time marriage dissoluble only by the state after a showing that one spouse had committed some egregious act against the other. The state's interest in the preservation of marriages was expressed in its power to deny a divorce even when both spouses wished to terminate the marriage. Thus, under this literal reading of doctrine, the state receded from marriage regulation when it adopted one of the several new grounds for divorce which have been labeled "no-fault." Such grounds include irretrievable breakdown, separation in fact, and separation pursuant to a negotiated settlement (Freed and Foster 1981, pp. 4049–4053).[3] At the very least, such grounds permit divorce by mutual consent of the parties; in their most expansive form, they effectively permit divorce at the will of one spouse. If doctrine were a fair representation of legal reality, no-fault divorce reform would indeed represent a major shift in the state's view of marriage and divorce.

Traditional divorce law, however, demonstrated a remarkable divergence between doctrine and practice. For most Americans the fault-based system did not erect serious impediments to divorce. The conditions of divorce were negotiated by the parties and one spouse, generally the husband, was designated the defendant in an uncontested collusive suit (Rheinstein 1972, pp. 104–105). Unseemly as this may have been for litigants and their attorneys, divorce at the joint will of the spouses has long been a feature of American life. One might even assert that fault divorce truly left the parties to their own devices, that they alone, acting jointly, carried the keys to their own divorce. In contrast, in the most polar version of no-fault—the irreconcilable differences ground—one spouse alone can unilaterally terminate the conjugal relation. To this extent, the state is a more active participant in divorce, coming to the aid of the party who wishes to end the relationship rather than relegating him or her to a process of private negotiation with the recalcitrant spouse.

On balance, no-fault divorce probably was a desirable reform.

Under prior law, there were extreme cases in which one party persistently refused the other a divorce. Migratory divorce, the last resort of the wealthy or leisured, was too expensive or time-consuming for many Americans.[4] It is probably preferable for the law to bury defunct social myths than to preserve them in doctrine while simultaneously evading them in practice. Nevertheless, requiring that termination of the conjugal relationship be negotiated by the parties tended generally to redistribute wealth from have-husbands to have-not-wives. This was, in the generality of cases, a positive result, but redistribution dictated by the relative bargaining power of the parties was capable, in particular cases, of producing unfair results.

I do not wish to argue that no-fault divorce is an unwelcome development, or that it is without consequences, both intended and unintended.[5] Rather, I wish to place it in the perspective of preexisting practice, of which it is largely confirmatory. It is not unfair, I believe, to assert that the legal profession is the primary beneficiary of no-fault divorce reform. Lawyers and judges are no longer required to systematically compromise professional ideals in the routine management of divorce cases (Foote, Levy, and Sander 1976, pp. 943–1010).

Similarly, excessive significance has been ascribed to doctrinal reformulation of alimony, or spousal support. It is true that most of our statutory law no longer even suggests that the divorcing homemaker is entitled to lifetime support at the standard to which she became accustomed during marriage. Support statutes now generally prescribe support payments only for the spouse who is unable to support herself because of ill health, lack of vocational training, or the presence of young children requiring full-time care. Except for permanently disabled or elderly homemakers, support is to be awarded, if at all, only for relatively short, fixed periods.[6] Recent statutory expression of the notion that a divorced wife is not entitled to lifetime support is not a new idea, however; in most jurisdictions, it merely codifies judicial language dating back at least to World War II and is reflective of actual trial court practice of an earlier period. Even the current less permissive reformulation grossly overstates the divorcing homemaker's past or present eligibility for spousal support. For the vast majority of divorced wives, alimony has long been no more than a theoretical right. Marshall and May, writing in 1932 and 1933, surveyed divorce judgments in Maryland and Ohio. They found that alimony was sought in approximately 12 percent of cases and was granted in only 6 percent (Marshall and May 1933). Surveying national divorce data from 1887 and comparing the incidence of California alimony awards before and after the 1969 enactment of no-fault divorce, Weitzman (1981) concludes that "the promise of alimony has always been a myth." With respect to those spouses singled out for solicitude under the modern support formulation, "those with full-time responsibility for young children, those who require transitional support to become self-supporting, and those who are incapable of becoming self-supporting by reason of age or 'earning disabilities' after a long marriage," Weitzman concludes that "California data indicate that the system in practice has failed to provide for these women." She found, for example, that "[o]nly 13% of the mothers of preschool children were awarded any spousal support in 1977" (Weitzman 1981, pp. 1221–1222).[7]

Commentators who posit the "withering away" of the legal institution of marriage also find support in the rise of the social institution of cohabitation without marriage and, particularly, in recent case-law recognition of this social development (Glendon 1976, pp. 691–697; Blumstein and Schwartz 1983, pp. 37–38). While I do not wish to minimize the importance to unmarried cohabitants of the manner in which the law regulates, or fails to regulate, their relationships, I think it is fair to say that recent developments in the legal treatment of cohabitation have had relatively little effect on the legal institution of marriage. Indeed, the entire thrust of case-law treatment of cohabitation has been to categorically refuse cohabitants access to the status-based incidents of marriage.[8] Cohabitants have merely been offered the panoply of general contract principles available to all persons but heretofore denied to cohabitants because of the meretricious nature of their relationship.[9] At most, contract offers cohabitants the opportunity to define and regulate their *inter se* relationship. Current law offers them no possibility of acquiring the many *extra se* status-based incidents of marriage, for example, derivative social insurance claims, such as social security old age, survivors, and disability spouses' benefits,[10] unemployment insurance benefits,[11] workers' compensation benefits for surviving spouses,[12] statutory life insurance benefits, "family" health insurance, federal estate and gift tax exemption for surviving spouses, preferred state inheritance and estate tax treatment, federal income tax splitting, and wrongful death[13] and loss of consortium[14] claims against third parties who have wrongfully injured one's spouse.

The law might, and perhaps should, have assimilated marriagelike cohabitation to marriage (Blumberg 1981), but it did not. Indeed, it has pointedly declined many invitations to do so. Such refusal can plausibly be read as resistance to the dilution of legal marriage. By imposing the incidents of marriage only on those who have clearly committed themselves to it—the lawfully wedded—and allowing an escape hatch for cohabitants who, were they assimilated into marriage, might subvert the institution from within, judges have effectively shored up the legal institution of marriage. The only trend in marriage law that can plausibly be related to contract treatment of cohabitation is increased judicial and legislative tolerance for contract ordering between married persons. Prenuptial contract regulation of possible future separation and divorce has, for example, been accepted in some jurisdictions. It should be noted, however, that the principal marriage contract cases[15] antedate *Marvin v. Marvin*,[16] the leading modern cohabitation case. Moreover, decisions permitting premarital contract ordering of divorce purport to find their sources in preexisting marriage law, namely, long-standing doctrine permitting antenuptial waiver of rights, such as dower and the elective share, that would otherwise accrue when a marriage is dissolved by the death of a spouse.[17] Still, it is likely that acceptance of contractual ordering of cohabitation will, over time, soften legal resistance to contractual ordering in marriage. In any event, this permissive development is not of great significance in the United States, where the overwhelming majority of people not only continue to marry[18] but also accept, without attempt at variation, all the incidents of marriage imposed by the state.[19]

Thus, I conclude that none of the changes discussed—the adoption of no-fault divorce, the recodification of spousal support obligations, or the judicial application of contract principles at the dissolution of informal conjugal relationships—represents a significant development for the sociolegal institution of marriage. With respect to the first two reforms, legal change largely confirmed prior practice; it was law reform that was "lagging" rather than "leading." With regard to judicial response to cohabitation, the contractual rubric chosen to regulate cohabitation had, and is likely to have, little impact on the legal regulation of marriage.

This is not to suggest that there are no new significant legal developments in domestic relations law. The three topics I have chosen to discuss—marital property, joint custody, and mediation—are "leading" developments in two senses. They are genuinely new in that they introduce concepts heretofore unexplored and results previously unknown in domestic relations law. They also have substantial potential for altering the way spouses think about marriage and divorce and the roles they play therein.

The wealth-redistribution function of negotiated fault divorce settlement was a potential casualty of no-fault divorce. It was not accidental that the first major irreconcilable differences provision, which effectively established a form of unilateral no-fault divorce, was enacted in California, a community property state in which each spouse owns a 50 percent interest in all property earned during marriage. In 1969, when California adopted no-fault divorce, such a reform was unthinkable in a state like New York, where title controlled property ownership during marriage and at divorce.[20] New York's additive introduction of fault-free divorce, effective two years earlier in 1967, necessarily took the form of divorce by negotiated settlement[21]: a spouse was entitled to divorce after living separate and apart for a specified period of time pursuant to a signed agreement between the parties.

No-fault divorce reformers were sensitive to the need for a marital property regime to replace the role of negotiated property settlements under fault law. The Uniform Marriage and Divorce Act, promulgated in 1969, proposed unilateral no-fault breakdown divorce and comprehensive equitable property distribution at divorce. In 1983, the Uniform Commissioners approved a newly drafted state Uniform Marital Property Act, which proposes a version of community property for nationwide adoption.

Most of the striking development of marital property law that has occurred in the past decade, however, has been accomplished by state legislatures and state courts operating independently but convergently. The concept of marital property is now almost universally accepted in the United States; Mississippi is the only state that persists in treating title as controlling at divorce. Ten years ago, many major states, including New York, Massachusetts, Virginia, and Pennsylvania, were still title states.

The doctrine of equitable distribution, that is, that the property of the parties shall be equitably distributed at divorce, has expanded not only in its frequency of general adoption but also in its frequency of specific application. Originally a doctrine reserved for special circumstances, it is now routinely applied. It has come, over time, to embody the community property view that marriage is an economic partnership in which both parties have a stake without regard to the actual distribution of market earnings. This trend has been evidenced over the last decade by the frequent rewriting of statutes to include the homemaker's contribution to the marriage and the nonmarket spouse's opportunity costs as factors to be considered in property distribution at divorce.[22] It is also evidenced by a legislative and case-law movement toward a presumptive 50–50 division.[23]

The most striking development is the ever-expanding definition of "property" available for distribution at divorce. To the extent that law conceptualizes the couple as an economic enterprise in which the parties invest as well as consume, it must be recognized that all the economic growth experienced by the unit will not be reflected in the tangible assets readily available for distribution at divorce. A true measure of assets acquired by the marriage must include the parties' enhanced capacity for future earnings. Since 1976, when the California Supreme Court decided the landmark *Marriage of Brown*,[24] a majority of state courts have followed *Brown* in holding that unvested as well as vested rights to future pension benefits are property divisible at divorce.[25] Professional good will is, in the case of divorce, a projection of that portion of postdivorce earnings attributable to practice-building efforts expended during marriage. Even though such good will is often nontransferable because it is inseparable from the person of the professional, it has been generally recognized in the last few years as property subject to division.[26] Most recently, the courts have been grappling with professional education. Most courts are unwilling to dismiss entirely such claims because of the clear investment aspect of professional education and the obvious continuum between already-recognized forms of intangible property and the value of enhanced future earnings due to education acquired during marriage. Yet judges have recoiled at staggering valuations and have generally fallen back on otherwise anomalous cost-reimbursement remedies.[27] Professional education does not necessarily mark the limit of this doctrinal development: in 1984, the California legislature considered a bill that directed the divorce court to classify as community property all accretion to earning power acquired during marriage.[28]

One effect of accounting for human capital gains made during marriage is to introduce, in more plausible and credible form, an analog to alimony, which has never been favored in this country and has been honored more in the breach than in the award. While alimony and marital property distribution of future earnings attributable to marital effort are similar in that they both generally are paid out of the obligor-spouse's postdivorce earnings, their rationales are very different. Alimony discharges a support duty that, implausibly, survives divorce, while distribution of an intangible asset that manifests itself in postdivorce earnings represents a return on marital investment. The courts, in perhaps conscious recognition of the similarities as well as the differences, tend to characterize professional education awards as alimony,[29] rather than property division, although they clearly are in the nature of property division.

Combining no-fault divorce and expanded concepts of property distribution, a picture emerges of conjugal freedom and economic constraint. The individual spouse may freely renounce the conjugal relation but is bound to honor the economic investments the couple has made. Either spouse is free to walk away from the associational aspect of marriage, but neither spouse may be unjustly enriched by the couple's joint efforts.

The development of marital property law did not, of course, occur in a vacuum. It was spurred by no-fault divorce, which removed property distribution from the relatively unprincipled negotiation of fault-based divorce and sent it on a search for coherent organizing principles. Marital property law owes a great deal to economics, which has presented an ample and sophisticated view of marriage as, *inter alia*, an economic enterprise (Becker 1973, 1981; Krauskopf 1980; Kiker 1971). Yet the law also takes on a life of its own, remodeling our relations so that we begin to think differently about them, giving conscious expression to inchoate concepts and thus bringing them to the forefront of our thought. Until recently, for example, few couples could consciously articulate that a spouse's presence in professional school represented a form of marital investment; now many comfortably do so. Their expectations develop accordingly.

As the economic distribution of marital assets may persist long after the conjugal relation has been terminated, so may the coparental relationship endure. This is the thrust of joint custody, which has experienced rapid and widespread legislative and case-law development equaled only by the growth of marital property law. Joint custody involves two basic notions: that each spouse's parental role persists after divorce and that the spouses' coparental relation persists as well. The first concept, the persistence of the parental role, is unexceptionable. Even though divorced fathers often abandon their social, as well as their economic, relationship to noncustodial children, the legal ideal has, at least in this century, included both parents in the child's postdivorce life. This ideal has commonly been expressed as weekday custody in one parent and weekend cutody, or visitation, in the other. The persistence of this primary-secondary pattern even in some joint custody arrangements has caused some observers to question whether joint custody works any change at all. The essential innovation of joint custody is conjoint parental decision making. Formerly, legal custody was coextensive with physical custody. The parent with primary custody exercised dominant control over the child's life while the parent with visitation rights exercised legal control, if at all, only during his short, intermittent custodial periods. Each parent was expected to maintain a parent–child relationship, but it was a relationship independent of the other divorced parent. Joint custody, however, expects both parents to exercise legal control conjointly as they did in marriage, regardless of the actual temporal allocation of physical custody. "Under a joint custody arrangement legal custody—the legal authority and responsibility for making 'major' decisions regarding the child's welfare—is shared at all times by both parents."[30] Whether this goal is attainable in most or many cases and, if so, whether its realization will serve the best interests of the child are issues beyond the scope of this paper. What is important here is the reconceptualization of divorce: the parents may freely terminate their conjugal relationship but conjoint aspects of the parental relationship will persist after divorce. Many courts will decree joint custody even if one spouse objects to the continuation of coparental relations; some will decree joint custody even if neither parent has requested it.[31]

In the past several years, twenty-eight states have enacted joint custody statutes.[32] Legislation is pending in another eight states.[33] Courts do not need legislative permission to order joint custody. Many courts have made joint custody awards without explicit legislative authorization.[34] The recently enacted statutes are, however, noteworthy because most of them go far beyond mere legislative authorization of joint custody.[35] Twelve statutes either announce that joint custody is the public policy of the state or express a preference for joint custody.[36] More moderately, sixteen say that parents should be encouraged to share child-rearing.[37] Only seven statutes require the agreement of the parties before the court can order joint custody.[38] Thirteen create a presumption affecting the burden of proof when both parents agree to joint custody or require that the court state its reasons for denial of joint custody when both parents have agreed to it.[39] Six states provide adjunctive mediation: two make it mandatory,[40] and four make it discretionary.[41]

The emergence of a model of divorce that is characterized by the persistence of property and coparental ties between divorced spouses has understandably encountered skepticism and resistance from those who have observed that divorced spouses are often unable to work together effectively.[42] The impediments to cooperation stem from two sources: the tensions that led to a breakdown of the conjugal relationship and the escalation of estrangement caused by the adversary process of divorce. The primary goal of a mediative approach to divorce is to eliminate the hostility engendered by adversary legal process (Folberg 1982, pp. 12–15, 41). An ancillary goal, often supported by public or private family counseling services, is development of the couple's capacity for continuing conjoint activity. It is possible to view divorce mediation as merely one aspect of a generalized growing disenchantment with adversary legal negotiation and litigation. From a domestic relations perspective, however, divorce mediation appears as a procedural handmaiden summoned forth by a new substantive model of divorce. It seems likely that practitioner interest in mediation arose from a generalized rejection of adversary process, and that divorce provided a propitious setting because continuing economic and coparental relations were becoming increasingly important to divorcing spouses.

L. Riskin, a lawyer, mediator, and legal scholar, gives a balanced description of mediation and compares it to adversary process.

> Nearly all mediators seek to help the disputants achieve an agreement. Most have educational objectives as well, especially where the parties will have a continuing relationship. There are, however, enormous differences in procedures and roles that mediators adopt. Some will act merely as go-betweens, keeping open lines of communication. . . . Some mediators will urge that the parties propose solutions; others will make their own proposals and try to persuade the parties to accept them and may even apply economic, social or moral pressure to achieve a "voluntary" agreement. . . .
>
> Mediation offers some clear advantages over adversary processing. it is cheaper, faster, and potentially more hospitable to unique solutions that take more fully into account nonmaterial interests of the disputants. It can educate the parties about each other's needs and those of the community. Thus, it can help them learn to work together and to see that through cooperation both can make positive gains. One reason for these advantages is that mediation is less hemmed-in by rules of procedure or substantive law and certain assumptions that dominate the adversary process. . . . [I]n mediation— as distinguished from adjudication and, usually, arbitration—the ultimate authority resides with the disputants. The conflict is seen as unique and therefore less subject to solution by application of some general principle. . . . Thus, all sorts of facts, needs, and interests that would be excluded from consideration in an adversary, rule-oriented proceeding could become relevant in a mediation. . . . In a divorce mediation, for instance, a spouse's continuing need for emotional support could become important, as could the other party's willingness and ability to give it. In most mediations, the emphasis is not on determining rights or interests, or who is right and who is wrong, or who wins and who loses because of which rule; these would control the typical adjudicatory hearing. The focus, instead, is upon establishing a degree of harmony through a resolution that will work for these disputants.
>
> A danger inheres in this alegal character: individuals who are not aware of their legal position are not encouraged by the process to develop a rights-consciousness or to establish legal rights. Thus, the risk of dominance by the stronger or more knowledgeable party is great. Accordingly, for society to maximize the benefits of mediation while controlling its dangers, it must carefully adjust the role of lawyers in the mediation process. [Riskin 1982, pp. 34–36].

Today, most mediation is voluntary, and tends to displace traditional adversary negotiation. With both processes, the desired final result is a divorce settlement. Thus, voluntary mediation represents neither growth nor decline in the state's involvement in divorce because traditional negotiation, like mediation, is a private dispute settlement process. Only the character of the process has changed, at least insofar as both unfold "in the shadow of the law" (Mnookin and Kornhauser 1979), that is, tend to follow legal norms.[43]

Some jurisdictions have, however, organized their own mediation programs. At the moment, state-organized and staffed mediation programs are generally restricted to child custody disputes. Unlike private mediation voluntarily undertaken by the parties, some state mediation is obligatory (McIsaac 1981; Pearson, Ring, and Milne 1983). Moreover, the reputed success of state programs has generated legislative impetus to expand subject matter coverage.[44] Thus, state-organized mediation may represent a significant state entry into divorce negotiation and settlement, aspects of the divorce process that heretofore had been left to the private activity of the parties.

The purpose of this chapter has been to use recent legal developments to construct a new model of divorce. These legal developments have not, of course, arisen in a doctrinal vacuum. Each has been generated or influenced by social change and insights supplied by other disciplines. The impetus for joint custody comes from the relaxation of traditional gender roles: fathers now frequently demand equal treatment as parents. Our increasingly sophisticated approach to marital property owes much to economics, particularly to human resources accounting and the economics of the family. More basically, the law became sensitive to these aspects of economic theory only when it no longer took gender-based economic roles for granted. For example, the value of a homemaker's services was accorded legal cognizance after most married women had entered the labor market.[45] The contention that human capital investment ought to be taken into account in property division at divorce becomes plausible when the identity of the individual beneficiary of a couple's human capital investment no longer seems predetermined or self-evident.

These legal developments, however, do not merely reflect social change; they fuel it as well. The divorced father who becomes the joint custodian of his children accelerates the breakdown of gender-based social roles. The spouse who claims a property interest in human capital acquired by her mate during marriage is making several radical assertions. She is challenging allocation of human capital investment resources on the basis of gender. More fundamentally, she is claiming an equality of social roles. This latter principle, which many feminist theorists consider vital for true gender equality, is gaining a toehold in American law. Its two entry points are marital property doctrine and the emergent fair employment practice standard of equal pay for comparable work.

In constructing a new model of marriage, I have mainly relied on three recent trends in the law and practice of domestic relations—burgeoning marital property development, joint custody, and mediation. I discount the significance of no-fault divorce as a reflector or cause of social change because I believe it largely confirms long-standing legal practice. In contrast, the developments I have identified reflect genuinely new ways of thinking about marriage and divorce. In the model of marriage and divorce that they imply, an unsatisfactory conjugal relation is readily terminable but the children and economic product of the marriage may engender ties between the divorced spouses that are far more enduring than the conjugal relation proved to be. To enable the parties to fairly define and effectively pursue their postdivorce relationship, the nonadversary conjugal termination process called "mediation" is helpful.

Thus, divorce, while nominally more freely available, dissolves less. In terms of the incidents of marriage, as the conjugal bond has become, at least nominally, more freely dissoluble, the economic and coparental bonds have grown increasingly indissoluble. A recent judicial decision, reported by a nationally syndicated columnist, has great heuristic value. A Michigan trial court readily granted a no-fault divorce to a couple with three minor children. After assessing the economic situation of the family and the needs of the children, the court ordered the divorced spouses to live together until the children reach majority and to continue to perform the economic and coparental roles performed during marriage (Goodman 1983). Such a divorce is, of course, no divorce at all. The trial judge made the error of inexorably following the principle of continuing economic and coparental relations to the point where it obliterated any notion of a conjugal divorce. This case, by over-statement, dramatically illustrates recent trends in American law.

NOTES

(This chapter was based on research completed prior to 1983. While research published since then has consistently borne out the assertions and predictions made in this chapter, the notes and references that follow could not be amplified to include those more recent items.)

1. But see Glendon, *Is There a Future for Separate Property?*, 8 FAM. L. Q. 315 (1974).

2. The state need not, of course, become significantly involved in every divorce to evidence a high level of state ordering. Much divorce is ostensibly private in that it is largely the product of negotiation between the parties. Nevertheless, the settlement achieved by negotiation will strongly reflect what the parties might expect if they took the case to court (Mnookin and Kornhauser 1979, pp. 968–969).

3. By 1981, seventeen states had adopted irretrievable breakdown as the sole or dominant ground for divorce. Those that adopted it as the major but not exclusive ground retained the preexisting ground of mental illness or insanity. See, e.g., Cal. Civ. Code Sections 4506, 4507; Uniform Marriage and Divorce Act Section 305. An additional eighteen states had added breakdown to their traditional fault grounds. Twenty states had adopted "living separate and apart" for a specified period, and seven states had adopted some form of divorce by mutual consent (Freed and Foster 1981). See, e.g., N.Y. Dom. Rel. L. Section 170(6) (McKinney's).

4. Nevada has long been a haven for divorce-seekers able to sojourn there for the jurisdictionally required six weeks. The United States Supreme Court, in a series of decisions, interpreted the Constitution to require that the parties' home state extend full faith and credit to most sister state migratory divorces. Bilateral divorces, those in which both spouses participate, are conclusively valid because both spouses are generally estopped to later question the domiciliary basis for the rendering court's jurisdiction. *Sherrer v. Sherrer*, 334 U.S. 343 (1948). See also *Johnson v. Muelberger*, 340 U.S. 581 (1950).

5. Some consequences are jurisdiction-specific, and turn on the particular characteristics of pre-reform and post-reform law. In California, for example, the pre-1969 fault regime required that the "innocent" spouse be awarded more than 50 percent of the community property. The no-fault law, in contrast, directed the court to divide the property equally without regard to marital behavior. While some commentators suggested that this reform was merely confirmatory of trial practice, that is, that courts had routinely been awarding 51 percent to the "innocent" spouse, Lenore Weitzman has persuasively demonstrated that this was not so. Instead,

"three-quarters of the [pre-reform] cases involved a substantially unequal division." Since the "innocent" spouse was predominantly the wife, California no-fault divorce has partially undercut the wealth redistribution function of marital property law (Weitzman 1981, pp. 1181, 1201, 1203).

Other outcomes are possible, however. In those states that enacted a fault-free divorce ground but did not extend no-fault principles to property division, one would expect little or no change in wealth distribution. Freed and Foster list fifteen states that treat marital fault as a factor in property division and/or alimony. In those states that adopted some version of no-fault and also, at or about the same time, initially enacted equitable distribution provisions, one would expect to see increased redistribution from the economic haves to the have-nots of marriage. Such states include, *inter alia*, Maryland, Massachusetts, New Jersey, New York, Pennsylvania, and Virginia. This result should also be expected in those states that ceased to treat fault as a bar to alimony. Only seven states still make marital misconduct an automatic bar to alimony (Freed and Foster 1981, pp. 4055, 4059).

6.   See, e.g., Uniform Marriage and Divorce Act Section 308; Cal. Civ. Code Section 4801 and recent annotations.

7.   Weitzman's data suggest, however, that women in these three categories are far more likely than others to receive spousal support awards.

8.   In *Marvin v. Marvin*, for example, the California Supreme Court specifically disapproved an earlier intermediate appellate decision that applied the provisions of the Family Law Act to a long-term stable cohabitation. 18 Cal. 3d 660, 679-83 (1976) (disapproving *Marriage of Cary*, 34 App. 3d 345 (1973)). The Court went on to hold that contract law provided the appropriate rubric for cohabitation.

Michelle Marvin's experience on remand is instructive. The trial court concluded that the parties had not made any contract but nevertheless found that Michelle needed economic rehabilitation and awarded her $104,000 for that purpose. The Court of Appeal vacated the award because it was not supported by any legal principle: rehabilitative support is a Family Law Act remedy, not a contract remedy. The Supreme Court of California presumably agreed when it denied review. *Marvin v. Marvin*, 122 Cal. App. 3d 871 (1981).

In *Hendrix v. General Motors Corp.*, 9 Fam. L. Rptr. (BNA) 2663, 2664 (1983), the First District California Court of Appeal aptly summarized *Marvin*:

> Contrary to popular misconception, *Marvin v. Marvin* . . . did not legitimize the cohabitation of unmarried persons, nor did it open Pandora's box by giving those cohabitants the same causes of action and other benefits as if they were married. *Marvin* did nothing more than establish the right of unmarried cohabitants to enter into valid contractual obligations so long as sexual services did not constitute the sole consideration therefor. (See also *Norman v. Unemployment Ins. Appeals Board*, 34 Cal. 3d at p. 6.) Other cases have recognized the limitations of *Marvin* and have refused to find that a

nonmarital relationship is the equivalent of a marriage (*People v. Delph* (1979) 94 Cal. App. 411; *Harrod v. Pacific Southwest Airlines* (1981) 118 Cal. App. 3d 155; *Garcia v. Douglas Aircraft Co* (1982) 133 Cal. App. 3d 870).

The case disapproved by *Marvin, Marriage of Cary*, 34 Cal. App. 3d 345 (1973), provided some of the support for Glendon's prediction (published shortly before *Marvin*) that the "distinction [between cohabitation and marriage] may someday be discarded" (Glendon 1976, p. 693). This prediction has, I believe, proven erroneous. With respect to the failure of efforts to constitutionalize recognition of cohabitation, see *Califano v. Boles*, 443 U.S. 282 (1979) (former cohabitant, mother of decedent's child, not entitled to "mother's" or "divorced mother's" social security benefits on decedent's account).

9.   *Marvin* has been followed on many jurisdictions. See, e.g., *Levar v. Elkins*, 604 P.2d 602 (Alaska 1980); *Marvin v. Marvin*, 18 Cal. 3d 660, 557 P.2d 106, 134 CAL. RPTR. 815 (1976); *Dosek v. Dosek*, 4 FAM. L. REP. 2828 (BNA) (Conn. Super Ct. 1978); *Rehak v. Mathis*, 239 Ga. 541, 238 S.E. 2d 81 (1977); *Glasgo v. Glasgo*, 410 N.E.2d 1325 (IND. CT. APP. 1980); *Tyranski v. Piggins*, 44 Mich. App 570, 205 N.W.2d 595 (1973); *Carlson v. Olson*, 256 N.W.2d 249 (Minn. 1977); *Kozlowski v. Kozlowski*, 80 N.J. 378, 403 A.2d 902 (1979); *Morone v. Morone*, 50 N.Y.2d 481, 413 N.E.2d 1154, 429 N.Y.S.2d 592 (1980) (recognizing express but not implied contracts); *Beal v. Beal*, 282 Or. 115, 577 P.2d 507 (1978); *Latham v. Latham*, 274 Or. 421, 547 P.2d 144 (1976); *Baldassari v. Baldassari*, 6 FAM. L. REP. (BNA) 2602 (Pa. Super. Ct. 1980); *In re Estate of Thornton*, 81 Wash. 2d 72, 499 P.2d 864 (1972). For a very early *Marvin*-like case, see *Torres v. Roldan*, 67 D.P.R. 342 (P.R. 1947).

10.   *Califano v. Boles*, 443 U.S. 282 (1979).

11.   See, e.g., *Norman v. Unemployment Insurance Appeals Board*, 34 Cal. 3d 1 (1983). (Voluntary termination of employment to follow a nonmarital cohabitant to his new job does not constitute "good cause" for unemployment benefits, as it would if the cohabitants were married.)

12.   Courts have historically refused workers' compensation recovery to surviving unmarried cohabitants on grounds of morality and public policy. A few courts have reversed the old precedents and now treat the unmarried cohabitant as an ordinary "dependent," a much less desirable status than "surviving spouse." For extended discussion, see Blumberg (1981, pp. 1141–1142).

13.   In wrongful death provisions naming the beneficiaries of the action, the word "widow" or "wife" has been interpreted to mean lawful widow or wife. See *Meisenhelder v. Chicago & N.W.P. Co.*, 170 Minn. 317, 320, 213 N.W. 32, 34 (1927); *Molz v. Hansell*, 115 Pa. Super. Ct. 338, 340, 175 A. 880, 881 (1934). See also *Drew v. Drake*, 110 Cal. App. 3d 555 (1980) (holding that a woman who cohabited continuously for three years with her lover and witnessed his negligent killing in an automobile collision was not

sufficiently "closely related" to the victim to sustain an action for negligent infliction of emotional distress).

14.   It has generally been held that marriage is prerequisite to a claim for loss of consortium, that is, a claim for compensation for services, society, and sexual relations lost because of tortious injury to one's mate. See, e.g., *Hendrix v. General Motors Corp.*, 9 FAM. L. RPTR. (BNA) 2663 (Cal. Ct. App. 1983); *Chiesa v. Rowe*, 486 F. Supp. 236 (W.D. Mich. 1980); *Tong v. Jocson*, 76 Cal. App. 3d 603, 142 CAL. RPTR. 726 (1976); *Tremblay v. Carter*, 390 So. 2d 816 (Fla. Dist. Ct. App. 1980); *Sostock v. Reiss*, 92 Ill. App. 3d 200, 415 N.E.2d 1094 (1980); *Sawyer v. Bailey*, 413 A.2d 165 (Maine, 1980). But see *Butcher v. Superior Court of Orange County*, 9 FAM. L. RPTR. (BNA) 2229 (Cal. Ct. App. 1983); *Bullock v. New Jersey*, 487 F. Supp. 1078 (D. N.J. 1980). See, generally, Meade, *Consortium Rights of the Unmarried: A Time for Reappraisal*, 15 FAM. L. Q. 223 (1981); Note, *Extending Consortium Rights to Unmarried Cohabitors: An Examination of Tong v. Jocson*, 14 U.S.F. L. REV. 133 (1979).

15.   *Posner v. Posner*, 233 So. 2d 381 (Fla. S. Ct. 1970); see also *Belcher v. Belcher*, 271 So. 2d 7 (Fla. S. Ct. 1972).

16.   18 Cal. 3d 660 (1976).

17.   See, e.g., *Posner v. Posner*, 233 So. 2d 381 (Fla. S. Ct. 1970).

18.   While the absolute number of American cohabiting couples is impressive (1.8 million in 1982), and there has been a substantial rate of increase in recent years (256 percent between 1970 and 1982), "unmarried couples [in 1982] still represent less than 4 percent of all couples (married and unmarried)." Bureau of the Census, March 1982.

19.   We lack data on the incidence of marriage contracts. It is generally assumed that they are made primarily by the very wealthy and by older persons who have grown children by a prior marriage.

20.   New York did not adopt equitable distribution until 1980. Laws 1980, Ch. 281, ch. 645, codified at Dom. Rel. L. Section 236 (McKinney's).

21.   Like many states, New York added a fault-free breakdown ground to its preexisting fault system. Laws 1966, ch. 254, amended and codified at Dom. Rel. L. Section 170(6):

> The husband and wife have lived apart pursuant to a written agreement of separation . . . for a period of one or more years after the execution of such agreement and satisfactory proof has been submitted by the plaintiff that he or she has substantially performed all the terms of the agreement.

22.   Compare, e.g., *Anderson v. Anderson*, 68 N.W.2d 849 (N.D. 1955) ($2,000 equitable distribution award to wife reversed because she had contributed no extraordinary service, that is, no services beyond those of an ordinary housewife) with recent case law and legislation requiring that homemaking services be taken into account in property distribution. See, e.g., Ark. Stat. Ann. 34-1214 (1981 Cum. Supp.); Burn's Ind. Stat. Ann.

31-1-11.5-11 (1980); Neb. Rev. Stat. 42-365 (Supp. 1980); Ohio Rev. Code Ann. 3105.18 (1981); Wis. Stat. Ann. 765.255 (1981).

23. See, e.g., Ark. Stat. Ann. 34-1214 (1981 Cum. Supp.) ("All marital property shall be distributed one-half to each party unless the court finds such a division to be inequitable. . . . The court must state its basis and reasons for not dividing the marital property equally. . . ."); *Paul W. v. Margaret W.,* 8 Fam. L. Rptr. (BNA) 3013 (Penn Ct. Com. Pls. 1981); N.C. Gen. Stat. Sec. 50-20; Wisc. Stat. Ann. 767.255 (1981). Equal division is the rule in four of the eight community property states: California, Idaho, Louisiana, and New Mexico. See, e.g., Cal. Civ. Code Section 4800; *Michelson v. Michelson,* 86 N.M. 107, 110, 520 P.2d 263 (S. Ct. 1974). While most jurisdictions continue to prefer the flexibility of variable distribution, I discern in the reported cases a strong trend toward more equal distribution.

24. 15 Cal. 3d 838, 842, 126 Cal. Rptr. 633 (1976).

25. *Van Loan v. Van Loan,* 116 Ariz. 272, 569 P.2d 214 (Ariz. S. Ct. 1977); see also *Johnson v. Johnson,* 131 Ariz. 38, 638 P.2d 705 (Ariz. S. Ct. 1981) (valuation); *Thompson v. Thompson,* 438 A.2d 839 (Conn. S. Ct. 1981); *Robert C.S. v. Barbara J.S.,* 434 A.2d 383 (Del. S. Ct. 1981). See also *Jerry L.C. v. Lucille H.C.,* 448 A.2d 223 (Del. S. Ct. 1982) (valuation); *Linson v. Linson,* 618 P.2d 748 (Hawaii Ct. App. 1980); *Shill v. Shill,* 599 P.2d 1004 (Idaho S. Ct. 1979); *Pieper v. Pieper,* 79 Ill. App. 3d 835, 398 N.E. 2d 868 (1979); *Marriage of Hunt,* 78 Ill. App. 3d 653, 397 N.E.2d 511 (1979); *Sims v. Sims,* 358 So. 2d 919 (La. S. Ct. 1978); *Deering v. Deering,* 292 Md. 115 (Maryland Ct. App. 1981) (dictum); *Boyd v. Boyd,* 323 N.W.2d 553 (Mich. Ct. App. 1982); *Janssen v. Janssen,* 9 Fam. L. Rptr. (BNA) 2387 (Minn. S. Ct. 1983); *Kuchta v. Kuchta,* 636 S.W.2d 663 (Mo. S. Ct. 1982); *Marriage of Laster,* 643 P.2d 597 (Mont. S. Ct. 1982); Neb. Rev. Stat. 42-366(8) (Cum. Supp. 1980); *Ellett v. Ellett,* 573 P.2d 1179 (Nev. S. Ct. 1978) (dictum); *Reed v. Reed,* 9 Fam. L. Rptr. 2396 (N.Y. App. Div. 1983); *Kalinoski v. Kalinoski,* F.C. No. 80-530 (Penn. C.P. Butler Cty. 12/1/82), 9 Fam. L. Rptr. (BNA) 3033; *Cearly v. Cearly,* 544 S.W.2d 661 (Texas S. Ct. 1976); *Woodward v. Woodward,* 656 P.2d 431 (Utah S. Ct. 1982) (overruling prior decisional law); Va. Stat. Ann. Section 20-107.3(E) (8) (1982 Cum. Supp.); *Wilder v. Wilder,* 534 P.2d 1355 (Wash. S. Ct. *en banc* 1975); *Bloomer v. Bloomer,* 84 Wis. 2d 124, 267 N.W.2d 235 (Wis. S. Ct. 1978).

In addition, some states, including Alaska, New Hampshire, New Jersey, New Mexico, South Dakota, and Tennessee, have held that vested pensions earned during coverture are marital, or community, property but have not yet been asked to characterize unvested pensions. See *Monsma v. Monsma,* 618 P.2d 559 (Alaska S. Ct. 1980); and *MacDonald v. MacDonald,* 443 A.2d 1017 (N.H. S. Ct. 1982), but see *Baker v. Baker,* 421 A.2d 998 (N.H. S. Ct. 1980); *Kikkert v. Kikkert,* 88 N.J. 4 (S. Ct. 1981) (vested but unmatured pension is subject to equitable jurisdiction); *Ridgway v. Ridgway,* 94 N.M. 345, 610 P.2d 749 (S. Ct. 1980); *Hansen v. Hansen,* 273 N.W.2d 749 (S. Dak. S. Ct. 1979); *Whitehead v. Whitehead,* 627 S.W.2d 944

(Tenn. S. Ct. 1982) (dictum). Related case law in a number of these states indicates that unvested as well as vested pensions will be included within the purview of marital property. See, e.g., *Rostel v. Rostel*, 622 P.2d 429 (Alaska S. Ct. 1961); *Dugan v. Dugan*, 9 Fam. L. Rptr. (BNA) 2305 (N.J. S. Ct. 1983); *Stern v. Stern*, 66 N.J. 340, 348 (1975); and *Hurley v. Hurley*, 94 N.M. 641, 615 P.2d 256 (N.M. S. Ct. 1980).

26.　*Rostel v. Rostel*, 622 P.2d 429 (Alaska S. Ct. 1981) (valuing non-transferable business good will); *Wisner v. Wisner*, 631 P.2d 115 (Ariz. Ct. App. 1981), rev. den.; *Marriage of Foster*, 42 Cal. App. 3d 577, 117 Cal. Rptr. 49 (1974); *Mueller v. Mueller*, 144 Cal. App. 2d 245, 252 (1956); *Marriage of Nichols*, 43 Colo. App. 383, 606 P.2d 1314 (1979); *Fucci v. Fucci*, 425 A.2d 592 (Conn. S. Ct. 1978) (dictum); *Watterson v. Watterson*, 353 So.2d 1185 (Fla. Ct. App. 1978); *Loveland v. Loveland*, 91 Idaho 400, 422 P.2d 67 (S. Ct. 1967) (dictum); *Marriage of White*, 98 Ill. App. 3d 380, 384 (1981); *Arnold v. Arnold*, 133 N.W.2d 53 (Iowa S. Ct. 1965); *Walters v. Walters*, 419 S.W.2d 750 (Ky. Ct. App. 1967); *Miranda v. Miranda*, 596 S.W.2d 61 (Mo. Ct. App. 1980); *Marriage of Herron*, 608 P.2d 97, 102 (Mont. S. Ct. 1980) (dictum); *Lockwood v. Lockwood*, 205 Neb. 818, 290 N.W.2d 636 (S. Ct. 1980); *Fox v. Fox*, 401 P.2d 53 (Nev. S. Ct. 1965); *Dugan v. Dugan*, 9 Fam. L. Rptr. (BNA) 2305 (N.J. S. Ct. 1983); *Hurley v. Hurley*, 94 N.M. 641, 615 P.2d 256, 259 (N.M. S. Ct. 1980); *Nehorayoff v. Nehorayoff*, 108 Misc. 2d 311 (N.Y. S. Ct. 1981); *Hirschfeld v. Hirschfeld*, 8 Fam. L. Rptr. 5403, NYLJ, May 4, 1982 at 7 (S. Ct. 1982); *Barton v. Barton*, 8 Fam. L. Rptr. (BNA) 1121 (N.Y. S. Ct. 1982); but see *Litman v. Litman*, 453 N.Y.S.2d 1003 (S. Ct. 1982); *Nastrom v. Nastrom*, 262 N.W.2d 487, 493 (N.D. S. Ct. 1978); *Marriage of Goger*, 27 Or. App. 729, 557 P.2d 46 (1976); *Marriage of Fleege*, 91 Wn. 2d 324, 588 P.2d 1136 (S. Ct. en banc 1979); *Spheeris v. Spheeris*, 37 Wis. 2d 497, 506 (S. Ct. 1967). But see *E.E.C. v. E.J.C.*, 457 A.2d 688 (Del. S. Ct. 1983); *Winn v. Winn*, 206 Kan. 737, 482 P.2d 16 (Kan. S. Ct. 1981) and *Nail v. Nail*, 486 S.W.2d 761 (Tex. S. Ct. 1972) (good will cognizable only to the extent it is transferable in the market).

27.　See, e.g., *Marriage of Horstmann*, 263 N.W.2d 855 (Iowa S. Ct. 1978); *Inman v. Inman* (Inman II), 8 Fam. L. Rptr. (BNA) 2329 (Ky. Ct. App. 1982), modifying 578 S.W.2d 266 (1979); *Moss v. Moss*, 264 N.W.2d 97 (Mich. Ct. App. 1978); *DeLa Rosa v. DeLa Rosa*, 309 N.W.2d 755 (Minn. S. Ct. 1981); *Mahoney v. Mahoney*, 91 N.J. 488, 453 A.2d 527 (N.J. S. Ct. 1982); *Hubbard v. Hubbard*, 602 P.2d 747 (Okla. S. Ct. 1979); *Lundberg v. Lundberg*, 318 N.W.2d 918 (Wisc. S. Ct. 1982).

But see *O'Brien v. O'Brien* (N.Y. Ct. App.), NYLJ, December 30, 1985; *Reen v. Reen*, 8 Fam. L. Rptr. (BNA) 2193 (Mass. Prob. Ct. 1982); *Kutanovski v. Kutanovski*, NYLJ August 25, 1982; *In re* Neuhaus, 9 Fam. L. Rptr. (BNA) 2168 (Wn. Super. Ct. 1982) (professional education is marital property and should be valued in terms of its capacity to augment future earnings).

Courts in Arizona, Colorado, Indiana, New Mexico, and Texas have declined to grant any form of marital property recognition to professional degrees. See *Wisner v. Wisner*, 631 P.2d 115 (Ariz. Ct. App. 1981); *Graham v. Graham*, 574 P.2d 75 (Colo. S. Ct. 1978); *Marriage of McManama*, 399 N.E.2d 371 (Ind. S. Ct. 1980), *Marriage of Muckelroy*, 498 P.2d 1357 (N. Mex. S. Ct. 1972); *Frausto v. Frausto*, 611 S.W.2d 656 (Tex. Ct. Civ. App. 1981).

28.   A.B. 525 (1983-84 Regular Session). The bill failed.

29.   See, e.g., *Zahler v. Zahler*, 8 FAM. L. RPTR. (BNA) 2694 (Conn. Sup. Ct. 1982); *Mahoney v. Mahoney*, 91 N.J. 488, 453 A.2d 527 (N.J. S. Ct. 1982); *Hubbard v. Hubbard*, 603 P.2d 747 (Okla. S. Ct. 1979). Another reason for such characterization may be that property division debt is dischargeable in bankruptcy while alimony, or spousal support, is not. 11 USC Section 523(a)(5).

30.   *Beck v. Beck*, 86 N.J. 480, 432 A.2d 63 (N.J. S. Ct. 1981).

31.   See, e.g., *id.*

32.   Freed, *Joint Custody Laws: An Analysis and Comparative Survey*, 9 FAM. L. RPTR. (BNA) 4025 (1983). These states include Alaska (A.R.S. Section 25.20.060); California (Cal. Civ. Code Section 4600); Colorado (CRS Section 14-10-123.5); Connecticut (Conn. Stat. Section 466-56); Delaware (13 Del. Code Section 701); Florida (Fla. Stat. Section 61.13(2)(b)); Hawaii (Hawaii Rev. Stat. Section 571-46.1); Idaho (Idaho Code Section 32-717 B); Illinois (Ill. Ann. Stat. Ch. 40, Section 603.1); Iowa (Iowa Code Ann. Section 598.1); Kansas (Kan. Stat. Section 60-1610); Kentucky (Ky. Rev. Stat. Section 403-270(3)); Louisiana (La. Civ. Code Art. 146, 157, 250); Maine (Maine Rev. Stat. Ann. Tit. 19, Section 214, 581, 752); Massachusetts (Mass. Ann. Laws Ch. 208, Section 31); Michigan (Mich. Comp. Laws Ann. Sections 722:23(3), 722:23(6a)); Minnesota (Minn. Stat. Ann. Sections 518:0003, 518:17); Mississippi (Miss. Code Ann. Section 93-5-23); Montana (Mont. Rev. Code Ann. Section 40-4-222, 223, 224, 225); Nevada (Nev. Rev. Stat. Section 125.140); New Hampshire (N.H. Rev. Stat. Ann. Section 458:17); New Mexico (N.M. Stat. Ann. Section 40-4-91); North Carolina (N.C. Gen. Stat. Section 50-13.2(6)); Ohio (Ohio Rev. Code Ann. Section 3109.04); Oregon (Ore. Rev. Stat. Section 107.105(1) (6)); Pennsylvania (Pa. Stat. Ann. Vol. 23 Section 1001-1005, 1011); Texas (Texas Fam. Law Section 14.06(a)); and Wisconsin (Wis. Stat. Ann. Section 767.24 (1) (b)).

33.   Freed, *supra* note 32. These states include Georgia (HB 592); Indiana (HB 1820); Maryland (SB 663, HB 753, HB 501); Missouri (SB 94); New York (A 6982); Oklahoma (HB 1141); Washington (HB 695, HB 403, SB 4027) and West Virginia (HB 1314).

34.   See, e.g., *Marriage of Burham*, 283 N.W.2d 269, 272 (Iowa S. Ct. 1979); *Beck v. Beck*, 86 N.J. 480, 432 A.2d 63 (N.J. S. Ct. 1981); *Dodd v. Dodd*, 403 N.Y.S.2d 401, 403 (N.Y. S. Ct. 1978); *Muller v. Muller*, 49 S.W.2d 349 (Va. S. Ct. 1948). See also Maryland Attorney General's Opinion No. 83-024 (6/2/83), reported at 9 FAM. L. RPTR. (BNA) 2504 (1983).

35.   Freed, *supra* note 32. The Connecticut, Kentucky, and Texas statutes

simply authorize joint custody. The North Carolina statute authorizes joint custody and formulates specific guidelines.

36.   *Id.* Alaska, California, Delaware, Florida, Idaho, Iowa, Kansas, Louisiana, Montana, Nevada, New Mexico, and Pennsylvania.

37.   *Id.* Alaska, California, Colorado, Delaware, Florida, Idaho, Illinois, Louisiana, Michigan, Mississippi, Montana, Nevada, New Jersey (by court decision; see *Beck v. Beck*, 86 N.J. 480, 432 A.2d 63 (N.J. S. Ct. 1981)), New Mexico, Pennsylvania, and Wisconsin.

38.   *Id.* Colorado, Illinois, Louisiana, Massachusetts, Ohio, Texas, and Wisconsin.

39.   *Id.* Alaska, California, Idaho, Iowa, Kansas, Kentucky, Louisiana, Mississippi, Montana, Nevada, New Hampshire, New Mexico, Pennsylvania.

40.   *Id.* California and Delaware.

41.   *Id.* Alaska, Colorado, Iowa, and Pennsylvania.

42.   See, e.g., *Lumbra v. Lumbra*, 136 Vt. 529, 394 A.2d 1139 (Ver. S. Ct. 1978) (presumption that joint custody is not in the best interests of a child because, *inter alia*, of "the problem of cooperation"); Adler and Chambers 1978.

43.   On the other hand, to the extent that private mediation represents an abandonment of legal norms in favor of a unique solution individually tailored to the particular divorcing couple (Riskin 1982, pp. 34–36), private mediation displaces state-developed legal norms and, therefore, represents a decline in state involvement in divorce. The role that legal norms should play in mediation is a subject much debated by mediator-lawyers.

44.   The California Advisory Commission on Family Law, for example, believes that state mediation is needed to resolve contested financial, as well as child custody, issues (California Senate Subcommittee on Administration of Justice 1979, pp. 16–17).

45.   By 1976, more than 50 percent of married women aged 20 to 54 were in the labor force (U.S. Department of Labor).

REFERENCES

Adler, Bobette, and Chambers, Carole R. "The Folly of Joint Custody." *Family Advocate* 3 (1981):6–10.
Becker, Gary S. "A Theory of Marriage." In Theodore W. Schultz (ed.),

Economics of the Family: Marriage, Children, and Human Capital. Chicago: University of Chicago Press, 1973.

Becker, Gary S. *A Treatise on the Family.* Cambridge, Mass.: Harvard University Press, 1981.

Blumberg, Grace. "Cohabitation Without Marriage: A Different Perspective." *UCLA Law Review* 28(1981):1125–1180.

Blumberg, Grace. "Intangible Assets: Recognition and Valuation." In *Valuation and Distribution of Marital Property*, vol. 2. New York: Matthew Bender, 1984.

Blumstein, Philip, and Schwartz, Pepper. *American Couples.* New York: William Morrow, 1983.

California Senate Subcommittee on Administration of Justice. *Second Report of the Advisory Commission on Family Law: Conciliation Courts, Mediation, Counseling and Family Court Coordination.* May 4, 1979.

Crouch, Richard E. "Mediation and Divorce: The Dark Side Is Still Unexplored." *Family Advocate* 4(1982):27–35.

Folberg, Jay. "Divorce Mediation: A Workable Alternative." In Davidson, Howard; Ray, Larry; and Horowitz, Robert (eds.), *Alternative Means of Family Dispute Resolution.*

Foote, Caleb; Levy, Robert J.; and Sander, Frank E. A. *Cases and Materials on Family Law*, 2nd ed. Boston: Little, Brown, 1976.

Freed, Doris Jonas, and Foster, Henry H. "Divorce in the Fifty States: An Overview as of August 1, 1981." *Family Law Reporter* 7(1981):4049–4076.

Glendon, Mary Ann. "Is There a Future for Separate Property?" *Family Law Quarterly* 8(1974):315–329.

Glendon, Mary Ann. "Marriage and the State: The Withering Away of Marriage." *Virginia Law Review* 62(1976):663–720.

Glendon, Mary Ann. *State, Law, and Family.* New York: Elsevier, 1977.

Goodman, Ellen. "Twisted Divorce: Is Court on Forbidden Ground?" *Los Angeles Times*, Part II, p. 7, November 29, 1983.

Kiker, B. F. (ed.). *Investment in Human Capital.* Columbia: University of South Carolina Press, 1971.

Krauskopf, Joan. "Recompense for Financing Spouse's Education: Legal Protection for the Marital Investor in Human Capital." *Kansas Law Review* 28(1980):379–417.

Marshall, Leon Carroll, and May, Geoffrey. *The Divorce Court*, 2 vols. Baltimore, Md.: Johns Hopkins University Press, 1932–1933.

McIsaac, Hugh. "Mandatory Conciliation Custody/Visitation Matters: California's Bold Stroke." *Conciliation Courts Review* 19(1981):73–81.

Mnookin, Robert, and Kornhauser, Lewis. "Bargaining in the Shadow of the Law." *Yale Law Journal* 88(1979):950–997.

Pearson, J.; Ring, M.; and Milne, A. "A Portrait of Divorce Mediation Service in the Public and Private Sector." *Conciliation Courts Review* 21(1983):1–24.

Rheinstein, Max. *Marriage, Stability, Divorce and the Law.* Chicago: University of Chicago Press, 1972.

Riskin, Leonard L. "Mediation and Lawyers." *Ohio State Law Journal* 43(1982):29–60.

Silberman, Linda J. "Professional Responsibility Problems of Divorce Mediation." *Family Law Reporter* 7(1981):4001–4012.

Steinman, Susan. "Joint Custody: What We Know, What We Have Yet to Learn, and the Judicial and Legislative Implications." *UCD Law Review* 16(1983):739–770.

U.S. Bureau of the Census. *Current Population Reports*, Series P-20, No. 38, Marital Status and Living Arrangements: March 1982 (1983).

U.S. Department of Labor, Bureau of Labor Statistics. *U.S. Working Women: A Databook* (1977).

Weitzman, Lenore. "The Economics of Divorce." *UCLA Law Review* 28(1981):1181–1268.

PART V

Calculation and Emotion in Marriage

14 Marriage Squeezes and the Marriage Market

AMYRA GROSSBARD-SHECHTMAN

FEW PEOPLE LIKE TO THINK of themselves as participants in a market when it comes to personal aspects of life. It is often degrading to participate in an organized job market, and generally discomforting to know that another employee might do our work just as well. We aspire to be unique. Even those who like the idea of competition tend to do so at an abstract level. While praising the free market, they build hedges against competition that could intrude into their own lives—be it at the workplace or in the home.

NOTE: *This is a revised version of a paper written in 1980, while I was a fellow at the Center for Advanced Study in the Behavioral Sciences, thanks to the financial support of the National Science Foundation (#BNS 76 22943 to the Center for Advanced Study in the Behavioral Sciences), and of a paper prepared for "Contemporary Marriage: Comparative Perspectives on a Changing Institution," a conference held at the Center for Advanced Study in the Behavioral Sciences, Stanford, August 1982. I would like to thank Muriel Bell, Nancy Chodorow, Kingsley Davis, Adam Kuper, Yochanan Peres, Alan Stone, and Myra Stroeber for helpful comments and discussions.*

Our need to be unique is intimately linked to our concepts of love. Western culture conceives the home as the place to find both romantic love and parental love. The family offers an escape from the impersonal and competitive outside world, a "haven in a heartless world" (in the words of Christopher Lasch, as cited in the chapter by Alan Stone).

When Westerners think about marriage, they tend to focus on its unique and romantic aspects and to overlook the routine of married life. They prefer not to think about the work involved in running a household, in part because a mate can so easily be replaced in most of these jobs. Yet being a wife—and to some extent, being a husband—largely constitutes a job; moreover, if it is a good job—that is, a job involving good working conditions—there are many possible candidates for it.

Although husbands also work in the home, women perform the preponderance of work in the household. Men compete to obtain the most desirable wife to work for them, relying on assets to win the wife they want—an increasing challenge in a world of high expectations for women. It is from these unromantic aspects of marriage that one can generate the concepts of marriage market and marriage squeeze.

How people get married or remain single, how they live a married life, and the frequency and manner of divorce are functions of a variety of factors. In this chapter I wish to emphasize the influence of one particular factor, the number of marriageable men relative to that of marriageable women, what demographers call the sex ratio. To see the importance of this factor for understanding contemporary trends in cohabitation, divorce, or feminist ideology, it is first necessary to delve into the concept of a marriage market.

The following section presents a market theory of marriage squeezes. The next sections present empirical evidence supporting the theory. The chapter ends with conclusions of a more general nature, including thoughts about the future of contemporary marriage.

A Market Theory of Marriage

The market theory of marriage is an expansion of labor economics.[1] Men and women are viewed as participants in markets for household labor. Men demand wife labor and supply husband services whereas women supply wife services and demand husband labor. The term labor, used here in a general sense, includes child-bearing, child-rearing, and any task a person performs for the benefit of a spouse and beyond one's own needs.

Markets for household labor are obtained by plotting aggregate demand and supply schedules and finding their intersection.[2] In a market for female household labor women are ready to work for various amounts of time depending on the hourly compensation involved. Consequently, the supply curve depicted in Figure 14.1 describes the relationship between rewards from work (vertical axis) and amount of work (horizontal axis). Such supply of work tends to have a positive slope reflecting people's tendency to work more for higher wages. The demand curve indicates how much female household labor men want to obtain at different levels of compensation. Generally, the cheaper a service, the more its users will rely on it, and therefore the demand is downward sloping. The equilibrium, obtained at the intersection of demand and supply, determines the average hourly compensation that men are willing to offer women to induce them to work in the home. This compensation will in part be translated into goods and services consumed by the wife, cultural norms and expectations about the distribution of power in the home, the rights of women to their husbands' earnings, and other legal and traditional arrangements regarding marriage and cohabitation. At the same time, within a normative framework, one expects individual variation depending on the characteristics of the women and men involved. Similarly, one can conceive of a market for male household labor, where men supply labor that women demand. Market forces will also establish a clearing price for husbands' household labor.

Individual marriages tend to occur when at the market "wages" for female and male household labor the amount of such labor a woman wants from a husband equals the amount of labor he wants to supply and when the amount of work this same man wants from a wife equals the amount of work she is willing to perform. Egalitarian marriages involve symmetric exchanges of household labor between husbands and wives.

Women's supply curve moves to the left, that is, their propensity to work as wives decreases, when their opportunities outside marriage (mainly a function of the regular labor market condi-

Figure 14.1

Market for Household Labor

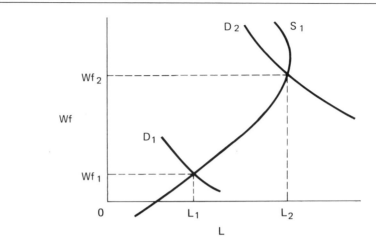

tions) improve. Likewise, the supply curve moves leftward in situations of relatively high nonwage wealth.[3] Men's demand curve moves to the right when either men's wealth or desire to marry increases. Symmetrically, wealth also affects markets for husband labor. Women are better off the higher the compensation for their own household labor, and the lower the compensation the market determines for husband labor. The opposite is true for men.

The groundwork for the analysis of marriage squeezes has now been set. A marriage squeeze for men occurs when there are relatively more men than women participating in the market for labor in the home.[4] The larger the number of men eligible for marriage in a society (that is, the higher the sex ratio), the larger the equilibrium compensation women expect from marriage, w_f, shown in Figure 14.1. This can be shown as an increase from w_{f1} to w_{f2} following a shift in aggregate demand from D_1 to D_2. Similarly, one could show that the equilibrium compensation for husband labor goes down if the sex ratio rises.

In a given cultural context, the increase in aggregate employment opportunities in marriage means a higher probability that women will marry.[5] This effect is seen in the increase of total hours that women work in the home from L_1 to L_2. This implication is straightforward: when more men are available (shift in aggregate demand) for a given number of women (aggregate supply unchanged), the number of women who marry increases.[6]

Marriage squeezes are also predicted to have an impact on the relative proportion of unmarried women to unmarried men. The effect of sex ratio variations on individuals' likelihood to get married depends on gender and type of marriage squeeze. Such asymmetry is caused by differential tendencies for men and women to select marriage versus its alternatives, cohabitation or a casual sexual relationship. I therefore discuss marriage squeezes' effects on cohabitation before returning to differential trends in percent of unmarried men and women.

There are two ways to derive a theoretical implication regarding the effect of a marriage squeeze on the likelihood of cohabitation. Again, I am taking the example of a marriage squeeze for men. First, it follows from the point just made that if the number of marriageable men increases and more women get married, fewer women will be available for possible cohabitation. A second, more subtle, implication of the theory is that the increase in men may cause the number of marriages to increase more than proportionately. In such a case, the underlying mechanism would be the transformation of nonmarital unions into marital unions. In order to explain this second mechanism by which the number of cohabiting couples would decrease as a result of a marriage squeeze for men, I need to discuss how marriage squeezes affect the market compensation for household labor.

As the aggregate demand for a wife's labor increases, the compensation determined at the market equilibrium is also expected to increase (from w_{f1} to w_{f2} in terms of Figure 14.1). Such improvement in the terms offered wives will be reflected in a number of ways, including better legal rights. Now that men are competing for women's services in the home, the latter command a better bargaining position in the form of more protection in case the marriage disintegrates.[7] One form that an improvement in legal rights can take is in the transformation of a common-law union into a marriage. Even though one notices many moves to equalize the rights of common-law and legal wives (Bruch 1981), it still remains true that under most circumstances legal wives are entitled to more protection in case of separation or husband's death.

Theoretically, a marriage squeeze for men leads to a higher ratio of legal unions to consensual unions, because some of the women who would have lived with a man will use improved market conditions to make the union legitimate. Moreover, unions being formed under circumstances favorable to women are more likely to take the form of a marriage than when fewer men are available.

Clearly the converse also holds. During a marriage squeeze for women, the theory of marriage squeezes dictates an increase in the ratio of nonmarital to marital unions. For instance, an influx of women to a constant number of men theoretically will lead to a higher ratio of nonmarital to marital unions. Either new consensual unions will form between previously unmarried men and some of the new women or some of the existing marriages will be broken, allowing nonmarital "recontracting" by some previously married men or women.

This effect of marriage squeezes on cohabitation helps explain an asymmetric effect of marriage squeezes on male and female proportion unmarried. A marriage squeeze for women leads to increased proportions of unmarried women for two reasons. First, fewer women are likely to be involved in any type of heterosexual relationship. Second, women's lower bargaining power encourages an increase in the ratio of cohabiting to married couples. The percentage of unmarried men is expected to rise less as a result of a marriage squeeze for women. On the one hand, more cohabitation occurs at the expense of legal marriages, but, on the other hand, some men who want to marry irrespective of marriage squeeze variations find a wife more easily. Conversely, a marriage squeeze for men is likely to reduce the percentage of unmarried individuals. However, the percentage of unmarried women is expected to decrease faster than the percentage of unmarried men.

Furthermore, if the number of men increases, women of given quality will be more selective in their mating choices and will marry men with more desirable qualities than the men they would have married under less favorable market conditions. An examination of sorting patterns would show less sorting between women who are young and single and men who are substantially older, divorced, unattractive, poor, or of a background that women for some reason prefer to avoid.[8]

Also, if married women can obtain more total revenue out of their work as spouses, they can spend more time on their personal leisure and will less often have to work outside the home. Assuming that it is the need for income that often pushes women to work outside the home, it follows that a marriage squeeze for men will cause a lower rate of labor force participation of married women. This will be particularly true among women with little education who are less likely to experience intrinsic rewards from work. Moreover, the total involvement of women in the work force will decrease, since fewer women will remain single. Traditionally, unmarried women participate in the labor force more frequently.[9]

Marriage squeezes are expected to affect divorce because women prefer marital stability more than men do and will try to enter marriages with a relatively long expected duration (see also Heer and Grossbard-Shechtman 1981). Expected marital stability may be considered part of the compensation that women receive for supplying household labor (Grossbard-Shechtman 1982). Whether the wife's preference for a marriage of long duration will dominate the husband's preference for shorter marriage depends, among other things, on the conditions in the market for household labor. If the wife's competitive value in that market is high, she is more likely to obtain a commitment toward a marriage of long duration from her husband. But if equilibrium conditions offer wives a low amount of compensation, they have little bargaining power to ensure either a marriage of long duration or an initial commitment to legal marriage. Therefore, divorce rates depend upon the sex ratio of men to women.[10]

Thus, variations in marriage squeeze influence cohabitation and divorce. They also influence other aspects of the compensation women receive for their labor in the home and more generally affect gender differentials in benefits from marriage. This can be reflected in the ratio of family expenditures benefiting the wife in relation to the husband, the value of alimony payments, and the willingness of women to have more children than they would, had they followed their own inclination.[11]

Feminism may also be related to marriage squeezes. An economic theory of feminism connects quite nicely with an economic theory of marriage. The feminist movement is a type of labor union protecting women who participate in markets for labor and marriage. According to this view, women can bargain collectively for better working conditions. A marriage squeeze for women, causing a significant worsening of market conditions for women, propels women to organize and to raise women's compensations above the market level. As in other types of labor unions, the mechanism that makes bargaining for higher wages possible involves restrictions on entry into that market. Many feminists have committed themselves to singlehood, in part a reflection of their willingness to trade higher wages for higher employment levels in markets for wife labor.

Alternatively, a psychological theory of feminism views the movement as an outlet for personal frustration. People whose position has worsened relatively to that of others often coalesce and form a group for protest, especially if group awareness develops easily. Both a marriage squeeze for women and the contraceptive revolution have contributed to a recent deterioration in the compensation for wife labor.[12] The dramatic growth of the women's movement, or the feminist revolution, can consequently be viewed in part as a response to the relative worsening in women's position in the market of household labor.

Testing the Effects of Marriage Squeezes

In estimating the effects of changes in marriage squeezes over time one faces conceptual problems, such as the problem of timing of a squeeze. In the theoretical discussion presented above, the perception of marriage squeezes at the onset of a decision regarding marriage or cohabitation affected the nature of the decision. However, marriage squeezes vary substantially during the life cycle (Davis and Van den Oever 1982). If people were to take expected variations into account before making a decision, they would assess market conditions in the market for household labor both in the present and in the future. For instance, the worse the marriage squeeze expected at a later stage in life, the lower the bargaining position now. In rational decisions, although the present would demand more consideration than the future, both existing and expected marriage squeezes would play an important role.

Another conceptual problem has to do with separating the effects on marriage that stem from a marriage squeeze and those that do not. A good test of the theory would require control for other variables influencing marriage patterns. These other factors may be categorized as financial (often termed "economic"), demographic (for instance, number of people born in a particular year), cultural (for instance, the emphasis on decision making without parental influence), or political (for instance, the onset of the Vietnam war). The findings reported in the next section do not attempt to control such other factors, and therefore must be interpreted very cautiously.

In the United States at various times each sex has experienced a marriage squeeze. Variations in marriage squeeze occur because, on the average, women marry men who are generally somewhat older and because the number of births fluctuates from year to year (Glick, Beresford, and Heer 1963). In the early 1950s men faced a shortage of women. This marriage squeeze for men resulted from a decline in the absolute number of births each year during the late 1920s and early 1930s. A man born in 1930 seeking a wife born in 1932, for example, would be at a disadvantage. In the mid-1960s, when the baby-boom generation started to reach marriageable age, the United States began to experience a marriage squeeze for women. A woman born in 1946, for example, would be most likely to marry a man born in 1944. During the post-World War II baby boom, many more children were born in 1946 than in 1944, so that women belonging to the 1946 cohort were facing a marriage squeeze. A marriage squeeze variable defined as the ratio of men between ages 20 and 29 to women between ages 18 and 29 and pictured in Figure 14.2 for the period 1951–1982 reflects this transition from a marriage squeeze for men to a marriage squeeze for women. It also follows from the most recent decline in fertility and from the difference in average male and female age at marriage that we are now entering into a new period of marriage squeeze for men. This explains why the sex ratio rose above 1.00 in 1980.

For simplicity, I will focus on simple measures of marriage squeeze: national averages for selected years and cohorts. In accordance with the theoretical discussion, data on marriage squeezes will be compared to measures of nuptiality and age at marriage, cohabitation, labor force participation of married women, and divorce. The next section reports preliminary evidence and summarizes some relevant results that have previously been published.

Recent Variations in Marriage Squeeze and Related Variables

Figures 14.2–14.7 compare trends in marriage squeeze with trends in a variety of indicators of female status. Taking 1.00 as the dividing line between a marriage squeeze for men and a marriage squeeze for women, Figure 14.2 illustrates that starting in 1951 a marriage squeeze for men occurred, heightening in 1953 and then tapering off. As of 1978 the sex ratio facing young unmarried people has tended to climb, passing the 1.00 mark briefly in 1980.

In the mid-1960s the sex ratio of young unmarried men to young unmarried women reached a level lower than 1.00, and a marriage squeeze for women became acute. Simultaneously, the downward trend in women's age at first marriage reversed and women's chances of being married decreased. Figure 14.3 shows that the onset of a marriage squeeze for women roughly coincided with the onset of an increase in the percentage of women aged 25–29 who have never married. The period of marriage squeeze for women also corresponds to an increase in the median age for women's first marriage from about 20 to about 22 as shown in Figure 14.4. The period of marriage squeeze for women also witnessed a growth in the percentage of never-married men. However, as predicted from the theory, such increase proceeded at a slower rate than the increase in the proportion of never-married women. For instance, between 1970 and 1980 the percentage of never-married women aged 25–29 grew at an average yearly rate of 9.9 percent, whereas the percentage of never-married men in the same age group grew by only 7.3 percent per year on average.

The recent softening of the marriage squeeze for women and the onset of a marriage squeeze for men has not been sufficiently deep or persistent to cause far-reaching effects observable by 1982 or 1983. However, Figure 14.4 shows that a recent slowdown in the increase in women's median age at first marriage has occurred. Also, although Figure 14.3 shows that the percentage of never-married women continued to climb after 1980, the rate at which such increase occurs in the 1980s (an annual average of 6 percent) is slower than the annual growth rate of 9.9 percent that characterizes the 1970s. Morever, juxtaposition with parallel time-series for men shows an interesting trend reversal. Where during the

Figure 14.2

Marriage Squeeze for Men, Aged 20–29, and Women, Aged 18–29

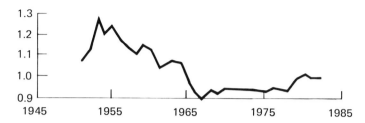

SOURCE: Heer and Grossbard-Shechtman 1981, p. 52; U.S. Bureau of the Census, *Current Population Reports*, Series P-25: Nos. 643, 721, 800, 917, 929, and Series P-20: Nos. 306, 323, 338, 349, 365, 372, and 380.

Figure 14.3

Never-Married Women, Aged 25–29 (Percentage)

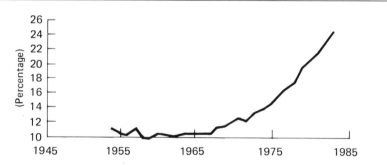

SOURCE: U.S. Bureau of the Census, *Current Population Reports*, Series P-20, selected reports.

Figure 14.4

Women's Median Age at Marrige

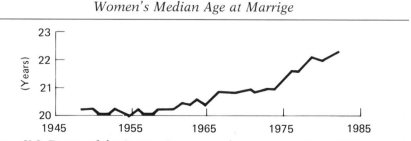

SOURCE: U.S. Bureau of the Census, *Current Population Reports*, Series P-20, selected reports.

Figure 14.5

Unmarried Couples Living Together (in Thousands)

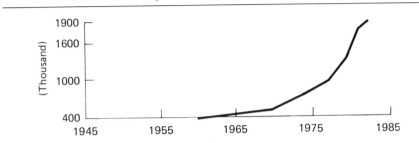

SOURCE: U.S. Bureau of the Census, *Current Population Reports*, Series P-20, selected reports.

Figure 14.6

Percent Employed, Women Aged 25–34

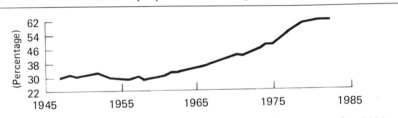

SOURCE: U.S. Bureau of Labor Statistics, Bulletin 2175, Table 15, December 1983.

Figure 14.7

Divorces per 1,000 Married Women, Aged 25–29

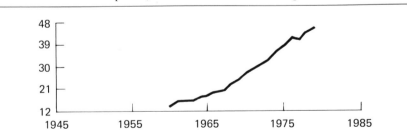

SOURCE: Carlson 1979; U.S. Bureau of the Census, *Current Population Reports*, Series P-20, Nos. 306, 323, 338, 349; National Center for Health Statistics, *Vital Statistics of the U.S., Vol. 3, Marriage and Divorce* for 1976 to 1979. Adjustments were made to the more recent data following Carlson 1979.

1970s the percentage of never-married women rose much faster than the percentage of never-married men (9.9 percent a year versus 7.3 percent a year), from 1982 to 1983 the percentage of never-married men grew at a rate of 5.8 percent, a rate almost identical to the corresponding annual increase in percentage of never-married women (6 percent). Thus, since the onset of a marriage squeeze for men we are now observing a slowdown in the tendency of people not to marry and a tendency for the excess growth in percentage of never-married women versus percentage of never-married men to disappear.

Figure 14.5 illustrates the number of unmarried couples living together in the United States.[13] It appears that a dramatic increase in cohabitation took place beginning in the 1970s and continuing up to the present. It is only in the last year for which data were available, 1982, that we observe a significant slowdown in this trend. Unfortunately, no data are available for the late 1960s, so that it is impossible to determine the exact timing of the jump in the popularity of cohabitation. It could well be that the upward trend in cohabitation significantly changed in the mid-1960s and not in 1970, thus coinciding with the shrinking popularity of marriage apparent in Figures 14.2 and 14.3. Moreover, the data on cohabitation include couples of all ages, and the popularity of cohabitation among young couples could have increased earlier. Young people tend to adopt new lifestyles more readily than older people, in part because of the interference of fewer vested interests and of greater future benefits from adopting a favorable change. Data for the 1970s also show that in the first part of that decade cohabitation rose fastest among people under 25, at a slightly slower pace among those aged 25 to 44, and much more slowly among those 45 and over. In the last years of the past decade, the fastest growth in cohabitation occurred among people aged 25 to 44.[14] The tendency for a more moderate growth in cohabitation corresponds to the onset of a marriage squeeze for men.

So far then, the data on young women demonstrate a correspondence between three trends: the onset of a marriage squeeze, a decrease in the tendency for young women to get married, and (with a possible lag) a dramatic increase in the popularity of cohabitation. This correspondence, however, does not offer absolute proof of the impact of marriage squeezes. More factors influencing marriage and cohabitation need to be controlled if the evidence is to be convincing.[15] While skeptics may point to the possible lag between the trend in the marriage squeeze and cohabitation, such skepticism can be dealt with by emphasizing the time it takes people to accept social norms about new lifestyles.

Such lags in the adjustment of social norms can also account for the apparent divergence between the squeeze trend and that in marriage and cohabitation in the late 1970s. It appears from Figure 14.2 that while the marriage squeeze for women aged 18–29 remained more or less constant after 1965, trends in marriage and cohabitation changed dramatically throughout the late 1960s and the 1970s. Such divergence could be the result of lags in the spread of new social norms. (It could also be due to the insufficiency of the marriage squeeze measure used here. A more accurate empirical measure of the marriage squeeze variable would have to take account of variations over time for a given cohort.) Similar lags may also explain why the number of cohabiting couples was still rising in 1982.

It would also be worthwhile to consider how perceptions about adjacent cohorts affect a particular age group experiencing a marriage squeeze. In the early 1970s, the effect of a marriage squeeze for women aged 18–29 in a particular year became cumulative. Women entering the market for household labor in 1970 had to cope not only with a relative scarcity of men aged 20–29 in 1965 but also with competition by unmarried women in their thirties. Thus, 28-year-old women faced a more unfavorable market of household labor in objective terms than their older sisters faced in 1965. Their perceptions and beliefs may also have been influenced by the unpleasant experience of cohorts immediately preceding them.

Women's liberation, whose major protagonists had been developing and had been presenting their ideas for more than a decade, suddenly became popular in the mid-1960s. The simultaneous occurrence of a market squeeze for women and its social response suggests a relationship between objective market factors and subjectively perceived ideologies such as women's liberation. Alternatively, the worsening in market conditions could have propelled women into organizing in a unionlike manner. The tremendous rise in popularity of feminist ideas was in part a reflection of the growing frustration among women who had a difficult time achieving the standard of living their mothers and older sisters had reached in the past, and in part a framework for collective action to improve market conditions.

It seems that the basic pattern of women's liberation followed closely that of the trends in marriage and cohabitation: a dramatic increase in the mid-1960s, when the concept of women's liberation reached the headlines, and a continuous growth throughout the 1970s. For instance, the magazine *MS.* for career-oriented women first appeared in 1972 and experienced a rapid growth in its readership. The feminist influence on higher education provides another indicator of the impact of the feminist revolution, among young women in particular. Women's studies first appeared in the last half of the 1960s. In 1970 the first integrated women's studies program was officially established at San Diego State University. "Between 1970 and 1975, 150 new women's studies programs were founded, a feat that was repeated between 1975 and 1980" (Boxer 1982, pp. 661–695).

The growth of the feminist movement not only coincided with the marriage squeeze and the movement away from marriage but probably also fueled a stronger reaction to the marriage squeeze. The feminist revolution may have shortened the lag between cause and actual behavior by making young women of the 1970s more aware of alternatives to traditional marriages, thereby encouraging a more widespread response to the unfavorable conditions in the market for household labor.

The marriage squeeze also relates to female employment and the divorce rate. From Figure 14.6 it is apparent that a dramatic upsurge in female employment started in 1963, about the time the sex ratio dipped under 1.00.[16] Again it appears that female employment grew fast throughout the 1970s. The divorce rate shows a similar pattern: a takeoff in 1967 for women aged 25–29 (and in 1969 for women aged 30–34; Carlson 1979), and steady growth thereafter (Figure 14.7).

Figure 14.6 also reveals a slowdown in the growth of the rate of employment of women aged 25–34 starting in 1979. Unfortunately no data on trends in divorce corresponding to the recent reversal in marriage squeeze are as yet available.

The evidence presented in this section shows that marriage squeezes affect U.S. marriage patterns in many different ways. The evidence presented here is impressive in its uniformity. Many different dimensions move in the predicted direction. More sophisticated statistical analyses, which control for other relevant factors such as income, wages, contraceptive technology, preference for various types of work, and discrimination, would be desirable, but even at this stage the importance of marriage squeezes seems difficult to deny.

Additional preliminary evidence on the effects of marriage squeezes is based on comparisons across different groups or areas.

Additional Evidence

Using data for the various states of the Union, Freiden showed that in states with a lower sex ratio—that is, with more of a marriage squeeze for women—a lower percentage of women got married (Freiden 1974). In the same vein, Keeley (1979) found that marriage squeezes delay women's expected age at first marriage.

An interesting question is how the marriage squeeze acts across races. It appears from the U.S. data that racial variation in marriage squeeze relates to a variety of indicators of women's status.

Spanier and Glick (1980) have noted that the sex ratio of marriage eligibles is considerably lower among blacks than among whites. This is in part a function of differences in the sex ratio at birth (Willerman 1979) and in part a result of higher mortality rates for blacks than for whites and for men than for women. In addition, for the years 1967–1970 more than three times as many marriages between black men and white women occurred as between white men and black women.[17] All these factors depress the equilibrium conditions for black women in the market for household labor. The marriage squeeze theory probably provides one important reason why in 1970 the percentage of women aged 25–34 who ever married was 83.3 percent among blacks, as contrasted to 91.0 percent among whites (U.S. Bureau of the Census 1973).

Black–white comparisons also lend support to the hypothesis that relates marriage squeeze to sorting patterns. Spanier and Glick found that a large proportion of black women marry men who are significantly older than the typical age at marriage for the population as a whole. They also discovered that black women are significantly more likely than white women to marry either men at lower educational levels than themselves or men who had been married previously. And the black–white differentials in cohabitation are substantial. In 1976, twice as many black adults as white adults maintained living quarters without being married (Glick and Norton 1979).

In addition, the theory of marriage squeeze offers a new explanation for the greater tendency of black married women than white married women in the United States to participate in the labor force (Cain 1966). The adverse marriage conditions that stem from a marriage squeeze cause black women to have a weak bargaining position for compensation. Consequently, many more black women, even those who are married, will be employed outside the home. A final black–white comparison shows that black women are more likely to be divorced. In 1970, 3.7 percent of all white women were divorced, whereas that proportion stood at 5.1 percent for black women.

Guttentag and Secord (1983) similarly argue that lower sex ratios among American blacks than among American whites account for the former's higher divorce rate and cohabitation rates. They also present a wide array of interesting evidence regarding the effect of marriage squeezes on women's relative status in marriage and on society in general.

Conclusion

Marriage squeezes thus seem to affect marriage, cohabitation, divorce, female labor force participation, and political consciousness. The existence of such effects implies that marriage markets must exist and must have important ramifications. As unappealing as such unromantic notions may sound, markets affect even the most intimate aspects of our lives.

Most readers with a Western cultural background will probably experience difficulty in accepting these views. However, in countries such as Japan and India marriage market awareness is a fact of life. These countries use widespread means to promote market clearance, such as go-betweens, newspaper advertising, and even creation of local marriage bureaus.[18]

The United States and other Western countries are clearly experiencing a downward trend in the popularity of marriage, as discussed in the chapter by Kingsley Davis. Are we moving toward general disillusionment with marriage in nonreligious circles of the Western world? Or will we follow the example of the Far East, where the ideal of romantic love has never been popular and where more down-to-earth marital institutions seem to enable a smoother adjustment to the frequent demographic and technological changes that are part of modern living? A deromanticization of love, allowing for awareness of marriage squeezes and of marriage market forces in general, could lead Western societies into a direction opposite to that experienced in the recent past, a trend toward more marriages but fewer marriages based on romantic attraction.

NOTES

1. This market approach to marriage has been influenced by Becker (1974) and was elaborated in Grossbard (1976) and Grossbard-Shechtman (1982 and 1984b).

2. Derivation of individual supply and demand schedules can be found in Grossbard-Shechtman 1984b.

3. Theoretically this is not always the case; see Grossbard-Shechtman 1984b.

4. The term "marriage squeeze" was coined by Paul Glick (see Glick, Beresford, and Heer 1963).

5. Previous theoretical contributions have discussed this relation between marriage squeezes and the likelihood that women will marry (see Becker 1974; Henry 1975; and Smith 1980, pp. 58–96).

6. If polyandry is permitted, an increase in the number of men beyond the point where all women are married once could be translated into a higher propensity for women to get married to more than one man.

7. This recognizes that women are more interested in legal protection in case a separation occurs. Women's preference for tying their husbands to familial obligations, particularly after dissolution, and men's relative emphasis on avoiding limitations to their freedom (including the freedom from responsibility to their children) is strongly rooted in biological differences between the sexes. In Grossbard-Shechtman (1982), I show formally how women's stronger desire for legal protection in marriage can be derived from gender differences in productivity levels (reproductive productivity in particular) and in life-cycle variations in two major kinds of productivity (reproductive and earnings-generating). Other biologically rooted gender differences have been related to the asymmetric desire for

legal protection at dissolution. This includes differences in morbidity, mortality, and sources of sexual satisfaction (see Davis and Van den Oever 1982).

It should also be kept in mind that women's relative preference for legal protection through marriage is not universal. For instance, women oriented toward a career outside the home and not toward childbearing may be less interested in stability and legal protection through marriage.

8.   Others have hypothesized this relation between marriage squeeze and sorting patterns, among them Lebergott (1965, p. 363) and Spanier and Glick (1980, pp. 707–725).

9.   For a more complete discussion of the effect of sex ratio variations on women's labor supply, see Grossbard-Shechtman (1984b and 1985).

10.   Some hypotheses similar to those presented here have been published by Guttentag and Secord (1983) well after the theory presented here went through its initial versions. For a partial comparison between our theories, see Grossbard-Shechtman (1984a).

11.   In Heer and Grossbard-Shechtman (1981) marriage squeezes are related to marital fertility, assuming wives are more willing to have children than husbands.

12.   The first explanation was suggested by Yochanan Peres. The second is also found in Heer and Grossbard-Shechtman (1981).

13.   Before 1977, no data were published on the number of unmarried couples aged 25–34. Therefore I could not present a figure using age groups comparable to the measure of marriage squeeze. A more detailed discussion of trends in cohabitation can be found in Graham Spanier's chapter in this volume.

14.   According to the U.S. Bureau of the Census (1981), the ratio of cohabitation in 1980 compared to that in 1970 was 9.46 for households where the householder was under 45 and 1.24 for households where the householder was 45 and over. That same ratio comparing 1980 to 1977 was 1.68 and 1.17, respectively.

15.   There are, however, serious statistical problems in testing a theory with annual data for such a short period.

16.   For more empirical evidence on the relationship between marriage squeeze and female labor force participation, see Grossbard-Shechtman (1984b and 1985).

17.   But the total racial exogamy is limited in the United States. "In 1975, about 4.4 percent of married black men and about 2.4 percent of married black women had partners of a different race, almost always white" (Spanier and Glick 1980, p. 724). This low exogamy justifies viewing markets for services by black and white wives as separate.

18.   This happened, for example, on the Japanese island of Hokkaido, where men who had been experiencing a shortage of brides organized an agency to bring potential wives from the mainland (*New York Times*, January 3, 1978).

REFERENCES

Becker, Gary S. "A Theory of Marriage." In T. W. Schultz (ed.), *Economics of the Family*. Chicago: University of Chicago Press, 1974.

Boxer, Marilyn J. "For Women and about Women: The Theory and Practice of Women's Studies in the United States." *Signs* 7(1982):661–695.

Cain, Glen C. *Married Women in the Labor Force*. Chicago: University of Chicago Press, 1966.

Carlson, Elwood. "Divorce Rate Fluctuations as a Cohort Phenomenon." *Population Studies* 33(1979):523–536.

Carter, H., and Glick, P. C. *Marriage and Divorce: A Social and Economic Study*. Cambridge, Mass.: Harvard University Press, 1970.

Davis, Kingsley, and Van den Oever, Pietronella. "Demographic Foundations of New Sex Roles." *Population and Development Review* (1982):495–512.

Freiden, Alan. "The U.S. Marriage Market." In T. W. Schultz (ed.), *Economics of the Family*. Chicago: University of Chicago Press, 1974.

Glick, Paul C.; Beresford, John C.; and Heer, David M. "Family Formation and Family Composition: Trends and Prospects." In Marvin B. Sussman (ed.), *Sourcebook in Marriage and the Family*. Boston: Houghton Mifflin, 1963.

Glick, Paul C., and Norton, Arthur J. "Marrying, Divorcing, and Living Together in the U.S. Today." *Population Bulletin* 5(1979): entire issue.

Grossbard, Amyra. "An Economic Analysis of Polygamy: The Case of Maiduguri." *Current Anthropology* 17(1976):701–707.

Grossbard-Shechtman, Amyra. "A Theory of Marriage Formality: The Case of Guatemala." *Economic Development and Cultural Change* 30(1982): 813–830.

Grossbard-Shechtman, Amyra. "Review of Guttentag and Secord's Too Many Women." *Sociology and Social Research* 68(1984a):390–391.

Grossbard-Shechtman, Amyra. "A Theory of Allocation of Time in Markets for Labor and Marriage." *Economic Journal* 94(1984b):863–882.

Grossbard-Shechtman, Amyra. "Female Labor Supply, Marriage, and Sex Ratios." Paper presented at the Meetings of the Population Association of America, Boston, March 1985.

Guttentag, Marcia, and Secord, Paul F. *Too Many Women: The Sex Ratio Question*. Beverly Hills, Calif.: Sage Publications, 1983.

Heer, David M. "Sex Roles in the United States, 1960 to 1975: A Demographic Analysis." Manuscript, University of Southern California, 1978.

Heer, David M., and Grossbard-Shechtman, Amyra. "The Wife Market, the Marriage Squeeze and Fertility." Paper presented at the Population Association of America, April 1979.

Heer, David M., and Grossbard-Shechtman, Amyra. "The Impact of the Female Marriage Squeeze and the Contraceptive Revolution in Sex Roles and the Women's Liberation Movement in the United States, 1960 to 1975." *Journal of Marriage and the Family* 43(1981):49–65.

Henry, Louis. "Schéma d'évolution des mariages après de grandes variations des naissances." *Population* 30(1975):759–779.

Keeley, Michael C. "An Analysis of the Age Pattern of First Marriage." *International Economic Review* 20(1979):527–544.

Lasch, Christopher. *Haven in a Heartless World.* New York: Basic Books, 1977.

Lebergott, Stanley. "The Labor Force and Marriage as Endogenous Factors." In James S. Duesenberry, Gary Fromm, Lawrence R. Klein, and Edwin Kuh (eds.), *The Brookings Quarterly Econometric Model of the United States.* Chicago: Rand-McNally, 1965.

Smith, Peter C. "Asian Marriage Patterns in Transition." *Journal of Family History* 5(1980):58–96.

Spanier, Graham B., and Glick, Paul C. "Mate Selection Differentials between Whites and Blacks in the United States." *Social Forces* 58(1980):707–725.

U.S. Bureau of the Census. *1970 Census of Population: General Population Characteristics.* "Women by Number of Children Ever Born." *Census Report* PC (2)-3A. Washington, D.C.: Government Printing Office, 1973.

U.S. Bureau of the Census. *Current Population Reports*, Series P-20, No. 365, *Marital Status and Living Arrangements: March 1980.* Washington, D.C.: U.S. Government Printing Office, 1981.

Willerman, Lee. *The Psychology of Individual and Group Differences.* San Francisco: W. H. Freeman, 1979.

15 *Emotional Aspects of Contemporary Relations*

From Status to Contract

ALAN A. STONE

I SHALL BEGIN by presenting the basic thesis of this chapter in its starkest form. Then I shall briefly report a human vignette that will help focus on themes of interest in the psychology of young adults. I shall examine three Eriksonian themes—identity, intimacy, and generativity—in light of what has been called the new narcissism, and shall attempt, through my analysis, to offer a psychiatric contribution to our understanding of the changing significance of marriage for this generation of young adults.

First, then, the thesis: for today's achieving young adults, the major stresses, the disappointments, and the most important causes of psychological suffering and alienation occur in the home and family. The workplace by comparison seems less stressful— even a relief.

Examining this claim from a social-historical perspective, one finds that an interesting transformation in social thought has taken place. A major theme in sociological commentary on the effects of the Industrial Revolution and mass production has been that these developments created a radical disjunction between the workplace and the home, and that the new workplace was an evil influence. The workplace took on a negative tone as a hostile environment exemplified most notably in Marxist indictments of alienated labor. "Misery springs from the nature of the prevailing mode of labor." By contrast, at least, the home was seen as a more natural, more positive, and, therefore, potentially more fulfilling environment.

As the postindustrial welfare state came into being, the disjunction between public life and private life received even greater emphasis. The domain of public life was impersonal, uncontrollable, alienating, and yet expanding. The domain of private life was seen as shrinking and, therefore, even more precious in that it offered the hope of love and intimacy and escape from the competitive stress and alienation of the real world (Lasch 1977). "An American dream" was based on this vision of the social reality. The nuclear family would, to use Christopher Lasch's language, create a "haven in a heartless world." In that dream, the world of the workplace and the public domain was hectic, demeaning, demanding, manipulative, and even corrupt.

Against this heartless world, marriage and the nuclear family were to create a haven of support, love, comfort, and moral order. I want to emphasize that part of this dream was based on the assumption that marriage and the nuclear family were the embodiment of a natural order, a natural hierarchy, and that therefore questions of power and domination need not be confronted. While the outside world was ordered by impersonal contractual relations, the haven of the family was ordered by personal relations of trust.

Most of the assumptions of this dream have been challenged. The natural hierarchy of the family has been called into question by a transforming array of social and economic forces, the availability of contraception, and the emergence of feminism (Firestone 1974). Power and domination within the family have become subjects of central concern to family therapists. Marriage has become the problem not the solution, or so it seems to many. This interpretation is a reversal of the nineteenth-century Marxist description of alienation in the workplace. The family has become the place of alienated labor, of stress, tension, and "misery." It is no longer considered a haven in a heartless world. People increasingly go to the workplace to escape the isolating, demeaning, and demanding pressures of marriage and family.

It would be wrong to assume that this account of social reality began in the nineteenth century. The contrast between the public and the private domain is, for example, a constant theme in Shakespeare's plays. In "The Merchant of Venice," the reality of the city and its corruption are contrasted with the natural harmony of Belmont. But Shakespeare was too great a genius to assume that Venice and Belmont could really be separate except in a dream. The social, demographic, and economic forces at work in the real world eventually intrude on the home and family. I wish to raise an important conceptual point here (Zaretsky 1976 and Lasch 1977 deal with such questions at length). If one assumes that the family somehow can function as a psychological and emotional haven, regardless of the economic, political, and social forces, then the family can save the society by socializing children in the proper fashion, inculcating whatever form of manners and morality that may be necessary to an ordered society. If, on the other hand, one believes that the family is deeply affected (even directly or indirectly shaped) by what goes on around it, then the family's role as a socializing force will be a casualty of the larger disorder. This theoretical distinction is of enormous significance for national social policy aimed at the institution of marriage and the family. Debate over this distinction fueled, for example, the controversy set off by the Moynihan Report (U.S. Department of Labor 1965).

My belief is that most of the people in the generation born before World War II believed in the American Dream. The dream, they realized, might not come true; the reality may have been closer to what Doris Lessing described in her remarkable novel, *The Golden Notebook.* "Behind every door," she wrote, "there is a disaster." But that generation, to which I belong, *believed* in the family, and that belief alone made a crucial difference in how we felt about the institution of marriage, in how we planned our adult lives as opposed to the next generation.

This generation, by contrast, faces a markedly more chaotic present as well as an unsettled future. The upheaval which has occurred for those born since World War II has developed in so many aspects of life that it has completely altered the background against which social and sexual relations are formed. Without attempting to construct a chain of cause and effect, I will present a brief catalogue of these changes and then attempt to analyze the developmental conflicts they pose for this generation.

Changing Context of Marriage

Perhaps the most incontrovertible developments are demographic. Women and men are both living longer, but, more important, female longevity is outrunning male longevity, causing the female majority in the population to grow. In addition, with the ability to control reproduction, women now have fewer children, and the rearing years consume a far smaller proportion of a woman's life. Elsewhere in this volume Davis and Van den Oever report:

> According to the 1980 life table for the United States, a white woman marrying at age 22 will live to age 79.4. Yet she will stop having children at about 30 years of age, much earlier than her grandmother did. Assuming that the last child will leave for college at age 18, the mother (at age 48) will still have more than 31 years to live free from the care of children.

With divorce rates also rising and remarriage rates declining, these authors conclude that the roles of both marriage and reproduction are becoming less important to women while the role of independent worker is rising in importance.

At the same time, the feminist movement, perhaps to some extent a response to these demographic changes, advocates the equality of women in the marketplace. The movement also appears to decrease the relative value that women place on marriage, reproduction, and mothering.

Factors besides demography and ideology, such as economics, education, medical technology, and the social welfare state, also may stimulate the higher divorce rate and the lower marriage rate. Increasing job competition and uncertainty, some argue, contribute to decisions to defer childbearing and marriage (Glick and Norton 1977). Economic uncertainty coincides with the increasing number of women completing college and entering graduate school rather than getting married (ibid.). Women who have spent time in graduate school are below average in marital stability, partially because of increased career options and pressures (ibid., p. 9). Thus, education for women and achievement can place a strain on "traditional" marriage. Birth control and legalized abortion reduce the risks of sexual activity outside wedlock, while welfare payments for unwed mothers reduce the economic premium placed on marriage as an insurance policy (Glaser 1978). In fact, about one in three births are now conceived premaritally (Glick and Norton, p. 3). People increasingly are delaying marriage (ibid., p. 5).

In short, the reasonably stable set of expectations, values, and institutions that the generation born before World War II faced no longer prevails. Instead, a situation of uncertainty, fluidity, and heterodoxy confronts the young adult. What do young adults make of their situation, and, in particular, how do these changes affect their psychological unfolding?

Subjective Elements of the Life Cycle Today

These, of course, are broad questions that have no simple, single answers. Therefore, I would like to examine these questions in light of a specific group of young adults and a specific theoretical framework—Erikson's life cycle. The clinical experience on which I shall rely is based on my experience over the past fifteen years with young men and women who attended Harvard Law School. They were admitted to Harvard Law School because of distinguished achievement in college and high scores in standardized aptitude tests. Certainly not lacking in ambition, they all are committed to a career. Indeed, "careerism" has become the central value in the lives of these young adults. If they follow in the footsteps of their predecessors, many of them will take their places among the power elite of this country. The majority come from privileged backgrounds, the women no less than the men; and even the so-called minority students are with few exceptions from reasonably affluent and educationally advantaged backgrounds. While these young adults certainly do not accurately represent their age group, they provide an interesting and important sample of achieving persons among whom a dominant value is careerism.

A word about the nature of my contacts with these students. I knew them in the most general and superficial way, as a member and chairman of the Admissions Committee for four years. Although we do not interview applicants, this was an excellent way to get some sense of the scope of their remarkable accomplishments (at least on paper). I have also known thousands of them from classrooms over the past fifteen years, where the Socratic method is practiced; and thus one has a sense of how they conduct themselves in public situations, and of their public values and attitudes. Finally, I have known hundreds of them particularly well as students in a course I have been teaching for the past fifteen years on interviewing, negotiating, and counseling. The course is an experience-based learning situation, and it allows me what can be called a clinical relationship. As a requirement of that course, students submit a lengthy, personal experience report and analysis. Almost half of these students elect to write about a "living together" relationship.

Erikson, in his outline of the life cycle, presents an ideal, ordered sequence: identity culminating in a career choice, intimacy culminating in a commitment to a personal relationship, and generativity culminating in children, creativity, or productivity. These sequences, as Erikson well knows, never occur so exactly in real life. Indeed, given the impact of changing sexual practices among young teenagers in all classes of American society, Erikson's sequence seems problematic—intimacy precedes identity perhaps at all class levels. The group of young adults that I have known at Harvard Law School have delayed the resolution of identity and have first made serious attempts at intimacy. As a result, deep conflicts arise between career choice, commitment to a mate, and the proper resolution of generativity. I shall discuss these conflicts at several levels.

First, let me say a few things about the delays in resolving identity. Law school, unlike all other graduate institutions, requires no fixed or extended prelaw curriculum. Furthermore, the decision to go to law school, though careerist, is often seen as a way to keep one's options open. Graduates of elite law schools possess a broad spectrum of career options in business, politics, government, and administration, not to mention the many alternatives within the practice of law itself. The ability to delay specific career choice contains an important psychological dimension which I examined at great length in a previous paper ("Legal Education on the Couch," 1971). Briefly summarized: the choice of a career is an important step in coming to terms with adolescent grandiosity. The young person must at the very least make a choice among his different dreams of glory. Testing his ego ideal against reality has crucial significance for his self-esteem. But the law student who has gained entrance to an elite law school can delay this day of reckoning; he can postpone his career decision and retain his dream of unlimited options. Although Erikson contrasts identity with role diffusion, in the special circumstances of the law student, keeping one's options open—which might be equated with role diffusion—is the norm.

Although they delay the resolution of their identity, this group of students does not delay the pursuit of intimacy. Yet according to Erikson (1964), the young adult should not make serious attempts at intimacy until identity has culminated in a career choice. He explains: "Thus, the young adult emerging from the search for and the insistence on identity is eager and willing to fuse his identity with that of others. He is ready for intimacy, that is the capacity to commit himself to concrete affiliations and partnerships and to develop the ethical strength to abide by such sacrifices and compromises."

A Clinical Vignette

I have my students read this section of Erikson in the context of discussion of the laws of marriage and divorce. The response I received from one woman student revealed much about the transformation in attitudes that young people express about intimacy. I quote her remarks as faithfully as I can.

"The laws of divorce and marriage should not be premised on the assumption that people will marry only once. Furthermore, it is seriously misleading for psychiatrists to construct a theory of maturity or normality based on the assumption that an enduring love relationship formalized in marriage is the norm or is even a meaningful ideal for society." The latter part of the woman's statement is a criticism of Erikson. She continued by stating that "such legal assumptions and psychiatric ideals condemn many, if not most of us, to a sense of personal failure. We will feel required to stay in unhappy marriages as my parents did who waited for ten years to get a divorce, though they hated each other. Or else we will get a divorce feeling that we have failed at intimacy or that we lack ethical strength."

"My own opinion is that if a man and a woman get along for five or ten years, that is as much as can be expected. People change and they stop sharing. It is much more sensible to plan on a series of relationships—perhaps three or four. The law should make it as easy as possible for this to happen, and psychiatrists should stop pontificating about one marriage being better than four."

I want to emphasize that her response seemed to be a carefully thought out position, not meant to be a tendentious argument. It produced a painful silence in the classroom not only because this woman had made a personal statement but also because we all sensed a chilling rationality in what she had said.

At the time, I waited out the silence. The comment one might have expected came from one of the other students in the class. "What about children?" The woman replied that she was not sure whether or not she would have children, and that she certainly did not intend to sacrifice her career for them. No one, by the way, asked her, "What about love?"

What are we to make of these remarks? What do they tell us about this generation of young adults, and what do they tell us about the assumptions of Eriksonian psychology? Psychiatrists have learned rather painfully that much of what they thought was scientific and professional was merely ideological, like the hagiography of the family and the good mother. Many of these young people are agnostic about family and marriage. However, in asserting this, I should call attention to the tremendous variety of both attitudes and practices which, as I mentioned earlier, are a predominant feature of the current landscape. In fact, the variety and uncertainty of options that young people find among their peer group may in turn contribute to the agnosticism. But dreams die slowly; a majority of college graduates today still report that they hope to be married some day (GAP 1975). And I doubt that many young men and women hope they will be married several times.

The Marriage Equivalent

In any event, the reality that this young woman described is even more problematic than she acknowledged. She, like many in the new generation, is a child of divorced parents; she thinks in terms of three marriages, but probably she and most of her friends have had more than casual sexual experiences in high school and at least two "marriage equivalents" before they begin to think of legal marriage. Indeed, many students have had at least one "living together relationship" before they even come to graduate school. Close to two million unrelated men and women not married to each other are currently sharing living quarters (Glick and Norton 1977, pp. 3, 34).

Psychiatrists who treat young adults share the clinical impression that these living-together relationships often have all of the substantial emotional complications of marriage. While demographers report that young people are getting married later, the psychological reality is that they are getting married sooner. And in addition to these premarital relationships, young people also experience cohabitation between marriages, not to mention extramarital affairs. Thus, when my student spoke of some norm of three she might just as well have spoken of five or six. Clearly the lifestyle I am describing does not apply to all young adults, nor does it apply to all Harvard Law students. However, mental health professionals who treat young adults from the middle and upper classes are certainly familiar with the pattern I am describing. Indeed, therapy for unmarried couples has become a common clinical practice. And the pattern of marriage equivalents and marriages is probably at least as frequent among the lower social classes of American society.

The nature of premarital relationships in the group I am considering requires further clarification. These relationships do not consist merely of casual sex. A great deal goes into them—allowing oneself to be vulnerable, loving and being loved, manipulating and being manipulated, exploiting and being exploited, sexual adventure, and discovery—all this and yet typically without "commitment." Indeed, when these relationships terminate, young people most commonly offer the explanation, "I wasn't ready to make a commitment." Thus, if Erikson's sequence does not describe the actual reality, he seems to have captured the psychological reality of human development. These achievement-oriented young people enter into premarital relationships on a theory of "non-binding commitments" with, as Lasch points out, no apparent awareness that this is a contradiction in terms. Thus, in these relationships very basic ambiguities exist which, according to experienced clinicians, the partners seldom articulate or explore (GAP 1983).

The remarkable human challenge for these young people is how to achieve intimacy, intimacy that they still seem very much to want, without making any clear or lasting promises. Even the most psychologically healthy of partners call into play psychological mechanisms such as denial, make-believe, and an avoidance of the future. These psychological mechanisms prevent young people from exploring or even articulating the ambiguous nature of their relationship. For those who, for psychological reasons, have difficulty making long-term commitments, such relationships provide a neurotic escape.

Even for those partners potentially capable of commitment, the lack of external definition in such relationships makes it difficult to integrate the relationship into family and other social networks (GAP 1983). It is therefore easy to understand why there has been so much talk about the "new narcissism." Many young people engage in intense relationships that lack commitment and appear to end solely on the basis of self-interest. But one should be leery about labeling a whole generation as narcissistic as Christopher Lasch has done, especially when the term has so many different meanings that the label itself is confusing. Lasch recognizes this problem and is very particular about what he means by narcissism. He believes that Eric Fromm and others have used the term so loosely that they say little more than that the present generation is selfish. Lasch, in contrast, attempts to make a more technical and stronger argument by claiming that this generation of young adults has been socialized to have the kind of narcissistic personality disorders that psychiatrists assert have replaced the classical neuroses. Lasch uses "the principle that pathology represents a heightened version of normality" and outlines the psychoanalytic version of early childhood experiences. He considers these experiences to be causes of narcissistic personality disorders. Relying on this perspective to explain the "non-binding commitment," he quotes one of Otto Kernberg's patients as a paradigm: "The ideal relationship to me would be a two-month relationship. That way there'd be no commitment." But the way Kernberg's patient expressed his feeling is far from typical. He was apparently incapable of any real attachment, being fearful of parasitic dependent needs and afraid of his own emptiness. Out of fear of vulnerability, he used his narcissistic defenses to avoid intimacy.

The young people at Harvard Law School, however, sincerely

desire intimate relationships. Since they often become deeply involved and their vulnerability is all too real, their serious living-together relationships are emotionally equivalent to marriage and their break-ups are often emotionally equivalent to divorce. In fact, such break-ups create strains not commonly encountered in divorce: "Because the living-together relationship has never carried the promise of permanence as does marriage, there is very little social support for those feelings of outrage, hurt, and anger which are considered 'justified' when marriage breaks up" (GAP 1985).

The formal social and legal mechanisms for disentangling a marriage provide a framework in which friends and relatives can respond supportively. For people "merely living together," the outcome of a break-up instead is an unexpressed and often not understood feeling of vague and generalized depression (GAP 1983). Often young people are perplexed about what moral attitude they should have about the break-up of these relationships. With no sense of what is morally correct, their emotional responses are confused and confusing to each other. Sometimes the partners feel betrayed and used; those who are psychologically minded may recognize in retrospect that they were playing "make believe" and may wonder about the depth of their own feelings for the other person.

I do not deny that really defensive narcissism exists in some young adults today, but it is not the kind of narcissism most commonly found in the successful young adults I have come to know. Most helpful in understanding the quality of their narcissism is a paper by Helen Tartakoff, "The Nobel Prize Complex" (1966). She describes a pattern of narcissism among men and women who have been highly successful. Even in early childhood, these people showed talent, ability, or qualities of personality that endeared them to one or both of their parents. As a result of this special and intense relationship, they not only avoided preoedipal trauma, they also managed either to win the Oedipal struggle or to soften its full impact. Their narcissism is not so much the product of primitive defenses as it is the result of precocious adaptiveness. Obviously, this narcissism does not result from some new trend in child-rearing in America. Those who know Freud's biography will recognize that the pattern Tartakoff described applies to him. He wrote, "If a man has been his mother's undisputed darling he retains throughout life the triumphant feeling, the confidence in success, which not seldom brings actual success along with it." This is the pattern of "narcissism" I see most commonly in the students who have made their way through the competitive maze that leads to Harvard Law School. Such people bring high expectations to their intimate relationships as well as to their careers. These two sets of expectations almost inevitably come into conflict, particularly when two such people are involved with each other.

The conflicts that emerge are easy to understand. Both partners yearn to recreate their special relationship, both want to be admired, and both understandably expect to be first in academic and career pursuits. The conflicts have evolved partially from the dramatic change in role expectations for women. Successful young people today may be more conservative and more religious, but they have abandoned the hagiography of the *Good Mother*. Women want a career and a successful one. An early marriage might limit their geographical options, even if it did not saddle them with children. Men certainly engage in the same calculus, and of course each partner will eventually know that the other is calculating.

Such calculation is unlikely to produce the kind of openness and vulnerability that love and intimacy necessitate. Thus a nonbinding and ambiguously articulated commitment is an understandable adaptation to the difficult conflict between the need for intimacy and the determination to advance one's career. These nonbinding relationships are still meant to fulfill the old Dream, a haven in a heartless world, a retreat from the stress of constant achievement, a wish to be valued not as a means to an end but for oneself. If such a relationship is not a marriage, it is, to say the least, a honeymoon. But the demands of career and the need for achievement inevitably intrude. They are so important to both parties that it would be impossible for them not to intrude. The couple may work at helping each other, may plan their careers together, and may share their ambitions—perhaps they may even legalize their union, but difficult hurdles crop up frequently, the most formidable being the narcissistic response to the other's success. I remember a very sensitive and sensible young man with remarkable self-insight who had experienced a double blow—he had not earned high enough grades to make the prestigious *Law Review* and the woman he was living with had. He wondered if their relationship could survive this blow to his self-esteem. Imagine how the young woman must have felt. She was deprived of the opportunity to glow in her success.

Unfortunately, these intimate relations are not only vulnerable to the hazards of dual careers, differing success, and geographical dislocations. They are also vulnerable to tensions over sexual fidelity and jealousy. Although the partners may have thought they had an implicit or even explicit understanding regarding sexual relationships with others, neither may be prepared for his feelings or the expectations of his partner when the contingency actually arises. Alternatively, the couple may not have confronted the issue at all. When such tensions occur, the "definiteness" of the arrangement and the degree of commitment by implication become seriously and explicitly tested.

Most important, however, is the fact that when these relationships terminate, they leave emotional wounds and the need to express grief. Because, as I mentioned, they are typically carried on in social isolation, there is no socially acceptable framework in which to do that grieving or work through the loss. As a result, young people engage in more "on the rebound" relationships, show a greater reluctance to be open and vulnerable, and tend to hold back more in the next nonbinding commitment. Young adults who experience a series of these relationships begin to develop a "comparison shopper's" mentality—in short, they bring to the relationship exactly the kind of calculating attitude and approach that will confound an intimate relationship.

Thus, this generation of young adults is neither more selfish nor more narcissistic than previous generations. They do not form their nonbinding commitments out of a fear of intimacy. Rather their relationships are a compromise between their desire for intimacy and their career ambitions. At the same time, however, when these marriage equivalents fail, they become an important social learning experience that teaches young adults to be wary and calculating. When Margaret Mead years ago suggested trial marriage as an antidote for the rising divorce rate, she did not consider the social learning that results from trials that fail. This social learning encompasses an expectation that the relationship will not work out, a readiness to walk away when things get difficult, and sometimes even a wariness that becomes an inability to fall in love. Despite all of the difficulties of these marriage equivalents, or perhaps paradoxically because of them, this generation of young adults has contradictory, almost sacramental ideals of love, intimacy, and marriage. Alongside their career ambitions, they have a bulwark against cynicism—namely the expectation that in a personal relationship they will achieve their unique identity. This ideal imagines more than a haven in a heartless world; it is the dream that a surpassing intimate relationship will lift the couple above the ordinariness of everyday experience. Their sex life and intimacy must be the vehicle of transcendence; their relationship must fulfill a personal destiny. This ideal is, of course, the antithesis of the matter-of-fact "realistic" approach articulated by my student in class. But it will not be misunderstood if a psychiatrist suggests that young people expect so much and so little—such, of course, is our view of human nature.

The Marriage Contract

But of course, despite the increase in unlicensed cohabitation, many young adults today do decide to get married. The question of what a marriage should be then arises because the traditional marriage roles and the so-called natural order of the family have been repudiated. Thus the couple must invent the form and structure of their marriage. To do that, they must negotiate. They must order their mutual lives by contract or by some equivalent, and this requires them to be calculating. If they do not calculate before marriage, then they will soon after, because the demands of career and the obligations of marriage inevitably conflict. What each partner owes to the marriage and wants from it has to be decided. The rise of marriage contracts detailing the most personal aspects of personal matters manifests this need for negotiation and compromise. Lon Fuller, an expert on contract and the jurisprudence of contract, once wrote that the rise of contract could be understood as a necessary legal form to deal with the emergence of market economies. Parties who did not know each other well enough to rely on personal trust utilized contract for specific transactions. Contract was suitable for the marketplace, he thought, but not for the more intimate relationships of the family.

Is it reasonable from this perspective to suggest that marriage is becoming more like a market transaction? Gary Becker has developed a school of social analysis that relies on economics and market analysis to examine social institutions such as marriage. Amyra Grossbard-Shechtman, who studied under Becker, has written a number of papers on the marriage market. Ironically, the foundation of her analysis is the assumption that the woman provides what she calls wife services (child-rearing, housekeeping, companionship) to the man in exchange for money, goods, and status. But the young women whom we are considering are not interested in that kind of exchange. They are much more likely to agree with the Italian women's manifesto (Zaretsky 1976, p. 139):

> We affirm that all labor hitherto carried out by women, that is, cleaning the house, washing and ironing, sewing, cooking, looking after children, taking care of the old and sick, are forms of labor like any other, which could be carried out equally by men or women and are not of necessity tied to the ghetto of the home.

These women want equal career opportunities, equal sharing of wife services, and a financial partnership. A unilateral exchange of money for services seems remote from their interests.

Admittedly, formal marriage contracts have not been very successful; indeed, proponents of the idea have emphasized that the real function of contracts is to insure that a recognition of the different interests of the partners takes place in advance and that potential conflicts of interest are negotiated before a commitment is made.

Whatever the use of marriage contracts, their popularity proves that young adults now need to reinvent the institution of marriage. A common element in many marriages today will be an agreement to postpone having children. Yet that decision transforms marriage into an institution not much different from a marriage equivalent. Recognizing this, many young adults postpone legal marriage until they are ready to bear children or actually have them on the way, or, less commonly, have already had them.

The difficulties in a childless marriage, as Erikson suggests in *Insight and Responsibility*, is the danger of self-absorption. Each partner tends to become his or her own infant or "pet." Parental "caring," on the other hand, overcomes this tendency.

Infantile self-absorption promotes frustration and heightens ambivalence toward the contractual obligations of marriage. Extramarital sex is a common reaction to this frustration and ambivalence. Interestingly, such affairs often occur with some person from the workplace. Obviously, convenience and opportunity play a role, but another element also deserves our attention—an element that offers insight into how young adults may solidify their marriage.

As more women enter the work force, new sexual problems arise. One of these is sexual harassment—a very real problem but only a small part of the larger sexual situation. More often what happens is that men and women increasingly come together in joint enterprises where they feel they are working to accomplish some worthwhile common goal or at least are sharing the same experience. The setting may not be ideal for romantic love, but it does provide a feeling of comradeship—the closeness of people who have coped together, who have helped each other to accomplish something, and who have gotten to know each other in real ways. Thus, in the context of a joint enterprise, comradeship may develop into intimacy. This intimacy, although a by-product of the working relationship, may generate intense erotic feeling. We have so often focused on the harassing, exploitative, and inappropiate nature of sex at the office, that we have failed to recognize that it has something to teach us—namely, that when a man and woman work together in a shared enterprise, intimacy, eroticism, and love may be enhanced.

When Erikson quoted Freud's famous maxim on love and work as the criteria of adult maturity I think he had in mind success in two separate domains, the world of work and the world of the home. This maxim of human fulfillment was of course male-oriented; women's work was in the home. Today both sexes participate in both domains. I want to suggest that somehow those domains must come together. The clue for stabilizing marriage is somehow to make of a marriage a joint enterprise. Children clearly fulfilled that role in the past and no doubt will continue to do so. Many women in traditional marriages vicariously and in practical ways participated in their husband's careers; thus, they made that career a joint enterprise. Similarly, some men vicariously and in practical ways participated in child-rearing.

Making marriage a joint enterprise is not easy. The stresses of competition and the need to dominate intervene. Perhaps even more difficult are the strains that other members of the workplace, perhaps unwittingly, create for the couple as well as the strains that the workplace itself engenders. Intimacy in the workplace may give rise to conflicting expectations with respect to other workers.

Where once intimacy was subordinate to the demands of the workplace, it may later demand so much attention that the subordination is turned around. On the other hand, the workplace may generate new tasks and upset the former personal arrangement. As the original basis of intimacy is lost or altered, the old intimacy itself may wither and may be replaced by another.

A recent survey regarding sexual tensions in the workplace indicates that the pull between intimacy and efficiency is a pervasive reality. Many women and men have found that the only way to resolve the tensions between sexual attraction, impersonal organizational goals, and workplace gossip is a strict professionalism amounting to "an iron fence" around one's emotions (*Wall Street Journal* 1981).

There is no final solution to the difficulties created by advanced education, professional careers, and workplace temptations, for both men and women. However, present reality should not be confused with absolute and eternal necessity. Particularly as social values regarding couples in the workplace move away from the "men's club" mores of old, the tensions may be ameliorated at the same time that workplace becomes more humane. The motivation underlying pair-bonding remains strong. If the social network in which the couple lives reinforces that motivation, many couples will be able to work out their professional problems, to keep loving each other, and thus yet find a way to create a haven in a less heartless world.

REFERENCES

Erikson, Erik. *Insight and Responsibility.* New York: W. W. Norton, 1964.

Firestone, Shulamith. *The Dialect of Sex.* New York: William Morrow, 1974.

Glaser, Nathan. "The Rediscovery of the Family." *Commentary* 66(1978): 49–56.

Glick, Paul C., and Norton, Arthur J. "Marrying, Divorcing, and Living Together in the U.S. Today." *Population Bulletin* 32(1977).

Group for the Advancement of Psychiatry (GAP), Committee on the College

Student. *The Educated Woman: Prospects and Problems.* New York: Mental Health Materials Center, 1975.

Group for the Advancement of Psychiatry (GAP), Committee on the College Student. *Friends and Lovers in the College Years.* New York: Mental Health Materials Center, 1983.

Lasch, Christopher. *Haven in a Heartless World.* New York: Basic Books, 1977.

Lasch, Christopher. *The Culture of Narcissism.* New York: W. W. Norton, 1979.

"Sexual Tension: Some Men Find Office Is a Little Too Exciting with Women as Peers." *Wall Street Journal,* April 14, 1981.

Stone, Alan A. "Legal Education on the Couch." *Harvard Law Review* 83(1971):392–418.

Tartakoff, Helen H. "The Normal Personality in Our Culture and the Nobel Prize Complex." In Rudolph Loewenstein (ed.), *Psychoanalysis: A General Psychology.* New York: International University Press, 1966.

U.S. Department of Labor, Office of Policy, Planning, and Research. *The Negro Family.* Washington, D.C.: U.S. Government Printing Office, 1965.

Zaretsky, Eli. *Capitalism, the Family, and Personal Life.* New York: Harper & Row, 1976.

INDEX

NOTE: References to tables are shown in italics.